ARISTOTLE
METAPHYSICS

ARISTOTLE
METAPHYSICS

Translated by RICHARD HOPE

With an analytical index
of technical terms

ANN ARBOR PAPERBACKS
The University of Michigan Press

First edition as an Ann Arbor Paperback 1960
Copyright © 1952 Columbia University Press, New York
All rights reserved
ISBN 0-472-06042-2
Published in the United States of America by
The University of Michigan Press and simultaneously
in Rexdale, Canada, by John Wiley & Sons Canada, Limited
Manufactured in the United States of America

1983   1982   1981   10   9   8

TO THE MEMORY OF

FREDERICK JAMES EUGENE WOODBRIDGE

PREFACE

This version of Aristotle's *Metaphysics* presents us with what may be described as a Postscript to Natural Science. The new translation aims to meet the needs of college and graduate students. It therefore renders his text into clear English, as accurately as possible, idea by idea rather than sentence by sentence or word by word. The glossary entitled "Analytical Index of Technical Terms," contains selected Greek terms listed by numbers corresponding to the numbers inserted into the text itself for purposes of ready reference. The Latin equivalents noted have been taken from the translation made by William of Moerbeke and the commentary based on it by St. Thomas Aquinas (*Tertia Editio stereotypa attente recognita*, Turin, Italy, M. E. Marietti, 1935).

(From the Preface to the original edition)

CONTENTS

SUMMARY

BEING AND BECOMING

ARISTOTLE
METAPHYSICS

I. BOOK ALPHA

I

ALL MEN naturally have an impulse to get knowledge[182]. 980a21
A sign of this is the way we prize our senses; for even apart
from their utility, they are prized on their own account,
especially sensing with the eyes. For not only from practical
motives, but also when we have nothing practical in view,
we could be said to prefer sight to any of the other senses.
The reason is that of all the senses it can best bring us
knowledge and best discerns the many differences among
things. Any animal is provided by nature[101] with its
senses; but in some animals sensing leads to memory,
whereas in others it does not. Animals with memory are 980b21
more intelligent[172] and teachable than those which are
not able to remember. Those unable to hear (such as bees)
are intelligent, but not teachable; whereas those which
have both memory and hearing are teachable. Thus, all
animals except man live by what they perceive[173] and
by memories, but have little experience[168]; whereas the
human race lives also by art[171] and reasoning.

From memory men can get experience; for by often remembering the same thing they acquire the power of unified 981a
experience. Experience, though it seems quite like scientific
knowledge[179] and art, is really what produces them; for,
as Polus rightly says,* experience brought art, and inexperience, luck. Art is born when out of the many bits of
information[169e] derived from experience there emerges a
grasp of those similarities in view of which they are a unified

* Plato *Gorgias* 448C, 462B, C.

3

whole[43]. Thus, a man is experienced who knows that when Callias was ill of this disease he was helped by this medicine, and so for Socrates and for many others, one by one; but to have art is to grasp that all members of the group[20] of those † who are ill of this disease have been helped by this medicine.

Now experience seems in no respect inferior to art in a situation in which something is to be done. On the contrary, we see experienced men succeeding even better than those who know the reasons[90], but who lack experience. The reason is that experience, like action or production, deals with things severally as concrete individuals[40], whereas art deals with them generally[43]. Thus, a physician does not cure "man" (except incidentally[3]), but he cures Callias, Socrates, or some other individual with a proper name, each of whom happens[3b] to be a man. If, then, someone lacking experience, but knowing the general principles[90] of the art, sizes up a situation as a whole[43], he will often, because he is ignorant of the individuals within that whole, miss the mark and fail to cure; for it is the individual[40] that must be cured.

Nevertheless, we believe that knowing[182] and understanding[186] characterize art rather than experience. And so we take experts in an art to be wiser[180] than men of mere experience; because wisdom presumably comes only with knowledge[182], and we believe that the experts can analyze and explain[83], whereas others cannot. Men of experience discern the fact "that"[202], but not the reason "why"[203]; whereas experts know the reason why and explanation[83]. Hence we also hold master workmen in each craft to be more valuable and discerning and wise than manual workers, because the former can discriminate the various factors[83] relevant to the various effects produced; whereas the latter, like inanimate objects, produce effects, as fire burns, without knowing what they are doing.

† A^bD^b. Other codices: those who have a certain high fever symptomatic of this disease, all the phlegmatic or the bilious, have been helped by this medicine.

Inanimate objects produce their effects somehow by nature[101]; and manual workers, by habit[157]. Master workers are presumably wiser[180], then, not because they are practical, but because they have their reasons[90] and can explain[83] what they are doing.

In general, too, it is a sign that a man knows[182] when he can teach. Hence we believe that art is more scientific[179] than experience. For men of knowledge can teach; whereas men only experienced cannot. So it takes more than being sensitive[165a] to make a master in art; for by the senses 10 we grasp things well as separate things, but the senses do not tell us the why about anything. They do not tell us why fire is hot, but only that it is hot.

The first person who invented an art beyond common sense[165] was fittingly looked upon by his fellowmen as a wonder; not only because there was something useful in his discoveries, but also because he was thought wise and superior to others. With the development of more arts, some for our necessities and others for our enjoyment, we invariably take the contributors to the latter to be wiser than the contributors to the former, because they are wise about what is not merely useful. Accordingly, after all such bodies 20 of knowledge had first been established, there followed those not directed either to our pleasure or to our necessities. They appeared first in those places where men had leisure. Hence, it was in Egypt that the mathematical arts were first developed; for there the priestly caste was set apart as a leisure class.

Now we have shown in the *Ethics* ‡ what differences there are between art[171] and science[179] and other such general disciplines. But what we intend to say in the present account is that all men take what is called "wisdom"[180] to be concerned with the first principles[82] of explanation[83]: so that, to sum up what we have said, the man of experience is deemed wiser than those who merely sense things, the 30 artist than men of experience, and the master worker than

‡ *Ethics* vi.3–7.1139b14–1141b8.

5

982a manual workers. Thus, wisdom is thought to consist in
  2   theoretical[187b] rather than in productive[189] kinds of
       knowledge. Clearly, then, wisdom is rational knowledge[179]
       concerning certain basic factors[83] and principles[82].

2

Since this is the knowledge[179] we are seeking, we must
inquire of what sort the reasons[83] and principles[82] are
which to know is wisdom[180]. The answer to our question
will perhaps become more evident if we state what we think
about the wise man. First, we assume that the wise man
knows all[150] so far as possible, though he does not know
anything in particular[40]. Next, that he is wise who under-
10 stands difficult matters, matters which it is not easy for
most men to understand; whereas sense perception[165] is
common to all, and therefore easy, and not a mark of the
wise man. Next, we assume that he who is more accurate
and more able to teach the reasons why[83] is the wiser in
his particular science. Also that those of the sciences which
are cherished on their own account and in the interest of
knowledge are closer to wisdom than those desired on
account of their by-products[112]. Finally, we assume that
the more controlling[82a] science is wiser than the subservient; for the wise man is a ruler rather than a subject,
and he should not be under another, since the less wise
should obey the wiser.

20   These, then, are the assumptions we entertain concerning
wisdom and the wise. But, of the traits specified, that of
knowing totally[150] must be his whose knowledge[179]
forms a systematic whole[43]; for in a way he knows something about any given subject[85]. And the features which
characterize the whole are precisely those which are most
difficult for men to know; for they are farthest removed
from the senses[165a]. Then, too, the most exact of the
sciences are those which are most concerned with primary[17a] considerations: for sciences based on few assumptions are more exact than those which employ ad-

ditional assumptions; for example, arithmetic as compared
with geometry. Such a theoretical[187b] science of explanation[83] is also most educative; for a teacher is one who
can tell in a given case what factors[83] are pertinent. Also, 30
knowledge[182] and science[179a] for their own sake are
found to the highest degree in the science of what is most
intelligible[179b]; for he who cherishes science on its own
account will cherish whatever is science par excellence, 982b
which is the science of what is most intelligible. But the
most intelligible matters are first principles[17a] and basic
reasons[83], since it is by and through them that any given
subject[85] becomes intelligible, not vice versa. Finally, the
most controlling[82a] of the sciences, the most suited to
rule the subordinate, is that which considers the "wherefor"[96a] of things, their good[98], and, taken generally[44],
that science which considers what is best in all nature[101].
In view of all that has been said, then, the knowledge we
are seeking can all have the same name; for this science is
the theory[187b] of first principles[82] and reasons[83],
among which is the good[98] or the wherefor[96].   10
    That this science, moreover, is not one of production[189]
is clearly illustrated in those who first began to philosophize.
For it was their curiosity that first led men to philosophize
and that still leads them. In the beginning, they were curious
about difficulties close at hand. Then they progressed little
by little in this respect and raised difficulties about matters
of greater consequence; for example, about behavior of the
moon and the sun and the stars and of all becoming[116a].
But whoever is perplexed and wonders thinks himself
ignorant. Hence, even the lover of myths is in a way a lover
of wisdom; for a myth is made up of wonders. Therefore,
inasmuch as men philosophized in order to escape ignorance, 20
it is evident that they learned[182] in the pursuit of knowledge[179a], and not for some useful end. This is attested
also by the fact that it was only after all the necessities for
commodious and enjoyable living had become common that
this sort of intelligence[172] began to be sought. Clearly,

then, we do not seek it for any other use; but, as we say that a man is free whose aims are his own and not another's, so we pursue this knowledge as the only one of the sciences that is free, since it alone is for its own sake.

Hence the acquisition of this knowledge may with some justification be regarded as not suited to man. For human nature is in many ways servile: so that, according to Simonides, God alone may have this prerogative; and it is fitting that a man should seek only such knowledge as becomes him. If, then, the poets are right, and the divine[208] is naturally jealous, this knowledge would probably most readily arouse such jealousy, so that those who excel in it would be unfortunate. But we should not believe in divine jealousy; for it is proverbial that bards tell many a lie, and we ought to regard nothing more worthy of honor than knowledge such as this. For the most divine knowledge is also most worthy of honor. This science alone may be divine, and in a double sense: for a science which God would most appropriately have is divine among the sciences; and one whose object is divine, if such there be, is likewise divine. Now our science has precisely these two aspects: on the one hand, God is thought to be one of the reasons for all things and to be in some sense a beginning[82]; on the other hand, this kind of science would be the only kind or the most appropriate kind for God to have. All other sciences, then, are more necessary than this; but none is more excellent.

Yet the acquisition of this science must somehow produce the direct contrary to its beginning. For all men begin, as we have said, by being amazed that things are as they are, as puppets are amazing to those who have not yet understood how they work, or the solstices, or the incommensurability of a square's diagonal with the side, for it seems curious that there is something which cannot be measured even with the smallest unit. Finally, however, in the progress of our science, the directly contrary and, as the proverb has it, the better state, is reached, the state reached by those who, as in the cases mentioned, have accepted in-struction; for there is nothing which would surprise a geometer more than if the diagonal of a square became 20 commensurable with the side.

We have now explained the nature of the knowledge we are seeking and the goal of our search and of our whole exploration[198].

3

We must clearly acquire knowledge of factors[83] that are primary. For we claim to know a thing only when we believe that we have discovered what primarily accounts for its being[83]. These primary factors are fourfold. First, we say the primary factor is a thing's essential character[26] or "what it meant to be that thing"[88]; for the question "why" leads us back at last to definitions[90], and the reason "why"[203a] is the primary[82] factor in explan-ation[83]. Secondly, we mean the material[84] or what persists in change[85]. Thirdly, "that whereby the move- 30 ment is started"[95b]. Fourthly, the very opposite factor, that is, the "wherefor"[96], or the "good"[98]; for this is the "end"[100] of any generation[116a] or change[109]. We have sufficiently inquired into these factors in the writings on nature.* Let us, nevertheless, here appeal for 983b confirmation to our predecessors in this inquiry into be-ings[1a] and in philosophizing about what is true concerning them. For, clearly they, too, speak of principles and ultimate factors. To go over what they say will therefore be profitable for the present exploration: for either we shall discover some other kind[19] of factor and explanation, or we shall rely all the more confidently on those we have just enumerated.

Most of those who first philosophized thought that in the materials of things would be found their only beginnings or principles. That from which all beings come, that from which they first arise and into which they at last go, the primary being[26] persisting through its many transformations, this 10

* *Physics* ii.3, 7. Cf. below, v.2.

9

it is, they say, that is elemental[103] and primary[82] in things. Hence they think that nothing is either originated or destroyed, since such a nature is always conserved; just as we say that Socrates neither is originated absolutely when he becomes beautiful or educated, nor is he destroyed when he loses those traits, because the Socrates in whom these changes occur remains. So, too, nothing else is originated or destroyed without qualification; for there must be a nature, whether one or more than one, out of which things are generated, but which itself endures.

Yet these men do not all give the same account either of the number of such primordial beings[82] or of what kind of
20 being they have. Thales, the pioneer[82c] in this kind of philosophy, declares that the primordial being is water (and therefore proclaimed the earth to be on water), probably having this idea suggested to him by the fact that the nutriment of everything is moist and that heat itself is born out of the moist and is kept alive by it. To be sure, that "wherefrom"[86] anything comes to be is its source or beginning. So he made this observation and acquired this way of explaining[174] things. He also noted that the seeds of everything have a moist nature and that water is the beginning of the growth of moist things. Some think that those ancients who, long before the present generation, were the first to theologize, had a similar idea of nature; because
30 they presented Ocean and Tethys as the parents of becoming and water as that by which the gods swore, which these people styled the "Styx." For what is oldest is most honorable, and what anyone swears by is the most honorable.
984a Although it may not be clear whether this opinion about nature is primitive and ancient, Thales at any rate is said thus to have explained the principles[17a] and origins[83] of things. Hippo no one would regard as worthy of a place in the company of these men, because of his intellectual limitations. Anaximenes and Diogenes, however, rank air before water as the chief primordial being of bodies; Hippasus of Metapontium and Heraclitus of Ephesus said it is fire;

and Empedocles used all four, adding earth to those mentioned as a fourth. These remain always and do not come into being, except that they come to be many or few as they 10 come to be combined into one or separated out of one. Then Anaxagoras of Clazomenae, who was older than Empedocles, but whose philosophic activities came later, declares that the beginnings are innumerable[130]: for, he says, nearly all things whose parts are like themselves[22a], such as water or fire, are thus generated and destroyed by combination[164b] and separation[164c] only; otherwise they are not generated or destroyed, but remain forever.†

By these considerations, then, one might be led to regard as the only basic factor the one which we have described as of a material kind[20]. But, as men progressed along these lines, the very state of affairs paved the way for them and coactively forced upon them continued search. For, if every disintegrative[117a] and originative[116a] process is from 20 some one or more elements, then, in view of this very circumstance, whereby[203a] does this come about, and what is here the crucial factor? Assuredly, the thing spoken of[85] does not itself effect its own transformation: I mean, for example, that neither wood nor bronze is the efficient agent transforming either of them and that the wood does not make the bed nor the bronze the statue, but that something else is the transforming[115] factor[83]. To search for this is therefore to search for another source or for what we are accustomed to call "that whereby the movement begins"[95b].

Now those who in the very beginning undertook such an exploration and said that there is a single persistent being[85] were not at all dissatisfied with themselves. However, at least some of those who held this view, as if defeated in this 30 search, maintained that this one being or nature as a whole must be immovable; not only as to origination and destruction (for this is old, and all agreed on it) but also as to every other transformation (and this is peculiar to them). 984b

† The elements of Anaxagoras were really qualities, not material.

None of those, then, who pronounce everything to be a unity, succeeded in locating an efficient cause, except perhaps Parmenides—and he only inasmuch as he posits that there is not only one, but somehow two factors in question. But, for those who believe in several elements it is most convenient[12b] to think in pairs: "hot and cold" or "fire and earth." Of these, they say fire has a motive nature; whereas water, earth, and the like they treat as its contraries.

After these men and such origins, which were inade-quate[6oe] to explain the generation of things, men were 10 again forced by the truth itself, as we have said, to search for the next kind of source. For it is not likely that fire or earth or any other such element should be, or that those men should have thought it to be, the factor explaining why things are or become good[98a] and beautiful[99a]; nor, again, would it be appropriate to relegate so momentous an issue[6d] to automatism[127] and chance[126]. When, therefore, someone said that mind[169] is present, as in animals, so in nature, as the crucial factor accounting for all order[149] and arrangement[207a], he spoke like a sound-minded man, in comparison with his fair-spoken predecessors. We know that Anaxagoras certainly maintained these views, although 20 Hermotimus of Clazomenae has prior claim[83] to having made this point. Those, then, who grasped things in this way posited both that the answer to the question of what explains the beautiful is also a principle explaining the being of things[1a] and that it is the sort of principle which explains the source of movement in things.

4

One would suppose that Hesiod would have been the first to look for something of this sort, or some other person like him, for example, Parmenides, who believed that love[159b] or desire[158] is the beginning[82] of all that is[1a]. For Parmenides, in giving his account of the genesis of all things[150], says: "Love was made by Aphrodite first of all the gods." And Hesiod says:

First of things was chaos made, and then
Broadbreasted earth. . .
And love, supreme among immortals.

Thus, it is suggested that among created beings[1a] there 30
must be[82f] some basic agent[83] which will move
things[188c] and bring them together. Now, who it was that
first had this idea and in what order these men followed each
other, we can determine later. Here we must proceed to
another thinker, who was aware that the stark opposites[50]
to the goods are likewise present in nature, not only
order[207a] and beauty[99], but also disorder and the ugly, 985a
and more evils than goods, more vile things than noble[99];
therefore he introduced both love[159c] and strife, each to
account for[83] one of the two opposites. For, if one follows
what Empedocles says and takes it according to its in-
tent[170] rather than its unintelligible expression, one finds
that love is introduced to explain whatever is good and
strife whatever is evil. Hence one might well claim in a
way[55c] that Empedocles believed and was the first to
declare that evil and good are principles[82]; for he explained
everything good by referring it to the good itself, everything 10
evil by referring it to evil itself.

These men, then, according to our interpretation, had a
firm grasp of two of the basic types of explanation[83] which
we distinguished in our writings on nature;* namely, the
material factor[84] and the agent or mover[95a]. They did
so obscurely, however, and not clearly[59c], as untrained
swordsmen strike out in a duel, rushing about and occasionally making fine strokes, but making them without scientific
expertness[179]; so these thinkers seem to talk without
knowing[182] what they are saying. For they evidently fail
to make use of their explanations, except very slightly.
Thus, Anaxagoras introduces mind[169] to create the
world[149b] mechanically, as a god is introduced on the
stage in a play. When he is confronted with the difficulty[200a] of explaining why a thing is of necessity, he 20

* *Physics* ii.3, 7.

drags mind in sideways; in other explanations, however, he uses everything rather than mind to account for[83b] the facts[116].

Although Empedocles makes greater use of his basic explanations than does Anaxagoras, he too fails to use them adequately[60e] and consistently[52]. For example, according to him love sometimes separates[164c] things, and strife unites[164b] them; thus, when everything is broken up[111a] into the elements by strife, fire is separated out[164b] by itself[24], and so is each of the other elements; but when everything is again brought together[111b] into one by love, each element is necessarily again dispersed[164c] among the parts of things. However, Empedocles, in contrast to his
30 predecessors, was the first to introduce a diversity of agents or movers[83], inasmuch as he does not present a single beginning[82] for all movements, but diverse[16] and contrary[50] beginnings. And he was the first to speak of material[84a] elements as four, though he used only two of
985b the four: fire he made a unique[2] kind of agent, whereas earth, air, and water he treated as having the same nature, being opposites[13] of fire. Anyone who reads the verses of Empedocles reflectively will get this doctrine out of them.

This is our version of what Empedocles said about the nature and number of the principles in things. But Leucippus and his disciple Democritus speak of two elements, the full and the empty, which they call "being"[1] and "nonbeing"[1b]: the full or solid is "being"; the void or empty space is "nonbeing." This is why they say that being has no higher claim to being than has nonbeing; for a solid or body has no higher claim to being than has empty space. Now, in identifying these as the crucial factors[83] in explanation[1a], they are giving attention to the material factors
10 only. Moreover, just as those who regard primary[85] being[26] as a unity and say that everything else comes into being as a mode[35a] of this one being, because[82] it comes by a process[35b] of rarefaction or condensation, in the same way these thinkers explain differences[76a] among things in

terms of the differences in their elements. The differences in the elements, they say, are three: shape[91a], arrangement[207a], and position[64]. For things vary[76] only in rhythm, contact, and rotation: rhythm is due to the shapes of elements; contact is due to their arrangement; and rotation, to their position. Thus, *A* differs from *N* in shape, *AN* differs from *NA* in arrangement, and *Z* differs from *N* in position. Like the others, then, these thinkers thoughtlessly neglected the other question about movement, the 20 whereby[95] or the how of a change among[82f] things[1b]. This is as far as our predecessors were able to go in their search for at least two of the factors in explanation which we have distinguished.

5

Contemporaneously, and even before them, the so-called Pythagoreans, the first to be absorbed in mathematics, not only advanced this particular science, but, having been brought up on it, they believed that its principles[82] are the principles of all things[1a]. Now, of these principles, numbers are naturally[101] the first. As a result, they seemed to see[187] in numbers, rather than in fire, earth, and water, many similarities to things as they are[1a] and as they come to be[116]: for one sort of modification[35a] of numbers, so to speak, is justice; another, soul and mind; still 30 another, opportunity; and so forth. Musical modes[35a] and relations[90], too, they saw in terms of numbers. And all other matters appeared to be ultimately of the nature of numbers; and numbers were for them the primary natures. 986a In view of all this, they took[65i] the elements of numbers to be the elements of all things[1a], and the whole heaven[143a] to be harmony and number. They were adept at finding numbers and harmonies, both in patterns of change[35a] and in the structure of parts. And they organized and unified[113h] the whole arrangement[149a] of the heavens to exhibit its harmony[56b]. And if they discovered defects anywhere, they invented the necessary additions in order to

15

make their whole system[197] hang together perfectly. I mean, for example, that since ten is thought to be complete[14], comprising every nature of numbers, they declare
10 that the number of moving[121] celestial bodies must be ten; and since only nine are visible[59d], they invent a tenth, the "counter-earth." We have discussed these matters more precisely elsewhere.* But the purpose[97] of going over them now is that we may learn[65] from these men what principles they posit[64] and how these fall under the basic kinds of explanation we have named. Evidently, then, these men regard number as a principle, both as the material of things[1a] and as the measure of their stabilities[33a] and instabilities[35a]. They say that the elements of number are the even and the odd, the latter limited[131a], the former unlimited[130], and that unity[24] is made up of both even
20 and odd, that numbers come from unity and, to repeat, that the whole heaven is numbers. Others among them say that the principles are ten, which they arrange[36] in columns[104]: limited and unlimited, odd and even, one and plurality[6b], right and left, male and female, rest and movement, straight and curved, light and darkness, good and evil, square and oblong. Alcmaeon of Croton seems to have believed[65i] this, and either he got this account[90] from them or they from him; for Alcmaeon was in the prime of life when
30 Pythagoras was old, and he expressed himself similarly to these men. For he says that many human affairs[151a] go in pairs, meaning not the particular contrasts[50a] which these men distinguished, but any at random[126a]: white and black, sweet and bitter, good and evil, small and great. Thus, he made indefinite[72g] suggestions concerning the
986b other contrasts; whereas the Pythagoreans proclaimed the number[27] and names[4] of the contrasts[50b].

From both of these groups, then, we may learn[65] this much, that contraries[50] are the principles[82] of things[1a]; and from the Pythagoreans we learn also how many and what principles there are. But how these may be brought

* *De caelo* ii.13.

into relation[113] to our factors of explanation[83] they have not made clear. However, they seem to regard[207] their elements as material[84a], for they declare that whatever exists[26] is composed and fashioned of them as if it were constituted by them[82h].

These considerations give us an adequate idea[187] of what the ancients intended when they said that the elements of nature are more than one. However, there were some who maintained that all things[150] have a single nature. These men varied considerably in the clarity of their expositions[99a] and in their fidelity to facts[101]. We can ignore them in connection with our present inquiry into types of explanation, since, unlike the other philosophers[101h] who try to explain[64h] natural processes as one unified being[1] which is generated out of unity as if unity were the world's material, these men have a different theory[36] of unity. For them how being[150] is generated is no problem, since they declare the world to be immovable. Nevertheless, this much is intimately related[55] to the present inquiry: Parmenides seems to grasp[137] unity as it exists in speech[90], while Melissus grasps a material unity. Hence, Parmenides declares that the world is limited; whereas Melissus declares it is unlimited. Xenophanes, however, who first expounded the theory of unity (Parmenides is said to have been his disciple), made no clear statement and seems not to have understood[137d] either material or formal explanation; but, gazing at the whole sky, he says: "Unity is God." These men, then, as we have said, are to be dismissed for the purposes of the present search: two of them, Xenophanes and Melissus, should be dismissed entirely, being a little too naïve. Parmenides, however, seems to reason[36] here and there more critically[166]; for when he insists that there is no nonbeing in competition with being, he must believe that there is only being, and nothing else. (We have examined this more clearly in our writings on nature.†) But when he is forced by factual evidence[173b] to interpret his doctrine of

† *Physics* i.3.

unity as applying to discourse and his doctrine of plurality as applying to sense he, too, assumes two kinds of factors and two beginnings, which he calls the hot and the cold, such as 987a fire and earth; and of these he ranges the hot with being, and the cold with nonbeing.

From what has been said, then, and from the sages who have sat in council with us during this discussion, we have acquired this much. On the one hand, the earliest sages assume that the beginning is bodily (for water, fire, and so forth are bodies), some assuming that the bodily beginnings are one, others that they are more than one; but all agree that they are of a material kind[84a]. On the other hand, certain sages assume in addition to this material factor that there is an active or moving principle[95a]; some say one, others, two.

10 Down to the Italians, then, and apart from them, other inquirers have spoken too restrictedly[146] concerning these matters; except that, as we have said, they happen[126a] to make use of two basic factors, and one of these (the agent or mover) some present as one and others as two. The Pythagoreans, too, have said that there are two beginnings, but they have added this, which is peculiar[42] to them: they believed that the limited and unlimited are not different[16] natural beings[101] (fire, earth, etc.), but that the unlimited-itself and the one-itself constitute the fundamental being[26] of natural beings, of which they are predicated[25a]; and therefore that number is also the fundamental being of all 20 things. In speaking thus of principles, they began to define[72] the question of what is[87], but conceived this project much too simply. For they defined it too superficially and held the first number to which a given definition applied[82f] to be "what"[26] the thing[188c] defined is; just as if one regarded "double" and "two" as identical, because it is first to the number two that "double" belongs[82f]. But, surely, "to be double" and "to be two" are not identical; if they were, one thing could be many, as, indeed, they concluded[3b].

This, then, is what we have learned from the ancients and their successors.

6

After the philosophies named came the enterprise[197] of Plato, which in many ways followed them, but went its 30 own way, diverging from the philosophy of the Italians. For in his youth Plato became familiar through Cratylus with the Heraclitean doctrines, that among things sensed there is a perpetual flux and that to know[179] such things is impossible, and he continued in this conviction also later on. 987b Socrates, however, concerned himself[197] with morals, and not with the whole of nature; in seeking general truths of morals as a whole, he first fixed thought[170] on definitions[72a]. Plato endorsed him and, having the background[5a] indicated, he believed that any knowledge of things as wholes must arise, not from objects of sense perception, but from another kind of beings[16]; for he thought it impossible to find a common definition[72b] for sensible things, since they are always undergoing transformation. Accordingly, he called beings[1a] that are as wholes[5a] "ideas,"[89] whereas all the objects of perception, he said, are defined[36] by and in terms of ideas; so that a multitude of things "participate"[93] in an idea[20] which desig- 10 nates[37c] them. The only novelty he introduced here is in the word "participation": for the Pythagoreans say that things are what they are[1a] by "imitating"[94] numbers; whereas Plato says that they "participate," thus making only a verbal change. For both alike neglected to investigate what it means to participate in or to imitate ideas[20]. However, he distinguished besides objects perceived and ideas a third kind of entity, the mathematical, which are intermediate, differing from things perceived in being eternal[135a] and unchanging[109e], and differing from the ideas in that there are many alike[57], whereas each idea is unique[24]. But, since ideas serve as principles of explanation for other beings, he believed their elements to be the elements

20 of all things[1a]. Thus, he thought that the "great-and-small"[147] [or quantity] is a material source[82] and that unity is a formal[26] principle; for arithmetical ideas come "from" the "great-and-small" [or quantities] and are related by "participation" in unity.

Like the Pythagoreans, then, Plato said that unity is itself a being[26], not an attribute[16] of[4] beings[1]. Like them, too, he said that numbers constitute the reason[83a] for the being[26] of other things. But unlike the Pythagoreans and in the place of their indeterminate "one," Plato interpreted infinity as great or small quantitatively and hence as partaking of duality.* He also taught that numbers are independent[74] of things perceived by sense; whereas the Pythagoreans teach that concrete things[188c] are numbers and hence do not place mathematical entities between[138a] ideas and things perceived by sense. Plato's belief that unity
30 and numbers are independent of concrete things (in opposition to the Pythagoreans) and his introduction of ideas[20] as beings were because of his interest in dialectic[90] (for the earlier men gave no consideration[93] to dialectic[78]), and his belief that duality is also[16] a being[101] resulted from his doctrine that numbers other than the prime can be neatly[101g] generated out of two as though it were a
988a pliable material.

But the facts[3b] are contrary to these theories, and the accounts they give are not reasonable. For they hold that the same material can produce many things, but that a form[20] has only one embodiment[116d]; whereas what we observe is that every table has its own material and that one artificer, using a single form or design[20], may make many tables. Formal and material factors are related as male to female; for the female becomes pregnant from a single impregnation, whereas the male impregnates many fe-

---

* The difference between Plato's and the Pythagorean idea of infinity seems to be that whereas the Pythagoreans thought of infinity as an indefinite continuum, such as the area of a geometrical figure without its circumference, Plato explained infinity in terms of discontinuous number series and their limits of great and small.

males. So sex is an analogue[94] of[82] matter and form.†

These, then, were Plato's answers to the question here under investigation. It is evident from what has been said that he made use of but two types of explanation: that which answers the question of "what" a thing is[87]; and that which gives the material basis[84]. For ideas[20] are related[83] by him to other entities as their "what"[4]; and unity is in turn the "what" of ideas. And it is clear to what material he refers[85] when he explains[36] how ideas are related to things perceived by sense and how unity is related to ideas; namely, that this material is a duality, the "great-and-small" of quantity. And as for the question[83] of the good[98a] and the bad [the "wherefor"], this, too, he assigned to the [material] elements, one accounting for good, the other for evil; in this doctrine[194] he followed, as we saw, some of the earliest philosophers, such as Empedocles ‡ and Anaxagoras. §

7

We have thus surveyed in a condensed and summary manner those who have spoken concerning first principles[82] and the truth[7a], and we have examined how well they have spoken. We have learned[33] from them that none of those who have spoken about a first principle or explanation[83] has mentioned any factors beyond those which we have distinguished in our writings on nature * and that all apparently have been groping[137d] for them, however blindly. Thus, some speak of the first principle as a material[84], whether they take it to be one or more than one and whether body or incorporeal: Plato speaks of the great and the small; the Italians, of the unlimited; Empedocles, of fire and earth and water and air; Anaxagoras, of the infinity of things composed of similar parts[22a]. All these men, then, have a hold

† According to Plato, the material factor would resemble the male, and the formal would resemble the female; according to Aristotle, the formal would be male ("informing" many), and the material would be female (providing the "formless" material, to be unified into a single organism).

‡ i.4.985a5.   § i.3.984b18.   * *Physics* ii.3, 7.

on this material kind of explanation, just as much as those
30 have who speak of air or fire or water or of something denser
than fire or subtler than air (for some have said that there
is such a first element). These men, then, have seized[137]
on this one material factor[83] only. Others have emphasized
the agent or effective source of movement[95b], such as those
who have reduced all beginnings[82] to the powers of friendship and strife, or mind, or love.

But no one has spoken clearly about what it means to be
something[88] or what constitutes the being of things[26].
988b To be sure, those speak of it who believe in ideas[20], for
they take ideas to be neither the materials of things perceived, nor materially compounded of unity, nor agents
(for they could not be agents[82] of change[109] when they
are used to account for[83] immobility and being at rest);
but they say that in the case of anything it is its idea that
explains what it means to be that thing and that unity explains what it means to be an idea.

Finally, they mention that for the sake of which[96]
activities[188b], changes[115], and movements[109] take
place; but though they use it as a principle of explanation,
they fail to use it accurately in the way it naturally functions[101c]. For those who explain things in terms[64]
of mind or love speak of the good of things; but they do not
10 explain how anything[4d] is[1] or comes to be[116] for the
sake of these goods; they merely say that they are sources of
movement. In the same way, those who assert that unity or
being[1] is such a good[101] say that it explains the being of
things[26], but not how anything is or comes to be for the
sake of another. Thus, they really[3b] both say and fail to
say that the good explains things; for they do not say this
explicity[105], but incidentally[3].

However, all these men, since they were unable to hit
upon any other factor in explanation, seem to attest that
we have rightly determined their number[27] and kinds[28].
In addition, it is clear that all principles must be sought
either in all four of these ways or in some one of them. Let

us next consider the possible difficulties[200] with regard to 20
the way in which each of these men has spoken and with
regard to the particular principles which each has stressed[33].

8

It is clear that those who reduce all to one and think[64] of
the matter of things as being some bodily nature, having
magnitude, err[128] in many ways[6]. For they consider the
elements of bodies only, not of incorporeal beings, though
there are incorporeal beings. In their eagerness to explain
generation and destruction and in explaining all things as
processes[101h], they ignore the very cause[83] of change.
And they err in failing to recognize the primary being[26] of
anything and in failing to answer the question of "what" a
thing is[87]; and besides, they too readily make a principle
out of any of the simple bodies except earth, without show- 30
ing how fire, water, earth, and air are generated out of one
another. For some things come from others by combination[164b], and others by separation[164c]; and it makes the
greatest difference which comes first[17] and which follows[18]. On the one hand, it would seem that the most elementary of all things should be the first out of which things
come to be by combination; and such would be the most 989a
minute-particled and the subtlest of bodies. Hence those
who posit fire at the beginning give an account most consistent with this argument[90], and each of the others agrees
to posit some such elementary body. At least none of those
who speak of one primary element posit earth, clearly because of its bulky parts. Of the three other elements, each
has found an advocate; for some select fire; others, water;
still others, air. But why, after all, do they not name earth
also, as most men do? For men often say all things are of
earth; and Hesiod expressly says that earth was the first 10
of bodies to come to be; it is an ancient and popular way of
accounting for[174] things. Nevertheless, they say, it is
wrong to regard as primary any of the elements other than
fire or denser than air; it must be finer than water. On the

other hand, if what is later in genesis is prior in nature, then what is concocted and compounded[164b], being later in generation, would be prior: water would be prior to air; and earth, to water.

Let these comments suffice about those who posit a single 20 material principle. The same might be said of those who posit more than one; for example, Empedocles describes his material as composed of four bodies. The same consequences[123] follow[3b] from some of his doctrines, though he has others peculiar[42] to him. For these bodies produce each other, so that the same body does not always remain fire or earth (we have spoken of these matters in the writings on nature *). Moreover, his explanations of movement in things seem to us neither right nor reasonable, regardless of whether there be one or two ultimate forces. For in general those who use such explanations necessarily ignore qualitative change[120]. Since hot cannot come from cold, or cold from hot, what is it that endures[35] these contrary states[50], 30 and what one nature could become now fire now water? Such changes he denies.

As for Anaxagoras, if one were to interpret him as believing in elements, one would make explicit the consequences of his theory[90] which he himself does not see[36c], but to which he would of necessity have been driven. To be sure, it is absurd on other grounds to assert that in the beginning all things were mixed[139]: for it would follow that they must 989b previously have been[82g] unmixed; and it is not reasonable to suppose that any chance form naturally[101c] comes to be mixed with any chance form or that things endure changes[35a] and happenings[3a] that are totally unrelated[73] to their natures[26] (for he thinks the same things endure both mixture and separation). Nevertheless, if one were to go along with him, coherently articulating what he wants to say, he would probably come close to the moderns. For, when nothing was separated out[164a], clearly there would be nothing which it would be true to say of that

* *De caelo* iii.7.

24

primal mixed being[26]: I mean that it was not white or black or gray or any other color, but of necessity colorless; for it would have had one of these colors, if any. Similarly, it 10 was flavorless, and by the same argument it had no other attribute; it could be of no kind[28], no quantity[27], no anything[4]. Otherwise, some[4] stated[36] that particular[22] form[20] would belong[82f] to it; but this is impossible if all things are mixed[139]; for it would clearly be unmixed[164a]. However, he declares that all things are mixed[139] except mind, and this alone is unmixed and pure. From such arguments it would follow that he would be driven to recognize as principles a "one" (for this is simple and unmixed) and an "other," which we think of[64] as like the indefinite before it is defined and before it participates in an idea[20]. Hence, though he talks neither rightly nor clearly, he wants to say something like what the later 20 men say and like what is now prevalent[173b].

The earlier thinkers seem to have been familiar[55] only with questions about genesis, destruction, and movement; for this is practically the only kind of primary being for which they seek beginnings and explanations. But those who began[34] to think[187a] about all kinds of entities[1a] and who believe[64] that some of them are perceptible and some imperceptible, clearly are beginning an inquiry concerning two kinds[19] of being. Hence we may dwell more on them, noting what they say well and what not so well with reference to our present inquiry.

The so-called Pythagoreans make an even stranger use of principles and elements than do those who give physical 30 explanations[101h]; for they have derived them, not from perceptible objects, but from mathematical entities[1a], which, with the exception of those in astronomy, belong to the realm of immovables. Nevertheless, all their discussions[78] and interests[197] concern nature: for they explain the generation of the heavens and carefully note the[22] events[3b], changes[35a], and revolutions[9c] in the celestial 990a regions. Thus, they employ all the principles and explanations, as if they agreed with the physicists, that all being[1] is perceptible and is contained under the so-called vault of heaven. But their explanations and principles, as we have said, are suitable[60e] for even more exalted beings, more suited[56a] to them, in fact, than to nature. For they fail to explain[36] motion in terms[85] of only the limited and the unlimited, and odd and even; and they fail to tell us how, without motion or change, it is possible to have genesis and destruction or any revolution of celestial bodies. And even granting that they have shown how spatial magnitudes can come from such elements, why should some bodies be light and others heavy? On the basis of what they assume[64h] and say, they should explain[36] perceptible as well as mathematical entities. If they have said nothing whatever about fire or earth or other bodies of this sort, I suppose it is because they have nothing peculiar to say about them. And how is one to believe[65] that number and its relations[35a] both explain how things are and come to be in the heavens from the beginning till now, and at the same time this same number constitutes the cosmos? And when in one particular region[22] they put right beliefs[175] and opportune times[134a] and a little above or below they put injustice and moments of decision[164] or indecision[139], and state by way of proof[63a] that though each one of these is a number there happens to be already in their places[132] a plurality of spatial bodies also composed of numbers (for these numerical relations belong[77] to the various places), are we to suppose that the number which each of these must be is the same number which is also in the sky, or is the heavenly number separate[74]? Plato says it is separate[16]; but even he thinks that though these bodies and their explanations are numbers the explanatory numbers are intelligible[169b], whereas the others are perceptible.

9

Now let us turn from the Pythagoreans, for we have said enough about them, and examine those who believe[64] that ideas[89] explain all. To begin with, in their attempt to 990b explain things[1b] visible[4a], they invented an equal number of other things, as if they thought it was easier to count many than few. For their ideas[20] are precisely equal in number to or not fewer than the objects which they are supposed[194] to explain by referring each object to its idea. For, corresponding to each thing[40] there is something which has the same name and is independent[74] of it, whether it be a primary being[26] or a composite[16b] being[24b], and whether sensible[4a] or eternal[135a].

As for the various ways in which we prove the existence[23] of ideas[20], none is clear[173b]: from some,* the conclusion does not necessarily follow; from others,† it would follow 10 that there are ideas even of matters of which we believe there are none. For, according to the arguments from the sciences there would be ideas of all matters of which there are sciences; according to the unity-out-of-multiplicity[24b] argument there would be ideas even of negations; and, according to the argument that we can think[169a] of something that has perished there would be ideas of things that have perished, since we have images[173a] of such things. Of the more accurate arguments, some imply[34] ideas[89] of correlatives[29], of which we admit that there are no separate[2] classes[19]; others assert a "third man" [between the perceptible and the ideal].

Also, in general the arguments for the ideas[20] destroy the very principles on which those who believe in ideas rely[177] much more than they rely even on ideas[89]. For it would follow that number would be prior to duality, that 20 being relative[29] would be prior to being independent[2], and all the other contradictions[50c] with their own principles on which those have stumbled who have followed the doctrine[175] of the ideas[89].

On the assumption[174] according to which we prove the being of ideas[89], there would be ideas[20] not only of primary beings but also of many other things (for not only

* For example, 991a8–b9.   † For example, 990b11–991a8.

primary beings, but other things, too, are intelligible[169d]; and sciences deal not only with primary being, but also with others); and a thousand other such difficulties arise. But, by logical necessity[123a] as well as by doctrinal tradition[175], if there is participation in ideas[20], then there can be ideas[89] only of primary beings; for participation is 30 not incidental[3], but is in an idea[20] in so far as the idea is not an attribute ascribed to a subject[85]. I mean, for example, that if something participates in the idea[15a] of "double" it also incidentally[3] participates in the idea of the "eternal"; for "double" happens[3b] to be eternal[88a].

991a Hence there are ideas[20] only of primary being; but the same terms designate[38] primary being both temporal and eternal—or else what would it mean to declare that a thing's unity[4] is apart[74] from the multiplicity which it unifies[24b]? And, if the ideas[89] and the things participating in them have the same idea[20], it will be something they have in common; for why should "duality" be identical with the perishable twos or with those dualities which though eternal are many and not be identical with "duality itself" and with a particular[4] two? But it they do not have the same idea[20] in common, then they have only the same name, and it would be analogous to calling both Callias and a wooden figure a "man" without observing any interrelation.‡

Then, above all, one might raise the question[200a] what on earth the ideas[20] contribute[58b] to the sensibles, either 10 to the eternal or to those that come to be and cease to be. For the ideas do not explain[83] any movement or change in perceptible objects. And as for imperceptibles[16b], the ideas do not in any way help towards their knowledge (for they do not constitute the definition of their being[26], else they would have been in them) or towards their being[23], if they do not belong inherently[82h] to the things which participate in them—although, if they did inhere in them, they might even be thought to be explanatory factors, like

‡ xiii.4.1078b34-1079b3.

the white with which a white object is painted[139]. But this argument[90], which first Anaxagoras and later Eudoxus and some others used, is quite easily upset[109d]; for it is easy to bring many impossibilities § to bear upon a doctrine of this sort.

In addition, other things do not come "from" the ideas[20] in any of the usual senses of "from." But to say that the ideas are patterns[89a] and that other things participate in them is to use empty words and poetical metaphors. For how[87] does one go about[9d] "looking up" to the ideas[89]? For anything may be or come to be like something else without being copied from it; so that whether Socrates exists or not a man like Socrates might come to be; and clearly this might be so even if Socrates were eternal. Also, there will be more than one pattern of the same thing, therefore more than one idea[20]; of man, for example, animal and biped and at the same time also man-himself. Again, the ideas[20] will be patterns, not only of perceptible objects but also of the ideas[89] themselves: a genus[19] would include[19] its species[20]; so that the same thing could be both pattern and copy.

Again, it would seem impossible for primary being and that whose primary being it is, to be dissociated[73a]. How could the ideas[89], if they are the primary being of concrete things[188c], be in isolation[73a]? In the *Phaedo* ‖ this doctrine is stated by saying that the ideas[20] are explanations for being and becoming. But though the ideas are, the things that participate in them do not come to be unless there is something to set things going[109a]; and many other things come to be, such as a house and a ring, of which we deny that there are ideas. Clearly, therefore, even the other things may be and come to be because of the same factors which govern the being and becoming of the things just mentioned.¶

§ For example, that "accidents" and "forms" could be without "substances" (Thomas Aquinas).

‖ Plato *Phaedo* 100C–E.   ¶ xiii.5.1079b12–1080a8.

Then, if ideas are numbers, how will they be explana-
10 tory[83a]? Is it because existing things[1a] are other numbers; for example, one number is "man," another is Socrates,
still another is Callias? What, then, do those numbers
explain[83a] about them? It will not make any difference
even if the former are eternal and the latter are not. But
if it is because things here, for example, harmony, are
ratios[90] of numbers, it is clear that the things between
which they are ratios are in some sense one. If, then, there
are such material somethings[4], it is evident that the
numbers themselves will be certain ratios of something to
something else. I mean, for example, that, if Callias is a
numerical ratio of fire and earth and water and air, then
also the idea[89] will be a number of certain other things
spoken of[85]; and "man-himself," whether or not it is in
some sense a number, will be a numerical ratio of certain
20 things, and not a number—nor because it is a ratio will it
therefore be a number.

Again, from many numbers, one number comes to be; but
how can one idea[20] come from many ideas? But if the
number comes, not from the numbers themselves, but from
the units in them, for example, in ten thousand, then how is
it with the units[24c]? If they are alike[57a], many absurdities follow; and also if they are not alike—neither the units
in the same number being like one another, nor all the units
in other numbers being like all the other units—for in what
will they differ, since they are without attributes[35d]?
Such views are neither reasonable nor consistent with our
thought[169c]. Again, it would be necessary to set up some
other ** inclusive kind[19] of number, with which arithmetic
deals, and all the things which some men call "intermediates"[138a]. And how would they be? From what beginnings
30 are they? Or why would they be intermediate between things
here and things-themselves? Again, each of the units in a
"two" would be from some prior duality; but this is im-
992a possible. Again, why is a number, taken together, one?

** Other than "species" or than "substance" of sensibles (Thomas Aquinas).

Again, besides what has been said, if the units are diverse[76a], it would have been needful to speak as do those who say that the elements are four or two: for each of those men designates[36] as an element, not what is common, such as body, but fire and earth, whether there is something common to them, for example, body, or not. But now the one is discussed as if, like fire or water, it were composed of similar parts[22a]; and if this is the case the numbers will not be primary beings. Clearly, if there is a one-itself, and this is a beginning, the "one" is being used[36] in more than one way[6]; or else that is impossible. 10

Moreover, when we want to reduce primary beings to principles, we derive[64] lines from short and long, that is, from a small and a great; and planes, from broad and narrow; and body, from deep and shallow. But how would the plane then contain[33] a line, or the solid, a line or a plane? For the broad and the narrow belong to a different kind[19] from the deep and the shallow. Just as number, then, does not belong[82f] exhaustively to these, because the many and the few are quite other than they, so it is clear that no other principles of the higher beings will belong to any of the lower. Thus, the broad is not a kind inclusive of the deep; for then body would have been a sort of plane.†† Again, from what would the inhering points have been derived? Plato even 20 objected to this genus as being a geometrical fiction[175]; but what he called the principle of the line, and this he often posited, was the individible[41] lines. Nevertheless, these must have a limit; so that, by the argument which proves the line, the point also exists.

In general, although wisdom seeks an answer to fundamental questions about matters open to public inspection[59d], we have given this up; for we say nothing to explain the source[95b] of change[115]. But, thinking we are discussing the primary being of such matters, we nevertheless maintain that there are other primary beings. But as to how the latter are the primary being of the former, we

†† xiii.9.1085a9–19.

talk in vain; for "participation," as we have said before,‡‡ is nothing. Nor do the ideas[20] have any connection[137] with
30 another basic factor in scientific explanation, with that "wherefor" any mind or any nature is in action[34]. This, too, we conceive[46] to be one of the principles. But mathematics has for men today become philosophy, although they assert
992b that it should be pursued[197] in behalf of other matters. Again, one might suppose[65i] that what is here called[85] primary being or matter is too mathematical and that it should be predicated as a differentia of primary being and of matter rather than being called matter itself; that is, the great and the small are like what the physical philosophers call the rare and the dense, which they assert to be the first differentiae of the thing spoken of[85]; for these are a sort of excess[148] and deficiency[148a]. And, as regards movement, if the great and the small are to be movement, it is clear that the ideas[20] will be moved; but, if the great and the small are not to be movement, whereby did movement come? So the whole inquiry concerning nature has been eliminated.

Also, though it is supposed to be easy to show that all
10 things are one, this is not accomplished; for, by the method of setting out terms apart[64a], the result is not to make all things one, but, if one grants all the assumptions, to maintain that there is a "one-itself." Not even this will result, if one will not grant that what is as a whole[43] is a genus; and in some cases this it cannot be. Nor is there any explanation[90] how lines and planes and solids, coming after numbers, "are" or "will be," or what validity[11], if any, they have; for they cannot be ideas (since they are not numbers) or intermediates (since those are mathematical entities) or perishable objects; they are evidently a fourth distinct kind or genus.

In general, if we search for the elements of things[1a] without distinguishing the various senses[6] in which the latter are said to be, it will be impossible to find them; es-

‡‡ i.9.991a22.

pecially if we search in this manner for the elements of 20
which things are composed. For it is surely impossible to
grasp[65] of what doing[34] is composed, or undergoing[35],
or the straight; but this is feasible[12b], if at all, only in the
case of primary beings. Therefore it is not true to say that
we may seek, or rightly think that we have, the elements of
all things[1a].

And how would anyone learn[184] the elements of all
things? For clearly it would not be possible[5b] to get a
start[82g] by having taken cognizance[181c] of anything
before. For, just as one who learns geometry, though he
may have previously acquired insight into other matters, has
not in advance acquired knowledge of the subject matter
of the science about which he is to learn, so it is in other
cases too. Hence, if there is a science of all things, as some
declare, then the learner would start[82g] with no acquired 30
knowledge[181c] whatever. Yet all learning proceeds by
means of demonstrations or by means of definitions: for
there must be previous insight into and familiarity[181d]
with the terms of the definition; and similar conditions must
be fulfilled in learning by means of induction[113e]. But,
on the other hand, if the science happened[126a] to be 993a
innate[101e], it would be surprising[191] how possession of
the greatest of the sciences would escape our notice[205].

Again, how would one come to know "of" what things
are; and how would this become evident[59a]? For this too
affords[33] a difficulty[200]; since one might quarrel about
it, as about some syllables—for some declare that the
syllable *sma* is composed of *s*, *m*, and *a*, whereas others
declare that it is a sound distinct[16] from any with which
they are familiar[181d]. Again, how would one recognize the
things of which we have sense perception if one did not have
the sense in question? But if the elements of which all
things consist are the same, we ought to be able to recognize
them in the way in which sounds consist[64g] of elements
of sound. 10

33

10

It is clear, then, even from what has been said before, that all the men discussed seem to seek the basic factors of explanation[83] we have mentioned in the *Physics* * and that we cannot[33] name any beyond these. But they seek these obscurely; and, although the factors have in a way been described before, they have in another way not been described at all. For the very first philosophy seems like unintelligible speech on everything, since it is young and still in its beginnings. Thus, even Empedocles says bones are because of their articulated structure[90]; though this explains what it meant to be[88] bones and the formal being[26] of the matter in question[188c]. But then it would be likewise necessary for flesh and each of the other related matters, or else none of them, to be likewise an articulated structure; that is, it is on this account that flesh and bone and each of the rest would be, and not on account of the matter, which he nevertheless names, that is, fire, earth, water, and air. If another person had argued thus, Empedocles would of necessity have agreed; yet he has not said this clearly.

Such points, however, we have previously illuminated[59]. But let us return † to the difficulties that one may raise about these matters; for we may, perhaps, gain[201] something from them for our later difficulties.

* *Physics* ii.3, 7.　† iii.

II. BOOK ALPHA THE LESS

I

To CATCH SIGHT[187a] of the truth is difficult, in one way; in 30
another, easy. A sign of this is that no one can see[126a] it
complete[60d] or completely[150] misses[126c] it, but each 993b
says something on nature;* so that, although he may individually contribute little or nothing, yet out of the collabor-
ation of all there arises a great mass[142a]. It reminds us of
the proverb: Who would fail[128] to hit a door? In this
sense, it is easy; but to be able[33] to hit the door[21] and
unable to hit the keyhole[22] illustrates[59] the difficulty[200d]. However, in view of this double difficulty, the
reason[83] for it may lie, not in the facts[188c], but in us:
for, as owls' eyes are[33] at noonday, so is our mental[154] 10
vision[169] blind to what in its own nature is the most
evident of all.

We do well, therefore, to give[33] heed[97] not only to
those whose opinions agree[92] with our own, but also to
those whose statements now seem trivial; for they, too, have
contributed something by giving us a realization[33a]. If
Timotheus had never lived, music would not be what it is;
but without Phrynis, Timotheus would not have composed
as he did. So among those who pursue truth, some have
contributed enduring doctrines, but they could not have
done so without[83a] the unrecognized work of others.

It is right, too, that philosophy should be called the 20
science of truth: for a theoretical science ends[100] in truth,
as a practical science ends in action[9c]; though practical

* Book Alpha the Less may have been written as an Introduction to the *Physics*.

men occasionally indulge in theoretical science, they have in view[187], not its eternal truth, but some practical[29] and present objective. To explain a thing it is necessary to know which among a number of things that have[82f] some trait in common[37c] gives that trait to the others. So fire, being hottest, is the reason[83] why other things are hot. So, too, what is most true is the reason why other things are derivatively[18] true. Hence, the principles of eternal things[1a] are necessarily most true; for they are true always and not merely sometimes; and there is nothing which explains their being[23] what they are[87], for it is they that explain the
30 being of other things. Consequently, status[33] in being[23] governs status in truth.

2

Thus, in spite of all, there is a definite[4] beginning[82], and
994a the reasons[83] for things[1a] are not infinite either in series or in kind. For there can be no infinite regress[114h] in the production of things[4a] from their materials[84], as flesh from earth, earth from air, air from fire, and so *ad infinitum*[111]. Nor in the agencies[82] whereby changes are effected[109], as a man is moved by air, air by the sun, the sun by strife, and so *ad infinitum*[131]. Similarly, the wherefor[96] cannot go on[114h] to infinity, as walking for health, health for happiness, happiness for something else, and so
10 on forever, one thing for the sake of another. So, too, in explaining what it means to be[88] among middle terms[138], conclusion[18a], and premise[17], the premise is necessarily the definitive factor[83] to which the later are referred. For, if we had to say which of the three is definitive, we would say the first[17a]; surely not the last, since the final term[100a] does not account for anything, and not the middle, since it accounts for only one. Nor does it make any difference whether the middle terms are one or several or even infinite in number. For in the infinite series here described and in infinites generally, all the parts down to the one before us are similarly middle terms; and hence where

there is no first term, there is no explanation[83] at all[44].

Neither can[5b] there be an infinite regress from firsts to consequences, so that, beginning with the higher term 20 (e. g., from fire, water; from water, earth; and so on forever), some other kind[19] of being is generated[116]. For a thing[4a] comes[116] from another[4a] in two ways (excluding the sense in which one thing comes after another, for example, the Olympian games after the Isthmian): either in the sense in which a man comes from a boy by the boy's changing[115] or in the sense in which air comes from water. Now, by the process of a man coming from a boy, we mean the change from what-is-coming-to-be to what-has-come-to-be, or from maturation to maturity; for, as coming to be[116a] is intermediate[138a] between being[23] and not being, so what is coming to be is always intermediate between what is[1] and what is not[1b]. The learner, for example, is in process of becoming a scientist; and this is what we mean when we say that from the learner comes the scientist. On the other 30 hand, water comes from air in another sense; namely, in the sense in which one of the things ceases to be[117]. Hence, the former process is not reversible, and the boy does not come from the man: for what comes to be by the process of becoming is not what is still coming to be, but what re- 994b mains after the process of becoming; thus, the day comes from (because it comes after) the morning, and therefore not the morning from the day. But the other processes are reversible. However, an infinite regress is in both cases impossible. For the terms[1] in the former, being intermediate, must have an end[100]; and the terms of the latter change into another, inasmuch as the destruction of the one is the genesis of the other.

Similarly it is impossible that the first or enduring[135a] being[1] should be destroyed. For, since the process of becoming cannot be traced back infinitely, a first thing which was destroyed when something else came to be would necessarily have perished [and hence would not be first].

The wherefor is an end, and an end of the sort which is not

10 for the sake of something else, but for the sake of which other things are. Hence, if there is a last term of this sort, the process will not be infinite; and if there is not there will be no wherefor. But those who assume[34] an infinite regress fail to notice that they remove[118d] the nature of the good. For no one would try to do[188a] anything if he were not going to arrive at a limit[131]. Rationality[169], at least, is incompatible with such an infinite series; for the reasonable man always acts for the sake of something, and this serves as a limit (for the end is a limit).

Moreover, what-it-meant-to-be-anything[88] cannot be indefinitely resolved[113a] into a chain of definitions which goes beyond what is meaningful[90]. For the earlier proposition is always more of a definition than the later; and if the first of a series does not define, neither will the next. And 20 those who deny this would abolish[118] science[179a]; for it is impossible to know[182] unless one arrives at an unexplained term[41]. Otherwise we would know[181a] nothing; for how could we understand[169a] things that are indefinitely explicable? This case is not like the case of the line which is indefinitely divisible; for we cannot know indefinitely, which is the reason why a geometer who follows an infinitely divisible line does not stop to count the segments.

A material[84] explanation[169a] would necessarily be made in terms of changes[109a], and nothing can be infinitely changing. And even if it could, such indefinite[130] being[88a] would not be an infinite[130].

In short, if the factors of explanation[83] were infinitely numerous[6b] in kind[20], it would not be possible to attain knowledge of them. For we think that we know[182] when 30 we know[181c] how to explain[83] adequately. But to keep on adding[64f] factors infinitely would take endless time.

3

The reception we give[3b] to a course of instruction depends on our habits[157]; for just as we welcome[46c] 995a familiar speech, so anything which is said in an unfamiliar way[74] is uncongenial[57] and seems unintelligible and strange. Hence the more familiar a thing is, the more intelligible[181d] it seems. A good illustration[59] of this power of habit is seen in the legal field, where mythical and puerile rules prevail over intelligent[181a] ones because they are customary. Accordingly, an instructor may fail to make an impression[66] because he fails to use the familiar mathematical language or because he fails to give concrete examples[89a] to those not accustomed to mathematical abstractions, or because he does not meet a demand for citing[113d] the poets as authorities. Some require accuracy[164d] in everything; others are irritated by accuracy, either because they cannot follow a closely reasoned argument, or because they fear hair-splitting. There is something 10 about accuracy that makes it seem unworthy to certain free spirits, either in business contracts or in rational exposition.

Hence, in any inquiry it pays to be trained[184a] in its method[66] and not to imagine that familiarity with the method of presentation implies knowledge of the subject matter itself, for neither is easily achieved[65]. Mathematically exact method, which is appropriate where the material factor[84] does not enter, is not to be expected in all the sciences. Such a method is evidently inadequate for the natural sciences[101a], where consideration must be given to the material factor. Hence, our first inquiry must be: What is[87] nature[101]? Then it will become clear what natural science is about and whether the theory[187] of explanatory analysis[83] and of principles[82] is a single 20 science or is distributed among the sciences.

III. BOOK BETA

I

In pursuing our science, we ought first to make a careful survey of the difficulties[200a] which confront us at the outset. Among them would be the diverse ways in which others have dealt with our problems and in addition any points that may have been overlooked. To have stated well the difficulties is a good start for those who expect to overcome[201] them; for what follows[18] is, of course, the solution of those very[17] difficulties, and no one can untangle

30 a knot which he does not see[190]. A difficulty in our thinking[170] reveals a tangle in existence[188c], since thought encountering a difficulty is like a man bound: neither the thought nor the man can move. Hence, we must first understand[187] our perplexities[200b], both for the reason given and also because whoever engages in a research[194] without having first stated his problems is like a person who does not know where he is going or whether or not he has found

995b what he wants. Such a person cannot see ahead[100] clearly, as can one who has begun with a statement of his difficulties. Then, too, a person who has heard all the contending parties, as if in a suit at law, is necessarily in the best position to judge[164].

Now, our first difficulty is related to those which we have raised in our introductory discussions—namely, whether the theory[187] of explanation[83] is a single science or belongs to several. Secondly, should this science properly examine the first principles[82] of primary being[26] only or, in addition, the principles on which all men base any explanation[63], such as whether or not is is possible[12b] to affirm[46] and to deny[48] one and the same thing at the same time and other such questions. Then, if this science 10 deals with primary being, whether one or more than one science deals with all primary beings; and, if more than one science does, whether they are all alike, or whether some are called "wisdom"[180] and others something else.

Next we come upon the inevitable[123a] problem whether only sensible[165c] primary beings exist or whether there are others. And if there are others, have they all the same kind of primary being; or are there several kinds[19], as those say who believe in[34] ideas[20] and in mathematical entities intermediate to ideas and sensible things? Having dealt with these questions, we must then ask whether our theory[187a] concerns only primary beings or also the essential[2] attributes[3a] of primary beings. And whose business is it to 20 examine[187] the relations of same[15] and other[16], like[57] and unlike[57f], identity[15b] and contrariety[50a], prior[17] and posterior[18], and other such terms about which the dialecticians dispute on the basis of more or less probable[60] premises? And what are the essential attributes of these relations? Not only what each is[87], but also whether each has its own contrary.*

Another difficulty is whether principles[82] and elements[103] are kinds[19] of being, or whether they are the intrinsic constituents[82h] into which things are divisible. And, if they are kinds of being, whether they are said to be nearest[100a] to or the furthest[17a] from what is not 30 divided[41], for example, whether it is "animal" or "man" that exists as a first and independent[74] principle[82] of a human individual[40].

Then, we must investigate very carefully whether or not something[4] besides[74] the material[84] of[83] things has its own[2] being; whether this exists separately[73] or not; and whether it is numerically one or more than one. For example, is there, apart from the composite thing[21a] (that is,

* iv. 2.1003b22–1005a18.

the union of a material and its attributes[25a]), something else, or nothing else, or sometimes something else, but not always? If so, what kind[28] of beings[1a] could they be?

996a   Then, are the number and kinds[20] of principles determinate[72], both logically[90] and ontologically[85]? Do perishables and imperishables have the same or different principles? Are they all imperishable, or are those of perishables themselves perishable?

Then comes that most difficult of all questions, whether unity[24] or being[1], as the Pythagoreans and Plato said, is not a particular[16] something[4] at all, but is the very being[26] of any being[1a]. Or is it not so? Is it itself some particular being? Is it a subject matter[85] such as Empedocles believed friendship to be and as others made similar claims for fire, water, or air?

10   And are principles wholes[43] or like concrete individual[40] affairs[188c]? Are they potential[11] or actual[9]? Are they principles only of movement? † These questions, too, afford considerable difficulty.

Finally, there is the question whether or not numbers, lines, figures, and points are primary beings. And, if they are primary beings, whether they are separate from sensible[165c] things or are, so to speak, funded[82h] in them. Concerning all these issues it is difficult to find the truth; even to state well these difficulties is not easy.

2

Now let us formulate the first problem mentioned:* Is the theory[187] of explanation[83] a single science, or distributed among several?

20   How, in the first place, could a single science embrace[181c] a variety of principles[82] that are not even the opposites[50] of each other? Secondly, not all principles apply[82f] to all things[1a]. Thus, among things immovable, how could one discover either a principle of movement[109] or the nature of the good? Since anything good in itself[2] or by its own

† ix.6.   * iii.1.995b6.

nature[101] is an end[100] and serves to explain[83] things only in the sense that it is for its sake that other things are or come to be, and since an end, or a "wherefor,"[96] is always an end of some action[188b], and all actions involve movement, there cannot be such a principle of movement or anything good in itself for things that are immovable. Hence it is that in mathematics nothing can be explained[63] in such terms[83], nor does any mathematical demonstration[63a] 30 throw any light on the better or the worse. No one would ever claim that it did. That is why some of the Sophists, such as Aristippus, vilified mathematics; for, in the other arts and in the trades, such as carpentering and cobbling, an action or a product is judged[36] in terms of better or worse, whereas mathematics takes no account[90] of goods and bads.   996b

On the other hand, if there is more than one science of explanation[83] and a different science for each principle, which of these is it that we are seeking? And who is a specialist in the scientific knowledge of explanation? A single thing[15] may need to be explained in terms of all kinds of factors. Take, for example, a house: the producer or agent[95a] of a house is the building art and the work of the builder; its "wherefor"[96] is the use[9c] to which the house is put; its material[84] is earth and stone; and its form[20] is its plan or definition[90]. Now, on the basis of our previous discussions † as to which of the sciences ought to be called "wisdom" it would seem reasonable[90] to apply the name to each of these types of explanation. The science of the end[100] or good[98], inasmuch as it is most controlling[82a] 10 and can lead the other sciences as if they were its unquestioning slaves, is certainly a kind of wisdom; for other things are always subservient to the end. But the science of primary being[26], inasmuch as it treats by definition[72e] of first factors[83] and of what is the most intelligible[179b], would be wisdom. For, in view of the many ways[6] in which men may know[179a] the same thing, we say that he knows[182]

† i.2.982a8–19.

better who knows[181c] well something in particular instead of merely being able to distinguish it from other things, and that such positive knowledge is always better than the negative; but we say that he knows best of all who knows "what" something is[87] rather than "how much"[27] it is or what it resembles[28] or what it can do[34] or what can[101c] be done to it[35]. And so we always believe that we know[182] what we are saying, even when we can
20 prove[63a] its truth, when we know its "what"[87]: "what" squaring a rectangle is—namely, the finding of a mean, and so forth. However, we know how things[116a] or acts[188b] or changes[115] come about when we know their source[82] or generation[109] (the opposite[13] of their end). Thus, any one of these types of scientific explanation would seem to be a different type of knowledge and yet may give us wisdom.

It is likewise debatable[51] whether one or more than one science deals with the foundations[82] of proof[63a]. By "foundations" I mean the common[92] beliefs[175] on which all men base their demonstrations: for example, that an assertion must be either affirmative or negative; that nothing
30 can simultaneously be and not be; and all the other assumptions[62a] of this kind. The question is whether the same science that deals with primary being also deals with these assumptions; and, if it is not the same science, which of the two it is that we are now seeking.‡

On the one hand, it does not seem reasonable that all these considerations belong to any one science. For why should an understanding[186] of them be peculiar to geometry or to any other science? But if they belong to any science
997a whatever and yet not to all, then getting such knowledge[181a] is not peculiar to that science which concerns[181c] primary beings any more than to other sciences. Anyway, how can there be a science[179] of these principles? For even now we are giving recognition[181c] to each of them; and any science[171] would certainly use them as well-known[181a] principles. But, if they can be proved[63a]

‡ iii.1.995b10; iv.3.

to be, there must be some class[19] of subjects[85] to which they belong: some of them may be demonstrable propositions[35a]; others may be axioms[67]. To demonstrate everything is impossible; for a demonstration must rest on something, be about something, and amount to something. Consequently, there is one kind[19] of being[4] common to all things demonstrated; for all the demonstrative sciences use the axioms. Now, if the science of primary being differs from the science of axioms, which of them is naturally[101c] more controlling[55b] and prior? Axioms are certainly most general[43] and serve as principles of all things. And, if it is not the philosopher's business to construct the theory[187] of truth and falsity applied to axioms, whose business is it?

Next among our general[44] problems is whether a single science deals with all the primary beings.§ If more than one science deals with them, which sort of primary beings shall we select[64] as our particular concern here? On the other hand, if one science deals with all, the consequences do not seem reasonable; for then there would be one demonstrative science of all propositions[3a], because every demonstrative science examines[187] assertions[85] in order to discern how essential[2] attributes[3a] are derived from common[92] beliefs[175], and because for every kind[19] of being there must be a single science to examine its essential attributes, as these are derived from common beliefs. Thus, statements of fact[202] belong together, and statements on which the demonstrations rest belong together, whether both belong to the same science or to another. Therefore, all attributes, too, belong together in both these sciences or in one compounded out of them.

The next problem is whether our theory concerns primary beings or also their attributes.‖ I mean, for example, if solids are primary beings and lines and planes are likewise, does the same science study[181c] them that studies the attributes of each kind (that is, the mathematical attributes), or does a different science do so? If the same science,

§ iii.1.995b11; iv.2.1004a2–9; vi.1.   ‖ iii.1.995b20; iv.2.1003b22–1005a18.

45

then the science of primary being would also be a demonstrative science; but we suppose that there can be no demonstration in answer to the question "what is"[87]? If a different science, then which science would contain the theory of the attributes of primary being? This is a very difficult problem.

Next comes the question whether the only primary beings there are, are sensible[165c], or whether there are others. And are these others all of one kind[19], or does there happen to
997b be more than one kind of such primary beings, as there are according to those who speak of ideas[20] and also of intermediates[138a] (the subject matter of mathematics)? ¶ We have already explained above ** in what sense we say that the ideas[20] are fundamental factors[83] and independent[2] primary beings[26]. Though there are many riddles[200c] in all this, the greatest absurdity is to declare that there are certain natures[101] independent[74] of the celestial motions, and then to declare that they are, nevertheless, like sensible and perishable natures, except in being eternal. For these men maintain that there is a man-himself, a horse-itself, health-itself, and so forth, about which they give no further information; and they establish[34] these after the manner
10 of those who assert[46a] that there are gods but that they are like men[151b]. For such theologians merely establish eternal men; and such philosophers represent ideas[20] as being merely sensible objects[165c] eternalized[135a].

There are many other difficulties[200] for anyone who believes[64] in intermediates[138a] between the ideas[20] and sensible objects[165c]. For they would have to suppose that besides[74] lines there are lines-themselves and visible lines; and similarly for all kinds[19] of things. Thus, since astronomy is a mathematical science, there must be a sky in competition[74] with the visible sky and another sun, moon, and so forth, as in the case of the sky. How can we believe[183] all this? For it does not seem reasonable that such a body would be immovable, but it seems altogether im-

¶ iii.1.995b18; xii.6–10; xiii, xiv.   ** i.6, 9.

possible that it should move. Similarly, with respect to the 20
objects of optics and mathematical harmony: these too, for
the same reasons[83], cannot be rivals[74] of the objects perceived; for if there are intermediate sensibles and their
corresponding sense perceptions evidently there must also
be "animals intermediate" between "animals-themselves"
and perishable animals. Suppose we ask[200a], further,
among what sorts[28] of beings[1a] one might find[194] the
objects of these sciences of intermediates. If geometry differs
from measurement of the earth only in that the latter deals
with what we perceive, whereas the former deals with the
unperceived, then, clearly, there should be also a science
besides medicine, intermediate between "medicine-itself"
and "this particular medical science"; and so with each of
the other sciences. But how is this possible? And there would 30
have to be healthy beings besides those seen to be healthy
and the "healthy-itself." Meanwhile it is not even true that
measurement deals with sensible and perishable magnitudes;
for then it would perish when they perish. On the other
hand, astronomy would not deal with perceptible magnitudes
or with these particular[4a] heavens; for perceived lines are
not the sort of lines of which the geometer speaks. Visible 998a
things are not straight or round in the geometer's sense; and
a round object does not in fact touch a straight edge at a
point, but in the way Protagoras, in his refutation of geometers, said it does. Nor are the movements and orbits of
celestial bodies like those on which astronomy bases[34] its
explanations[90]. Nor do points[38a] have the same nature
as the stars.

There are some, however, who say that these so-called
intermediates between the ideas and the sensibles are not
separate[73a] from things, but in them. It would require too
elaborate an account[90] to go over all the impossible consequences of this view; but reflections[187] such as the fol- 10
lowing may suffice. It is not reasonable that this should be so
of the intermediates only; for clearly the ideas, too, might be
in sensible things. The same argument[90] would hold for

both. Again, two solids would of necessity be in the same place; and the intermediates, being in the moving sensible things, would not be immovable. And, in general[44], what end is gained[96a] by supposing[64] their being[23] to be[23] in sensible things? For the same absurd consequences would follow as those previously mentioned: there would be a sky besides the sky, except that it will not exist separately[73a], but in the same place; and this would be even more impossible.

3

20 Turning now from these problems, which raise very serious difficulties for anyone who tries to get at their true solution, we come to similar difficulties concerning first principles[82]. Should we regard[65i] the kinds[19] into which things are grouped as their elements[103] and principles? Or should we turn rather to the primary constituents[82h] of things? * In the case of speech, for example, words are analyzed into their primary sounds, and these are said to be their elements and principles, not "speech," though all words are instances of it. So, too, in the case of geometrical problems, we call those theorems "elementary" which enter into[82h] all other proofs or into most of them. And physicists, whether they believe bodies have one element or several elements, agree[36] that an element or principle is that of which bodies are compounded and constituted. So

30 Empedocles declares that fire, water, and so forth, are the elements of which things consist and are their ingredients[82h], but he does not speak of these elements as if they were the "kinds"[19] of all things[1a]. And anyone who wants

998b to examine the nature of anything would examine its parts; for example, to learn[181c] the nature of a bed, he would see how it is put together. On the basis of such arguments[90], we would not regard the kinds[19] of things[1a] as their principles.

* iii.1.995b29; vii.10, 13.

But, since we come to know[181c] a thing by defining[72a] it, and since genera or kinds are the principles of definitions, we could regard kinds as also the principles of the things defined. And if we get[65] scientific knowledge[179] of various species[20] by knowing their kinds or the genera in terms of which we speak about them, then genera are controlling principles at least for their species. Accordingly, some of those who conceive the elements of things[1a] in terms of unity[24] or being[1] or the great and the small, appear to treat them as kinds[19] of being. But to speak of principles as both elements and kinds is confusing, since there can be only one constitutive order or system[90] of primary being and it makes a difference whether we define[72a] things in terms of their kinds[19] or in terms of their constituents[82h].

Moreover, even if a genus is an excellent principle, ought the principle to be the first genus or most inclusive kind, or the least[18a] inclusive kind, the one nearest[25a] to individual[41] things? † Here is another question that has two sides[51]. On the one hand, if kinds are principles in the degree in which they are general[43], then it is evident that the most inclusive kinds are primary principles; for they apply[36] to all things. There will then be as many principles of things[1a] as there are primary kinds. Hence, being and unity will be principles and primary beings, for they, most of all, apply to all things. Yet neither unity nor being can be the sole genus of all things; for the differentiating traits[76a] within each kind must also be and each be one; but neither a species nor a genus apart from its species can be predicated[25a] of the traits[55] that differentiate them, so that if unity or being is a genus, then no differentiating trait will be either a being[1] or a unity[24]. However, if unity and being are not genera, they cannot be principles (if any genus is a principle). As for the intermediate kinds, which are related[65h] by their differentiating traits, they would have to be genera down to the least species[41]; but some of them are

† iii.1.995b31; vii.13.

30 thought to be genera, and others not. Besides, differentiating traits are principles, even more so than are genera; but, if they, too, are principles, the principles will, so to speak, come to be infinite in number, especially if anyone takes[64] 999a the first or primary genus as a principle. On the other hand, if unity is more like a principle[82d], and if the indivisible is a unit, and if everything indivisible is so either in quantity[27] or in kind[20], and if the indivisible in kind is prior, and if a genus is divisible into species, then unity should rather be predicated of the least[18a] species, for example, of individual men ("man" is not the genus of "men"). And as for a series of "prior and posterior," such an attribute of things does not exist separately[74] from them; for example, if two comes first in a number series, there will not be "number" [genus] separate from the species of numbers, and similarly there will not be the genus "figure" besides the 10 species of figures. And if this is so in these cases, it will also be so in cases in which a genus is supposed to be separate from its species; for if anywhere there is a separate genus, it would seem to be in numbers or figures. In the case of individuals[41], however, there is no such series of prior and posterior. But where there is a distinction of better and worse, the better is always prior; hence there would be also in such series no separate genus.

It follows from these considerations that those kinds which are predicated of individuals could sooner be principles than could other kinds. On the other hand, it is not easy to say in what sense they are to be taken[65i] as principles. For a principle must be explanatory[83] beyond[74] the particular thing[188c] of which it is a principle and must be capable of being independently[73] of them. But why should anyone assume any such principle to exist beside the con-20 crete individual case[40], unless it exists as predicated of the whole[43] or of all[150]? But if this is the reason, then whatever has generality[43] of being would serve[64] best as a principle, so that the first and most general kinds would be principles.

4

In this connection there is a difficulty * which is the greatest of all and theoretically[187] the most necessary; let us now face it and make an analysis[90] of it. If there is nothing apart[74] from concrete individuals[40], and if these are infinite, how is a science[179] of infinite individuals possible? For whatever things we come to know[181c], we come to know in so far as they are one or the same and in so far as some general[43] attribute[4] belongs[82f] to them all. But, if this is necessary and there must be something 30 apart from the concrete individuals, then either the least inclusive[18a] or the most inclusive[17a] kinds must be separate beings; but we have just shown that this is impossible. Now, if there really is something apart from the composite being[21a] which is constituted[25a] by a qualified[4] material[84], is whatever[20] it may be something apart from all individuals, or only from some and not others, or from none?   999b

But if there is nothing apart from concrete individuals, then nothing would be conceived[169b]; all things would be perceived, and there would be no science of anything, unless one were to say that sense perception is itself scientific knowledge. And nothing would be eternal or immovable, for all things sensed perish and change[109]. But if there is nothing eternal, then there can be no becoming: for there must be something which undergoes the process of becoming, that is, that from which things come to be; and the last member[18a] of this series must be ungenerated, for the series must start with something, since nothing can come from nothing[1b]. Besides, if there is becoming and movement, the process must also arrive at a limit[131]; for no movement is infinite, and every movement has an end[100]. And nothing 10 can come to be which could not have come to be, so that whatever has come to be exists necessarily once it has come to be. However, if there is a material because it is un-

* iii.1.995b36; vii.8, 13, 14; xii.6–10; xiii.10.

generated, it is even more reasonable to suppose that the kind of being which a material becomes from time to time, should be primarily[26]; for, if neither the form nor the matter is separate, then nothing whatever is so. But, since that is impossible, there must be something besides the composite thing—namely, its shape[91] or form[20].

On the other hand, if this be admitted[64], the difficulty arises of deciding in which cases to posit[64] the existence of the form and in which cases, not. For certainly it cannot exist in all cases; we would not, for example, assume[64] the being of a "house" besides[74] the particular[4] houses.

20 Besides, would the primary being[26] of all men be one? But this would be absurd; for if things have a single primary being, they are one. But if each has his own peculiar primary being, this, too, would be unreasonable. Above all, how is it that a material comes to be each of several individuals; and how is any concrete thing[21a] a union of both material and formal elements?

Another difficulty † that can be raised regarding principles is: if things are one only in kind[20], then nothing will be numerically one, not even unity-itself and being-itself. And how will there, then, be scientific knowledge[179a], if there is nothing in all things that is one?

On the other hand, if the unity is numerical and each of the principles is one, not, as in the case of sensibles, different for different things, and if the principles of things[1a] have only numerical unity, then there will be nothing except the elements; for example, since a given[4a] syllable is always the

30 same in kind[20], its elements[82] are also the same in kind, for the same elements exist[82f] in the numerically different instances of the syllable. For there is no difference between saying "numerically one" and "individual"[40]. We speak of the individual in the sense of the numerically one; whereas

1000a we speak of something general[43] in the sense that it is predicated of individuals. Consequently, if individuals were all there is, there could be only so much language as there

† iii.1.996a2; vii.14; xii.4, 5; xiii.10.

are linguistic elements; since the elements of articulate sound are fixed[72] in number, and there would not be two or more instances of the same letters.

Another difficulty, as great as any and overlooked today as formerly, is whether things perishable and imperishable have the same or different principles.‡ If the same, how and why is it that some things are perishable and others imperishable? The disciples of Hesiod and all the theologians have been satisfied with explanations that seem to them credible, but 10 that make no sense to us. For when they present the principles as gods and say that anything that has not tasted nectar and ambrosia is born mortal, it is clear that they are using words which, though familiar[181d] enough to them, are explanations[83] completely above our heads. If the gods take nectar and ambrosia for the sake of pleasure, their doing so does not explain[83] their being[23]; and if the gods do so for the sake of their very being, how could beings who need nourishment be eternal[135a]? But why should we examine[195a] seriously the spurious wisdom of myths? We must look for information to those who use the language of 20 demonstration, and we must ask them why it is that if all things[1a] consist of the same elements some are by nature eternal, whereas others perish. Now, since they give us no reason[83] why things should be[33] as they are, it would seem clear that the principles[82] and explanatory factors[83] of different kinds of being are not the same. One would expect Empedocles, of all men, to speak most consistently[52], but even he fails us[35]: for he explains[83] that it is strife that governs[82] processes of destruction[117a]. But strife would seem to generate[116d] all other things as well, except unity[24], since all things except God proceed from strife. At any rate, he says:

> From them [strife and friendship] all that was and is and will be,
> Trees, and men, and women, have taken their growth,   30
> Beasts and birds and water-nourished fish,
> And long-lived gods.

‡ iii.1.996a4; vii.7–10.

53

It is clear even aside from these words that if things[188c]
1000b had not been in strife all things would have been united[24];
or, as he puts it, "When they have come together, then strife
has taken[111] flight[18a]." Hence, it would follow[3b], on
his view, that the most blessed God is the least intelligent[172]; since he does not contain strife and since like
knows[181] like, he could not know[181c] the elements. As
Empedocles says:

> For, by earth, we see earth; by water, water;
> By ether, godlike ether; by fire, destructive fire;
> Love, by love; and strife, by sad strife.

However, to resume the argument, this at least is evident
10 that according to his view it follows that strife no more
explains[83] destruction than it does being[23]. Similarly,
friendship does not explain being specifically; for, having
brought things together[113h] into one, it destroys the rest.
At the same time, he gives no reason[83] for change[115]
itself, except that things are naturally[101c] so.

> But when strife at last waxed great in the limbs of the sphere
> And sprang to make good its claims when the time was fulfilled
> Which was fixed in turn for them by a mighty oath.

Thus, it is necessary that changes come about; but he fails
to[59] explain[83] the necessity. However, he at least speaks
consistently; for he does not present some things as perishable and others as imperishable, but says all things are
20 perishable except the elements. But the difficulty which we
are now facing is why[203a] some things are perishable and
others not, if they consist of the same principles.

Let what has been said, then, suffice to show that the
principles should not be the same. Now, granting that they
are different, the difficulty remains whether they, too, will
be some imperishable and others perishable. For, if they are
perishable, they, too, must clearly consist of certain elements, since all the things that perish, perish by returning to
the elements of which they are composed; so that it follows
that there are other principles prior to the principles, which

is impossible, either for a finite[111] or an infinite[130] series[112a]. And how can there be perishable things, if their principles, too, are gone[118]? But if their principles are imperishable, why are things composed of imperishable 30 principles nevertheless perishable, whereas things composed of different principles are imperishable? This does not seem reasonable[60c], but either impossible[11f] or in need of a good deal of argument[90]. Moreover, no one has even tried to formulate[36] the different principles, since men seek[36] 1001a the same principles for all things. However, they swallow the prime difficulty we have been stating as if they took it to be insignificant.

Then there is the question § which is most difficult in theory[187] and most necessary in truth: whether being[1] and unity[24] are the primary beings[26] of things[1a], and whether each of them is being or unity without being anything[4] else[16], and what being and unity themselves are when they are[85] among other natures[101]. For some think that they are their own nature; others, that they have a nature. Thus, Plato and the Pythagoreans think that being 10 and unity are not something else, but that this is their nature; namely, that their essential being[26] is just[15a] to be[23] one[24] and to be[4] being[1]. Not so those who deal with nature. For example, Empedocles says that the one is a being, as though by way of reducing[113a] the one to something better known[181d]; for he seems to say that to be is friendship, at any rate, that friendship is in all things what explains[83] their being one. Others say that this unity and being, of which things[1a] both are and have come to be, is fire; others, air. Those who posit several elements speak in the same way; for they, too, must say that unity and being are as often[6d] as are those things which they declare to be principles.

If, then, on the one hand, we were not to posit that unity 20 and being constitute somehow primary being, it follows that none of the other general terms[43] could be primary being;

§ iii.1.996a9; vii.16; x.2.

55

for these are the most general of all. And if unity-itself and being-itself are not beings[4], neither would any of the others be anything[4] apart[74] from what are called individuals[40]. Thus, if unity is not primary being, then no number would be a nature separate[73] from things[1a]; for number is units[24c], and a unit is in some sense precisely what unity[24] is[87].

If, on the other hand, unity-itself and being-itself are beings[4], unity and being would of necessity be essential[26] to all things; for nothing but unity and being themselves would be predicated generally of them all. But if being-itself and unity-itself are beings[4], there is the great difficulty of conceiving how anything can be apart from them; I mean, how things[1a] will be more than one. For what is different[16] from being[1] is not; so that according to the argument of Parmenides it would necessarily follow that all things[1a] would be one and that this is being[1].

However, both of the alternatives are puzzling[200c]. For both if unity is not primary being and if unity-itself is a being[4], it is impossible for number to be primary being. We have shown above why this would be so on the former alternative. On the latter alternative there would be the same difficulty; for whence would there come to be another one besides[74] unity-itself? It would of necessity be not-one; but all things[1a] are either one or many, and each of the many is one.

Again, if unity-itself is indivisible, then according to Zeno's axiom it would be nothing. For he says that anything which when added effects[34] no increase and when subtracted effects no decrease would not be any thing[1] at all; clearly he talks as if a being[1] were a spatial magnitude[142a]. And if it is a spatial magnitude, it is bodily; for a body has being[1] in all ways. Whereas other things, such as a plane or a line, when added, will in some way effect an increase, but not in other ways; a point or a unit adds nothing in any way. However, since he theorizes[187] in a troublesome manner and since indivisibles may, indeed, have such consequences as would make them defensible[53] even against him (for indivisibles, when added, increase their number, though not their size), still the difficulty remains how from one or more than one such indivisibles a magnitude could be generated. It is like asserting that a line is generated out of points. But even if we get[65i] the point at issue, as some do who say that out of unity-itself and something else, which is not-one, there arises number, we must nonetheless investigate[194] why and how, if this "not-one" is an inequality or at least of the same nature, the being thus generated is sometimes a number and sometimes a magnitude. For it is not clear how magnitudes can come to be from adding such a nature either to unity or to any other number.

5

A related difficulty is whether numbers, bodies, planes, and points are primary beings[26] or not.* If not, the idea[87] of being[1] becomes elusive[161], and we do not know where to look among things[1a] for primary beings. The primary being of things is apparently not to be found[38] among qualities[35a], movements[109], relations[29], conditions[64c], and ratios[90]; for all of them are attributed[36] to some subject[85], and none is a this-something[4b]. The things of which compound[64g] bodies[102] are composed[111b] seem most obviously to be primary beings: water, earth, fire, and air. But their hot and cold, and so forth, really modify [35a], not them, but the compound bodies, and they are not primary beings; the body which bears[35] them is what persists[107] like an existing something[4c] and like a primary being.

On the other hand, a body is surely less primary being than is its surface; and a surface, than a line; and a line, than a unit or a point. For a body is defined[72] by these, and they seem able to be without body; whereas a body cannot be without them. Hence, though many of the earlier philosophers regard[175c] body as being[1] or primary being and

* iii.1.996a15; xiii.1–3, 6–9; xiv.1–3, 5, 6.

10 regard all else as modifiers[35a] of body, so that the principles
of bodies are the principles of things[1a], the later and wiser
philosophers regard[175] numbers as principles. And, as we
said, if they are not primary being, there is no primary
being, no being at all[44]; for it would not do[60d] to call
their accidents[3a] beings[1a].

However, if this is admitted, that lines and points rather
than bodies are primary being, we do not see to what
sort[28] of bodies they may belong; for they cannot belong
to sensible[165c] bodies. Then where is our primary being?
Besides, all of them are evidently divisions of body: one, in
20 breadth; another, in depth; another, in length. And no one
figure is in a solid body more than is any other; so that, if
Hermes is not in the stone, then neither is the half of a cube
something existing[72d] in the cube. Therefore, surfaces are
not in it either; for, if any surface were there, the one which
divides[72d] the cube in half would be there. And the same
account[90] may be given of a line, a point, and number
one[24c]. Consequently, whether it is body that is the most
primary being, or whether the mathematical elements are
more primary than body, even though they do not exist as
primary beings, we fail to find what being[1] is and what is
the primary being[26] of things[1a].

In addition to these difficulties, absurd consequences follow
with respect to generation and destruction. For if a primary
30 being that has not been before now is, or if one that was
ceases to be, it seems to be in process[35], coming to be and
perishing; but points, lines, and surfaces cannot come to be
and perish, though they may be at one time and not at
another. For, when two bodies touch, there is something
1002b which becomes one as soon as they touch and becomes two
when they are divided; so that when they have been united
the boundary between them no longer is, but has perished,
and when they have been divided boundaries exist which
before were not. (For it is not a point, which is indivisible,
that has been divided into two.) And, if these things come to
be and perish, from what do they come to be? The case is

similar with respect to the present in time; for this, too, cannot come to be and perish, but still seems to be always different[16], not being a primary being. And, clearly, the problem and explanation[90] are similar with respect to points, lines, and surfaces: they are all similarly limits or 10 divisions.

6

In general[44], the difficulty arises why, after all, we should look for[194] objects besides those sensed and the [mathematical] intermediates; why do we set up[64] forms or ideas[20]? Suppose it is because the [invisible] mathematical entities are not like objects before our eyes, but are, nevertheless, like them in that there are many of the same kind[57a], and hence their principles are not numerically determinate[72d]. Just as the elements of language are not numerically limited[72], but only in kind[20] (unless one takes[65] as elements the elements of actual[4a] syllables, or sounds; for such elements are numerically limited). Sim- 20 ilarly, the elements of mathematical intermediates are, even when of the same kind[57a], numerically infinite. Hence, if there are not, besides sensible and mathematical objects, others such as some say ideas[20] are, then primary being cannot be numerically one, but only one in kind[20]. And [if there are such beings,] the principles of things[1a] need not be so many[27] in number, but only in kind[20]. If this need is real, then it is also necessary for this reason to posit[64] ideas[20]. Even if those who say this do not make it explicit[36c], this is at any rate what they want[177]; and they must say what they do because each of the ideas[20] is in some sense primary being, and none is incidentally[3]. However, if we are to believe[64] both that there are ideas[20] 30 and that their principles are one in number, but not in kind[20], we have already stated * what impossible consequences necessarily follow.

Related to these is the difficulty whether the elements

* iii.4.997b27–1000a4.

exist potentially or in some other manner.† If in some other way, something else must be prior to the principles. For what 1003a is potential[11] is prior to any actual factor[83], since not everything that is potential[11b] need ever be[33] actual. On the other hand, if the elements are potential, it is possible that what is[1b] may never be[23]. For what is[1] not yet, may[11b] be[23], since what is not[1b], comes to be[116]; but of the things which cannot possibly be, none comes to be.

These, then, are the difficulties that we must raise concerning the principles; and we must also ask ‡ whether principles are general[43] or, as we say, "individuals"[40]. If they are general, they are not primary beings[26]; for what many beings have in common cannot itself be a this-something[4b], but is a "what"[5]; whereas a primary being is a 10 "this"[4b]. If we were permitted to suppose[64a] that what is predicated in common is itself a this-something, then Socrates would be many animals: himself and "man" and "animal"—if each of these indicates a this-something, or a separate thing[24]. These are the consequences of supposing principles to be general. But if they are not general, but individuals, they are not knowable[179b]; for knowledge of anything is general. Hence, if there is to be knowledge of such principles, there must be other principles prior to them; namely, what is[25a] general to them.

† iii.1.996a11; ix.8; xii.6, 7.   ‡ iii.1.996a10; vii.13, 15; xiii.10.

IV. BOOK GAMMA

1

THERE IS a science[179] which takes up the theory[187] of 21 being[1] as being[1] and of what "to be" * means[82f], taken by itself[2]. It is identical with none of the sciences whose subjects are defined as special aspects of being. For none of them looks[195a] upon being on the whole[43] or generally; but each, isolating some part, gets a view[187] of the whole only incidentally[3a], as do the mathematical sciences. Since we are searching for the first principles[82] and most general factors[83] of being, these must clearly be distinctive traits of some nature. If those who have sought the elements[103] of things were also engaged in this same search, we must interpret their "elements," too, as intrinsic (not merely 30 incidental[3]) aspects of being itself. Accordingly, we too must grasp the primary[17a] factors[83] of being[1] as being[1].

2

Now, "being" has several meanings;** but they all have a central reference[24a] to some one nature[101] and are not entirely different things that happen to have the same name. So, for example, everything called "healthy" has some reference to health, such as preserving it, or producing it,

---

* The expression "being as being" is to be understood in terms of verbs, in the sense of *esse qua esse* rather than of *ens qua ens*.

** Aristotle does not distinguish between the different meanings of "terms" and the different ways of "being," and his metaphysics is based in part on the attempt not to make such a distinction. However, it is difficult to translate this attempt into our English idioms, which take the distinction for granted.

or being an indication of it, or being capable of it. So, too,
1003b the "medical" is relative in various ways to the art of
medicine: anything is said to be "medical" because it
possesses the art of medicine, or because it is naturally
suited for this art, or because it is what the art of medicine
does. We could mention other terms with analogous varieties
of meaning. So "being," too, has various meanings, but they
all refer back to a single root[82]: some things are said to
"be" because they are themselves primary beings[26];
others, because they modify[35a] primary beings; still
others, because they are on the way to becoming a being, or
are destroying it, or are its defects[106] or its qualities or its
producers or sources or whatever else may be relative to a
10 primary being or to the negation of such a being or of its
relations. Thus, we declare even nonbeing[1b] to "be"[23]
what-is-not[1b]. As there is, then, one science of all that
pertains to health or to any other distinctive subject matter,
so whatever is said of one subject matter belongs to one
science. Accordingly, whatever is said in reference to a
single nature is a single science; for such statements, too, in
some way or other, refer to a single subject matter. Clearly,
then, the theory[187] of beings[1a] as being[1a] constitutes a
single science. And since any science deals chiefly with what
is primary[17a] to its subject, other considerations being
derived from and dependent upon the primary, the philosopher must have within his province the first principles[82]
and primary factors[83] of primary beings[26].

Furthermore, as any class[19] of things is united in sense
20 perception and in a science (for example, grammar is one
science and unites in theory all articulate sounds), so the
theoretical science of being as being includes as its parts the
sciences of the species[20] of being within the general
class[19] of being as being.

Now let us see whether unity and being are the same and
are one nature.† They accompany each other as do a principle[82] and an explanation[83], but not in the sense that

† iii.1.995b27, 2.997a25-34.

they have a common[24] definition[90]. (If they had the same definition, our argument would follow even more clearly.) Let us illustrate: "one man" and "an existent man" are the same being as "a man." The verbal difference between "one man" and "a man is" does not imply[59] that each refers to a different[16] being[4]; for both expressions apply to only a single man that comes into being and passes away. So if we add "one" [to "an existent[1] man"], the addition is not of another being, but to the same being. Thus, unity is not a being apart from single beings[1]. Similarly, any primary being is a unity, not additively[3] (a being "and" one), but essentially, being one[4c]. In view of all this, we may conclude that there are precisely as many kinds[20] of being as there are of unity; and the theory[187] about these kinds[87], for example, identity[15], similarity[57], and so forth, belongs to a single science. So, also, nearly all contraries[50] exhibit[113a] this same principle of union. But let us regard this theory as already covered in the "List of Contraries."

There are, then, as many parts of philosophy as there are kinds of primary beings[26]; accordingly, there must be a first philosophy and another following it.‡ Since it is a trait[82f] of being and unity to have kinds[19], the philosophic sciences will correspond to kinds of being. The philosopher, as we call him, is in this respect like the mathematician, whose science, too, has parts—a first and a second branch, and then others following them, all within mathematics.

The theory[187] of opposites[13] is not a separate science, but belongs to whatever science the particular opposition belongs to. So, for example, plurality[6b] belongs to the science of its opposite, unity; and the theories of negation[48] or privation[106] of being belong to the science of being. For this theory concerns that of which there is a negation or a privation. Sometimes we negate simply by saying that a given attribute does not belong[82f] to a given being; sometimes, however, we say merely that the attribute does not

‡ iii.2.997a15-25.

belong to a whole class[19]. In the latter case a privation positively differentiates[76a] one member from its class, in addition to the negation concerning the class. The negation of anything is merely its absence[23a]; whereas, in privation a member of a class is deprived of an attribute of his nature as a member of that class. In view of all this, our science 20 includes plurality; for it is the opposite of unity, and through it we get to know[181c] the opposites of the kinds of being and also their diversities[16], dissimilarities[57f], inequalities[57g], and whatever else is attributed to these or to unity or to plurality. We should also include contrariety[50a]; for contrariety is a kind of difference[76a], and difference, a kind of diversity[16a]. Consequently, though "unity" has several meanings, and hence these correlatives of unity, too, must have several, still the knowledge[181c] of them all belongs to one science. For a term belongs to different sciences, not merely because it is used in many ways, but when its definitions[90] can be referred neither to a single[24] subject matter[39a] nor to a common ground[24a]. But all attributes refer to something primary[17a]: things called "united" refer to unified being; likewise for "the same"[15], "the diverse," and contraries generally. Hence, after going over the various ways[6a] in which each may be taken, we must explain[46d], by reference to the primary[17a] subject related to each predicate, how the predicate is related to it: 30 some will be attributes because their subjects possess them; others, because they produce them; and still others, for other reasons. It is evident, then, as was said in our account of difficulties,§ that a single science must explain[90] these relations as well as primary beings[26] as such. This was one of the topics in our list of problems.

Next, it is the philosopher's task to be able to view[187] 1004b things in a total way[150]. For, if this is not the philosopher's task, then whose will it be to inquire, for example, whether Socrates and "Socrates seated" are the same, or whether "one" thing has only one contrary, or what it means to

§ iii.1.995b18–27.

be[87] contrary and how many ways of being contrary there are, and other considerations of this sort? Since these are essential[2] attributes[35a] of unity and being themselves, not their properties as being numbers or lines or fire, it is clear that this science must seek to know[181c] both what this subject matter is[87] and what can be said about it[3a]. Those who take up these problems are likely to go wrong, not because they fail to philosophize, but because, in their ignorance of primary being, they overlook what comes first. For, just as numbers as such have peculiar[42] attri- 10 butes[35a], such as oddness and evenness, commensurability and equality, too much[148] and too little[148a], and as these belong[82f] to numbers in themselves or in relation to one another, so what is solid, what is unmoved, what is moved, what is heavy, and what is not heavy, each has its[42] properties, which differ[16] from those of the others. So, too, being as being[1] has certain properties, and it is into the truth about these that the philosopher must inquire. This is indicated by the fact that dialecticians and sophists appear to be philosophers; for sophistry is but apparent wisdom, and dialecticians converse about any and all affairs on the ground 20 that being is common to all. But, evidently, they converse about all these matters because all are appropriate to philosophy. Sophistry and dialectic, indeed, revolve about the same kind[19] of concerns as does philosophy; but philosophy differs from dialectic in degree of power, and from sophistry, in kind[178] of life[153]. For dialectic puts questions[196a] about matters which philosophy knows[181e], and sophistry appears to be, but is not, philosophy.

In the list of contraries, one of each pair is a privation, and all can be reduced to either "being" and "nonbeing" or to "unity" and "plurality": rest, to unity; and motion, to plurality. And nearly all thinkers agree that beings[1a], 30 including primary being[26], consists of contraries—at any rate, all of them give pairs of contraries as their first principles: some, odd and even; others, hot and cold; others, limited and unlimited; and still others, friendship and strife.

Evidently all these and others are reducible to unity and
1005a plurality—at least, we shall assume this reduction; and the
principles stated by others thus fall entirely under these
two kinds[19].

These considerations, too, make clear that a single science
examines[187] being[1] as being[1]. For all things are either
contraries or are composed of contraries; and the basis[82]
of all contraries is the contrast between unity and plurality.
Whether they are used in a single sense or, as is more
probable, in several senses, they still fall within this science.
Even if "unity" is used in several senses, the other meanings
are related to the primary. The same is true of the contraries; so that, even if being is not as a whole[43] unified and
if it is the same as all its instances or is not separable from
10 them (as seems probable), there is, nevertheless, in some
cases a central meaning[24a] and in other cases a single
sequence[136c]. Therefore, it is not the geometer's business
to answer questions[187] about what contrariety is, or
perfection[14], or being, or unity, or sameness, or diversity;
for him these remain postulates[64h].

Now, to sum up, there is a single science that must view
systematically[187] being as being and whatever belongs to
it as being. And the same science examines[187b] both
primary beings[26] and whatever attributes[82f] they have,
including the considerations named, and also "before"
and "after," genus and species, whole and part, and so forth.

3

It is necessary to decide whether the same or different
20 sciences deal with what in mathematics are called
"axioms"[67] and with primary being[26]. Now, clearly the
examination[195] of axioms also belongs to one science, to
the science of the philosopher; for they refer[82f] to all
beings[1a], not to some special kind[19] among others. All
men use them, because all the various classes of things to
which axioms apply have being[1]; hence axioms refer to
beings[1] as being[1]. Men use them to an extent sufficient for

their purposes; that is, as far as the class of beings extends to which their demonstrations are relevant. But it is clear that the axioms extend[82f] to all things as being (since they all have being in common); hence the theory[187a] of axioms also belongs to him who knows[181c] being as being. For this reason no one among those who devote themselves to limited[22] inquiries undertakes to say anything about the 30 axioms, whether they are true or not. Neither the geometer nor the arithmetician does this. True, some of the physicists have done so, and for the simple reason that they thought of themselves as engaged in viewing[195a] nature as a whole[21] or being as such. But, since there is someone above even the physicist, inasmuch as nature is one particular[4] kind[19] of being, therefore he whose investigation[187b] is most inclusive[43] and concerns primary being, can best examine[195] axioms. Physics, too, is a kind[4] of wisdom, 1005b but not primary. And as for those physicists who have attempted to discuss truth and the way in which it is to be accepted[66], they show in this their lack of training in logical analysis; for when they have arrived at the level of physics, they should already know about these matters and not be still investigating[194] them while attending to their special studies.

It is clear, also, that the philosopher, who examines[187] the most general[150] features[101c] of primary being, must investigate[195] also the principles[82] of reasoning[62]. For he who gets the best grasp[181c] of his respective[19] sub-ject[188c] will be most able to discuss its basic principles. So that he who gets the best grasp of beings as beings must 10 be able to discuss the basic[68] principles of all being; and he is the philosopher. And the surest[68] principle of all is that about which it is impossible to be mistaken; for such a principle does not rest on assumptions and must be best known[181d]. (All men may be deceived about the things they do not know[181c].) For a principle which one must have in order to understand anything whatever is not an assumption; and what one must know to know anything one must have acquired before having arrived at this stage of specialized knowledge.

It is clear, then, that such a principle is the most certain of all and we can formulate it thus: "It is impossible for the same thing at the same time to belong and not to belong to 20 the same thing and in the same respect"; and whatever other distinctions we might add[72f] to meet dialectical[36] objections[200b], let them be added. This, then, is the most certain of all principles, since it meets the specifications[72a] stated above. For no one can believe[65i] the same thing to be and not to be; though, as some hold, Heraclitus may have denied this, he did not necessarily believe it in the way in which he stated it. Hence, if contraries cannot at the same time belong to the same thing (and we must add to this proposition[62a] the usual qualifications), and if an opinion stated in opposition[49] to another is directly contrary to it, then it is evidently impossible for the same man at the same 30 time to believe the same thing to be and not to be; for whoever denies this would at the same time hold contrary opinions. It is for this reason that all who carry out a demonstration rest[113a] it on this as on an ultimate[18a] belief[175]; for this is naturally a beginning also of all other axioms.

4

There are some who, as we have just said, declare it 1006a possible for the same thing both to be and not to be, even when the principle is understood[65i] in our way. Many, including writers on nature, use this language[90]. But we have now taken it to be impossible for anything at the same time to be and not to be; and we have therewith shown that this is the most certain of all principles.

Some, indeed, from lack of education, demand[46c] that this principle too be demonstrated; for it is a lack of education not to know[181a] that it is necessary to seek demonstration of some propositions and not of others. For there cannot be a demonstration of everything altogether[44];

there would then be an infinite regress, and hence there would still be no final demonstration. But if there are propositions of which it is not necessary to seek a demonstration, then those who refuse to admit ours ought to say what principle they would rather accept.

It is possible, however, to demonstrate by way of refutation[80a] that a contrary position is untenable, whatever other proposition the opponent[51] may formulate. Of course, if he does not propose an alternative, it is ridiculous to try[194] to prove[90] our principle to one who cannot demonstrate[90] his own. For such a man is, as far as this trait is concerned, no better than a plant. What I mean by "demonstrating by way of refutation" differs from demonstrating, because one who demonstrates may be held to beg[83d] the question; but if the other party is guilty[83a] of something like it, there may be refutation, even though there is no demonstration. However, the proper beginning for all such debates is not a demand for some undeniable assertion that something is or is not (for any such assertion someone might take as a begging[83c] of the question), but a demand for expressing[38] the same idea[4] to oneself and to another; for this much is necessary, if there is to be any proposition[36] at all. If a person does not do even this, he is not talking[90] either to himself or to another. If, on the other hand, he grants this, there can be demonstration; for then something definite[72] will be proposed. However, not he who demonstrates, but he who settles the issue[83a] acquiesces; for though he disowns discourse[90], he acquiesces in it. And he who concedes this, has conceded that something is true even without demonstration. Thus, not everything can be so and also not so.

Clearly this much at least is true that the words "be" and "not be" signify something determinate[4a]; not everything can be so and also not so. Suppose "man" has the meaning[38] "two-footed animal." By "having a meaning" I mean this: if "man" is "two-footed animal," then if anything is a man, its "being-two-footed" will be what its

"being-a-man"[88a] is. Now it makes no difference if we take a word that has more than one meaning, provided only 1006b that these be limited[72] in number; for one might use[64] a different symbol for each meaning[90] of the word. I mean that we might agree that "man" has, not one, but more than one meaning, of which one is denoted by "two-footed animal," and that there are also several others, for each of which a special word might be used; but, if these were not used and we were to declare merely that "man" has infinite meanings, then it is evident that there would be no discourse[90]; for not to have some specific meanings is to have no meaning, and when words have no meaning conversation with one another, and indeed with oneself, has been annihi-
10 lated, since it is impossible for one who does not think[169a] something to think anything. Even if this were possible, a word might be used to designate such a state of affairs[188c]. Let us suppose, therefore, what we supposed in the beginning, that a word has a meaning and a specific meaning. It is not possible, then, for "being a man"[88a] to mean what "not being a man" means; for "man" not only means something about certain beings, but has a definite meaning. As to having a meaning, what we insist on is that the meaning is not the object referred to (since then "musical" and "white" and "man" could have a single meaning or referent, and all would be one, and those terms would be synonymous). [What we mean is that] it will not be possible to be and not to be the same thing, except ambiguously; for example, if we call a
20 "man" what others were to call "nonman." The question[200a] is not whether the same thing can at the same time be and not be a man in name[37a], but in fact[188c]. However, if "man" and "nonman" mean nothing different, it is clear that also "not being a man" will mean nothing different from "being a man"[88a]: so that "being a man" will be "not being a man"; for they will be one. For this is what "being one" means, as in the case of "garment" and "vestment," whose definition[90] is one. If, therefore, they are to be one in fact, "being a man" and "being nonman"

must have the same meaning. But it has been shown that they have different meanings. Therefore, if it is true to say of anything that it is a man, it follows necessarily that it is a two-footed animal (for this was the meaning we assigned to 30 "man"). And, if this is necessary, it is then impossible for this two-footed animal not to be a two-footed animal; for "being necessary" means that it is impossible that the thing, for example, a man, should not be. Accordingly, it cannot be at the same time true to say that the same thing is a man and is not a man.

The same account applies also to "not being a man": for 1007a "being a man" and "not being a man" have different meanings, since even "being white" and "being a man" are different; for the former terms are much more opposed[13] and, consequently, have different meanings. If anyone should maintain that "white" could also have the same meaning, we would again say precisely what we have said above; namely, that then not only opposites[13] would be one, but all things would be one. But if this is not possible, what has been said follows. These conclusions follow from any reply which might be given to our question.

However, if when the question is asked for a direct reply one were to reply by merely adding negatives, then the question is not really answered; for, though there is nothing 10 to prevent the same thing from being besides a man also white and countless other things, still when one is asked if it is true or not to say that this is a man, an answer with a definite meaning must be given, and it will not do merely to add that this is also white and large. For, among other things, it is impossible to enumerate all the accidental attributes[3a], since they are infinite in number; therefore, either all of them must be enumerated, if the enumeration is to be an answer, or none of them. Hence, even if the same thing is ten-thousandfold a man and something else besides, the answer to be given to him who asks whether this is a man, cannot be merely that it is at the same time also "what is not man," unless the answer adds all the other

accidental attributes, whatever else besides man it is or is
20 not; but to do this would end conversation[78].

Generally[44] those who argue in this manner overlook[118]
both the being[26] of things and what it means to be[88]; for
it is necessary for them to assert that all attributes are
accidental and that there is no such thing as "being a
man"[88a] or "being an animal." Now, if there is such a
thing as "being a man," it will not be "being nonman" or
"not being a man" (its negatives): for it has one meaning;
namely, to define the being[26] of something. And to signify
its being[26] means that its being[23] is not something else.
But, if "being a man" means "being nonman" or "not being
a man," then a man's being will be something else. Hence
30 they must argue that there cannot be such a definition[90]
of the being of anything, but that all attributes are accidental[3]. The being[26] of a thing and its accidents[3a]
differ[72e] thus: whiteness is accidental[3b] to man because,
though he may be white, his being is not that of whiteness.

But if all statements merely predicate accidents[3], then
there will be no first point of reference[43], since accidents[3a]
always are predicated[25] about something as a subject[85].
1007b It would be necessary, accordingly, to proceed thus to
infinity; but this is impossible. For not more than two terms
can be thus combined, since the accidental is not accidental
to the accidental, unless two accidents are both accidental
to the same thing. Let us assume that "the white is musical"
and "the musical is white"; if these statements are true, it is
only because both "white" and "musical" are accidental to a
genuine subject, say, a man. But "Socrates" and "musical"
are not related in this way, that both are accidental to
something else. Since, therefore, some accidents are referred
to subjects and others to other predicates, those which refer
to subjects (for example, Socrates is white) cannot be pro-
gressively extended into infinity: "the white Socrates" does
10 not have still another accident; for nothing would give unity
to such a series. And "white" cannot have its own accidents
(for example, musical); for "musical" is no more accidental

to "white" than "white" is to "musical." We have already noted[72e] that some accidents are related to each other in this way, while others are related to subjects, as "musical" is accidental to "Socrates"; and an accident is an accident of an accident only in this latter sense, so that not all predicates can be accidents. There must, accordingly, be some meaning in the sense of indicating a thing's being[26]. And if so, it has been shown that contradictories[49] cannot at the same time be thus predicated[25a].

We observe, next, that if all contradictories were true at the same time of the same thing, it is clear that all things would be one. For if anything may be affirmed[47] or 20 denied[48] of everything (as those must maintain who say what Protagoras says), then the same thing would be a trireme, a wall, and a man. For, if someone should hold that a man is not a trireme, clearly he is not a trireme; then, if the contradictory be also true, he also is a trireme. Things will then be as Anaxagoras described them, all things[163] being mixed together, and nothing would truly belong[82f] to anything. These men, then, seem to be describing[36] the infinite[72c], and though they think they are describing being, they are describing nonbeing; for the infinite is potential[11c], not completely actual[10]. But of any particular being they must either affirm something or deny 30 something; for it is absurd to believe that anything can be its own negative and yet to exclude from it the negatives that do not belong to it. I mean that, if it were true to say of a man that he is not a man, it would certainly be true that he is also not a trireme. Now, if they admit this much, then they would be obliged (by their principle) to admit also its negative. But if the affirmative is not true of the man, the negative of trireme will certainly be truer of him than the negative of the man himself. If, then, even "nonman" is 1008a true of him, the negative of trireme will also be true of him; and if this, then also the affirmative. Not only do such consequences follow for those who maintain the view[90] under criticism; but it follows also that it is not necessary either to assert or to deny. For if it is true that a thing is a man and notman, then it is clear that it will be neither man nor notman; for to the two assertions correspond the two denials. And if the one is a single proposition composed of two, the other is also a single proposition opposed[13] to it.

Now, either this doctrine is so in all cases and a thing is both white and not white and both a being[1] and not a 10 being, and so forth or it is not so, but only in some cases, not in others. And if not in all cases, then at least these exceptions have their own attributes; but if in all, then, again, either any assertion whatever may also be denied, and any denial whatever may also be asserted, or, though any assertion may be denied, not any denial may be asserted. If the last alternative is so, there will be something which definitely is not, and this much at least is known[175] for certain[68]. And if something is certainly known[181d] not to be, the opposed assertion is even better known. But if it is equally possible to assert what it is possible to deny, one 20 who makes a distinction[75] (such as that a thing is white and again that it is not white) must either be saying what is true or not. And if he who makes this distinction does not say what is true, he is not saying anything, and nothing is anything. But how can things that are not speak or think? Besides, then all things would be one, as has been said before;* and man, god, and trireme, and their contradictories will all be the same. For if contradictories apply to anything, one thing will not differ from another; for if it differs, this will be something true and peculiar to it. So what has been said follows if whoever makes a distinction speaks truly. It would follow, besides, that all men may be speaking truly and all men may be speaking falsely, and therefore our opponent must admit that he speaks falsely. 30 At the same time, it is evident that in examining[195] him we have examined nothing at all; for he says nothing. For he says neither "so" nor "not so," but "so" and "not so." Yet he again denies both of these and says "neither so nor

* iv.4.1006b17, 1007a6.

not so"; for otherwise there would be something[4] definite[72]. If when an affirmation is true its denial is false, or when the denial is true its affirmation is false, then it will not be possible at the same time to assert and to deny the same thing truly. But this may be stating the very issue 1008b proposed at the beginning.

And can he be wrong who believes[65i] something is either so or not so, and he be right who believes both? If the latter is right, what could he mean by making such a statement about the nature of things[1a]? And if he is wrong, but not as wrong as he who believes things are either so or not so, then things[1a] must have some sort of order; and this order would be true, not at the same time also not true. If, however, all men alike are both right and wrong, no one can say anything meaningful; for one must then at the same time say these and also other things. And he who means[65i] 10 nothing, but equally thinks[175c] and does not think, in what respect does his condition differ from that of a plant?

But clearly no man who says these things or anyone else really is so stupid. For if he wants to go to Megara, why does he go there instead of staying where he is? Why doesn't he, as soon as he gets up in the morning, wander into any well or fall into any abyss that happens to be there, instead of carefully avoiding it, if he really thinks falling in equally good and not good? It is clear, therefore, that he takes one alternative to be better and another not better. If so, then it is also necessary to take one thing to be man and another not a man, and one thing to be sweet and another not sweet. 20 For one is not indifferent to all things alike when one wants a drink of water, or when one tries to see a man; yet he ought to be indifferent if the same things were man and not man. But, as has been said, there is no one who does not consciously[173b] avoid some things and not others. Hence, all men know[65i] that situations call for decisions[105], if not in all matters, certainly in matters of choice. And if in such matters they do not have knowledge[179a], but only opinion[175], they must be all the more concerned for truth,

just as the sick have more concern for health than do the
30 healthy. For he who has only opinion is not as healthy in
matters of fact[7a] as he who knows.

In any case, whether things be so or not so, still things are
more or less; for we could not say that two and three are
both even, and if we say four is five we are less mistaken than
if we say it is a thousand. If, then, not all are equally mistaken, it is clear that one is less mistaken, and therefore more
1009a right. If, then, one quantity is more nearly right, something
must be true to which the more true approximates. And even
if this truth does not exist, still some things must be more
certain and truer than others; and we are far from that
irresponsible doctrine[90] which would prevent us from
making definite[72] judgments[170].

5

This same doctrine[175] gives rise to the system[90] of
Protagoras; and both alike must be true, or they must both
be false. For if all opinions and appearances are true, they
must all be both true and false, since many men hold
10 beliefs[65i] contrary[50] to those held by others and
think[175f] that men are mistaken who do not share their
opinions[175]. It follows necessarily that the same thing
must both be and not be. And if this is so, any opinion must
be true; for when those who speak falsely and those who
speak truly oppose[13] each others' opinions, they exhibit
the similar opposition among things[1a]. Hence they all
represent the truth. It is clear, then, that both doctrines[90]
proceed from the same way of thinking[170]. But they do
not both require the same treatment. The one group can be
persuaded; the other must be compelled to agree. For those
who hold such opinions[65i] because they are confused by
real difficulties[200a], can easily be cured of their ignorance[190] by someone who addresses himself, not to their
20 arguments[90], but to their meaning[170]; whereas those
who argue[36] for argument's[90] sake can be cured only

by refuting[80a] each of their explicit arguments verbally by other arguments.

Those who are genuinely perplexed[200a] believe this notion[175] that contradictories are both valid[82f] at the same time, because they seem to see visible things actually giving birth to contraries. Hence they conclude that since nonbeing cannot come to be, this copresence of contraries is an elementary fact[188c]. So Anaxagoras declares everything to be mingled in everything; and Democritus, too, says that the void and the plenum are alike present[82f] in any part, though the one is being, and the other is nonbeing. To men who base their ideas[65i] on such considerations, 30 we can say that in one way they are right, but in another way they are wrong. For "being" means two things; there is one way in which something can come to be out of nonbeing, and another way in which it cannot, so that the same thing can at the same time be a being and a nonbeing—but not in the same respect: for the same thing can at the same time be potentially[11] contraries, but not actually[10]. In addition, we shall ask them to believe that there is among things[1a] another type of primary being[26], which is not subject[82f] to change[109], destruction, or generation.

It has also occurred to some observers, on the basis of what they could perceive[165c], that appearances[173b] 1009b are true. For they do not think that truth depends on the judgment[164] of large or small numbers of men, seeing that the same flavor is sweet to some who taste it and bitter to others; and if all men were ill or mad except only two or three who were well or mentally sound, these few would be judged ill or mad, not the many. Also, they point out that many other animals do not perceive as we do and that even the same human being does not always perceive the same objects in the same way. Which of these, then, are the true or the false appearances? Either compared with the 10 other may be true or false. Hence, Democritus concludes that either nothing is true or that the true is at any rate not evident to us. In general[44], it is because these men take[65i] intelligence[172] to be sense perception[165a] and suppose sense perception to vary as things vary[120] that they believe[46] sense appearances to be necessarily true. For it is by these considerations that Empedocles, Democritus, and practically all the others were trapped into holding such opinions[175]. Empedocles, for example, maintains that when men change[115] their condition[33a] they change their intelligence: "for good sense increases in men with what is before them." And elsewhere he says that "as men themselves changed, so came a corresponding change of mind." And Parmenides declared himself[46b] in the same way:

> For, as each has his mixture of flexible limbs,
> So is man's mind: in each and all,
> As he naturally bends his limbs, so, too, his mind;
> For what fills his body, fills his thought.

And it is reported that Anaxagoras told some of his friends that things[1a] are as they are experienced[65i] to be. Homer, too, is said apparently to have held the same opinion; for he had Hector, though lying unconscious from a blow, "thinking other thoughts"—as if even those deprived of thought could think changed thoughts. It is clear, that if the mind can hold to both, then things[1a], too, will be at once "both so and not so." Here we come to a conclusion which is hardest to bear: if those who have been most keen in the pursuit of whatever truth is possible for us, if they who seek and love it most, hold such opinions and make such pronouncements[46b] about truth, how can beginners in philosophy fail to lose heart? For thus to seek truth would be like pursuing flying game.

However, the reason[83] why these men believed[175] what they did is that, though they inquired into the truth about the things that are[1a], they thought[65i] that all the things that are[1a] must be sensible[165c]. But things contain[82h] a large amount of the kind of being which is by its nature indeterminate[72c]—the kind of being[1] we have described above.* Hence, though these men speak plausibly, they do not say what is true. (This is a more fitting way to put it than as Epicharmus did against Xenophanes.) And as they saw this whole world of nature changing[109a], and as nothing true had been said about what changes[115], they concluded that nothing could possibly be said truly about what is always and everywhere changing[115]. And from this conviction[174] there blossomed the most extreme 10 of their doctrines, the philosophy of Heracliteans, as Cratylus held it, who finally[100a] thought one ought not to speak at all, but who simply pointed his finger and censured Heraclitus for saying that it is impossible to step twice into the same river—for he himself believed[175c] that one could not do this even once.

To this argument we can also reply as before that indeed there is a valid reason[90] for thinking[175c] that the changing[115], while changing, could not be. But this is after all debatable[51]; for what is passing away must still have something of what has passed away; and of what is coming to be, something must already be. And in general[44], when anything is perishing, something[4] is[1] present[82f]; and 20 when anything is coming to be, there must be something from which it comes to be and something by which it is generated, and this process cannot go on to infinity. But leaving those arguments, let us point out that to change[115] in quantity[27] and to change in quality[28] are not the same. Let us suppose things to be perishing quantitatively, still there remains their form[20] by which we get knowledge[181a] of them. We should add another criticism against those who hold these views[65i]: they have been reporting[46b] what they observe in only a few sensible things as if it were true of the whole cosmos[143a]. For it is only the region[132] of what is sensible round about ourselves that is continually in process of destruction and generation; but this is, so to speak, not even a small part of the whole, so 30 that it would have been more just to acquit this small bit

* iv.5.1009a35.

because of the whole than to condemn the whole because of this small bit. Here, again, we may reply to them as we did above;† we must show them and persuade them that there is immovable nature. Certainly anyone who asserts that things at the same time are and are not ought in consequence to maintain that all things are at rest rather than in motion; for there is nothing into which they change, since everything already belongs[82f] to everything.

1010b As to truth, we must say that not everything which appears is true. First, because, granted that a perception when it perceives its own object[42] is not false, an appearance is not the same as a perception. Then, too, we may well be surprised that they raise the question[200a] whether bodies are as large and colors are of the same shade as they appear to people at a distance, or whether they are as seen closer at hand and as they appear to the healthy or to the ill, and whether those things are heavy which appear so to the weak or to the strong, and whether those things are true which appear so in our sleep or to us awake. They certainly
10 do not believe[175c] that a person who dreamed one night that he was in Athens, though he was asleep in Libya, would go next morning to the concert hall. And, as to the future, surely, as Plato says,‡ the opinion of the physician and that of the nonexpert are not equally authoritative[55b] in predicting whether a man will get well or not. And two sense perceptions are not of equal[57] value[55b] if one is of a strange object[55a] and the other of a familiar object[42], or one has an appropriate, the other an inappropriate object; so color is judged by sight, not by taste, and flavor by taste, not by sight; and these senses never at the same time perceive the same thing to be at once so and not so. Not even at
20 different times does the same sense disagree[51] about a quality[35a], but rather about that to which the quality happens to belong[3b]. I mean that the same wine might seem, if it has changed[115] or if the body has changed, at one time sweet and at another time sour; but at least the

† iv.5.1009a36–38.   ‡ Plato *Theaetetus* 178B–179A.

sweet taste itself has never yet changed to sour, and one is always right about it, since whatever is sweet is of necessity like it. But all these doctrines[90] ignore[118] this, allowing nothing to be of necessity, as they also allow nothing to have an essential nature[26]; for what is necessary cannot be now this way, now that, and if anything is of necessity, it cannot be both so and not so. 30

In general[44], if there were only the perceptible, there would be nothing if there were no animate beings[154]; for there would not be sense perception. It would undoubtedly, then, be true that there would be neither perceptible objects nor perceptivity[165b] (for this is a quality[35a] of the perceiver); but it is impossible that the subjects[85] which stimulate[34] perception should be only in perception. For perception itself is surely not of itself, but there is something else besides the perception, and that is necessarily prior to the perception; for what moves is prior in nature to what is moved, and even if these are correlatives, this is no less 1011a the case.

6

There are some who, either seriously or for the sake of argument, raise a difficulty[200a] by asking[194] who decides[164] who is healthy and, in general[44] on any issue, whose judgment is right. Such perplexities are like asking whether we are now asleep or awake. For all such questions arise because men demand a reason[90] for everything; they seek to prove that they can reach[65] ultimate principles[82], 10 but their very actions[188b] prove that they are not convinced. We have already explained the source of their trouble[35a]: they seek a reason[90] for things which have no reason, since the beginning of demonstration cannot be demonstrated. Serious philosophers may readily be convinced of this, for it is not difficult to grasp[65]. But those who insist on being refuted by argument[90] seek the impossible; for in insisting that they be proved to be self-contradictory[50], they already contradict themselves. For, if not all things are relative[29], and some things are what they are in themselves[2], not every appearance can truly be; for an appearance is an appearance to someone, so that 20 anyone who says that all appearances truly are, believes[34] that all things[1a] are relative[29]. Hence those who insist on proof[90] and insist at the same time on proving their proof, must beware of saying that appearances truly are; they should say that any appearance is for him to whom it appears and when and in so far as and in the way in which it appears. If they give any other reason[90] for the reasons they give, they will[3b] fall into contradiction[50]. For one and the same thing may appear to sight to be honey and to taste not to be honey; moreover, since we have two eyes, it may not appear to be the same thing to each eye, if the eyes differ. So that when they say, for the reasons[83] stated 30 above,* that things are as they appear and that therefore all things are alike false and true, since things do not appear the same to all or always the same to the same man, and even appear contrary[50] at the same time (as when we cross our fingers, we feel two things but see only one), we may reply: "Yes, but things are not both so and not so to the same sense, in the same respect, in the same way, and at the same time; 1011b to be truly, they must satisfy all these conditions." Hence those who are not serious, but argue for argument's sake, ought probably to say that nothing truly is in this sense, that anything must be true for something else, and that necessarily all things are relative to each other, both in judgment[175] and in sense perception[165a], so that nothing has been or will be except as it has been believed to be. Hence, if anything really has been or will be, this proves that not everything is relative to opinion. So, for example, if anything is one, it is one relative to something definite or to a definite number of things; and if anything is both half and equal, it is at any rate not equal to the same thing of which 10 it is the double. If, therefore, a man and his thoughts are

* iv.5.1009a38–1010a15.

the same thing so far as thinking goes, the man will not be a thinker, but a thought. And if each thing is relative to a thinker, and each thinker to his thoughts, a thinker must be infinitely relative.

So much, then, for the most certain opinion of all (namely, that opposed statements cannot be at the same time true) and for the consequences which have been drawn from it and for the reasons given for it. And if it is impossible for contradictories[49] to be at the same time true of a given thing, it is evident that contraries[50], too, cannot at the same time be true[82f] of it. For one of the contraries is also a privation[106], and a privation of a thing's very being[26] is a denial[48] also of its genus[19]. If, then, it is impossible at the 20 same time truly to affirm and to deny, it is also impossible for both of two contraries to hold good[82f] at the same time, at least if both refer to the same aspect, or if one to some particular aspect and the other generally[105].

7

And the possibility of a middle[138a] between contradictories[49] is excluded; for it is necessary either to assert or to deny one thing of another. This is clear from the definition[72] of truth and falsity; for to deny what is[1] or to affirm what is not[1b] is false, whereas to affirm what is and to deny what is not are true; so that any judgment that anything is[23] or is not states either what is true or what is false. Hence, either what is[1], is affirmed or denied, or else what is not[1b] is affirmed or denied. [There can be no middle ground.] A middle might be asserted as gray is 30 between black and white, or one might say that between man and horse there is something that is neither. If a thing were "between" in the latter way, it could not change[115] (as nongood might change to good, or vice versa). But all existing things and intermediates in fact change into their opposites[13]. However, if a thing were really an intermediate [like gray], it would have to change into one of the opposites; 1012a

83

but a thing does not change to white unless it was nonwhite.

Similarly, every concept[170a] and thought[169b] is expressed[170] either as an affirmation or a negation; this is clear from the definition of truth and falsity. When a proposition either asserts or denies, it says either what is true or what is false. And unless this is an idle dispute[90], there would have to be [intermediate] statements between contradictories, such that they neither tell the truth nor fail to tell it; and there would have to be some sort of change[115] (neither generation nor destruction) between being and not being. Even in those cases in which the negation of one proposition implies the affirmation of its opposite[50], for example, in numbers there would have to be a number neither odd nor even. But this is impossible, as is clear from the definition. Such intermediates would lead to an infinite regress; existing things[1a] would be multiplied many times. For these intermediates, since each has its own nature[26], would have their positive and negative opposites; and each of these in turn would be something[4] with its own nature; and so forth.

It is also said by some that when one denies that a thing is white one merely denies that it is[23] anything; so that the negation refers to a nonbeing.

There are other paradoxical opinions; for when men are unable to refute captious[80] arguments, they are supposed to admit the argument and to agree to its conclusion. Some argue in this way for this reason[83]; others, because they wish to explain[90] everything. But basic[82] to all these arguments are definitions[72a]. And definition arises out of the necessity of stating what we mean; since the statement[90] of which the word is a sign becomes a definition. Now the argument[90] of Heraclitus, to the effect that all things are and are not, seems to present[34] all things as true, whereas that of Anaxagoras, that there is an intermediate between contradictories, seems to present all things as false; for when things are mixed, the mixture is neither good nor not good, so that one cannot say anything true.

8

After this analysis[72a], it is evident that both in particular[24d] and in general[150] those are wrong who assert 30
that nothing is true (for they maintain that nothing prevents any proposition from being as true as that the diagonal
of the square is commensurable with the side), and those are
likewise wrong who assert that everything is true. For these
arguments[90] are almost the same as that of Heraclitus;
for he who says that everything is true and everything false
also states each of these arguments separately[73a], with 1012b
the consequence that, since they are impossible, the two
together are an impossibility. Again, there are evidently
contradictories which cannot both be true. Nor can they
all be false; although from what has been said this would
be more feasible.

Against all such arguments, however, it must be
asked[83d], as has been said * also in the previous discussions[90], not that something is or is not, but that something
has meaning; so that we must converse on the basis of
definition by grasping what falsity or truth means. But,
if what is true to assert is nothing other than what it is false
to deny, then it is impossible for all things to be false; for 10
one of a pair of contradictories must be true. Again, if it is
necessary in every case to assert or to deny, then it is impossible for both to be false; for it is one of a pair of contradictories that is false.

Hence, also, the frequent saying befalls[3b] all such arguments, that they destroy[118] themselves. For he who says
that all things are true presents[34] even the statement[90]
contrary[50] to his own as true, and therefore his own as not
true (for the contrary denies that it is true); whereas he
who says that all things are false presents also himself as
false. But, if the former makes an exception[118d] of the
contrary, as if it alone were not true, and the latter makes
an exception of his own statement as not false, they will 20

---

* iv.4.1006a18–22.

nonetheless in consequence beg[83d] an infinite number of statements as true and false; for that which says that the true statement is true is true, and this process will go on to infinity.

Also, it is evident that those who say that all things are at rest do not speak the truth; nor do those who say that all things are in movement. For if all things are at rest, the same things will always be true and the same things will always be false. But this evidently changes[115]; for the speaker himself at one time was not and again will not be. But if all things are in movement, nothing will be true; everything will therefore be false. But it has been shown that this is impossible. Again, only beings[1] can change; for change is from something to something. Neither can all things be now at rest and now in motion, so that nothing is eternal[135]; for there is always a mover of things moved, and the first mover is itself unmoved.

V. BOOK DELTA

I

"Beginning"[82] means[36]: (1) The first point whence a thing's[188c] movement proceeds, such as the beginning of a line or of a road which has an opposite[50] end. (2) The point 1013a whence a thing develops[116] best; for example, in learning the learner starts not at the first point or beginning of the subject[188c] to be learned, but at the point that makes learning easiest. (3) The guiding part[82f] of any process[116]; for example, the keel of a ship, the foundation of a house, and in animals the heart, or the brain, or some other part (depending on which of the various theories one believes[65i]). (4) The external source whence a process or movement has[101c] developed—a parent starts a child, or an insult starts a fight. (5) The decisive[178] factor which 10 moves whatever is moved or changes whatever is changed[115]; so political "princes," "principal" or ruling classes, and "first men" in monarchies or tyrannies; so, too, those arts are called "principal" or "primary" that give direction[82b] to the other arts. (6) A principle of knowledge, the basic idea for understanding[181b] any body of knowledge[188c]: such as, the premises[64h] of proof[63a].

Explanatory factors[83], or principles, have these same meanings, for they are all beginnings.

What all beginnings have in common is that they are points of departure[17a] either for being, or becoming, or knowing[181a]. Some of them are internal[82h] controls; others, external. Illustrations of beginnings or principles 20 [besides "an explanatory factor," just mentioned] are:

a nature[101], an element[103], an intention[170], a choice[178], a primary being[26], and an ultimate "wherefor"[96] (for such ends as the good and the beautiful are also beginnings both of knowledge[181b] and of motion).

2

"An explanatory factor"[83] means[36] (1) from one point of view, the material constituent[82h] from which[86] a thing comes to be: the bronze of a statue, the silver of a cup, and their kinds[19]. (2) The form[20] or pattern[89a] of a thing, that is, the reason[90] (and the kind of reason) which explains what it was to be[88] that thing; for example, the factors in an octave are based on the ratio of two to one and, in general, on number. This kind of factor is found in the parts[22] of a definition[90]. (3) The agent whereby[95]
30 a change[115] or state of rest[110] is first[17a] produced[82]: a decision is "responsible"[83a] for a plan, a father "causes" his child, and, in general, any maker "causes" what he makes[34], and any agent causes some change[115]. (4) The end[100], or the wherefor[96]; when we take a walk for the sake of our health, and someone asks why we are walking, we answer, "in order to be healthy," and thus we think we have explained[83] our action. So any intermediate means to the end of a series of acts: as means of health there are re-
1013b ducing, purging, drugs, instruments, and so forth; for all these are for an end, though they differ from one another in that some are instruments, and others are actions[9c].

Since what we call an "explanatory factor" may be any one of these different aspects of a process, it follows[3b] not only that anything actually has several such factors which are not mere accidental[3] differences of meaning (as both the sculptor's art and the bronze are needed to explain a statue as a statue, the bronze being its material[84], and the sculpturing, its agent[95a]), but it follows also that these factors are reciprocal: exercise explains good health, and
10 good health explains exercise; though they explain each other differently (good health as end[100], and exercise

as[82] means[109]). And the same thing may explain contraries[50], for the same thing which by its presence explains[83] a given fact[4a] is "blamed"[83b] by its absence
for the contrary fact; for example, a shipwreck is "caused"
by the absence of the pilot, whose presence is responsible[83]
for the ship's safety. Thus, both the presence and the privation[106] are factors in the sense that they account for
some event[109a].

All the factors here mentioned clearly fall under four
varieties. From letters come syllables; from building materials come buildings; from fire, earth, and so forth, come
bodies; from parts come wholes; and from assumptions come 20
conclusions. The first factor in each of these pairs is the
subject matter[85] or the parts[22]; the second is what it
meant to be[88] that particular whole[21], or synthesis[64g],
or form[20]. A "cause" in the sense illustrated by a seed, a
physician, an adviser, and any agent[34] generally is the
factor whereby[95] a change or state of being is initiated[82].
Finally, there are the ends[100] or the good[98] of the others;
for all the others tend toward[96] what is best as toward
their end. It makes no difference now whether we say "their
good" or "their apparent good."

These, then, are the kinds[20] of explanatory factors. But
they fall into many lesser varieties, which can also be sum-
marized under a few heads. There are several ways[6] in 30
which explanatory factors explain, even when they are of
the same general kind[57a]. Thus, one factor is prior[17]
to another, which is posterior[18]: health is prior to both the
physician and the technician; the octave is prior to the ratio
of two to one and to number; and so always the inclusive
factor is prior to individual[40] factors.

Then there are accidental[3a] factors of various kinds[19];
for example, a statue is, we say, by Polyclitus, but it is also
by a sculptor; the sculptor happens[3b] to be Polyclitus. And 1014a
so the kind (sculptor) and the accidental (Polyclitus) which
it embraces are both factors in the statue; thus, a man is
responsible[83a] for the statue, and so is the more general

species "animal"; for Polyclitus is a man, and man is an animal. These accidental factors are sometimes remote and sometimes proximate; for example, between Polyclitus in particular and man in general there would be such intermediate factors as "a white man" and "an artist."

Besides, any factor, whether essential[55] or accidental[3], may be actually in operation[9a] or merely capable of acting[11a]: a house being built is the work of "builders," but more actually of the builder who is building it. The same is
10 true of the things to which explanatory factors refer—they may be singled out or referred to more generally: "this statue," or "a statue," or even more generally, "an image"; and "this bronze," of "of bronze," or, generally, "of matter"; and likewise with reference to the accidental factors.

Moreover, both accidental and essential factors may be combined: instead of Polyclitus or the sculptor, we say "Polyclitus the sculptor." However, these varieties reduce to but six, each being taken either individually[40] or collectively[19]: the accidental factors (individual or collective); combined or separate[105] factors; and actual or
20 potential factors. There is another difference among them: the operating and individual causes exist and cease to exist simultaneously with their effects (this man actually healing is correlative with this man who is now being healed, and this actual builder, with this thing-being-now-built); but potentially they do not exist together (for the house and the builder do not perish with the act of building).

3

An "element"[103] means[36] the first inherent[82h] component out of which a thing is constructed and which cannot be analyzed[75a] formally into a different form[20]; for example, the elements of speech are the parts of which speech consists[21b] and into which it is ultimately[18a] divided, whereas they cannot in turn be divided into other forms of
30 speech different from them in kind. If an element is divided, its parts are of the same kind[57a]; as a part of water is

water, whereas a part of a syllable is not a syllable. Similarly, those who speak of elements of bodies speak of the parts into which bodies are ultimately divided, whereas the parts are not divisible into others of a different[76] kind; and whether there is only one such part or more than one, they call them "elements." There are, likewise, the so-called "elements" of geometrical proofs and of demonstrations in general: for those theorems which are primary and belong inherently to many theorems are called "elements" of demonstrations; so 1014b there are syllogisms which are primary, having only three terms, one of them the middle term.

Also, by transfer of meaning people call an "element" whatever, being single and small, has many uses. For this reason the small and simple and indivisible is called an "element." Hence, too, whatever is most general[43] comes to be called an "element"; because any universal, being single and simple, is exemplified[82f] in many instances, in all, or in as many as possible. For this reason, too, some hold the one and the point to be first principles. And some say that since the so-called highest genera are general and indivisible (for they are indefinable) they, too, are elements, 10 more elementary than the differentia[76a], because more general; for a genus is always to be found where there is a differentia, but a differentia does not necessarily go with every genus. What is common, therefore, to all the meanings of "element" is that it is primary and inherent.

4

"Nature"[101] means[36] (1) the generation[116a] of "growing"[101b] things, as if one were to emphasize the "native" in nature.* (2) It means also an inherent something out of which[86] a thing begins to grow. (3) It means that in natural beings there inheres a source of their motion[95a]. Things are said to "grow" when they increase because they 20 are in contact with something that causes them to develop together with it or, as in the case of embryos, adherently.

* Pronounce the *y* in *physis* long.

And growing together[101f] differs from contact[137]: for in the latter there need be no union besides the contact; whereas in cases of growing together there is something which is the same in both bodies by which they develop together instead of merely touching, and they are thus a single and continuous body, though they differ in quality. (4) "Nature" also means the primary material of which an artefact is made and which cannot in its raw state be transformed by its own power; for example, bronze is said to be

30 the nature of a statue or of bronze utensils, and wood, of wooden objects, and so forth. For in each of these things their primary material is preserved. In this sense men call the elements of natural things their nature: some call it fire; others, air; others, water; others, something else of the sort; some regard an assortment of these, others regard all of them together, as the nature of things. (5) And "nature" means the primary being of natural beings. Thus, there are those who say that the nature of a thing is its primary mode of composition[64g]. And it is in this sense that Empedocles

1015a says:

> Nothing that is has a nature,
> There is only a mixing and separating,
> And nature is but a name men give to the mixture.

Hence, also, we say of things that are or come to be naturally, that even though they contain the source[86] of their being, they do not have their nature until they have their form[20] or shape[91]. A natural being, then, such as an organism[152] or its organs[22], is composed of both; so that nature is, on the one hand, prime material (prime either relative to the particular thing or generally prime, as in bronze objects the bronze is their first material, but in general the first material

10 of bronze is, perhaps, water, if all things that can be melted are water). On the other hand, a thing's nature is also its form or primary being or the culmination[100] of its becoming.

(6) Hence, by an extension of meaning any primary being

whatever has come to be called a "nature"; because the nature of anything is in some sense its primary being.

On the basis of what has been said, then, nature in the primary and chief sense is the primary being of those things which have in them their own source of movement; for a material is called a "nature" because it is capable of receiving[12] it, and the processes of becoming and growing are natural because they are movements proceeding from it. And in this sense nature is the source of movement in things, which are natural because this source is inherent in them, either potentially[11] or completely[10].

5

"Necessary"[123a] means[36] (1) being such a contributory 20 factor that without it there could be no life (for example, breathing and food), or good, or possibility[116] of good, or avoidance[58d] of evil, or riddance[106] of evil (for example, drinking medicine is necessary in order to get well, and sailing to Aegina is necessary in order to collect money).

It means, also (2), the compulsory and compulsion; that is, what impedes and obstructs some impulse[155] or choice[178]. For what is compulsory is said to be necessary, and therefore also painful, as Evenus says: "What is necessary is irksome." And compulsion is a necessity, as Sopho- 30 cles says: "Compulsion makes it necessary for me to do this." And necessity is held, and rightly held, to be not subject to persuasion; for it goes contrary to whatever course may have been chosen or intended[176].

(3) We say that what cannot be[33] otherwise is of necessity as it is. And this seems to be the sense of "necessary" from which the other senses are derived. For what is compulsory is said to be necessary only when a compelling force makes us do or suffer something not desired[155]; so that 1015b necessity is the reason given when something turns out otherwise. Similarly, the contributory factors of living and of the good; for when either the good or living and being

require certain conditions, these conditions are said to be necessary, and such a factor is said to be a necessity.

(4) Demonstrations[63a], when they are strictly[105] demonstrative, are necessary in the sense that no other conclusion is possible; and the reason[83] for its necessity lies in the fact that the premises on which the syllogism rests cannot be otherwise.

10 Some things are necessary because of some external[16] factor that necessitates them; whereas others are the factor explaining a necessity within things. Consequently, the necessary, in the primary and chief sense, is the simple, for it cannot be in more than one way; hence it is not subject to variation, since it would then be in more than one way. If, therefore, there are any things eternal and immovable, nothing can be compulsory for them or against[74] their nature.

6

"One"[24] may mean[36] either an accidental[3] unity or a unit by itself[2]. (1) An accidental unity is the identity of meaning of two such phrases as "Coriscus and the musical" and "musical Coriscus," which refer to the same thing; so, 20 also, "the musical and the just" and "musical just Coriscus." For these are all united in an accidental sense: the just and the musical, because both are accidents[3b] to a single primary being; the musical and Coriscus, because one of them is accidental to the other. Similarly, also, "the musical Coriscus" is one with Coriscus, because one of the terms, "musical," is accidental to the other, "Coriscus"; and "the musical Coriscus" is one with "just Coriscus," because each accident belongs to one and the same individual. So, too, when an accident is attributed to a genus or a general term; for example, "man" is united with "musical man," either 30 because "musical" is an accident of a class "man" taken as a single primary being, or because both are accidents of some individual man like Coriscus. But they do not both belong to him in the same way; one may be his genus and inherent in him as a primary being, and the other may be the primary being's state[33a] or quality[35a]. These are all illustrations of accidental unity.

(2) Things are said to constitute a unit or to form an essential unity (*a*) because of their continuity[136a]: a   1016a bundle is unified by a binder, and pieces of wood, by glue; a line, even when bent, is said to be one if it is continuous; and any organ, such as a leg or an arm, is united with the organism. But of these, those that are naturally continuous are more united than those unified by art. Things are continuous which move together and cannot do otherwise; and their movement is one when it is continuous and temporally indivisible [or simultaneous]. And things constitute a continuous being when they are not one by contact merely; for if you arrange[64] pieces of wood touching one another, you will not say they are one piece of wood or one body or any other one continuum. Things genuinely continuous are said to be one, even if they can be bent; and they are still 10 more so when they cannot be bent; for example, the shin and the thigh are each more unified than the leg, because the movement of the leg need not be one. And the straight line is more unified than the curved. But when a line is bent into an angle, we say it is both one and not one, because its movement may be simultaneous or not simultaneous; whereas that of the straight line is always simultaneous, and no part of it which has magnitude can rest while the other moves, as in a bent line.

(*b*) There is another sense in which things themselves are united in a single subject[85]: when they do not differ[76b] in form[20]. But things do not differ whose form is indistinguishable[75a] to sense; and their subject may be closely[17a] or only remotely[100a] what unites them. So all wines are 20 said to be one, as water is said to be one in so far as it is indivisible in form; so also all fluids (such as oil and wine) are said to be one, and all things that can be melted, because in all of them there is a single ultimate subject, such as water or air.

(*c*) And things are said to be one when they are of the same kind or genus, though their differentiae separate them. All such things are said to be "one," because the genus to which the differentiae refer is one; for example horse, man, and dog are "one something," because they are all animals, and, indeed, in a way similar to that in which things are united materially. In this way things are sometimes said to be "one." But sometimes the more inclusive kinds unite
30 things that in their least species are different, when their species themselves are united in a genus; an isosceles and an equilateral triangle are "one and the same figure," because they are both triangles, though they are not the same triangles.

(*d*) Also, things are said to be "one" when their definition[90], which states what it meant to be such a thing[88], is indistinguishable from the definition of another thing; though in itself any definition is divisible. Thus, a thing does not lose its unity when it becomes larger or smaller, because its definition remains the same; and many plane figures are the same when the definition of their form is one.

1016b In general, those things are really united which must be conceived[169c] by the same formula for their essential being, or which cannot be separated in time or place or definition. Of these, those are especially unities which are primary beings. For in general whatever cannot be divided is for that reason said to be a unity. So, if two beings cannot be divided as men, they are humanly one; if not divisible as animals, they are alike animals; and if both are magnitudes, then as magnitudes they are one. Most things, then, are said to be one in so far as they do, undergo, have, or relate to something in common; but things are said to be one primarily whose primary being is one; and their being may be one in continuity, in form, or in definition; for we count
10 as more than one things that are either not continuous, or whose form is not the same, or whose definition differs.

(*e*) Although we say that in a sense anything is one if it is a magnitude[27] and continuous, yet, in another sense, we deny it unless the thing is a genuine whole[21], that is, unless its form has unity: we should not, on seeing the parts of a shoe scrambled together, say that it is a single thing, except that the parts have continuity; but it is genuinely one only if they are put together so as to be a shoe and thus to have some one form. For the same reason the circle is of all lines most unified, because it is whole and complete[14].

(3) To be one[88a] means to be an arithmetical beginning: for a primary measure[146] is a beginning; it is that by which we first measure how a thing belongs to a kind[19]. Hence, 20 unity is the beginning of knowing anything individually. But not all kinds have the same units. For here it is a quarter-tone, and there it is the vowel or the consonant; there is a different unit of weight, and another of movement. But everywhere the unit is something indivisible, either in quantity or in kind. An indivisible quantity is called a unit if it is indivisible in every dimension and is without position; it is called a point, if it is indivisible in every dimension and has position; a line, if divisible in a single dimension; a plane, if divisible in two dimensions; and a body, if quantitatively divisible in all three dimensions. In reverse order, then, what is divisible in two dimensions is a plane; divisible in a single dimension, a line; divisible in quantity in no dimension, either a point or a unit, the unit being without position, 30 and the point having position.

(4) And just as things are numerically one, they are also one in form, or in kind, or by analogy: those numerically one have a single matter; those formally one, a single definition; those generically one, a single pattern[91a] of classification[25]; and those analogically one bear to each other the same ratio or relation that another pair has. Unities follow the order here given: those numerically one are always also formally one, but those formally one are not always numerically one; all things formally one are generi- 1017a cally one, whereas things generically one are not all formally one, but only by analogy; and things one by analogy are not all generically one.

It is evident, also, that "many" has the same variety of meanings that its opposite[13], "one," has: for some things are called "many" because they are not continuous; others, because their material elements are different (either immediately[17a] or in last analysis[100a]); still others, because their definitions indicate that in each case the essential being[88] is different.

7

"Being,"[1] too, may mean[36] either an accidental[3] or an essential[2] being. (1) In an accidental sense; for example, we say the just *is* musical, the man *is* musical, and this musical 10 being *is* a man; just as we say that a musician builds, when the builder happens to be a musician, or the musician a builder, since "this *is* that" here means[38] that one is accidental to the other. So, too, when we say "the man is musical" and "this musical being is a man," or "this white thing is musical" or "the musical is white," the last two statements mean that both musical and white are accidental to the same thing; the first statement means that what is asserted is accidental to a being; so "the musical is a man" still means that the musical is accidental to the man, not vice versa. So, too, the nonwhite is said to be because there are beings to which it can be attributed. Hence, whenever 20 anything is said to be in an accidental sense, the meaning is that both attributes belong to the same being, or that an attribute belongs to a being, or that an attribute belongs to something which is.

On the other hand, (2) the varieties of essential being are indicated by the categories; for in as many ways as there are categories may things be said to "be." Since predication asserts sometimes what a thing is[87], sometimes of what sort[28], sometimes how much[27], sometimes in what relation[29], sometimes in what process of doing[34] or under-going[35], sometimes where[30], sometimes when[31], it follows that these are all ways of being. For there is no difference between "the man *is* getting well" and "the man

gets well"; or between "the man *is* walking" or "cutting" and
"the man walks" or "cuts," and so forth.   30

(3) The "is" in a statement also means that the statement
is true; and "is not," that it is not true, but false. These
meanings obtain for affirmative and negative forms of
speech alike: that Socrates is musical means that this is
true, or that Socrates is a nonwhite thing means that this is
true; but "it is not the case that the diagonal of the square is
commensurate with the side" means that it is false to say
that it is.

(4) Finally, to "be" and "being" mean sometimes that   1017b
what is said is true potentially[11]; and at other times,
actually[10]. For we say that a being is a seeing being both if
it can see and if it does see; likewise, an intelligent being is
one which either can use or does use its knowledge; and a
thing is stable either because it is standing still or can do so.
Similarly, primary beings may be in either sense; for we
say Hermes is in the stone, and a half line is in the line, and
that a growing stalk *is* wheat. But what the difference is
between being potentially and not being must be explained[72e] elsewhere.*

8

"Primary being"[26] may mean[36]: (1) a simple body, 10
such as earth, fire, water, and everything of this sort; and
in general bodies and the bodies composed of them, both
animals and superior beings,** as well as their parts. But all
these are called "primary being," because they are not
attributed[36] to[39a] something else[85]; whereas other
things are said of them.

(2) It may also mean the explanation[83] of being[23],
because primary being is never attributed as a predicate to
something else; for example, we do not say that a living
being *is* soul or life.

* ix.7.

** Apulejus: "Daemones sunt animalia corpore aerea, mente rationalia, animo
passiva, tempore aeterna" (quoted by Thomas Aquinas).

(3) It may mean whatever is intrinsic[82h] to primary beings in the first sense, limiting[72] them and marking[38] them as a this-something[4b], or whatever when destroyed[118] destroys such a primary being[21]: the surface of a body, as some say, or the lines of the surface; and, in 20 general, number is by some thought to be of this sort, for if it is destroyed, they say, then there is nothing, for it bounds all things.

(4) It may mean "what it meant to be"[88] a given thing; this is determined[72a] in its definition[90], and this is called a thing's primary being.

It follows, accordingly, that "primary being" has a double meaning: the ultimate[18a] subject matter[85], which is never an attribute, and that which, being definitely a this-something, may have a separate[73] being,† and such is a thing's shape or form.‡

9

The "same"[15] means[36], (1) among accidents[3], being attributed[3b] to the same thing: "white" and "musical" are the same when one man is both; and "man" and "musical," when the latter is accidental to the former; and "the 30 musical is a man" when the former is accidental to the latter. In these cases each term is the same as any other and as all together, since they all refer to one and the same musical man; and in such cases the sameness is not general[43], for it would not be true to say "every man is the same as musical": for such a general statement would apply[82f] to the subject essentially[2], whereas acciden-1018a tal[3a] attributes are not of things in their own character[2], but of individual cases[40] severally[105]. Thus, "Socrates" and "musical Socrates" are meant[175a] to be the same; but "Socrates" does not apply to more than one, and therefore

† Cf. viii.1.1042a29.

‡ Thomas Aquinas: "Essentia enim et forma in hoc conveniunt quod secundum utrumque dicitur esse illud quo aliquid est. Sed forma refertur ad materiam, quam facit esse in actu; quidditas autem refertur ad suppositum, quod significatur ut habens talem essentiam."

"every Socrates" and "every man" are two different uses of "every."

In addition to this accidental sameness, "the same" has (2) an essential[2] sense, and in the same ways as does "the one"[24]: for things are the same when either their matter[84] is one (in kind[20] or number[141]) or when their primary being[26] is one. Hence it is evident[59d] that sameness[15b] is in a sense a unity: whether it unites the being of more than one thing or of a single thing when taken[163] as two; for when we say that a thing is the same as itself, we take it as two.

Things are called "other"[16] if their forms[20], materials[84], or definitions[90] (of their primary being) are more than one; and in general[44] "other" means the opposite[13] of the "same." Things are said to be "different"[76a] when they are "other," but are in some respect[4] the "same": other not merely numerically[141], but formally[20] or generically[19] or analogically[54]. To be different, things must be generically other, or contraries[50], or other in their very being[26]. Things are called "alike"[57] (1) when they all have the same modifiers or attributes[35], (2) when they have more modifiers the same than other, (3) when they are of the same sort[28], or (4) when in the course of their changes[120] from contrary to contrary they change in the same way most of the time[6c] or in the most important ways[55b]. Things are "unlike"[57f] in the opposite ways to those in which they are "alike."

10

"Opposite"[13] has a variety of meanings[36]: contradictory[49], contrary, correlative[29], privation-possession, beginning-end (extremes[18a] of generation[116a] and destruction[117a]), and incompatibles (accidents which cannot[12b] be simultaneously co-present[23c] in the same subject[12]) or elements[86] of incompatibles. Gray and white cannot at the same time belong[82f] to the same thing; hence their elements [white and black] are opposites.

"Contrary"[50] means[36] (1) attributes whose genera[19] are different[76] and which cannot[11b] at the same time be present in the same thing; (2) things which differ most[6c] within the same genus; (3) attributes which differ most in the same subject; (4) things which diverge most from the
30 same potentiality[11]; and (5) things that differ widely either in themselves[105], in genus[19], or in form[20]. Other things are said to be "contrary" by derivation from these kinds of contraries, as their possessors[33], their subjects[12], their producers[189] or sufferers[35c] (potential or[34] actual[35]), their losers[58d] or acquirers[65], their possessions[33a] or privations[106].

Moreover, since "one"[24] and "being"[1] have several[6] meanings, anything related[39a] to them must vary[77] with them; hence, the "same" and the "other" and the "contrary" must have different meanings in each category[25].

Things are said to be "other[16] in kind"[20] (1) when, being of the same genus, they belong to co-ordinate species;
1018b or (2) when, being of the same genus, they have a difference[76a]; or (3) when they are contrary in their primary being. Contraries are related to each other as "others in kind," if not all of them, at least those primarily so called. And (4) members of the last[100a] species in any genus are "other in kind" if they differ in definition[90] (for example, a man and a horse belong to indivisible[41] species of a genus, but their definitions are different); and, finally, (5) things which are the same in their primary being are "other in kind" if they are distinguished by a differentia.

Things are said to be "the same in kind" in ways opposite to these.

11

"Before"[17] and "after"[18] are applied[36] to cases in
10 which there is a first[17a] or a beginning[82] in each genus[19], for then things may be nearer to some beginning, which is determined[72] either intrinsically[105] and naturally[101]

or relatively to something[29], or some place[30], or some person: some things are located before others because they are nearer either to some place[132] determined by nature (for example, the middle[138] or the end[18a]) or to some chosen[126a] object; whereas what is farther away comes after. Other things are temporally[134] "before": some because they are farther from the present (that is, a past event, the Trojan war, came before the Persian, because it is farther removed from the present); others because they are nearer to the present (that is, a future event, like the Nemean games, is before the Pythian, because it is nearer to the present); in these cases we treat[163] the present as a beginning or a first. In cases of movement[109], what is nearer to the first mover is "before": the boy is before the 20 man. The first mover is in itself[105] a beginning. Other things take precedence by their power[11], since a greater[148] power comes before a lesser; hence, a being whose choice[178] determines subsequent events comes before them, for had he not caused them to follow, they would not have occurred, whereas his decision set them in motion; and thus choice or decision is a beginning. Other things take their place, before or after, in some order[207a] starting at some point according to some rule[90]: the dancer in second place comes before the one in third place, measured from the leader of the chorus; and on a lyre, the next to the highest string comes before the highest, because the middle string is the starting point.

In addition to this sense of "before and after" there is another sense, (2) the order of priority in knowledge[181]; 30 here, too, priority is determined by an intrinsic point of reference. Thoughts come before or after either according to definition[90] or according to sense perception[165a]. According to definition, the general[43] propositions are prior; but according to sense perception, particulars[40] are prior. In definition, too, the attribute[3a] is prior to the whole[21] which is being defined (that is, "musical" is prior to the musical man); for a definition is not a whole without the part[22]. However, as[12b] a being[23], "musical" comes after an[4] actual[1] musical man.

(3) Qualities[35a] of prior things are prior: the straightness
1019a of a line is prior to the smoothness of a surface.

There is another distinct use of "before" and "after": (4) natural[101], or ontological[26], priority; that is, things are thus prior when the being[23] of others depends on theirs, though they themselves are[12b] independent—a distinction[75] which Plato used[163]. Since there are many ways[6] of being[23], however, there is, first, priority according to subject matter[85]; here primary being[26] is prior. Then there is priority according to potentiality[11] and actuality[10]; here some things are prior in power (for example, the half line is prior to the whole, the part to the whole, and material[84] to primary being), and others, in
10 actualization; here these same things are subsequent. For it is only after a whole has been analyzed[206a] that these things are actual beings. In a way[55c], therefore, all things that come before or after are ordered in accordance with these distinctions: for some things are independent of others in their origins[116a] (the whole is independent of its parts); and others are independent in decomposition[117a] (the part is independent of its whole); and so forth.

12

"Power"[11] means[36] (1) the external[16] source[82] of a movement[109] or change[115]; or, if internal, a distinct otherness[16] in the thing moved: the building art is a power which is not present[82f] in the thing built; whereas a curative power may reside[82f] in him who is being cured, but it is a distinct capacity, not his function as a patient. In general[44], the beginning of a change or movement is called
20 a power, which may be in something else or be another capacity of the same thing, and this beginning is also an external or distinct agency; for it is by this agency that a process proceeds[35] and by which, as we say, a thing is "enabled"[11b] to suffer change[35], although we sometimes

say this, not about any change[35a] whatsoever, but only about a change for the better.

(2) A power implies doing[100] something well[99a] and deliberately[178]; for those who walk, but not well, and those who talk, but not as they wish, we are likely to describe as not "able"[11a] to talk or walk; similarly, when something changes[35].

(3) The tendency[33a] to remain impassive[35d], to resist change[115], or at least to[200e] resist change[109d] for the worse, is a "power": for when things are broken, battered, bent, or in any way destroyed, it is not because they have this ability[11a], but because they do not have ability; they 30 lack something, whereas things that are impassive to such processes, being barely and slightly affected by them, enjoy a power[11] and a capability[11a] in a positive sense[33].

Since "power" has these various meanings, "ability"[11b] also varies: (1) it means having the power to begin a movement or a change in something else or oneself as distinct (for even stability is an ability). "Ability" means (2) something over which another thing has such power. (3) It means any 1019b power of change[115], whether for better or for worse: for even what perishes is said to be perish-able[11b], otherwise[11f] it would not perish; it has, in fact, a certain disposition[64c] or cause[83] or principle[82] for suffering such change[35a]. Sometimes ability seems to imply possessing[33] something, and sometimes it means to be deprived of something. But, if privation[106] is itself a possession[33a], then all things are capable, because they possess[33] something. And we would use the same term[37b] to describe[36] a thing[1] that is capable because it has some condition or principle and one that is capable because it has the privation of what the other has, if it is possible[12b] to have a pri- 10 vation. So (4) a thing may be capable because there is no power or source, either external or distinct, to destroy it. Finally, (5) things are "able" in so far as something may or may not happen[116] to them or may or may not turn out[3b] well[99a]. And such power is found even in lifeless things, for example, in instruments; for men say one lyre is playable, and another not, if the latter does not have a good tone.

Incapacity[11d], on the other hand, is the privation of a power and an absence of such a source as has been described; it may be general[44], or in a particular thing that would normally[101c] be capable, or at a particular time when the power would normally be present[33]. Thus, it is not in the same[57] sense that a boy, a man, and a eunuch are[11f] impotent[116d].

20   Opposed to each kind of capacity, whether for change[109c] generally or for improvement, there is, of course, the corresponding incapacity[11d].

An impossibility[11f] may mean such an incapacity; but it may also mean the opposite of a possibility. In this case the "impossible" is the direct contrary[50] of what is necessarily[123] true[7]: that the diagonal of square is commensurable with its side is impossible, because contrary to fact[8], and its direct contrary, incommensurability, is not only true but also necessary; that it is commensurable is, therefore, not only false but also necessarily false. On the other hand, the direct contrary of this, the "possible"[11b], holds when it is not necessary[123a] for its direct contrary to be false: it is possible for a man to be seated, for it is not of

30   necessity false that he is not seated. The possible, then, means[38]: (1) what is not of necessity false; (2) what is true; (3) what may[12b] be true.

The term "power" is also used metaphorically in geometry.

Such "possibilities" do not refer[39a] to a power. Possibilities in the sense[39a] of potencies[11] all relate[29] to the

1020a first meaning given; that is, to a source[82] of change[115] that is external or distinct. Other things are called "capable," some because something else has such power over them; some because nothing has such power over them; and some because there is a power over them in some way or other. Likewise for things incapable. Hence, the strict[55b] definition[72b] of power in the primary sense will be the external or distinct source of change.

13

A "quantity"[27] is[36] what is divisible[75] into two or more constituent parts[82h], each being naturally[101c] a[24] unit[4] or a "this-something"[4b]. A quantity, then, is a plurality[6b] if it can be counted; and a magnitude[142a], if it can be measured. A plurality is what is potentially[11] divisible into what is not continuous[136a]; magnitude, into what is continuous. A magnitude continuous in one dimension is length; in two, breadth; in three, depth. Of these, a limited[131a] plurality is a number[141]; length, a line; breadth, a surface; and depth, a body[102].

Some things are said to be quantities in an essential sense[2], and some in an accidental sense[3]: the line is a quantity essentially; the musical, accidentally. Of those which are quantities in their own character[2], some are so in their primary being[26], for example, the line is a quantity (since in the definition[90] stating[36] what it is[87] a[27] quantity[4] is stated[82f]); others are modifications[35a] and states[33a] of such primary being, for example, much and little, long and short, broad and narrow, deep and shallow, heavy and light, and the rest of this sort. Also great and small and greater and smaller, when taken[36] by themselves[2] or relatively to each other, are both essential[2] attributes[35a] of quantity; although these terms[37a] are transferred[121] to other matters also.

Of the things said to be quantities in an accidental sense, some are meant according to our illustration of the musical and the white as quantities, because that to which they belong[82f] is a quantity, and others in the sense in which motion[109] and time[134] are quantities; for these also are said to be quantities of a sort and continuous, because the things of which they are modifications[35a] are divisible. I do not mean the divisibility of what is being moved, but of [the spatial magnitude] through which it has been moved; for it is because this space is a quantity that movement is a quantity, and it is because the latter is a quantity that time is also.

14

"Quality"[28] means[36] (1) the differentia[76a] of primary being[26]: a man is an animal of a certain quality (two-footed), and a horse is of the quality four-footed, and a circle is a figure of a certain quality (without angles), and so 1020b each quality is the differentia of a primary being. This is one meaning of quality, the differentia of primary being. Another is (2) applicable to immovable[109e] and mathematical[140] entities, as numbers[141] have certain properties; for example, the compound[64g] numbers which are not in one dimension, but which are illustrated by surfaces and solids (those which have two or three factors[27]), and in this sense[44] quality belongs[82f] inherently to any primary being except[74] quantity itself. For the primary being of a quantity is what it is once, for example, the number six is defined, not by what it is two or three times, but by what it is once, that is, six is once six.

(3) All modifications[35a] in moving primary beings 10 (such as heat and cold, whiteness and blackness, heaviness and lightness, and the like), in terms of which bodies change[115], when they are said to be altered[120]. So also things change according to virtue and vice and, in general[44], according to evil and good[98].

Quality, therefore, has practically[69] only two meanings, and chiefly[55b] one of these: in the primary sense[17a] quality is the differentia of a primary being. And of this the quality in numbers is a particular[4] case[22]: for it is in a sense a differentia of primary beings, though not of things moved or of moving things as such. Secondly, there are the modifications of moving things as such and the differentiae of movements. And of these modifications, virtue and vice are[22] instances[4]: for they make evident[59] differentiae of

movement[109] and activity[9], according to which things 20
that are in movement act[34] or are acted upon[35] well or
badly; since what is able to be moved or to act[9a] in one
way is good, whereas what can do so in another or the
contrary way is vicious. Especially, however, do good and
evil indicate[38] quality in living beings; and, among these,
especially in those which have the power of deliberation[178].

15

"Relations"[29] are[36] (1) quantitative, as double to
half, threefold to third, and in general the manifold to the
correlative fraction; also what is greater[148] than another
is relative to it. (2) In the sense in which fuel is relative to
what it heats, or a cutting instrument to the cut, or in
general an agent[189] to what it acts upon[35c]. (3) In the 30
sense in which the measurable is relative to the measure[146],
and knowable[179b] to knowing[179], and the perceptible[165c] to perceiving[165a].

Relatives of the first kind are numerical, and they bear
either a general[105] or a specified[72] relation to numbers or
to unity[24a]: the double is in a specified numerical relation
to one; whereas the manifold is numerically related to one,
but not in any specified ratio. And $\frac{1}{2}$ has a specified relation 1021a
to $1\frac{1}{2}$; $\dfrac{n+1}{n}$ and $\dfrac{n}{n+1}$ are indefinitely related to a number, as
nx is to x. And "greater than" is indefinitely related to
what is less; numbers are commensurate, whereas "greater
and less" need not be; the greater is, in relation to what is
less, "so much and something more," and this "something
more" is indefinite, for though it is whatever it happens to
be, relative to "what it is more than" it may be equal or
unequal.

All these relations are numerical and are expressed[35a]
by numbers; and so, in a sense, are "equal," "like"[57],
"same"[15], being all relative to[39a] "one." For things are 10
"the same" when they have one primary being, "alike"
when they have one quality in common, and equal when

they have one quantity; and since "one" is the beginning and measure of number, all these relations are numerical, though not in the same way.

Secondly, active[189] and passive[35c] things are said to be related either as[39a] potentially[11] active and passive or as actually[9] so: what can be heated is relative to fuel, because it can heat; but fuel actually burning is relative to what is being heated, as a knife is to what is being cut, in the sense that they are active or operating[9a]. But there are no active operations of numerical relations, except in the way which has been stated elsewhere; for operations in the sense of movements are not relative to them[82f]. Among the relations that relate potentially, there are temporal[134] relations: what has made is relative to what it has made; and what will make, to what will be made. So, too, a father is called the father of his son; for the father has been actively related to the son, who passively has been conceived.

Finally, there are some relations that relate according to privation[106] of a power, such as "incapable," "invisible," and whatever is said in this way. Things are related numerically or potentially when they are what they are said to be because they refer to each other, not because something else is referred to them; but things "measurable" or "knowable" or "thinkable" are relative, because something else is referred to them. For a thing is "thinkable" when[38] it is possible[23] for a thought[170] to refer to it; but the thought is not relative to what is being thought, for these are two ways of saying the same thing. Similarly, seeing is always seeing something, not just seeing the seen, although it is, of course, true to say this; but seeing is relative to color or to something else of the sort, whereas "seeing" and "the seen" are not relatives, for "seeing the seen" is redundant.

Thus, things are relational when they are said to be in one of these ways; but they may also be relational when they are included in a relational genus[19]; for example, medicine is relational because it is a species of scientific knowledge[179], which is thought to be relational. So, too, traits are said to be relational when the things that have them are relative: "equality" and "similarity" are relational beings because equal or similar things are relative. Some things are relative only accidentally: a man is relative because he happens[3b] to be[88a] the double of something, and double is relative; or white may be accidentally relative if the same thing happens to be double and white.

16

"Complete"[14] means[36] (1) that beyond which it is not possible to find[65] even a single part[22]; one's time[134] is complete when it is no longer possible to find a moment of one's time.

It means (2) what cannot in its own kind[19] be surpassed in excellence and goodness; a physician or flute-player is accomplished or complete when nothing in his proper[55] kind[20] of excellence is lacking[148a]. And thus, transferring the meaning also to the bad, we speak of an "accomplished" schemer and a "perfect" thief; indeed, we even speak of a "good" thief and a "good" schemer. For any excellence is a kind[4] of completion; and anything is complete, as every primary being is complete, when, as regards its proper kind of excellence, it lacks no part of its natural magnitude.

(3) Those things are called complete which have achieved[82f] a reputable end[100]; for to be accomplished means to have arrived[33] at the end. Hence, since any end is something ultimate[18a], we transfer the meaning to the bad and say that something has been "completely" spoiled and "completely" destroyed, when it lacks nothing of destruction or corruption, but when it is in its last extremity. That is why death, too, is by a figure of speech called our "end," because goals and endings are finalities. And so the final[18a] goal[96] is doubly an end.

Thus, things are complete which in their own kind[2] are perfected in these various ways: because in goodness[98a] they either lack nothing or cannot be excelled or have nothing proper to them outside of them; and, in general[44],

because they cannot be excelled in their own kind[19] or
1022a have nothing proper to it outside of them.

Other things are, in dependence on these meanings, said
to be complete, because they do[34] or have[33] or are
adapted[56a] to some such complete being, or because they
are related[29] in one way or another to what is called complete in these primary senses.

17

"Limit"[131] means[36] (1) the last point[18a] of anything; that is, the first point[17a] beyond which it is not
possible to find any part, and the first point within which all
the points are. (2) It means the form[20], whatever it may
be, of a spatial magnitude[142a] or of what has magnitude.
(3) It means also the end[100] of anything, that to which,
not from which, a movement[109] or action[188b] proceeds;
but sometimes it means both beginning and end. (4) It
means, finally, the wherefore[96], the primary being[26], the
"what"[88] of anything; for these are the limits of knowl-
10 edge[181], and, if of knowledge, then also of known
things[188c].

Thus, it is evident[59d] that "limit" means as many
different things as does "beginning"[82], and even more; for
a beginning is in a sense[4] a limit, but not every limit is a
beginning.

18

"According to"[39] has many[6] meanings[36]. (1) It
means the form[20] and primary being[26] of anything[188c];
that according to which a good man is good[98] is the good
itself. (2) It means the primary[17a] way in which a thing
naturally[101c] comes to be[116]; a thing is colored according
to its surface. Thus, it is primarily the form that is "according to"; but, secondarily, the material[84] of a thing, too,
and any subject[17a] matter[85] is "according to." In
general[44], "according to" has meanings as varied as "ex-
20 planation"[83] has[82f]; for we say either "With regard to

what has he come?" or "Wherefor[96] has he come?" Also, we say that a conclusion is unwarranted or warranted either "according to" or "because of"[83] its premises. Again, "according to" may relate[39a] to position[64]; a man stands "accordingly" (at a place[132]) or walks "accordingly" (in a direction).

Hence also, "of its own accord" or "by itself"[2] must[123] have many meanings. (1) What a thing is "by itself" is "what it meant to be[88] that thing": Callias "by himself" means "Callias" and "what it means to be Callias." But "by itself" also means (2) whatever belongs[82f] inherently to a thing's being[87]: Callias is "by himself" an animal. For "animal" is a constituent[82h] in the definition[90]; since Callias is a particular[4] animal. (3) Thirdly, "by itself" means anything, or part of anything, as having re- 30 ceived its own primary property: a surface is "in itself" white, and it is "in himself" that a man[151] is alive[152]. For his soul[154] is a particular[4] aspect[22] of the man, and his primary property "by himself" as a living being. (4) "By itself" means also whatever factor[83] of a thing's being cannot be also a factor of some other being. So, a man can be explained[83] as an animal, a biped; but "by himself" a man is a man. Finally, "by itself" means (5) whatever belongs[82f] to anything alone and as alone; hence, whatever is isolated[73] is "by itself."

19

"Disposition"[64c] refers[36] to the order[207a] among a 1022b thing's parts[22]; it may be order as to place, power, or form. For parts must[124] have some position or other, as the very word[37a] "disposition" makes evident[59].

20

A "habitude" or "state of being"[33a] means[36] (1) an active[9] habit or "having," a kind[4] of action[188b] or motion[109] on the part of a "haver" to what is "had"; for, between a doer[34] and his deed there is the doing. So, too, between him who has a garment and the garment he has there is a having. It is evident, then, that it is impossible[12b] to "have"[33] this sort of having; for there would be an infinite[130] regress[112a] if it were possible[23] to have the having of what one has.

10 The same term also means (2) a state or disposition[64c], being well or ill disposed, and that either with regard to itself or in relation to something else; for example, health is a state of being, since it is such a disposition. (3) A "state of being" may also refer to the disposition of some part of the whole; for to have excellence of parts is a state of being.

21

Things are said[36] to "endure"[35a] what befalls them or "happens" to them. "Happenings" may, accordingly, refer (1) to those qualities through which a thing suffers modification, as when it changes[120] from white to black, sweet to bitter, heavy to light, and so forth. But they refer also (2) to the actual[9] modifications which have been produced by the endurance of a happening. And (3) we refer especially to "enduring" or "suffering" a modification when the hap-
20 pening is injurious and painful. Accordingly, (4) we speak especially of great misfortunes and pains as happenings which we endure or undergo.

22

"Privation"[106] means[36] (1) the lack of some available[101c] property, even though it does not belong to the deprived being; for example, a plant is said to be deprived of eyes. It means (2) such a lack in a being or class[19] of beings which normally [101c] possesses the property; for example, a blind man and a mole are in different ways "deprived" of sight: moles as a whole class of animals are so deprived, whereas only individual[2] men are. (3) A "privation" may mean that under the conditions when a being would normally[101c] enjoy a possession, it is deprived of it; so blindness is a privation, not in general, but when sight fails to come to those who would naturally[101c] have it; similarly, there is privation to the extent, degree, or relation in which a 30 lack occurs which normally would not occur. (4) The violent taking away[118c] of anything is called a privation or deprivation.

Indeed, there are as many "privations" as there are negatives[48]: for a thing is called "unequal" because it does not have the equality it would naturally have; "invisible," because it has no color or a poor color; "footless," because it has no feet at all[44] or very poor ones. Or it may be defective in some degree, such as "seedless" fruit, which 1023a is in a sense imperfect. Or it may have something, but not easily or not well; for example, a thing is "uncuttable" not only when it cannot be cut at all but also when it cannot be cut easily or well. However, it may be total[150] deprivation only; for a man with one sightless eye is not called "blind," but one who lacks sight in both eyes. This is why not every man is either good or bad, either just or unjust; for there is an intermediate[138a] state.

23

"To have and to hold"[33] means[36] (1) to treat[113] something according to one's own nature[101] or desire[155], which is why fever is said to hold a man, or a tyrant, a city. 10 And when we are clothed, we "have on" or "wear" our clothes. (2) A thing "has" another in the sense of receiving[12] it: bronze "has" the form[20] of a statue; and a body "has" a disease. (3) In still another way, what contains is said to "hold" what it contains, for that in which something is contained is said to be held by it: we say that the vessel holds the liquid; the city, its people; the ship, its sailors; and any whole[21], its parts[22]. (4) What hinders[129] anything from moving or acting according to its own tendency[155] is said to "hold" it: pillars hold the weights above them; and the poets represent[34] Atlas as holding the heavens as if they were about to fall onto the 20 earth, and there are some natural philosophers[101h] who believe[46] this. It is in this way, too, that what holds things together is said to "hold" them, as if they would otherwise separate, each according to its own tendency.

"To be in something" is used in ways similar and corresponding to the meanings of "to have."

24

"To come from[86] something" means[36] (1) to come out of a material[84], and that in two ways, either out of the most[17a] inclusive[19] material or out of the least[20]; for example, all things that can be melted "come of" water, and the statue "comes out of" bronze. (2) It means to come
30 out of the[17a] starting-point[82] of a movement[109a]: "From" what did the fight come? "From" an insult; because this was the beginning of the fight. (3) It means to come from an individuated thing[64g] (matter[84] and form[91]), as the parts come out of the whole, a verse out of the Iliad, and stones out of a house. (4) As a thing ends[100] in its shape[91], and thus attains completion[14], so the form[20] "comes from" its parts[22]; for example, man from being two-footed, and a syllable from its letters. This is
1023b different from the sense in which a statue comes from bronze; for the composite, individual, primary being "comes from" its sensible[165c] material, whereas the form comes from its own material.

In these ways, then, things "come from something"; but there are others. (5) In any one of these ways things can[82f] "come from" some part; when a child comes from father and mother, or a plant out of the earth, they come from a part of these. (6) Things may "come from" others in time[134]: night from day, and storm from fine weather, because the one comes after the other. In some of these cases, things change[115] into one another, as in the cases just mentioned; in others there is merely a succession[136c] in time,
10 for example, the voyage started from the equinox, because it took place[116] after the equinox, and the festival of the Thargelia from the Dionysia, because after the Dionysia.

25

A "part"[22] means[36] (1) any kind of a division[75] of a quantity[27], for what is taken[118b] from a quantity as a quantity is always[135] called its part; two is in this sense a part of three. However, sometimes only those divisions which measure the whole are said to be its parts; which is why two is in one sense called a part of three, but in another sense it is not.

A "part" means (2) also the elements into which a form[20] (not a quantity) may be divided: thus, we say that species are the parts of their genera. So, also, the elements into which any whole[21] is divided or of which it consists[21b], whether the whole is a form or has a form: a bronze sphere 20 or cube has as one of its parts the bronze, which is the material in which the form is; and it also has as parts its angles. Thirdly, (3) the elements in a proposition[90] which serves[59] as a definition are parts of a whole; in this sense the genus is called a part of a species, though in another sense a species is part of its genus.

26

A "whole"[21] means[36] something from which none of those component parts are lacking that naturally[101] make up[36] the whole; or a container whose contents compose a kind[4] of unity[24], in one of two ways: either in that each is a unity, or in that all together make up a unity. For a universal[43] or a general[44] proposition[36] is a kind[4] of a whole and is general[43] in that it embraces 30 many things, because it is predicated[25a] of each[40] and because each is an instance of one whole: a man, a horse, and a god are all "living beings." So, also, a continuous[136a] and limited[131a] entity is a whole when it is one thing which consists potentially[11] of many constituents[82h], though it may be a whole even if its many constituents are actual[9]. Moreover, things are especially wholes which are such by nature[101] rather than by art[171]; the same is true also of the "one," because wholeness is a sort of unity.

1024a   Quantities whose beginning[82], middle[138], and end[18a] may change their position[64] without affecting[34] the aggregate[76a] are called totals[150]; those whose parts have fixed positions are wholes; those in which both of these features are possible[12b] are wholes and totals. This last class retains its nature when its parts are transposed[64e], but not its shape[91], such as wax or a coat; they are called wholes as well as totals, for they have both features. But water and all liquids and number are called totals; for we do not say "the whole number" or "the whole water," except by an extension of meaning. Things which have the kind of unity called "totality" are also said to be "all" when their parts are treated as separate[75]: "this total number" or 10 "all these units."

27

    To be "damaged" or "mutilated" is not possible[36] for any chance quantity whatsoever; it must be divisible[22] and a whole[21]. Thus, "two" is not damaged when either of the two "ones" is taken away[118b] (since the part removed must be less than the damaged whole which is left), and in general[44] no number can be damaged; for a damaged being must still retain its essential character[26]. If a cup is damaged, it must still be a cup; but a number from which something is subtracted is no longer the same. Besides, even things consisting of unlike parts cannot all be mutilated: for a number may have unlike parts, such as two and three, and in general[44] things whose parts may be transposed, such as water or fire, cannot be mutilated; their being[26] must in- 20 volve some structure or position among their parts. And they must be continuous[136a]; for a musical scale[56] consists of unlike parts, and its parts have position, but it cannot be mutilated. In addition, not even the things that are wholes can be mutilated by being deprived[106] of any part at random. For the parts removed must be neither[55b] essential[26] nor taken at random: a cup is not damaged if it is perforated, but only if the handle or some projecting part is removed; and a man is not mutilated by merely removing some flesh or the spleen, but only by removing the kind of extremity which when wholly removed[118b] cannot grow[116a] again[33]. Hence, bald men are not said to be mutilated.

28

A "genus"[19] is[36] (1) the continuous[136a] generation[116a] of beings having the same form[20]; for example, 30 "as long as the race of men lasts" is said, because "as long as it lasts" means "as long as their generation goes on continuously." (2) It refers to what first[17a] brought[109a] things into being[23]; for it is thus that some men are called Hellenes by race and others Ionians, because the former came from Hellen, and the latter from Ion as their first[17a] begetter[116d]. And the word is used more with reference to the begetter than to the matter; although races are also named from the female, such as the descendants of Pyrrha.

(3) A genus means also "plane," as the genus of plane figures[91a], and "solid," of solid figures: for each of these 1024b figures is, in the one case, a plane of such and such a sort[5] and, in the other case, a solid of such and such a sort; and this it is to which the differentiae[76a] are referred[85]. Thus, the first[17a] constituent[82h] in a definition[90], which is given[36] in answer to the question of what something is[87], is the genus[19], whose differentiae the qualities are said to be.

"Genus," then, means: first, the continuous generation of the same kind[20]; secondly, the first[17a] mover[109a] which is the same in kind[57a]; thirdly, the matter, for the subject[85] to which the differentia or the quality is referred is also called its "matter"[84].

Things are said to "differ in genus" in whose cases the 10 proximate[17a] referent[85] is different and which are not analyzed[206a], one into the other or both into the same thing; form[20] and matter[84] are of different genera. Also, things have different genera when they are described[39a] by different[91a] categories[25] of being[1]: some signify[38] what[87] a thing[1a] is, others of what sort[28] it[4] is, and still others as we have previously * specified[75]; these, too, are not analyzed into one another or into some one[24] thing[4].

29

The "false"[8] refers[36] (1) to a state of affairs[188c] as false: and this, on the one hand, because it is not put together[21b] or cannot[11f] be[23] put together[64g]; as when the diagonal of the square is said to be commensurate with
20 the side, or you are said to be a seated being, since the former is always[135] false, and the latter sometimes[31]; in these two senses states of affairs are[1a] not. On the other hand, there are affairs that, indeed, are[1a], but that naturally[101c] appear[173b] either not to be such as they are or to be affairs that are not, such as a sketch or dreams; for these are, indeed, something[4], but are not the affairs whose appearance[173] they occasion[34] in us. States of affairs, then, are said to be false either because they themselves are not or because the appearance derived from them is of something that is not[1b].

Next, (2) a false account[90], in so far as it is false, is the account of things that are not[1b]. Hence, every account is false which is an account of something other than that of which it is true[7]; for example, an account of a circle is false of a triangle. In a sense, any answer to a question regarding a thing's essential character[88] has a single object, but in
30 another sense it has several; since a thing itself and a thing with an attribute are not the same. With reference to such a question "Socrates" and "musical Socrates," for example, have the same essential character. But a false account is an account of nothing, except in a qualified sense. Hence, it was simple-minded of Antisthenes to insist[46c] that nothing is properly affirmed save in the strict[55] form[90] of saying one thing of another thing; from which it was concluded[3b]

* v.7.1017a24–27.

that there can be no contradiction[49a], and hence there can be no falsity. But it is possible to give an account of an object, not only by referring to the object itself, but also by referring to something else. This may be either false or true; for example, eight may be shown to be a double 1025a number by means of the definition[90] of two.

These considerations, then, are in these ways said to be false. But a false man is one who is prone and partial to such accounts, not for the sake of something else, but for their own sake, and who is able to instill such accounts into other people, just as we declare states of affairs to be false which occasion a false appearance. Hence, the argument[90] in the *Hippias* * that the same man is false and true is misleading. For it takes[65] him to be false who is able to speak falsely, though he is discerning[182] and intelligent[172]; and takes him to be the better who is consciously false. Such falsehood is based on analogy[113e]; for example, one who limps con- 10 sciously is better then one who does so unconsciously; where by "limping consciously" is meant the imitating of lameness, since, if a man were consciously lame, he would probably be worse. We may deal with the analogous case of moral character in the same way.

30

The "accidental"[3a] is attributed[36] to what belongs[82f] to something and what it is true to say, but not of necessity[123] or for the most part[125]; for example, if someone digging a hole for a plant finds a treasure. This, the finding of a treasure, is accidental for the one digging the hole; for neither does this of necessity come from or after that, nor if a man plants does he usually find a treasure. And a particular musician might be white; but since this does not 20 happen[116] of necessity or for the most part we call it an accident. Consequently, since there is something that belongs[82f] and something to which it belongs, and some instances of the former belong to instances of the latter at

* Plato *Hippias Minor* 365–376.

some place[30] and at some time[31], therefore what belongs to something, but not because the latter was this[4a] or the time now or the place here, will be an accident. Therefore, also, there is no determinate[72] factor[83] accounting for the accidental, but a chance one; and this is indeterminate[72c]. Thus, it was an accident[3c] for a man to come to Aegina if he went there, not in order to get there, but was driven out of his way by a storm or was captured by pirates. The accidental[3a] has happened and is, but not in so far as the affair in question is what it is, but in view of other considerations; for a storm was responsible[83a] for his coming to a

30 place for which he was not sailing, and this was Aegina.

There is also another meaning of "accidental"; namely, whatever belongs to something with regard to itself[2], but is not an aspect of the characteristic being[26], as a triangle has its angles equal to two right angles. And these accidental considerations may[12b] be eternal[135a], as none of the others is. But an account of this matter is given elsewhere.*

* *Posterior Analytics* i.75a18–22, 39–41, 76b11–16.

VI. BOOK EPSILON

1

CLEARLY it is any being[1a] as being[1a] whose principles[82] 1025b
we are trying to explain[83]. Any science, in so far as it is[93]
rational and reasonable[170], is concerned with principles
and explanations more or less fundamental[105] and explicit[164d]; thus health or any state of well-being has its
grounds or causes, and mathematics has its principles, elements, roots, and branches. But all such sciences circum-
scribe some particular being or kind of being as an object of
special concern[197] and never treat it simply as a being[1]
or as simply being; they never raise[34] the question[90] 10
"What is"[87]? Some regard this as too obvious, as evident
to sense; others say that, assuming what is, they must
explain[63a] as best they can what pertains[82f] essentially[2]
to the kind of being their particular subject matter is. It is
evident that such a method[113e] provides no theory[63a] of
primary being and no answer to the question "What is?"
There must be some other way. The specialists are even
unable to tell whether their special kind of being is or is not;
for the same theory[170] that tells us what is tells us whether
or not a given thing is.

Let us consider, for example, the natural sciences. They
deal with a special kind of being, namely, the sort of primary
being which has its source of movement or rest in itself. 20
Clearly, the science of this kind of being is neither practical[188] nor an art[189]. For in an art the source of motion
is in a mind or skill or some power in the artist; and in
practical sciences the source is in some decision of the doer,

since "practical" and "deliberate" are the same. Consequently, if all thinking[170] is either practical or artistic or theoretical, the natural sciences are theoretical and theorize about the kind of being that has the power of movement and defines primary being as a system of propositions only in so far as they are for the most part not independent of the facts which they define. We must not lose sight of definition and of what-it-means-to-be; otherwise our investigation would get nowhere. Now, things defined, or considered as they are, are in two different ways: some, such as "snub," are not independent of material being; others, such as "concave," are independent. A being may be concave without being anything else; but a "snub" being must be a nose. If all natural entities, therefore, are like the "snub," that is, nose, eye, face, flesh, bone, and animal generally or leaf, root, bark, and plant generally, we cannot define or explain them without reference to movement, since they are always material. But in natural science we must also investigate and define what it is to be a body, hence, also, what it means to be a living body, and hence the soul, too, in so far as its being is not independent of living bodies. This makes it clear how the natural sciences are theoretical.

But mathematics, too, is theoretical. Whether it deals with immovable and independent entities is at present not clear; still, it is clear that some parts of mathematics theorize about entities as immovable and independent. However, if there is something eternal and immovable and independent, it is evident that knowledge[181b] of it must be theoretical. But this theory does not belong to the natural sciences, since they deal with movable things; nor to mathematics; but to a science prior to both. For natural things are neither independent nor immovable; and mathematical entities, though immovable, are for the most part not independent of material reference. The first science, however, is a theory of entities both independent and immovable. Though all ultimate factors are necessarily eternal, these objects of first science are especially so, since they explain those divine beings which are accessible to us [the celestial beings].

Consequently, there are three theoretical branches of philosophy: the mathematical, the natural, and the theological. For it is clear that, if the divine belongs anywhere, 20 it belongs inherently to such a nature, the supreme[159a] philosophy being the theory of the supreme kind of being. The theoretical sciences, then, are preferable to others; and theology, to the other theoretical sciences. One may well ask whether this first philosophy is general or is concerned with some particular kind or nature of being. For the mathematical sciences, too, are not alike in this respect; geometry and astronomy are concerned with a particular nature, whereas general mathematics is common to all. If, then, there is no other primary way of being besides natural being, natural science will be the first science; but, if there is immovable primary being, the science of this will be prior, and first philosophy will thus be general, both 30 because it is first and because it is the theory of being as being; it examines what is and whatever belongs to beings as being.

2

Now, a being as such may be in several ways. One of them, as we saw, is to be accidental; another, to be true (nonbeing is to be false); besides these, there is the list[91a] of categories, that is, what, of what sort, how much, where, when, and anything else that "being" as such may mean; 1026b also, a being may be, as such, either potentially or actually.

In view of these many ways of being, we must first consider the accidental and point out that there can be no theory of it. Witness, no practical science, no art, no theoretical science troubles itself about it. Thus, a house builder is not also a builder of all the accidents that come into being along with the house, for they are infinite; and though there is nothing to hinder the house once built from being pleasur-

able to some, being hurtful to others, being useful, and in any case being different from all other things, none of these
10 effects concerns the science of building. Nor does the geometer have a theory about the accidents of his diagrams[91a], or whether "triangle" is different from "triangle having its angles equal to two right angles." There is a good reason[60c] for these facts[122a], since the "accidental" is, in a way, but a name. Hence, Plato * was, in a way, not wrong when he maintained that sophistry is the study of nonbeing. For the arguments of the Sophists, we may say, deal above all with the accidental: whether "musical" and "literate" are different or the same; whether "musical Coriscus" and Coriscus are the same; whether if everything that is, but is not always, has come to be, it follows that a musical person who has become literary must have been
20 literary and become musical—and all the other arguments of this sort; for accidental being is apparently something akin to nonbeing. And this is clear also from arguments such as this: any other type of being undergoes generation and destruction, but accidental being does not.

However, we ought to explain accidental being as far as possible, its nature and its grounds[83]; for thus we may at the same time make clear why there is no science of it. Some things, then, are always and of necessity as they are, not in the sense of being compelled, but in the sense in which we say that they cannot be otherwise; others are so,
30 not of necessity or not always, but usually; and this is the principle or ground by which the accidental is distinguished, for what is as it is neither always nor usually we say is accidental. Thus, when in the dog-days there is wintry and cold weather, we say this is an accident, but not when the weather is hot and sultry; because the latter is so always or usually, but not the former. And it is an accident that man is white (for this is not so always or for the most part); but he is not by accident an animal. And that a carpenter pre-
1027a scribes for disease is accidental: because it is not the carpen-

* Plato *Sophist* 237A, 254A.

ter who naturally[101c] does this, but the physician; yet a
a carpenter may happen to be a physician. And a cook, seeking only to please the palate, may concoct something having
remedial virtue, but this is not essential to his culinary art;
hence we declare it an accident—that is, though in a sense
it is the case that he did it, he did not do it as a cook. Though
in other cases the capacities of the agent explain the fact,
there is in the cases instanced no determinate art or power
that explains them; for when things are or happen accidentally, their explanations are also accidental.

Consequently, since not all things that are or come to be
are of necessity, most of them being as they are for the most 10
part, there necessarily is accidental being; for example, a
white man is neither always nor normally musical, but since
this sometimes happens it is an accidental fact. If not, everything will be of necessity. Therefore, whatever may be
otherwise than it normally is, will serve to explain accidents.
If we ask as our basic question: "Is there nothing which is
neither always nor normally so?" we see that this is an
impossible state of affairs. Accordingly, there must be
among events those which "happen"[126a] accidentally.
But, admitting accidents and normal events, does nothing
ever happen "always," or are some things happening
eternally? Let us postpone this question.† Meanwhile, it is
evident that there is no science of accidental being; for every 20
science is concerned with what is always or normally so.
For how can anyone learn or teach otherwise? Something
must be determined as occurring either always or normally;
for example, honey-water is normally good for a fever. But
there can be no systematic account of the extraordinary,
such as when something fails to happen at the new moon.
For even what happens at the new moon, happens then either
always or normally; but there is no telling what may then
happen accidentally.

Now we know what it means to be accidental and why,
and why there can be no science of such being.

† xii.6–8.

3

Evidently there are beginnings and explanatory factors which, though they may come and go, do not share in the 30 gradual coming and passing of beings. For if this were not so and if the factors accounting for events were not necessarily accidental, everything would be of necessity. Let us consider a particular event. Will it happen, or not? It will, if this other happens; if not, not. And that other will, if something else will. So is is clear that taking time from finite 1027b time we must arrive at the present. This man, therefore, will die of a disease or by violence if he goes out, and he will go if he becomes thirsty, and this will happen if something else does, and thus we shall come to an actual fact[82f] or to something that has happened. Suppose he becomes thirsty if he eats something bitter, and he either has or has not done so; then his dying or not dying will be of necessity.

Similarly, if one jumps over to past events, the same reasoning holds; for something that has happened now exists as present in something. Everything that follows will accordingly be of necessity; for example, this living person will die, for already, let us say, there are contraries in his 10 body; but whether he will die by disease or by violence, is not necessary until something else happens.

Thus, it is clear that the process continues to some starting-point, which in fact points to no necessary consequence. This, then, will be the starting-point for whatever happens by chance; and nothing else will explain its coming to be. But to what sort of starting-point and to what sort of factor such chance events can be referred[113a], whether to a material factor or to an end or to an agent, is a question which deserves careful examination.

4

So much, then, for accidental being; for it has been sufficiently clarified[72e]. Now, being in the sense of being true and nonbeing in the sense of being false are concerned with union[64g] and division[75] and, taken together, with the relation of contradictories[49]. For there is truth when an 20 affirmation corresponds to a combination[21b] in beings and when a denial corresponds to a dissociation among beings; whereas there is error [or nonbeing] when the opposite relations hold.

But how it happens that we think[169a] things together or apart is another question, where by "together" and "apart" I do not mean in succession, but so that some unity comes to be. For the false and the true are not in things[188c], as if the good were true and the bad were forthwith false; but they are in the judgment[170]. And in the case of single terms or in the question "What is?" truth and error are not present even in the thinking[170]. But the problems arising from "being" and "nonbeing" in this sense we must postpone for later inquiry.*

However, since unification and separation are in judgment 30 and not in things, "being" in this sense differs from "being" in the chief sense. For to predicate[137c] or deny[118b] what something is, or that it is of some sort, or that it is so much, or the like requires thinking.

Hence, "being" in the sense of being accidental and in the sense of being true must be dismissed. For the explanation of the former is indeterminate, and that of the latter is something that befalls a mind; both are concerned with 1028a the remaining kind of being, and neither explains any kind of being or nature of being. Hence, they may be dismissed; and we must seek to explain the principles of being as being. But it was evident in the distinctions we have made concerning the many ways in which things are said † that things may "be" in many ways.

* ix.10.   † v.7.

VII. BOOK ZETA

I

10 "Being"[1] has many meanings, as we have previously *
pointed out in our account of the various ways in which
things are said[6a]. For "being" means, on the one hand,
what a thing is or a "this-something" [or subject]; on the
other hand, it means that a thing is such, or so much, or
any of the other types of predicates.

Although "being" can be used in these various ways, it is
evident that of these meanings it is the first that answers
the question of what the particular thing designated is;
hence it defines "being" in a primary way.† For when we
say of what sort a designated thing is, we indicate that it
is (for example) good or bad, but say nothing about its
being three cubits long or a man; and so, when we tell
"what" a thing is, we do not indicate whether it is white
or warm or three cubits long, but that it is (for example) a
man or a god. However, the meanings other than primary
being are also said to indicate being, because they are in
some cases quantities of what a thing is in the primary sense,
or its qualities, or what happens to it, or some other feature
20 of that thing's primary being.

Hence, one might even question whether walking, being
healthy, sitting, and the like "are" or "are not": for none
of them is naturally[101c] self-dependent[2] or capable of

---

* v.7.

† Thomas Aquinas: "Licet modus significandi vocum non consequatur immediate
modum essendi rerum, sed mediante modo intelligendi; quia intellectus sunt
similitudines rerum, voces autem intellectuum, ut dicitur in primo Perihermenias."

being separated from some primary being; but rather it is whatever is walking or sitting or being healthy that may be said to be a being[4] among other such beings[1a]. The other ways of being are always referred[72] to some subject[85]; and it is this subject that in the primary sense "is" an individual[40], to which must then be referred such predicates as "good" or "sitting." Hence, it is clear that only because there is primary being can the other ways of being be and, 30 consequently, that what is first or simply, not derivatively, is primary being.

Things can "be first" in several ways; but primary being is first in all ways, first in discourse[90], in knowledge[181], and in time[134]. For temporally none of the kinds of being that are expressed through the other categories can be independently, as this alone can. In discourse, too, this is first; for the definition of anything must always give its primary being. And as for knowledge, we assert[175c] that we know[182] anything best when we recognize what it is (for example, a man or a fire) rather than of what sort or how much or where it is, since we know these others 1028b only if we first know what it means to be a quantity or a quality, and so forth.

In short, the question that has always been asked and is still being asked today, the ever-puzzling question "What is being?" amounts to this: "What is primary being?" Some say this being is a unity; others, a plurality; some, that it is limited in number; and others, unlimited. Hence we, too, must reflect[187] especially, primarily, and almost exclusively concerning what it is that "is primarily."

2

Primary being[26] is thought to belong most evidently to bodies; and therefore, when we seek illustrations of primary being, we point not only to animals and plants and their parts, but also to such natural bodies as fire, water, earth, 10 and the like, and to anything that is either a component part of these or is composed of them, whether of the parts or of the whole bodies, such as the heavens and their parts, stars, the moon, and the sun. But we must inquire whether these alone are beings primarily, or whether there are others also; or whether only some of these are, or whether there may be others too; or whether none of these are, but only something else. Some hold that the limits of body, that is, surface, line, point, and unit, are more primary beings than are bodies or solids. Again, some think that there is nothing primarily beyond objects of sense; but others, that there are eternal beings greater in number and of a higher 20 order. Thus, Plato declared ideas[20] and mathematical entities to constitute two forms of primary being, and as a third he added the primary being of perceptible bodies. Speusippus spoke of still more forms of primary being, beginning with unity, and sought to establish independent principles for each, principles for numbers and for magnitudes and for soul; in this fashion he extended the number of kinds of primary being. Others, however, say that ideas and numbers have the same nature and that everything else is derived therefrom, including lines and planes as well as the heavenly sphere and whatever is sensible.

These are the matters into which we must inquire: whether a proposition is well said or poorly stated; what primary beings there are; whether there are or are not any beyond those sensible; how the sensibly perceived beings are; 30 whether or not there is besides these sensible beings a separate primary being, and, if so, why and how. We begin with a clarification of what is meant by primary being.

3

"Primary being" means four, perhaps more, ways of being: (1) being a what[88]; (2) being a generality[43]; (3) being a kind[19]; and (4) being a subject matter[85]. Now, a subject of discourse is that about which anything is said and which is itself never said of anything else. Hence, we 1029a should begin by making this fourth meaning clear[72e];

for to be a subject seems really to be the first meaning of primary being.

This principal way of being is attributed in one way to the material; in another way to the form; and in a third, to their product. By "the material" I mean, for example, bronze; by the form, the shape or figure; and by their product, the statue, their union as a single whole[21a]. Consequently, if the shape be prior to the material and more strictly speaking a being, it will also, for the same reason[90], be prior to the product of both.

We have now briefly stated what one sense of primary being is; namely, being not what is said of a subject, but being the subject for whatever is said. However, we must not stop here; for this is not enough. The statement is itself not clear; and, besides, it implies that primary being is 10 really the material. For, if primary being is not the material kind of being, it baffles[161] us to say what it is. If all attributes are removed, nothing but material appears to remain. For all else is merely what bodies undergo or do or could do, or it is their length, width, and depth, which are quantities, and these are not themselves primary beings. Thus, a quantity is not a primary being; but there must first be a primary being *whose* quantity it is[82f]. However, if we disregard the length, width, and depth of things as not of their being, we see nothing left except that which is thus qualified[72]; so that those who approach[195a] the problem in this way are compelled to conclude that in the material of things alone can their primary being reside.

By "material" I mean that which is in itself[2] not a 20 particular thing[4] or a quantity or anything else by which things[1] are defined[72]. For there is something of which each of these is predicated and whose being is different from that of any of the predicates. Everything else is predicated of primary being; whereas primary being must be predicated of being-a-material. Hence, in the last analysis a subject is itself not a particular something or quantity or anything of the sort; not even their negations, for the negations, too, would belong to it only accidentally. It follows from these considerations that primary being is material. But this is incompatible with what we said about primary being as "a something"—something in particular. Therefore the form, or else the product of both form and material, would seem to be primary being rather than the 30 material itself. We may disregard the product of both, I mean of a material and of a form; for its being is both derivative[18] and familiar[59a]. Material, too, is in a sense clear. We must inquire therefore concerning the remaining meaning; for this is most perplexing. Some objects of sense are commonly said to be primary beings; accordingly, we must first search among them.

4

1029b Since we have pointed out at the start * in how many ways we conceive[72] primary being[26], and one of them was the "what-it-is"[88] of anything, we must examine[187] this. In thus proceeding to the more intelligible,† our inquiry will make progress, for learning always proceeds in this way: from what is by its nature less intelligible to what is more intelligible[181d]. Just as in practical problems, we ought to start from what is good for each toward the knowledge of how what is good generally can become good for each, so here, starting from what is more intelligible to us, we must make what is by its nature intelligible also intelligible to us. Now, things that strike us first and are familiar to us as individuals often are poorly understood and have little or 10 no being; nevertheless, by starting from what is inadequately known, but familiar to us, we can learn to know what is intrinsically[44] intelligible, using what we do know, as I have explained, to guide us.

Accordingly, let us first make some comments on the

* vii.3.1028b33–36.

† Bonitz put this passage (lines 3–12) at the end of chapter 3 and made it refer to sensibles.

topic in hand from the standpoint of discourse. When we speak of "what" anything is[88], we mean what it is of itself[2]. For "what you are"[88a] is not "that you are (for example) musical," since it is not in and by yourself that you are musical. "What you are," accordingly, means what you are of yourself. But "what anything is" is not the whole of its intrinsic being. For a thing is not what it is in the way that white is of a surface; because "being a surface" does not imply "being white," nor does it mean the two together, "being a white surface." Why? Because "surface," added to "white," cannot define its own being, for the definition must not repeat what is to be defined; it must express it. Thus, the definition states "what a thing is." Consequently, if "to be a white surface" is defined as "to be a smooth surface," then to-be-white and to-be-smooth are one and the same.

Now, there are such composites[64g] in the case of other categories, too; for in each case there is a subject matter (such as the qualitative, the quantitative, the when, the where, and the changing); and we must therefore inquire whether there is a definition stating what for each category it means to be and whether each thus has its own way of being—whether, for example, the being of a white man is a subject that must be defined by its own intelligible constitution or "what-it-is-to-be-a-white-man," not by compounding definitions of "white" and "man." Let a name for this composite, therefore, be "clothes" or X: What is it to be X? But perhaps this X is not something by itself? Now, there are two ways in which an X fails to be something by itself: one, by addition; the other, by omission. The one X adds the very term to be defined to something else; as if in defining "what-it-is-to-be-white" we were to add "white" to "man" and then define the combination of the two. The other X merely adds something else as an attribute, instead of defining what it is to be X; as if X meant "white man," and one were to define X as white. A white man is white, to be sure; but what it means to be X is not what it means to be white.

So we return to our question: Is what it means to be X a genuine "what"? No. For the "what" of X must state precisely what it is to be X. But when X includes an accidental predicate, the composite does not designate an individual being: thus, "white man" does not define a single being[4b], for only primary beings have such individuality.

Consequently, "what it is to be" belongs only to those things whose being can be stated in a definition. And we do not have a definition whenever we have a term which identifies something (for then all terms would be definitions, since there is some term or other that identifies anything, so that "the Iliad" would be a definition), but only when the term refers to something primary; and those terms refer to primary beings which attribute nothing to some other being. Accordingly, "what it is to be" will belong only to beings that are included in a genus; for only these are understood to be without being merely participants[93], modifiers[35a], or accidents[3a] of other beings. Everything else, if it has a name, will have its meaning stated by saying that this belongs to that, or instead of such a simple statement there may be one more precise; but it will have neither a definition nor a meaning which imports "what" it is.

Perhaps definition, too, like the statement of what a thing is, may have several meanings; for "what-a-thing-is" may refer to primary being (to a this-something), or it may refer to one or another of the predicates (quantity, quality, and the like). For, though all things "are," they "are" not in the same way; but some things are primarily, and the rest dependently. So, also, the statement of what a thing is refers essentially[105] to primary being; and to the other categories, only in some sense. We might ask even of a quality, What is it? so that even a quality is an instance of "what" is, but not essentially. As in the case of nonbeing, some declare nonbeing, according to the very form of speech, to "be," yet not in the primary sense, since its being is nonbeing; likewise in the case of the being of qualities.

We must, to be sure, inquire how we should express our-

selves in each case; but it is more important to know what
the facts are in each case[33]. Now that we know what we
mean, we can see that "the what it was to be"[88] of a
thing will belong, just as does the "what"[87] of a thing, 30
primarily and simply to primary being; and derivatively,
also, to the other categories, but not simply "what it was
to be," but merely what it is to be a quality or a quantity.
For when we declare these to be beings it must be either by
an equivocation[37b] or by way of an extension[64f] or
restriction[118b] of meaning; as when we say the unknown
is known. In truth, we use these terms neither in an equivocal
nor in the same sense, but as "medical" may refer to a single
object by various relations which are neither identical nor 1030b
ambiguous; thus, a patient, an operation, and a surgical
instrument are all called "medical," not equivocally or to
denote[39a] a single subject, but because all have some relation or other to a common point of reference[24a]. However,
it makes no difference exactly how we describe these facts,
since it is evident that definition and "what it was to be"
belong primarily and simply to primary beings only; they
belong, though not primarily, to other considerations as
well. If we agree[64] on this, it does not follow necessarily
that there must be a definition for every term that denotes
an object, but only that a definition indicates a particular
kind of object. It defines anything that is a unity, not by
continuity (like the Iliad) nor by connection (as some things
are linked together), but in one of the principal ways in 10
which a thing is "one." What I have in mind is that "one,"
like "being," implies primarily a "this-something," but
may refer to a quantity or quality. Hence, there is a concept[90] as well as a definition[72a] even of "white man"; but
not in the same way as there is either of "the white" or of
a primary being.

5

There is a difficulty here: if one denies that a composite[64f] term[90] is a definition, can there be a definition of

any paired concepts which are not simple, but are necessarily stated[59] by terms in combination? I mean, for example, there are "nose" and "concavity"; and "snub nose" is therefore a compound something, because "snub" is in "nose" not by accident. The nose has the attribute of concavity or snubness as its own attribute, not as "white" 20 belongs to "Callias" or to "a man"; Callias, who is a man, happens to be white, but, being an animal, he does not "happen to be" male any more than equality happens to be a quantity. Here "snub," "male," and "equality" belong to something essentially and are concepts in which the definition or the name of that to which the respective attribute belongs is an integral part; and they cannot be understood[59] independently[73a]. "White" can be understood apart from man; but "female" cannot, apart from "animal." In these cases of essential attributes, therefore, "what it is to be," or the definition, may not belong to them any more than to other attributes, or they may belong to them, as we have said, in some other nonprimary way.

There is another difficulty concerning them. For if "snub nose" and "concave nose" are the same, then "snub" and 30 "concave" are the same; but since the latter are not the same, because it is impossible to speak of the snub apart from the object to which it belongs as an essential attribute (since "snub" is "concavity in a nose"), then to say "snub nose" is either impossible or is redundant, meaning "concave-nose nose" (since "snub" nose is equivalent to "concave-nose" nose). And so it is absurd to maintain that "what it is to be" should belong to such things; for if this is not absurd, then there will be an infinite regress, since in "snub-nose 1031a nose" there will be still another combination to be defined.

It is clear, then, that there is definition of primary being only. For if other categories also have it, they involve an addition; what is true in the case of "quality" [which we have analyzed], would hold also for a quantity like "odd," for "odd" cannot be defined apart from number any more than can female apart from animal. In saying "with an addition," I mean cases in which the same thing must be said twice, as in the examples given. And, if this be true, there will be no definition of terms in any coupled form (for example, of odd number); but we fail to notice this, because our definitions are usually not precise. However, if such terms, too, have definitions, it will be in some other way; then, as has been said, "definition" and "what it is to be" must have more than one meaning. Consequently, in one sense definition and "what it is to be" belong to nothing 10 except to primary beings; to other terms, only in another sense. It is clear, then, that definition states what it is to be; and "what it is to be" belongs to primary beings either solely or especially, primarily, and simply.

6

We must inquire also whether "what it was to be" is identical with or different from particularity. For this is of some importance[9e] to our inquiry into primary being, since each particular thing is held to be identical with its own primary being, and "what it is to be" anything is accordingly said to be the primary being of that particular thing.

Now, in the case of being an accidental attribute this does not seem to obtain; for example, "a white man" is not "what 20 it is to be a white man"[88a]. For, if they are the same, then for someone to be a man and to be a white man would also be the same: since, as people say, the man and the white man are the same being; so that to be a white man would be the same as to be a man. But perhaps it is not necessary that accidental attributes have the same kind of being that the essential attribute or "what it is to be" of a thing has; for terms predicated of a subject do not need to be related to it in the same way. Perhaps at least in a syllogism the extreme terms ought to relate to the middle term in the same way, such as when a man is said to be white and to be musical; however, even this is not true.

On the other hand, in the case of beings that are said to be in themselves, are the intelligible constitution and the being not necessarily the same? Let us suppose that there are some primary beings to which no other primary beings or other natures are prior; that is, primary beings such as some declare the ideas[89] to be. If, now, the good itself is to be different from what it is to be good, and "animal itself" from what it is to be an animal, and being[1] itself from what it is to be, then there will be other primary beings and natures and ideas beyond[74] those recognized[36]; and if "what it is to be" belongs to primary beings, those others will be the prior primary beings. Similarly, if the being of ideas and the meaning of ideas are disconnected from one another, there will be no knowledge[179] of the former, and the latter will not be[1a]. By being "disconnected," I mean if what it is to be good does not belong to the good itself, or if the meaning of good is not itself good. For we have knowledge of any particular thing only when we know[181b] what it is to be that thing. And the case is the same for other beings as it is for the good; so that, if the meaning of good is not good, then "what it is to be" (the meaning of anything) itself has no being[1]; and "what it is to be one" is not one. And so for all cases or for none what it is to be, is; and, if not, nothing else is. Obversely, whatever does not have "what it is to be good" is not good. It is necessary, accordingly, for the good to be one with what it is to be good; and the beautiful, with what it is to be beautiful; and so in the case of all things that are not said "of" something else, but are primary and in themselves.* For it is enough if beings have this trait, even if there are no ideas[20]; or rather, perhaps, even if there are ideas. It is also clear at the same time that if ideas[89] are what some declare them to be, the [sensible] things to which ideas refer[85] cannot be primary beings; for the ideas must be primary beings, not attributed to subjects, since in the latter case they would be only participating[93] in being.

* But cf. viii.3.1043b2.

From these arguments, then, it is clear that, whether thing or idea, such a being must be identical with what it is to be that something; and this identity is not accidental. 20 This is clear, also, because to know[179a] an object is to know what it is to be that object; so that even in the explication[64a] both must be one. But, because accidental[3] being, such as "musical" or "white," is two-dimensional, it is not true to say of it that it is identical with its meaning, for both the accidental trait[3a] and that to which it attaches[3b] are white: so that the accident "white" and what it is to be white are, in one sense, the same; but, in another sense, they are not the same, since "to be white" is not the same for "man" as for "white man," though it is the same with the attribute[35a].

It would evidently also be absurd if one were to assign[64] a name to each successive instance of what it is to be: for there would then be another beyond that; for example, what it is to be a horse would then have its own meaning 30 added to the meaning of "horse." If primary being is, as we say, what it is to be, what, indeed, is there to hinder some things from being immediately and at once what-it-is-for-them-to-be? Not only are these one, but both are also one with their definition, as is clear from what has been said; 1032a for it is not accidental that "one" and "what one is" are one. Were they different, there would be an infinite regress; for there would be "what one is," which would be something belonging to "one," and these would be one; and, consequently, the same distinction could be made concerning the being of "what it is to be one."

It is clear, then, that in the case of being primarily and essentially the being is one and the same with its "what" or intelligible constitution. The sophistical objections to this position and the question whether "the intelligible constitution of" Socrates and "to be" Socrates are the same thing are answered by the same solution; for there is no difference either in the considerations out of which the

question arises or in the considerations by which it may be
10 successfully answered. We have now explained when a thing
is the same as "what it is to be" that thing, and when not.

7

The things that come to be are generated: some by nature;
others, by art; still others, "automatically." But whatever
comes to be is generated by the agency of something, out of
something, and comes to be something[4]. And I speak of the
something it comes to be to include all the categories—
particularity[4a], quantity, quality, and place.

Natural productions are those whose beginnings are
natural. That out of which[86] they come to be is what we
call the material[84]; the agency by which they come to be
is some natural being[4d]; and what[4] they come to be is a
man or a plant or some other one of the beings which we
20 have especially called primary. All things produced, whether
by nature or by art, come from a material; for their capacity[11b] to be or not to be indicates their material nature.
In general[43], nature includes that out of which things are
produced, that according to which they are produced (for
what has been produced, such as a plant or an animal,
has a nature), and that by which they are produced, another
member of the same natural species, having the same
form[57a] (thus, men generate men). This is the way things
are generated naturally.

Other productions are said to be "made"[189] either by
art or by some power or by thought[170]. Some of them,
indeed, seem automatic and ruled by chance, just as do
30 some of the works of nature; for even naturally the same
things are produced with or without seed. Concerning these
we must inquire later.* In any case, it is by art that those
1032b products come whose form[20] dwells in the mind[154],
where by "form" I mean what it is to be that product, its
first or primary being. For even contraries have in a way
the same form, inasmuch as "what"[26] a privation is must

* vii.7.1032b23–30, 9.1034a9–21, b4–7.

be stated in terms of the "what" of its opposite, such as health in relation to disease; since it is by the absence of health that disease is recognized[59] and health is the pattern[90] kept before the physician's mind and in his knowledge. Now the health of a patient comes to be in this way: health being a state of bodily equilibrium, it is necessary, if health is to be the patient's, that this condition belong to him; and if this equilibrium is his, he must have warmth, and so forth. And so the physician continues to think[169a] until he arrives at something which he himself can produce. It is then, from this point onward and towards health, that the process is called in the "making." Hence it follows that in a way health comes to be out of health, and a house, out of a house, that is, the material being, out of the immaterial; for in medical science is to be found the form of health, and in architecture, the form of a house. And here by "primary immaterial being" I mean "the what it is to be" of anything.

One phase of the productive process, therefore, is called "thinking," and another, "making": that which proceeds from the starting-point and from the form is "thinking"; that which proceeds from the end-point[100a] of the thinking is "making." In a similar way the intermediate[138a] states are produced. I mean, for example, that if a body is to be healthy, it must be brought into equilibrium. What, then, is this state of equilibrium? So and so. And to attain so and so, the body must be made warm. What, then, is this in turn? That other. And that is present potentially; it is, therefore, under the physician's control.

In this sense the agent[34] and the starting-point[95] of the process of healing, if it happens by art, is the form in thought; but if the process happens spontaneously it is whatever would start the making if a man were to make it by art. So in healing the starting-point may be the warming; and this the physician produces by friction. Warmth in the body, accordingly, either is an essential part of health or is followed, directly or through several stages, by something of the kind which is an essential part of health. And that is the minimal factor in the production, and so is an essential 30 part of health, as are of a house, the stones; and so in other cases. Hence, as is often said, it would be impossible for anything to come to be if nothing were present previously[82g]. It is evident, then, that some part of the production necessarily be present: thus, the material part is 1033a essential, since it is in process, and it is this material that comes to be something.

However, is the material ever an essential part of the definition of the completed object? It is certainly only by referring to both that we can state what bronze rings are[87]: we mention the material by saying that it is bronze, and the form, by saying that it is such and such a figure, figure being the nearest genus into which it can be placed. A bronze ring, therefore, cannot be defined without reference to its material.

There are, indeed, many cases in which something, when produced, is named in terms of the material out of which it is produced, yet its name is not the name of its material, but the name indicates *of* what material it is; for example, a statue is not called "gold," but "golden." However, a man brought to health is not called a well sick-man. The reason is that the product comes to be both out of a privation and out of the subject matter, which we call the material; that is, 10 it is both "the man" and "the sick" that become healthy. Yet the product is more especially said to come out of the privation; that is, the healthy man, out of the sick, rather than out of the man. It is for this reason that a healthy person is not said to be nonsick, but to be a man; and the man, to be healthy. On the other hand, anything whose privation is obscure[59b] and nameless, such as the absence of a particular figure in bronze and the absence of the figure of the house in bricks and timber, is held to be produced out of these materials; as health has been established out of abnormal bodily processes. And so, as the healthy man is not named according to the material which has been altered in the way described, the statue is not said to be wood, but rather (by a change in the word) wooden, not bronze, but of bronze, not gold, but golden, and the house, not bricks, but of bricks; although if one were to examine closely, one would not say simply that a statue is produced out of wood, or a 20 house out of bricks, because the production requires the transformation, not the permanence of the material out of which it proceeds. However, we employ this mode of speech for the reason given.

8

Whatever is produced, is produced not only by some agency (I mean, that by which the production is begun) but also out of something (not out of its privation, but out of a material, in the sense in which we have defined * it); and it is also a product, something brought into being (a sphere, a ring, or anything it happens to be). Now, just as this product is not mere bronze (its substance), so it is also not merely a sphere; to be sure, incidentally the bronze sphere, 30 which is the real product, is a sphere. For to make an individual thing is to make a "this-something" out of an indefinite[44] substance or subject[85]. I mean that in making the bronze round one makes neither the round nor the spherical, but something else; one puts this form into something other than itself. For if one were to make a form, one would make it out of something other than itself; for this 1033b is what "making" means. Let us consider making a bronze sphere; out of this, bronze, one makes that, a sphere. If the substance, bronze, is also made, it, too, must be made similarly out of something, and so the making would go *ad infinitum.*

It is evident, accordingly, that the form, or whatever we want to call the shape in the perceived object, is not produced; nor is there ever any production of it; no intrinsic nature[88] is ever made. For an intrinsic nature comes to be *in something else* made by art or by nature or by some power.

* vii.7.1032a17.

It is a bronze sphere that is made out of bronze and "sphere,"
10 since one makes a form enter into this matter, and thus the
result is a bronze sphere.

Hence, if there were production of "sphere in general,"
something would be produced out of another something.
For the product would also have to be analyzable[75] and
to be, on the one hand, matter and, on the other hand, form.
If, therefore, a sphere is "a solid figure the points on whose
surface are equidistant from the center," then one element
of this being will be a subject matter of "sphere" and the
other element will be in that subject matter; the whole will
be "a sphere" produced, corresponding to the bronze sphere.
It is evident, therefore, from what has been said, that what
we have called the form or essential being[26] is not produced, but that it is the combined form-in-matter that is
produced, and that in everything that is produced there is
matter, and that any object is, on the one hand, matter
and, on the other hand, form.

20 Is there, then, any sphere except particular spheres or any
house over and above the bricks; if so, how would any
particular thing ever have come to be? But "form" means a
"such"[5] and is not a "this"[4a] or a definite[72] particular
existence. And the maker or begetter makes or begets a
this out of a such; and what has been begotten is, then, a
"this-such." And the whole "this," Callias or Socrates, is
analogous to this bronze sphere; and man or animal, to
bronze sphere in general. Accordingly, it is evident that if
the formal factor, or the "ideas," as some are accustomed to
call them, have being beyond the particulars[40], they have
nothing to do with origins and with primary beings, and
they need not, at least not for these reasons, be independent[2] primary beings.

30 It is also evident in the case of many objects produced in
the course of nature that what is generated is similar to
that by which it is generated and that, different as they are
numerically, they are one in form; for man generates man—
unless, indeed, nature fails of her usual goal, as when a

horse produces a mule. And even here there is similarity, for that which would be common to horse and ass, the proximate genus, has not received a name, but would 1034a doubtless be both and something like a mule.

It is evident, therefore, that there is no need of setting up[149c] an idea as an exemplar[89a]; though men have sought to discover such forms, especially in cases like these, which concern primary beings. An agent or producer is adequate to account for the production and for the embodiment of the form in the matter. There is in the composite, for example, in Callias or Socrates, such and such a form in their particular flesh and bones; and though they differ in matter, for each has his own, father and son may share one form, for the form is indivisible[41].

9

We may ask why some productions, such as health, come to be by both art and nature[127], whereas others, such as a 10 house, do not. The reason is that in the case of production by art the production arises from a material in which some part of the thing[188c] inheres[82f], so that the material can in some cases move itself, in others not; in some cases it can move in particular ways, in others not; for many things can move themselves, but acquire certain movements by art, as in dancing. Things made of such material (such as stones) cannot be moved in certain ways except by external force, though in other ways they can, as with fire. This is the reason why some productions require the intervention of art, and others not; for some things which can begin to move without art can also be moved either by other things without art or because they themselves embody a part of 20 the product.

These observations make it clear that as natural productions proceed from like to like, so does art, in a way. Production may come from a like part, as a house comes from a house in mind[169] (since the art is the form) or from some other part or from something that has such a part. Otherwise the production is accidental; for the first essential factor in making anything is that a part be already there. Thus, warming by friction brings more warmth to the body, and warmth is health, or part of it, and is therefore followed by other parts of health or by full health; and so warming is said to create health, because it creates that 30 upon which health naturally follows. Hence, all things begin in their primary being, as syllogisms begin by stating what a thing is[87]; so from being come all becomings.

Natural growths[111b] follow this same pattern. For the seed is productive in a manner analogous to art, since it has 1034b the form potentially; and that from which the seed comes is somehow like its offspring. Not all productions are perfect reproductions as a "human being" from a "human being," for from a man may come a woman, and there are also cases of deformed or imperfect offspring: mules do not come from mules. There are some natural products which, like the artificial ones previously considered, can be produced arbitrarily[127], for their material is able to move itself in the way in which seed usually moves; but those products which do not have such material can be produced only by parents.

Now that we understand why among primary beings no forms are produced, we can show that this is true among the other forms of being as well—among quantity, quality, and 10 the other categories. For, as it is the bronze sphere that is produced, not "sphere" or bronze, and likewise in the production of the bronze itself there must always be present[82g] both a material and a form in the production of any primary being[87], so also in the cases of quality and quantity and the other categories; for what is produced is not a quality as such, but the quality of this particular wood; not a quantity as such, but the quantitative modification of this particular wood or animal. However, we may note[65] a peculiarity[42] of the production of primary beings: another primary being, the producer, must pre-exist in complete realization[10]; for example, an animal, if an animal is to be produced. But this is not necessary in qualitative or quantitative production, where the producer need not pre-exist except potentially.

10

Since a definition[72a] conveys a concept[90], and every 20 concept has parts[22], and since as the concept is related to the object[188c], so the part of the concept is related to the part of the object, it may be asked on this basis whether the concept of the parts must inhere[82h] in the concept of the whole[21] or not. It appears that in some cases the concept is divisible into parts [just as the object is divisible]; but that in other cases it is not. For the concept of the circle cannot be divided into concepts of sections, whereas the concept of a syllable can be divided into concepts of the letters; although the circle may be divided into sections, just as the syllable is divisible into letters.

Again, if the parts are prior to the whole and an acute angle is a part of a right angle, then the acute angle is prior to a right angle; and if a finger is a part of an animal, a finger is prior to a man. But it is the latter that are held 30 to be prior; for the concepts of the former are conveyed by means of reference to the concepts of the latter, and the latter are prior also from the standpoint of being independently of the others.

Perhaps we should point out that "part" has several meanings and that one of these is "what measures according to quantity." But, disregarding this kind of part, let us rather inquire about the parts of which primary being consists. Given a material, a form, and the composite of 1035a these, the primary being is this union of matter and form; therefore, its material is in a sense a part of it; but in another sense it is not, for its parts are only the elements which are stated in its definition. For example, flesh is not a part of concavity (though it is the material in which a concavity may be produced), but is a part of "snub"; and the bronze is a part of the statue as an object[21a], but forms no part of the statue as a concept. For only the form, or the object as having form, can be expressed in the concept; whereas the material element by itself cannot be expressed in the concept.

This is why the concept of the circle cannot be divided
10 into concepts of sections, whereas the concept of the syllable can be divided into concepts of letters: for the letters are parts of its form, and are not merely its matter; but the sections are parts in the sense of being a matter on which a form supervenes; nevertheless, they are nearer the form than is bronze when roundness is produced in bronze. But in a sense not even all its letters are parts of the concept of a syllable, for letters made in wax differ from letters in articulate speech; they are parts of a syllable when they are its perceptible matter. So even if a line, when divided, passes away into its halves, or a man into bones, sinews, and
20 muscles, these do not therefore compose their very being, but are merely their material; they are parts of the thing[21a], but not of its form, that is, of the concept, and hence they are not in the concepts.

In some cases, then, the concept of such parts will be present, but not in other cases, where the concept does not refer to the concrete object[65h]; for it is for this reason that some things have for their constituent principles parts into which they pass away, whereas others do not. Those objects, then, which are the form and the matter taken together, such as the snub nose or the bronze sphere, pass away into these materials and have matter as a part; but those which do not have matter, but are without matter, and whose concepts are of the form only do not pass away
30 at all or at any rate not in this way. Therefore, these materials are principles and parts of the concrete object, but are not parts or principles of their forms. Therefore, the clay statue is resolved into clay, the sphere into bronze, Callias into flesh and bones, and the circle into sections; for there is a sense in which the circle is taken as material,
1035b since "circle" is equivocal—it may mean any circle in

general[105] or an individual[40] circle, there being no special name for the latter.

The truth, then, is as has now been stated; nevertheless, let us state it more clearly[59c] and therefore take up the question again. On the one hand, the parts into which a concept is divided are prior in all or in some cases. On the other hand, the concept of the right angle does not have as a part the concept of the acute angle, but the concept of the acute angle has as a part the concept of the right angle; for one who defines the acute angle makes use of the right angle, since the acute is less than a right angle. The circle and the semicircle are similarly related; for the semicircle is defined with reference to the circle, as is the finger with reference to the organism, since the finger is such and such a part of a man. Hence, those parts which are material and into which as material anything is divided are posterior; whereas those which are parts of the concept and a thing's very being[26] are prior in all or in some cases.

Now the soul[154] or life of animals (their primary being as animate) is conceptually, too, their primary being; that is, it is their form and what-it-means-to-be a body[102] of this kind[5]. At least, if each organ is well defined it will not be defined without reference to its function[9c]; and in functioning it involves the sense organs [and hence the life of the whole organism]. Consequently, all or some aspects of the soul are prior to the concrete animal; and so with each individual animal. And the body and its parts are posterior to this primary being; for it is not the primary being of life, but the concrete living thing, that is divided into these material parts. These are, then, in a sense prior to the concrete animal; but in another sense they are not. For they cannot be independently of the whole; since it is not any sort of a finger that is a finger of an animal, a dead finger being a finger in name only. But some parts are neither prior nor posterior, that is, the chief parts or the first in which the concept or the primary being of life is present, perhaps the heart or the brain (for it makes no difference to the argument

which of these is of this sort). However, "man" and "horse"
and general terms which can be applied to individuals are
not primary beings, but are in a sense compounded out of a
30 particular concept and a particular matter taken generally.
Of course, an individual, Socrates, already has a material as
an ultimate constituent; other beings likewise.

A part, then, may be a part of the form (and by "form"
I mean what-it-meant-to-be-that-thing), or of the composite
of form and matter, or of the matter itself. But only the
parts of the form are parts of the concept, and the concept
1036a is of a universal; for being a circle[88a] is the same as "the
circle," as being a soul is the same as "the soul." But as to
the concrete object, for example, this circle, that is, one of
the individual circles, whether perceptible[165c] or intelligible[169b] (by the "intelligible" I mean the mathematical,
and by the "perceptible," for example, those of bronze or
of wood), there is no definition of them; but it is denota-
tively[169c] or perceptually[165a] that they are known[181c].
And when they pass out of this known state[10], it is not
clear whether they still are or are not; but always they are
defined and known through the concept which expresses
them generally, since matter is with regard to itself un-
knowable. But matter is either perceptible or intelligible:
10 perceptible, as are bronze, wood, and all matter undergoing
movement; intelligible, that which belongs to perceptible
objects, but not as perceptible, that is, mathematical
entities.

These comments explain the relations between whole
and part and prior and posterior. But, when anyone asks
whether or not right angle, circle, or animal are prior to
their parts, of which they consist, we must meet the question
by saying that it cannot be answered simply. For if even
"soul" is animal or living being, or if the soul of each individual is the individual, and being a circle is the circle, and
being a right angle (or the primary being of a right angle)
is the right angle, then the whole in one sense must be declared to be posterior to the part in one sense; that is, to

the parts of the concept and to the parts of the particular 20
right angle. For both the material right angle of bronze and
that which is formed by individual lines [are posterior to
the parts]. But the immaterial is posterior to the parts of
the concept, but prior to those of the individual instances.
So the answer is not simple. If, however, the soul is something
different and is not the animal, then even so some parts
must be declared to be prior and others not, as has been
said.

11

One may also properly ask what sorts of parts belong to
the form and what sorts do not, but belong to the concrete
object[65h]. If this is not clear, it is not possible to define
anything; for definition has to do with the general and with
forms; so that as long as it is not evident what sorts of parts
are material and what sorts not, it is impossible to have a 30
clear idea of anything.

Where the same forms, then, are found under diverse
material embodiments, such as the circle in bronze, wood,
or stone, it seems clear that, because bronze and stone are
readily differentiated, they are no part of the primary being
of the circle. Where the same form and matter are regularly
found together, though there is nothing to prevent the same
distinction being made, it is hard to make the appropriate
discrimination. If all circles ever seen had been of bronze, 1036b
the bronze would nonetheless be no part of their forms. So
the form of man is always found in flesh and bone and such
parts: are these, then, also parts of his form, that is, of the
concept of "man"; or are they not rather his material? It is
because man is not found with other material embodiments
that we are unable to distinguish readily.

Since this distinction is possible[12], but not always clear,
some men raise the question even concerning the circle and
the triangle, as if these may not properly be defined by lines
and planes, but as if all these figures were analogous to the 10
flesh and bones of man and the bronze or stone of the

statue; so these men reduce all things to numbers and declare the concept of the line to be that of the number two. And among those who believe in ideas[89] some identify the dyad with the line itself, and others, with the form of the line; for in some cases, they say, the form and that of which it is the form are the same, for example, the dyad and the form of the dyad. But this, they say, is no longer the case with the line. It follows, therefore, that many things which appear to differ in form have one and the same form, as indeed the Pythagoreans also concluded; and it is possible 20 to present the form itself of all things as one, and the others as not forms at all; thus, all things will be a single unity.

It has been shown, then, that the question of definitions has some difficulty and for what reason. Hence, it is futile[9f] to reduce all things by this method and to eliminate matter; for some things are undoubtedly particular embodiments of form in matter or particular things in a particular state. And the comparison which Socrates the younger * was accustomed to make concerning the animal is not a good one; for in assuming it possible for a man to be without parts, as there may be a circle not of bronze, it leads away from the truth. For the two cases are not similar; an animal is something perceptible and cannot be defined without reference to movement, hence not without reference to its 30 parts in a certain organization. For not any old hand is a part of the man, but only when it is able to perform[100] its activity[9c], hence when it is alive; and when it is not alive, it is not a part.

As to mathematical entities, on the other hand, why are concepts not parts of concepts; for example, semicircles, of circles? For though concepts are imperceptible, does this make any difference? For even some things which are not perceptible will have matter, since there is matter in some 1037a sense in the case of everything which is not "what-it-meant-to-be" anything, that is, not its own[2] form itself, but is a "this-something"[4b]. The semicircle, then, is not a part of

* Plato *Theaetetus* 147D; *Sophist* 218B; *Statesman* 257C; *Epistles* 358D.

"the circle" in general, but of the individual circles, as has been said before;† for as there is perceptible matter, so there is also intelligible[169b] matter.

It is clear, also, that the soul is man's first and primary being, that the body is his material, and that "man" or "animal" is the composite of both taken generally. And if even the term "soul" may be thus used,‡ then "Socrates" or "Coriscus" have two meanings, the soul and the concrete individual[21a]. If "Socrates" or "Coriscus" means simply "this soul" or "this body," then these names are analogous to general names.   10

Later § we must inquire whether there is some other kind of matter besides that of such primary beings, and then we must also investigate other primary beings, such as numbers or something of this sort. For it is with these questions in mind[97] that we are trying to fix distinctions in the case of perceptible primary beings, since the theory of perceptible primary being is, in a way, the task of natural (that is, of second) philosophy; for the philosopher of nature must get knowledge not only about matter but also, and more especially, about concepts, and we must later ‖ consider definitions, and how the parts in a concept are parts of a definition, and why the definition is a conceptual unit (for, clearly, must not an object, being single, though having parts, have some basis for its unity?).   20

We have now explained in general what any[150] intelligible identity[88] is and how it is self-identical; also, why in some cases the concept of what-it-means-to-be contains the parts of the thing defined, and not in other cases; and also that in the concept of a primary being there are no material parts. For there are not even parts in the primary being as such, but in that which is individual[21a]. Of this there are concepts in a sense, and in a sense, not. For there is no concept of an individual including its matter (since that is indefinite[72c]); but there is a concept of an individ-

† vii.10.1035a30–b3.   ‡ vii.10.1036a16, 17; viii.3.1043b2–4.
§ xiii, xiv.   ‖ vii.12; viii.6.

ual's first and primary being, for example, in the case of man his concept is of the soul. For the primary being is the imanent form, from which, together with the matter, the
30 so-called concrete primary being is derived: concavity is the form from which, together with the nose (matter), "the snub" (that is, a snub nose) arises, and thus in it nose is doubly present. But in any concrete primary being, such as "snub nose" or Callias, there will be also a matter. And it has
1037b been stated that in some cases "what it meant to be that thing" is identical with the thing, as in first and primary beings; for example, "curvature" and "being curved," for this is primary. By a first and primary being I mean one whose being is not in something else, as in the material or the subject matter. But things which are material or are generals that include [65h] matter are not the same; nor are things that are accidentally one, such as Socrates and musical, for these are the same only by accident.

12

Let us now first give an account of definition[72a], in so far as it has not been discussed in the *Analytics;** for the
10 question there treated is of use in our account of primary being. I mean why a thing which can be defined by a concept is a unity[24], as in the case of man, whose concept we shall represent by "biped animal." Why is this being one, and not more than one—animal and biped? For in the case of "man" and "white" the concepts are more than one, for the one does not belong[82f] to the other; but when the attribute does belong, and the subject[85], man, possesses the attribute, something single comes to be, "a white man." In the case of "animal" and "biped," however, the one does not share[93] in the other; for a genus does not have the attribute of its species, since the same thing would then
20 share in contraries at the same time, because the species by which a genus is subjected to differentiation are contrary. But even if a genus did share in them the same argument

* *Posterior Analytics* ii.3–10, 13 (cf. 97a29).

would hold, since the differentiae are many, such as footed, biped, and featherless. Why are man and his attributes one, and not many? Not because they are present[82h] in the subject; for on this basis it would be possible for any trait to form a unity with its subject. It is definitive traits that must constitute a unity: for the definition is a concept that is unitary and is of a primary being, so that it must be the concept of something that is one; and "primary being" means something that is one and is a "this-something," as we maintain.

We must first examine definitions based on division[75]. In such definitions there is nothing but the genus, named first, and the differentiae. The lower genera are the first 30 genus together with successive[65h] differentiae: for example, the first, animal, and the next, animal that is biped; and, again, animal that is biped that is featherless; and so forth. And in general it makes no difference whether many 1038a or few terms are used or, therefore, whether few or but two: of the two, the one is the differentia, the other is the genus; for example, in "biped animal" animal is the genus, and biped is the differentia. If, then, the genus by itself[105] is not separable[74] from the species included in it, or is separable only as matter (so "sounds" designates a genus and also the matter of words, whereas the differentiae indicate the species of sounds, that is, the letters, derived from the genus), it is evident that the definition is the concept containing the differentiae.

However, it is also necessary for the division to proceed through the differentia of the differentia: for example, footed 10 is the differentia of animal; and it is necessary to know[182] the differentia of the footed animal in turn as footed. Hence, if one is to speak rightly and classify expertly one will not say that footed animals are either feathered or featherless, but will divide footed animals into cloven and uncloven, for these are differentiae according to the characteristics of the foot, since having cloven feet is a way of being footed. Thus one should proceed until one arrives at what is no longer capable of differentiation[76b]. Then there will be as many kinds of feet as there are differentiae, and the kinds of footed animals will be equal in number to the differentiae.

If this is so, it is evident that the last [100a] differentia
20 will be the primary being of the object and its definition, because one must not state the same thing more than once in definition, since that would be superfluous. And this does happen: for when one says "biped footed animal" one has said nothing other than "animal having feet, having two feet"; and, if one divides this according to the proper division, one will say the same thing more than once and as many times as there are differentiae.

If, therefore, a differentia of a differentia be taken, then one, the last, will be the form, that is, the primary being; but, if the division is based on accidents[3], as if one were to divide the footed into white and black, there will be as many differentiae as there are dividings. Hence, it is evident that the definition is in the concept which consists of the dif-
30 ferentiae or, according to the correct method, of the last of them. This would be clear if one were to change the order of such definitions, for example, that of man, saying that man is "an animal which is biped and is footed"; for when one has said "biped," "footed" is superfluous. But there is no order of parts in the primary being; for how can we think[169a] the one posterior and the other prior? Let this be our introductory exposition of definitions based on division and of their properties[28].

13

1038b   Since our inquiry concerns primary being, let us return to this topic. We have attributed primary being to subject matters, to "what-it-meant-to-be," to concrete individuals composed of these two, and to general terms. Concerning two of these we have given an account: "what-it-meant-to-be" and subject matters; and we have said of the latter that they are either individual[4b] subjects[1], for example, an animal may be the subject to which attributes are referred, or they are materials to be given actualization[10].

However, general terms[43] are held by some to be in the fullest sense explanatory principles[83] and beginnings[82]. Let us therefore proceed to discuss this problem. It would seem to be impossible that anything general should be a primary being. For in the first instance what constitutes the primary being peculiar to an individual object is that it does not belong to another, whereas anything general is common to a class; for we mean by "general" what naturally[101c] belongs to more than one object. Of which particular object, then, would what is general be the primary being? Either of all or of none. Of all it could not be; and if it is to be of one then all the other objects would become that one. For the objects whose primary being is one are themselves one; and "what-it-means-for-them-to-be" is then also one.

Moreover, primary being is not an attribute of a subject; whereas what is general is always attributed to a subject. However, though what is general cannot for this reason be primary being as "what-it-meant-to-be," may it, perhaps, inhere in such being and in the things themselves as subject? For example, may "animal-in-general" appear both in man and in horse? Clearly, this is a concept arrived at from particulars. However, it makes no difference that the concept does not include everything inherent in the primary being that is being considered; "animal" may nonetheless be the primary being of *an* animal, just as the concept "man" designates the primary being of any man in whom it inheres. Here the same consequence follows again; that is, the primary being "animal" will be the primary being in it which differentiates it from others as something peculiar to it.

It is, indeed, impossible and absurd that a concrete[4a] primary being, if it be made up of other things, should not be made up of primary beings or of individual things[4b], but of quality[28]; for a quality, which is not primary being, would then be prior to primary being and to a "this"[4a]. But this is impossible; for attributes cannot be prior to primary being, whether in concept or time or genesis, since they would then also be separately. Moreover, primary being would then inhere in Socrates, a primary being; so 30 that a primary being would be two individuals. And it follows, in general, that if a man and other such things are primary beings nothing in the concept of them is the primary being of anything and that nothing general exists separately from species or in anything else; I mean, for example, that there is no "animal" beyond particular animals and that nothing else in the concepts has separate being.

To those, then, who reflect[187] on the basis of these considerations, it is evident that no whole belonging to objects in common is a primary being and that none of the 1039a predicates common to them indicates a "this-something," but a "this-such"[5]. If not, then many other difficulties follow, especially the "third man." This is clear also from the following consideration. It is impossible for a primary being to be composed of primary beings inhering in it and completely actual[10]; for two things that are thus actual can never be actually one; though they may, if they are potentially two, be one, for the double consists of two potential halves, since it is the complete realization of the halves that separates them. Consequently, if a primary being is single, it will not consist of two primary beings inhering in it. Democritus is right when he declares it impossible for one 10 to be made out of two or two out of one; since he presents his indivisible magnitudes as primary beings. Similarly, it is clear that this will be the case also with number, if number is a synthesis of units, as is said by some: either two is not one, or there is no unity actual in one.

However, our conclusion has a difficulty. If no primary being can consist of generals, because "general" indicates a "this-such," and not a "this-something," and if no primary being can actually consist of primary beings, then every primary being must be simple, and then there would not be a concept of any primary being. Yet it is held by all and was long ago said * that it is only primary being or it primarily 20 that can be defined; but now it seems that even it cannot. There will, then, be no definition of anything; or in some sense there may be, but in another, not. But what we are now saying will become clearer from the considerations which follow.†

14

It is also evident from these considerations what consequence follows for those who believe that ideas[89] are primary and separate beings and at the same time believe that forms[20] are composed of genus and differentiae. For if the forms are so that there would be, for example, an "animal" in a man and a horse, we may ask whether this "animal" is numerically one and the same in both or whether there is a different animal for each. Logically[90] it is clearly one and the same; for the concept[90] would be expressed identically in either case. But if there is really a "man-in-30 himself" who is a "this-something" and is separate, then his components, "animal" and "biped," must also be "these-somethings" and be separate, primary beings; hence "animal" must be such a being. If, then, that "animal" is one and the same with the horse and with the man, as you are one and the same with yourself, how can what is one with separate beings be one? And what reason is there then 1039b for assuming that this "animal" will not be separated from itself? Then, too, if it participates in "biped" and "quadruped," an impossible conclusion follows; for contraries will then at the same time belong to it, although it is both one and a "this." But, if it does not so participate, in what sense would one then say that the animal is biped or has feet? Perhaps, it may be replied, by composition[21b] or coincidence[137] or mixture[139]. All these expressions, however, are meaningless[61].

On the other hand, suppose the animal to be different in

* vii.5.1031a11–14.　† vii.15; viii.6.

each. In that case there will be, so to speak, an infinite variety of things whose primary being is animal; for it is not by accident that man is constituted an animal. Moreover, this "animal-itself" would be many in number; for in each
10 variety the animal would be its primary being, since the species must be classified as animals. Otherwise man would belong to some other kind or genus. And besides, if man's genus is an idea, all his other constituents would also be ideas[89]. None of them, accordingly, could be the idea of one thing and the primary being of another; for that would be impossible. "Animal-itself" would accordingly be at the same time each concrete animal in all their varieties. And whence comes this "animal"? And how can "animal" come from itself? Or how can this "animal," whose very being[26] it is simply to be animal, be itself apart from animal?

The same consequences and others even more absurd will follow with respect to any sensible thing. If, therefore, these consequences are impossible, it is clear that there are no forms of perceptible objects in the manner in which some say there are.

15

20 Hence, concrete or individual[21a] primary being[26] differs from logical[90] primary being. I mean that being in the former sense is a logical being taken together with a material; whereas in the latter sense a logical being is taken generally. Whatever beings, then, are so called in the former sense come into being and pass away, whereas logical being does not thus come into being and pass away; for "house" as an intelligible form[88a] never comes to be, rather it is *this* house which is built. But concepts are or are not independently of processes of coming into being and passing away; for it has been shown * that no one originates or produces them.

Hence, there is no definition or demonstration of the primary being of sensible things; because they have matter,

* vii.8.

and the nature of the combination is such that it may either be or not be, and all individual instances of them are there- 30 fore perishable. If demonstration deals with the necessary, and definition is scientific, it is impossible for scientific knowledge to change from scientific knowledge into ignorance. Opinions are, of course, subject to such change; but it is impossible for demonstration and definition to vary thus. Hence, it is opinion which deals with what may be otherwise 1040a than as it is, and it is clear that there can be no definition or demonstration of concrete individuals. For, when perishable objects have passed beyond sense, they no longer appear[59b] to those who have scientific knowledge; and it will no longer be possible to apply definitions or demonstrations to them, even though the concepts of them remain in the mind[154]. Anyone, therefore, who tries to define a concrete individual must not ignore the fact that it is always possible that he may be refuted because of the impossibility of applying his definition.

Accordingly, it would be impossible to apply definition to an idea if it should exist as an individual, separately. A definition must consist of words, but he who defines must 10 not invent[34] terms; for they would be unintelligible. Terms in usage are common to all objects of a class; these terms, accordingly, must belong to more than one being; that is, if one were to define "you," he would say "an animal which is lean" or "white" or has some other attribute, which might also belong to another being.

However, someone may object that there is nothing to hinder any one attribute from belonging separately to a number of objects, though all taken together in a definition apply to one only. But it must be said in reply, first, that they would then belong also to both of the elements in the definition, such as "biped animal," to "animal" and to "biped." Indeed, this would even be necessary if they were eternal entities, whose elements are prior to and parts of the compound[64g]. They can be separately only if "man" can be separately; for either neither can or both can. If neither

20 can, a genus will not be independent of its species; but, if it
is independent, the differentia will also be independent. And
if they were assumed to be prior in being, they in fact do
not destroy anything from which they are taken. And if
ideas[89] consist of ideas (since constituents are simpler
than compounds), then the elements also of which an idea
consists, such as "animal" and "biped," must be predicated
of many beings. If not, how could they be known[181c]?
For then there would be an idea which it would be impossible
to predicate of more than one, and this could not be the case,
since every idea is held to be capable of being shared.

As has been said, the impossibility of defining concrete
individuals is easily overlooked[205] in the case of things
eternal, especially of unique beings such as the sun or the
30 moon. For a definition misses its mark[128] when it uses
attributes inessential to the sun's continuing to be; for
example, "going round the earth" or "nightly concealed."
For if it should stand still or not set, it would by that
definition no longer be the sun; but it would be strange if a
definition could do this to a primary being. A definition also
misses the mark when it uses attributes which may belong
to another object; for then, if another object with these
attributes arose, it clearly would be a sun. A concept,
1040b accordingly, must be common to more than one object; but
"the sun" presumably designates an individual object,
analogous to Cleon or Socrates.

Why doesn't some believer in ideas define an idea? He
would then make clear that what has now been said is true.

16

It is evident that most of the beings that are supposed to
be primary are powers[11]. Such are the organs of animals:
none of them can be an organ separately from its organism,
and if separated they all continue to be[1a], but as matter.
Such are also earth, fire, and air: none of them is a unity,
but they are as the milk before it has thickened—materials
10 out of which some unity may be formed. One might be

inclined to suppose that some parts of living bodies and of their living selves[154] possess individual being[1a], both actually and potentially, seeing that these parts have a source of movement in them, so that they can move from their normal places, especially in those cases in which animals, even when divided, continue to live. Nevertheless, such parts are only potentially individual beings so long as they are naturally united and continuous; and if they are held together by external force or accidental cohesion[101f], they constitute an abnormal individual.

Since "unity" is a term that is used like "being," and since the primary being of any unity is one, and objects whose primary being is numerically one are numerically one, it is evident that neither unity in general nor being in general can be the primary being of individual objects[188c]; just as being[88a] an element or being a principle cannot. Accordingly, we ask what a principle is, in order that we may 20 reduce it to something better known. Of these terms, then, being and unity are more primary than principle, element, and explanatory factor, though not even they are primary being, since nothing that can be common is primary being; for primary being belongs to nothing but to itself and to what has it, that is, to that of which it is primary being. What is one cannot at the same time be many; whereas what is common can at the same time belong to many objects. Consequently, it is clear that nothing that is general[43] can be so when separated and removed from concrete individuals[40].

However, those who assume that forms are primary being are to be credited, in one respect, with having rightly attributed independence to them, if they are, indeed, primary beings; but they are wrong in believing that a form is unity-in-multiplicity[24b]. The reason they believe this is that 30 they are unable to say what these primary beings are which are imperishable and independent of individual, sensible things. So they represent them as being of the same kind as the perishable (for with these we are familiar). Thus, man-in-himself and horse-in-itself are nothing but ordinary, sensible things with the words "in itself" attached[64f] to 1041a them. But even if we had never seen the stars, they would, I suppose, still be eternal beings beyond the range of our acquaintance; so here, too, though we cannot say *what* forms are, we must, nevertheless, say *that* they are. It is clear, then, that none of the things called "general" is primary being and that no primary being is composed of primary beings.

17

Now, taking another starting-point, we ought to say what primary being is and what kind of being it is; for thus it may also become clear what to say about the primary being that is separate from those primary beings which are sensed. Since primary being involves a beginning and an explanatory
10 factor, let us begin our explanation at this point.

Ordinarily we try to explain why[203a] by telling why something belongs[82f] to something else. For to ask why the musical man is a musical man is either, as has been said, to ask why the man is musical or something else. It is pointless to ask why anything is itself. For *a* fact, such as that it is true that, let us say, a lunar eclipse is, must be clear at the start. But the fact that anything is itself is the one and only reason that can be given in answer to all such questions as why a man is a man or a musician is a musician; unless one were to add that this is so because everything is inseparable from itself and that just this is what is meant by
20 "being one"[88a]. But this fact is common to everything and is a short-cut explanation. We may properly ask, however, why man is an animal of a certain sort. This, then, is clear, that we are not asking why he who is a man is a man. We are asking why something belongs to something. But the fact that it belongs must be clear; for if it is not, the question why is futile. For example, "Why is it thundering?" means: "Why does this noise occur in the clouds?" For what

is here sought consists in affirming something of something else.

And why are these materials, the tiles and stones, a house? It is evident that we are here seeking the explanation; and this,* in some cases, perhaps in the case of a house or of a bed, is the "wherefor"; in other cases it is the source of the movement or the efficient factor, for this is also an 30 explanation. Whereas it is the efficient factor that is sought in the case of a process of becoming and passing away, it is the final factor that is needed in explaining a case of being[23]. However, that it is an explanation which is sought easily escapes notice, especially when one thing is not expressly attributed to another—when it is asked why † a 1041b man is; because the expression is simple and does not single out[72e] this or that property. But the meaning of the question should be made explicit[36c]; otherwise, what happens will be something intermediate between no investigation and a definite investigation. Since the existence of the thing in question must be supposed and maintained, it is clear that what is asked is why the thing is what it is: Why are these materials a house? Because precisely these materials are present, and it is precisely this that it meant for them to be a house. And why is "this" or this body having this form a man? Hence the explanation is sought in terms of the material, that is, that by which it has been definitely formed[20] into a primary being[87]. It is evident, therefore, that there is no investigation or instruction concerning simple entities; but there must be some other way of dealing 10 with them.

Now, as to things that are organized[64g] so that the whole[150] is one, not like a heap, but like a syllable: the syllable is not its elements, for *ba* is not the same as *b* and *a*; nor is the flesh fire and earth. For when these are separated,

---

* Apparently spurious: "to speak logically, is a search for 'what-it-meant-to-be.' And it. . ."

† Preferable to the reading "what."

the wholes (flesh or syllable) no longer are; but the letters are, and so are fire and earth. Accordingly, the syllable as a whole is something distinct[4] and is not only the letters, vowel or consonant, but also something else; and the flesh is not only fire and earth, or the hot and the cold, but also something else. If, therefore, that something must either be 20 an element or be composed of elements, then if it is an element the same argument will again apply; for the flesh will be composed of this and fire and earth and something else, so that there will be an infinite regress. But if that something is composed of elements, it is clear that it will be composed, not of one, but of more than one; or else that one will be the object itself, so that we may apply to it, again, the same argument as for the flesh and the syllable. Therefore, this other would seem to be, not an element, but the factor explaining why this is flesh, or that is a syllable, and so forth. And this is the primary being of anything; for this is the first reason of its being. Although some features of objects are not their primary being, those that are primary being are natural and are established[111b] by nature; 30 hence the nature of a thing is clearly its primary being, and it is, not an element. but a principle. An element, on the other hand, is that into which something is divided and what inheres[82h] in it as material; for example, *a* and *b* are elements of the syllable.

VIII. BOOK ETA

1

LET US NOW pull our argument together[62], recapitu- ^{1042a}

LET US NOW pull our argument together[62], recapitu- 1042a
late[113h] the main points, and thus come to a conclusion[100]. We said that our investigation concerns the
fundamental factors[83], the principles[82], and the elements[103] of primary beings[26]. Some primary beings are
accepted by all; whereas others are explained differently by
different men. Those commonly accepted are the natural
beings, such as fire, earth, water, air, and other simple
bodies, then plants and their parts, as well as animals and
the parts of animals, and finally the heavens and the celestial 10
bodies; whereas ideas[20] and mathematical beings are
recognized as primary beings only by certain men in a
special sense. There are also arguments leading to the conclusion that there are other primary beings: namely, the-
what-it-was-to-be[88] of things; also, subject matters[85].
From another point of view, a genus is primary to its species,
and general classes are more primary than particular things.
And with genera and general classes are also connected the
ideas[89]; for it is by the same line of argument that all
these are held to be primary beings. And since the primary
beings that constitute "the-what-it-was-to-be" of things
must be formulated by definitions, we have been obliged to
discuss definition and essential attributes[2]. And since a
definition is a formula, and the formula has parts, it was
necessary for us also to examine parts in order to discover 20
what sorts of parts are parts of primary being and what
sorts, not; and whether the parts of primary being are also

parts of a definition. We saw that neither a general class nor a genus is a primary being. Concerning ideas[89] and mathematical entities we must inquire later;* for some say that these are primary beings independent of sensible primary beings.

For the present, however, let us consider only the commonly accepted primary beings. These are those evident to sense perception. And all perceptible primary beings are of some material or other. A subject matter is primary being in one of three ways: it may be a material (and I mean by material whatever, though it is not actually[9] a this-something or an individual, can become one); or it may be the formula or the shape, which, being a this-something, can have its own separate being only logically[90]; or it may be 30 the synthesis of these, which alone is generated and destroyed and is in an unqualified sense a separate being. (For of the primary beings in discourse, some are separable, but others are not.) Concerning the first way, it is clear that to be material is a primary way of being. For in all changes[115] to the opposite[13] there is something that remains[85] itself throughout the changes: in locomotion, the same thing may be now here, now there; in growth, what now has one size, at other times is smaller or larger; and in qualitative alteration, the same thing may be now 1042b in good health, and then in bad. Similarly, in changes involving primary being, a thing may now be something coming into being, and then something being destroyed; or it may be now a subject matter with a particular "this-something," and then it may be a subject matter deprived of such particularity. In such a change the other types of change are involved[77], whereas such a change is not involved in the other two; for it is not necessary that if a material be subject to change of place it must also be subject to generation and destruction. But the difference between becoming in a simple and in a qualified sense has been stated in the writings on natural beings.†

* xiii, xiv.   † *Physics* v.1.225a12–20; *On Generation and Corruption* i.2.317a17–31.

2

Since there is general agreement on the primary being of subject matter and of material, and since such being is potential[11], it remains to be said what primary being of 10 perceptible things is actual[9]. Democritus seems of the opinion that things differ in only three ways: having the same body, either as subjects or as materials, they differ in pattern, that is, shape, in turning, that is, position, or in their contacts, that is, arrangement. However, the kinds of difference among things appear to be more manifold. Thus, things differ in the way their materials are synthesized: some by blending, as honey-water; some by being bound together, as a bundle; some by being glued together, as a book; some by being nailed together, as a casket; or in more than one of these ways. Other things differ in position, such as a threshold and a lintel (for these differ in the way in which they are placed); and others, in time, such 20 as dinner and breakfast; others, in direction, such as the winds; and others, in sensible quality, such as hard and soft, thick and thin, dry and wet. Some objects differ in only some of these qualities, and others, in all of them, or, in general, some by excess, and others by deficiency.

Hence, it is clear that things are said to "be" in as many ways. To be a threshold means to lie in a certain position, and for a threshold its being is its lying in such a position. To be ice means to have been solidified in a certain way. The being of some objects may be defined by all these differences, because some of their parts are mixtures, others are blended, others are bound together, others are solidified, 30 and others have still other differentiae, as in the case of hands or feet. We must, then, grasp the kinds of differentiae, for these will be principles of the being of things: things differing by more or less, by thick or thin, and by other such qualities; all these are cases of being by excess or deficiency. And all things differing in shape, smoothness, and roughness are different by being straight or curved. As for other things,

1043a their being will consist of their being mixed; their not being, the opposite.

It follows from these considerations that since primary being is the factor in terms of which a thing's being is to be construed, we must seek among these differentiating characteristics what difference is the determining factor in the being of each separate thing. Now, a thing's primary being is none of these differentiating characteristics, not even when they are joined[141a] with the thing's material, and yet each is analogous to primary being. And, as in primary being, what is predicated of a material is what it actually does[9], so, too, in other definitions, the differentiating characteristic is most analogous to the thing's action or functions. For example, if a definition of a threshold is required, we should say "wood or stone in a certain position"; and in the case of a house, "stone or wood in a certain position," but here we might add the "wherefor."

10 In the case of ice, "water frozen or solidified in a certain way"; and harmony, "a certain blending of high and low"; and so forth.

It is evident from these considerations, therefore, that action[9] and definition[90] differ according to the material: it is in some cases a synthesis; in others, a mixing; in others, one of the other differentiating characteristics mentioned. Therefore, of those who give definitions, they who in answering the question of what a house is say that it is stones, tiles, and timbers speak only of a potential house, for these factors are material; whereas those who say that a house is an enclosure sheltering bodies and possessions, or something else of the sort, tell how a house functions; and those who combine both of these definitions speak of primary being in the third sense, as a synthesis. For definition by means of

20 the differentiae seems to be in terms of form and function; and definition by means of the components is in terms of the material. And so, also, with the definitions which Archytas was accustomed to accept; for they use both. For example, what is calm weather? "Absence of motion in a large expanse

of air"; here "air" is the material, and "absence of motion" is the behavior and formal being. And what is a calm sea? "Smoothness of sea"; where the "sea" is the subject matter, and smoothness is the action or shape. It is evident, therefore, from the things that have been said, what perceptible primary being is and how it is; for it is on the one hand material, on the other, formal, that is, a function, and, thirdly, it is the composite of the two.

3

We must not ignore the confusion which may arise when a term signifies either a composite being[64g] or its action[9] 30 or form[91] alone: whether "house" signifies the composite[92], a shelter made up of tiles and stones placed in certain ways, or the action[9] and form[20] of sheltering; whether a "line" is defined by two points in extension or merely by the two points; whether an "animal" is soul-in-body or soul (here a soul is the essential being[26] or action of its body). "Animal" might even be applied to both; not, indeed, as a subject with a single definition, but as a complex with a single point of reference[24a]. Such considerations make a difference in their bearing on other issues, but none for our investigation into the primary being evident to sense perception. For what it is to be[88a] pertains[82f] to the 1043b form[20] or function[9]. For "soul" and "to be soul"[88a] are the same thing; but "man" and "to be man" are not the same, unless the soul can itself be said to be man. Thus it is that in one way a concrete being and what it is to be it are the same; but in another way, they are not.

Anyone who reflects seriously will not think that a syllable is composed of letters and their synthesis or that a house is tiles and their synthesis. For synthesis, or mixture, does not arise out of the things snythesized, or mixed. Likewise in any other case: if a threshold is what it is by position, the position does not arise out of the threshold, but rather the latter out of the former. Accordingly, man is animal and 10 biped; but there must be in addition to such material factors

something else, something that is neither an element nor composed of elements; and it is precisely this [essential being of a thing] that is omitted when only the material factor is stated. If, then, this is the determining factor of being and of primary being, a statement of it would be a statement of primary being itself. And it would be necessary that this be either eternal or if perishable be so without actually perishing, and if it has become, it became not by a gradual coming to be. It has been shown clearly elsewhere * that no one makes or generates a form[20], but that it is a particular something[4a] that is produced, that is, something composed of material and form. But it is not yet clear whether the primary being of perceptible things is separate;
20 except that this is clearly impossible in some cases, where there cannot be anything separate from the particular beings, such as house or utensil. Perhaps, then, these products and others also not formed by nature, are not primary beings; and one might suppose that nature alone is primary being among perishable beings.

Hence the difficulty which the followers of Antisthenes and other ignoramuses have raised carries some weight: namely, that what is[87] cannot be defined, since a definition is merely talk and tells only of what kind a thing is; for example, they thought it impossible to tell what silver itself is, but merely that it is like tin. Hence, the only kind of primary being of which there may be definition and explanation is the composite, whether it be perceptible or in-
30 telligible; but of their primary constituents there can be none, since a definition relates something to something, referring partly to the material and partly to form.

It is evident, also, that if numbers are somehow primary being they are so in this sense, not, as some say, as numbers of units. For a definition is like a number, since it is divisible, and into parts not further divisible, inasmuch as definitions, like numbers, are not infinitely divisible. Just as when one of the parts of which a number consists has been subtracted

* vii.8.

or added it is no longer the same number, but a different one, even if a very small part has been taken or added, so a 1044a definition, or what-it-is-to-be, will cease to be itself when something has been taken from or added to it. And there must be something according to which a number is a unit, and there are men who seem unable to account for the unity which any one number has; for either it is not one, but a mere heap, or if it is one there must be something to constitute the one out of the many. So a definition, too, is one; but there are men who seem likewise unable to explain how it is one. Their inability to account for unity is natural, since the same argument applies to both cases: a primary being is united as we have explained, not, as some say, by being a sort of unit or point; each is rather an integration[10] and a 10 nature. Just as a number is precise, not more or less, so, too, is a primary being as far as its form goes; if it can be more or less what it is, this is due to its material.

Let this be enough of an analysis[72e] of the coming into being and passing away of what we have called primary beings, of how these processes are possible and how impossible, and of the reduction of things to number.

4

Concerning material being it is important to note that even if all things ultimately have the same source or come from the same antecedents, and even if their generation begins in the same material, each, nevertheless, has some material which is its own[55]: of phlegm it is the sweet or the fat, and of bile, the bitter or something of the sort; however, these may come from the same material. And the 20 same thing may have several materials, as when one material is the material of another: sweet phlegm comes from the fat and the sweet; and so it also comes from bile when bile is analyzed into its primary material. For one thing emerges from another in two senses: either by proceeding from it or by being the result of the analysis of a thing into its elements. So, also, the same material may yield diverse products when a different moving factor is involved; for example, out of wood can come a chest and a bed. But in some cases the material must be different for different objects[1a]: no one can make a saw out of wood even if he should try, nor out of

30 wool. However, when the same product is made out of different materials, clearly it is the art or the mover that is the same; for if both the matter and the mover were different, the product also would be different.

Hence, in seeking explanatory factors, one must look for all the relevant[12b] kinds, since the meanings of explanation are various. For example, what is the material factor out of which man comes? Is it not the menstrual fluid? What is the moving factor? Is it not the seed? What is the formal factor? It is what it meant to be man. And what is the final

1044b factor? The complete man. But perhaps the last two are the same. In any case, one must give the proximate factors; so man's matter would not be fire or earth, but the material peculiar to him.

In explaining physical and generable primary beings, then, this is the proper way to proceed if the factors involved in their generation are as we have stated and if these are what we seek to know. But in explaining natural primary beings that are eternal, another account is needed. For perhaps some of them have no material, or not a material of generation, but merely of locomotion. And in explaining natural beings that are not primary beings one must not look for a material, since their primary being is in their subject matter.

10 For example, what explains an eclipse materially? Nothing; for an eclipse has not a material, but a subject eclipsed. And what is the source of motion by which the light was destroyed? The earth. And wherefor? Perhaps there is no wherefor. And the formal factor is the definition, which would be obscure if it did not include the efficient or moving factor. For example, *what* is an eclipse? Deprivation of light? Yes! But we should add "by the interposition of the earth" in the definition, which then includes the efficient factor. In the case of sleep, however, it is not clear what it is

that goes to sleep. Shall we say that it is the animal? Yes!
But the animal with regard to what primarily—the heart
or some other organ? Then, by what agency? Then, what
does the organ undergo, but not the whole? Shall we say
that it is immobility of a certain kind? Yes! But by way of
what process in the organ primarily affected?   20

5

There are some beings which may or may not be, but
which never come to be or cease to be; for example, points,
if they indeed are, and in general forms[20] or figures[91]
(for it is not "white" that comes to be, but wood that
becomes white), if a coming-to-be means to be *from* something and to come to be something in particular. Therefore, not all contraries[50] can come from one another; for
it is in different senses that a white man comes from a black
man and that white comes from black. Not all things have a
material, but only those which come to be and change into
one another. Those beings which either are or are not, without changing[115], have no matter.

Another problem is how a thing's material is related to
its contraries. For example, if the body is potentially 30
healthy and disease is contrary to health, is the body then
potentially both? And is water potentially wine and vinegar?
Is it not rather a single material, one of whose contraries is
its positive state[33a] and form[20] and the other, its privation[106] of form, or corrupted state[117a] contrary to
its nature? Then there is the problem why wine is not the
material of vinegar or potentially vinegar, even though
vinegar comes from it, and why a living man is not potentially dead. Is it not because a thing's corrupted conditions
are accidental[3] to it? Is it not an animal's matter that 1045a
by being corrupted becomes potentially the matter of a
corpse, and is not water the material of the souring of wine
into vinegar? For the one comes from the other as does night
from day. And all things which thus change into one another
must pass through their material state: if an animal comes

from a corpse, the corpse first returns to its material and only then becomes an animal; and vinegar becomes a formless fluid and only then becomes wine.

6

Now, to return to the problem which has been mentioned *
concerning definitions[72a] and numbers[141]: what is the
factor that explains[83] their unity[24]? In the case of all
things that have several parts and in which the whole[21] is
not like a heap, but is a particular something besides the
10 parts, there is some such uniting factor. In bodies it may
be the fact that their parts are in contact[137] that gives
them unity, or it may be their cohesiveness or some other
such quality; whereas a definition is a unity, not by attachment of part to part, like the Iliad, but because it defines a
single object. What, then, is it that gives a man his unity,
and why is he not a mere aggregate of things, such as an
animal plus a biped; as though, according to certain theories,
there were an animal as a thing by itself and a biped by
itself? Why are not these two together a man, so that a
man would be, not by himself, but by participation in
more than one being, in the two, animal and biped? In
20 general, then, would not a man be not one, but more than
one, namely, animal and biped?

It is evident, therefore, that if men proceed in this way,
as they are accustomed to do in definition and discourse, the
difficulty is insoluble. But if, as we say, there is a material
and a form, and the material is a power[11], whereas the
form is operation[9], the explanation sought avoids this
difficulty. For the difficulty is the same as that which would
arise if "bronze sphere" were the definition of "cloak":
"cloak" would then mean "bronze sphere," and the question
would arise how the unity of a cloak can be explained by
two beings, sphere and bronze. But for us this is no difficulty,
because the one word denotes the thing's material[84], and
30 the other, its form[91]. What, then, can explain how what

* vii.12; viii.3.1044a2–6.

was potentially becomes actual, except the effective agent (at least for things which are generated)? There is no other factor that explains how a potential sphere becomes an actual sphere; since the two kinds of being (what it means to be[88] a material and what it means to be a form) define precisely this relation of potential-actual.

However, a material may be either intelligible[169b] or perceptible[165c], and one part of any definition is always a thing's material, and another part is its operation; for example, a circle is a plane figure. And whatever has no matter, either intelligible or perceptible, but is an individual, is forthwith a[24] unity[4]; for it is a distinct being[4c], 1045b either a this-something[4a], or a quality[28], or a quantity[27]. Hence, neither being[1] nor unity[24] is to be found in the definitions of such beings; for in order to be such a being a thing must by its very nature[88] have unity as it also has being[4c]. Thus, such beings require no further explanation for their unity or for their being; for each is forthwith a being and a unity, not because it comes under the genera "being"[1] or "unity," and not as if being and unity could themselves be separately[73] and independently[74] of the being of particulars[40].

However, because of this difficulty some speak of participation[93] and raise the question of some factor to explain participation and the meaning of participation. Others speak of a thing's being united[23e]: Lycophron says that sci- 10 ence[179] is a marriage of knowledge and the soul[154]; others say that living[152] is a synthesis or connection of the soul with the body. Here the same explanation[90] applies to all: being healthy would be a marriage or connection or synthesis of soul and health; the fact that a triangle is of bronze would be a synthesis of bronze and triangle; and being white would be a synthesis of surface and whiteness. The reason is that these explanations try to show how potentiality and complete realization[10] are both one and different. But, as has been said, the proximate[18a] matter and the form are merely two aspects of the identical reality, the one with respect to a thing's capacities, the other with respect to its actual operation. Therefore, to seek a reason for their unity is like explaining 20 how one is one; for each individual is a unity, and its powers and actual functioning are somehow united. Hence, there is no other explanation needed, unless it be the moving factor which effects the change from a power into an actual operation. But as to the individual beings which have no matter, they are simply one.

IX. BOOK THETA

I

We have dealt with primary being[26]; that is, with what "is" in the primary sense of the word, or with that to which the other categories of being refer. For it is with regard to the concept of primary being that we speak of the being of the others, quantity[27], quality[28], and so forth; since all of them implicitly contain a reference to the concept of primary being, as we have said in our introductory words on this topic.* But since "being"[1] applies not only to a particular something[4] or to a quality or a quantity but also to a power[11] or to a fulfillment[10] or to a working[9], let us now explain[72e] "power" and "fulfillment." † And let us first deal with "power" in the strictest sense of the term, which is, indeed, not the most useful for our present purpose; for "power"[11] and "act"[9] have application beyond things in process[109]. After speaking of the stricter sense, we shall, in our discussion of "act," clarify the broader sense also.‡

Now, we have pointed out § that there are several ways in which we can speak of power and capability[11a]. Of these, we may dismiss those powers that are so called by an equivocation; for some are so called by analogy, as in geometry, where on the basis of the presence or absence of a certain relation we speak of one thing as a "power" or not

* vii.1.

† Like "being," so "operation," "fulfillment," and cognate terms are to be interpreted in the sense of verbs.

‡ ix.6.   § v.12.

a power of another. But [genuine] powers, that are really
10 related, are a kind of source or beginning[82] and are so
called in relation to one primary kind of power, which is the
source of change in another thing or in another aspect of the
same thing. For there is a passive[35] power residing in
anything acted upon which is the source of its undergoing
change through the action of some other thing or through
its own activity upon itself; so, also, there is a state[33a]
of insusceptibility[35d] to deterioration or destruction
(that is, to change) through the agency of another thing or
of its own action upon itself. There is implied in all these
definitions the meaning of power in the primary sense,
whether the things called powers are powers of acting or of
being acted upon, and whether they refer to acting well or
to being acted upon well; so that even the passive powers
imply conceptually[90] the active powers. It is evident,
20 then, that the active and passive powers are in a sense the
same, since anything has a capacity[11b] both because it
can itself be acted upon and because another can be acted
upon by it; but in a sense these powers also differ. For the
one power is in the object acted upon. When a thing is
acted on by another, it must be the passive source[82] of
the action, and this source may even be its very matter[84].
For what is oily can be burned; what yields in certain ways
can be compressed; and so forth. But the other power is in
the agent: heat, in what can heat; and the builder's art,
in one who can build. Hence, if a thing is essentially[101d]
a unit it cannot be acted upon by itself; for it is identical
with itself.

An incapacity[11d], or what cannot be done[11f], is merely
30 the lack or privation[106] of the corresponding active
capacity; so that any power in a given object related to a
given process has a corresponding incapacity. But a thing
may suffer privation or lack in two ways: not only by not
having a certain quality but also by not always having
what it naturally[101c] has, because there is either a general
deficiency or an occasional departure from the normal either

wholly or to some degree. And in some cases, when objects which naturally have a quality fail to have it because they have suffered violence, we say that they have been deprived of it.

2

Such sources[82] of change * are sometimes in inanimate objects, and sometimes in animate beings; some in any organism's life[154] in general, and others characteristic of a life in so far as it has reason[90]. Hence, all the arts, or 1046b capacities of knowing how to make things, are powers, since they are capacities of initiating change in something else or in another aspect of the agent himself. Powers with reason have contrary effects, whereas any power without rational control has its specific effect: what is warm can produce only warmth; but the science of medicine can be employed to produce either disease or health. This is due to the fact that knowledge states reasons, and the same formula explains[59] both a normal and an abnormal[106] state of affairs, though differently: hence, it explains both, in a sense; but it explains especially the positive state[82f]. 10 Hence, such sciences necessarily involve the knowledge of contraries. They produce the positive results essentially[2], and the others not essentially; for they explain the constructive effects by their very nature, but the privations they explain accidentally[3], so to speak[55c]. The contrariety is explained by denials and deprivations. For the direct contrary of a thing is its primary privation, the deprivation of its positive state. Since contraries, however, do not occur in the same object, and since science is a rational power and the living self[154] has the power to initiate movement, therefore the scientist may produce contrary effects; whereas a healing drug produces health only, and the warm, warmth only, and the cold, cold only. For a scientific statement[90] applies to both contraries, 20

* "Powers" are here discussed "in the strictest sense of the term, which is indeed not the most useful for our present purpose" (cf. ix.1.1045b36, 6.1048a25–30).

though not in the same way, and comes from a living self[154] which can initiate movement; so that the self[154] may set in motion, as from the same source, events that may result in either of the ends conceived[137c]. Hence, the rational powers operate in a way contrary to that of the nonrational powers; namely, they have their source of motion in rational statements[90].

It is evident also that a capacity of doing or undergoing well implies the corresponding active[34] or passive[35] power, but not always vice versa. For one who does something well necessarily does it; but one who does something does not necessarily do it well.

3

There are some, such as the Megarians, who say that
30 there is a power[11a] only in act[9a] and that there is no power apart from its operation: that when not engaged in building, a person is not able to build, and that he is a builder only when he is in the act of building, and so forth. But it is not difficult to see the absurdities which follow on this view.

Of course, it is clear that a person who never builds cannot be a builder; for to be[88a] a builder is to be able to build; and similarly in the case of the other arts. Now, if it is impossible to have such arts unless at some time the art is learned and acquired, it is also impossible to cease to have
1047a them unless at some time they are lost, either by forgetfulness or by some misfortune or by the passage of time; but they never can be lost by the destruction of their objective contents[188c], since these remain always. Hence, when a man ceases to practice his art and is supposed no longer to have it, how can he have acquired the art anew when he subsequently readily knows how to build? Likewise in the case of inanimate objects that are cold or hot or sweet or in any way perceptible: they will not be anything at all when they are not in process of being perceived; so that those who maintain this position will have to conclude with the doctrine of Protagoras. Moreover, those who are not per-

ceiving, that is, exercising perception, can have no power of perceiving. If, then, one who has normal organs of vision, but is not exercising them, is blind even though he has eyes and is normal, then a person will be blind or deaf many 10 times a day.

Also, if what has been deprived of a power is incapacitated, then whatever has not yet come into being cannot possibly come into being. Now, of whatever is incapable of coming into being it can never be truly said that it is or that it will be; for incapacity means precisely this impossibility. Consequently, these doctrines take away all possibility of change and of coming into being. Accordingly, whoever is standing must always have stood, and whoever is seated must remain seated, since, if he is seated, he has no power of rising; for it would be impossible for anything to rise which is not able to rise. If, then, we cannot say these things, it is evident that power and act differ; hence, those doctrines which present power and act identically, are trying to deny a 20 difference that is far from trivial. Consequently, something may be capable of being without actually being, and capable of not being, yet be; similarly, one may be capable of walking, but not now walking, or be walking, though capable of not walking. A thing is "capable," therefore, when there results no impossibility from its actually doing what it is said to have the power to do. I mean, for example if a thing is capable of sitting and it is possible for it actually to sit down, there would be nothing impossible in this act; likewise, if it is capable of being moved or of moving something, or of standing or causing something to stand, or of being or becoming, or of not being or not becoming.

The word "actuality"[9], which is associated with "ful- 30 fillment"[10], has been derived from movements, though it can be applied in other ways; for to be in act seems, above all, to be a movement. Accordingly, we do not attribute being in motion to things that do not exist, though certain other predicates may be attributed to them: things that are not may be thought or desired, but they may not be moved.

For, if nonbeings were actual, they would have to be actually
1047b in motion; so that among nonbeings some are potentially,
but they "are" not in being, because they are not completely
or in fulfillment.

4

If what we have said * is the truth about possibility[11b],
clearly it cannot be true to say that something is possible,
but will never be; for then there would be no impossibilities.
I mean, for example, someone who failed to take the impossible into account[176] might say that the diagonal of the
square could be commensurate with the side, though it
never will be measured, on the ground that there is nothing
to hinder anything from being capable of being or of coming
into being, though it neither is nor will be. But he would
10 be obliged to suppose that it is not impossible that a nonbeing, which is a possible being, now is or sometime was;
this is, nevertheless, impossible, for it is impossible that the
diagonal of the square be commensurate with the side. The
false and the impossible are not identical; since it may now
be false that you are standing, but it is not impossible.

It is also clear that if when A is, B must also be, then
when A is possible, B must also be possible; for if B need
not be possible, there is nothing to hinder it from not being
possible. Now, let A be possible. Then, when A was possible,
nothing impossible followed if AB were assumed; hence, B
20 must also be. But that was impossible. Let it, then, be
impossible. If, therefore, B must be impossible, A must be
so too. But A was impossible; hence B is so too. If, accordingly, A is possible, B will also be possible; if, indeed, they
are so related that when A is, B must be. If, therefore, A and
B being related as has been stated, B is not possible on the
condition stated, neither will A and B be related as has been
assumed; and if when A is possible, B must be possible,
then, if A is, B must be too. For to say that if A is possible,
B must be possible also, means that if A actually is, both

* ix.3.1047a24–26.

at the time and in the way it was supposed capable of being,
B must also be at the same time and in the same way.   30

5

All our powers are either innate[19a], such as the senses,
or are acquired by practice, such as flute-playing, or by
education, such as the arts. And possession of those which
we acquire by practice or by reason requires their previous
exercise, whereas this is not required in the case of those
which are not of this sort or which are passive.

Moreover, since what is capable is capable of something at 1048a
some time and in some way, and whatever other qualifications must be added in the definition, and since some
things can produce movement rationally and have the power
of reasoning, whereas other things are nonrational and do
not have the power of reasoning, and since the former
powers must be in living things, whereas the latter may be in
both animate and inanimate beings, it is necessary in the
case of nonrational powers that when an agent[189] and a
patient[35c] are brought together the action[34] and affect[35]
take place, whereas in the case of rational powers this is not
necessary; for every one of the nonrational powers can have
but a single effect, whereas the rational can have contrary
effects, so that if they were under the same necessity as
are the nonrational they would have contrary effects at the
same time. But this is impossible. It is necessary, accordingly, 10
that something else be decisive in rational action; I mean
desire[156] or deliberate choice[178]. For whatever alternative a rational being desires decisively, that will he
do whenever he is capable of acting and when he is brought
into connection with the chosen object to be acted upon.
Consequently, every being which has a rational power must,
when it has the desire, do what it has power to do and in
the way in which it has it. And it has the power when the
object of corresponding passive power is present and is in a
certain state. If not, it will not be able to act. Nor need we
add the proviso that there be no external hindrance; for

what has power has the power of acting, and it has this, not in all circumstances, but in those circumstances in which
20 external hindrances are by definition excluded. Hence, even if one were to wish or desire to do two incompatible things at the same time, one would not do them; for no one has such a power. There is no power of doing both at the same time; hence, we do what we can and as we can.

6

Having now discussed power relative to movement, let us investigate actuality to determine what it is[87] and what kind[28] of a being[4] it is. The analysis will throw further light on power, by showing that we ascribe power not only to what naturally moves something else or is moved by something else, either simply or in some special sense of
30 movement, but also that we use the word in another sense, a sense which concerns our present inquiry and previous discussion.

Actuality in things is a state[82f] of being[188c] unlike the potential state which we have described. We say that potentially a Hermes is in a block of wood, because it can be derived[118b] from it; or, for the same reason, that the half-line is in the whole; or we say that a person knows if he is capable of reflection, even when he is not engaged in reflection. The contrasting state in each of these cases is called an actual state. What we are trying to say is clear by induction from these particular cases[40], and we must not seek a definition of everything, but rather comprehend
1048b the analogy: as the process of building is related to the ability to build; as waking is to sleeping; as seeing is to closed eyes; as what has been molded out of a material is to the material; as what has been shaped is to the unshaped. Actuality[9], then, may be defined by one pole[22] of this antithesis[76a]; potentiality[11b], by the other. But actuality is not always so called in the same sense, but by analogy: as *A* is in or for *B*, so *C* is in or for *D*. Actuality is related to potentiality in some cases as movement is related to the

power to move and in other cases as a primary being is to
its material. In addition, the infinite and the void and the
like are said to be potentially or actually in a sense different 10
from that applied to many other things[1a], such as beings
that see or walk or are seen. For these beings can sometimes
be truly said to be potential or actual without qualification;
for the seen is sometimes so called because it is actually
seen, and sometimes because it can be seen. But the infinite
is potential, not in the sense that it will ever be actual as a
separate being, but in the sense of being potential for
knowledge[181]. For division, being limitless, warrants[46d]
the potential being of this infinite activity, but not the
separate being of the infinite.

Moreover, any action[188b] which has a limit is in itself
not an end, since it is directed to an end outside itself:
the process of reducing one's weight has slenderness as a
limit, and the bodily parts themselves, when one is reducing 20
them, are thus in process, since the movement is directed
toward states of affairs which are not as yet present. This
movement is therefore not an action, or at least not complete[14] in itself; for it is not an end. But a movement
whose end inheres[82h] in it is perfectly active[188b]; for
example, in seeing, one *has* sight. And he who is thinking
has his thought[172], and he who is knowing is in possession
of knowledge[169a]; whereas he who is learning has not
yet learned, and he who is being healed is not in possession
of health. So, too, one who lives well has at the same time
achieved the good life, and one who is happy has happiness
in his grasp. If not, the process must at some time come to a
limit; as when one undertakes reducing. But this does not
happen; rather it is in living that one has laid hold upon life.

Of these activities, therefore, we may call some "processes"[109], and others "acts"[9]. For every process is
incomplete—reducing, learning, walking, house-building are
processes—that is, they are incomplete. For walking is not 30
at the same time having had a walk; or house-building, hav-
ihg built a house; or coming to be, having come to be; or

being moved, having been moved. What now moves is different from what has moved. But it is the same thing that at the same time has a view and is seeing, or is knowing[169a] and has knowledge. It is the latter sort of process, then, that I call "an act"; and the former, "a process." These and similar considerations, then, may be taken as having made clear what an act is and what kind of being it has.

7

We must now distinguish the conditions under which a thing may and may not be said to have a power; for this 1049a may not be said under all conditions. For example, is earth potentially a man or not? It is so only when it has become seed; and perhaps not even then? Similarly, it is not any organism whatever that may be healed by medical art or by chance, but only those which are capable of being healed; they alone are potentially healthy. In those cases in which the change from the potential state to fulfillment[10] is brought about deliberately[170], the process takes place as willed on condition that nothing external hinders; and, on the other hand, when a healing process is brought about by chance rather than by art the necessary condition is that there be nothing to prevent it in the body to be healed. So, too, a house is potentially if there is nothing 10 in the building material to hinder it from becoming a house and there is nothing else which needs to be added or removed or changed; under such circumstances the material is potentially a house. And so it is with other objects which have the source of their becoming outside themselves.

As to the things which have the source of their becoming within themselves, they are potentially all that they will be of themselves, if nothing external prevents. That is, the seed is not yet potentially a man; for it must be in something other than itself and undergo change. But when the seed has by its own initiation become of a certain sort, then it is potentially a man; whereas in its former state it requires some other initiation. So ore from the ground is not yet potentially a statue; it must first undergo change before it is the bronze [which is the material of a statue].

Moreover, we have a clue to what "potential" means in our way of saying that a thing is not a something else[4a], but "of" something else; for example, that a chest is, not wood, but wooden, and that wood is, not earth, but earthen. 20 If earth, in turn, is likewise not something else[16b], but is "of" something, then we would have a series in which the last is always potentially what precedes it. That is, a chest is not earth or earthen, but wooden, and "wooden" denotes what is potentially a chest and the material of a chest: the wood specifically[105] of a chest, or this[4a] wood of this chest. If, therefore, there is something primary, so that it cannot be said to be "of" anything else, this is prime matter: if earth is of air, and air, though not fire, is "of" fire, then fire is prime matter; that is, it is not itself a particular being[4b] or a primary being[26]. For a material differs from a subject matter[85] by not being a particular something: in the case of an attribute[35a] predicated of a subject matter, for example, of a man, both body and soul, the attribute is 30 "musical" or "white"; and the subject matter of the attribute is not called "music," but musician, and the man is not "a white," but a white man, and not a walk or movement, but someone walking or in motion, and the attribute indicates what kind of a man he is. Wherever this is the relation between subject and predicate, the final[18a] subject is primary being[26]; but wherever this is not so, but the predicate is itself a[20] form[4] and a particular something[4b], the final subject is a material or material being. Hence we say rightly in the case of both a material and an accidental attribute that things are "of" them; for both are 1049b indeterminate[72c]. It has been shown, then, when something may be said to be potentially, and when not.

8

Since we have previously * distinguished the various ways
* v.11.

in which things are "prior"[17], it is evident that actuality is prior to potentiality. And I mean prior not only to the definite[72] power which is said to be the source of change in something else or in some other aspect of the same thing, but to any source of motion or of rest generally. For nature, too, may from this point of view be placed in the same genus with power, since it is a source of change; not of change in something else, but in a thing's own being.

Actuality is prior to such potentiality both logically[90] and in being[26]; it is also prior in time in one sense, but not in another sense. The logical priority of actuality, then, is clear. For what is potential in the primary sense is potential because it can become actual: what has the capacity to build means what can build; what has the capacity to see means what can see; and what is visible means what can be seen. And the same reasoning applies to other cases; so that the reason[90] or knowledge[181] of the actual must be present before[82g] there is knowledge of the potential.

The actual is temporally prior, too, in the sense that an actual being is ahead of another[141] being of the same kind[20] that is only potential. I mean that this man who already is active and this corn and this seeing animal are temporally ahead of the material for a man, the grain of corn, and the animal whose eyes are not yet open; for they are not yet in operation, but can become an actual man, plant, or seeing animal. Prior in time to these there were other actual beings from which these came to be. For whenever something potential becomes something actual, it does so always by the agency of some actual being: man, from man; and a musician, from a musician. There is always a first mover, and the mover is actual. We said in the discussions † concerning primary being that everything that comes into being, comes into being from something and by some agent who is of its own kind.

This is also the reason why it is held impossible for one who has never built anything to be a builder, or for one

† vii.7, 8.

who has never played the harp to be a harpist; for one who learns to play the harp learns to play by playing it, and so forth. Hence arose the sophistic paradox that the learner who does not have knowledge will, nevertheless, be doing that which implies knowledge. However, because there is always something in what is coming to be that has already come to be and in general there is always something in what is changing that has already been changed (as is made clear in the discussions ‡ of change), therefore the learner must presumably have some element[4] of this knowledge. But 1050a here, too, it is clear that actuality is in this sense, too, prior to potentiality; that is, it is prior in the order of genesis and of time.

Then, too, actuality is prior to power in being[26]. One reason is that what comes later in genesis is prior in form and being: the man is prior to the son, as a human being is prior to the seed; for the one already has form, and the other does not. Also, everything that is produced proceeds according to its principle[82], for its wherefor[96] is its principle, and at the same time its coming into being is directed by the end[100]; hence the actuality is the end, and it is thanks to it that a power is possessed[65]; for animals do not see in 10 order that they may have the power of sight, but they have the power of sight in order that they may see. Similarly, men have the capacity of building in order that they may build, and the capacity of knowing[187] in order that they may know; but they do not know in order that they may have the capacity of knowing, except, perhaps, in so far as this is done for the sake of further training (and then they do not perform acts of knowing, except in a limited sense or because they do it without an immediate need). Again, a matter is potential because it may attain to form; it is when it is actual that it is in its form. And it is the same in other cases, even those in which the end is a process. Hence, as teachers consider that they have attained their end when they have exhibited their students actually performing their learning,

‡ *Physics* vi.6.

so it is with nature. For, if this were not so, it would be a
20 case of Pauson's Hermes; and we would not be clearer about
knowledge than about the figure in that painting, whether
it is painted or stands out in relief. For the activity or
work[9c] is the end; and the actuality is the activity or
work. And so even the word "actuality" is derived from
"action" and points to its fulfillment.

Now, the doing of an action[163] is its own end[18a], as
seeing is the end of vision; and from the activity of seeing
no further product results. But there are other activities
which produce something: house-building produces a house,
which exists apart from the activity of building. Nevertheless, in both cases the action is final when compared with
the potential, being in the former case not less an end, and
in the latter more of an end, than the power is. For the
construction of a house is realized in the house constructed
and is begun and completed simultaneously with the house.
30 Hence, in those cases in which something beyond the
activity is produced, the action lies in the product: the
activity of building lies in the house being built; weaving
is in the textile being woven; and so forth. In general, a
movement is in the thing being moved. But where there is
no other product beyond the activity, there the action is
inherent in the agent: seeing is in him who sees; knowing,
1050b in him who knows; and living[152] is in the actually living
being[154]. Hence living well, or happiness, is an actuality;
for it is a kind[28] of living. Consequently, it is evident
that the primary being or form is actual. According to this
argument, therefore, it is evident that actuality is prior to
potentiality in being; and, as we have said,§ one act always
precedes another in time up to the eternal prime mover.

However, actuality is prior in an even more fundamental
sense[55b]; for eternal[135a] beings are by their very being
prior to those that perish, since nothing eternal is potentiality. The reason[90] is this. Every power may eventuate
in one of two opposite[49] ways; for whatever is not even

§ ix.8.1049b17–29.

potentially real will never be realized[82f], but whatever 10
is potential may possibly not become actual. Accordingly,
whatever is potentially in being may either be or not be;
thus, the same thing is potentially being and not being.
But what potentially is not may possibly cease to be; and
what may cease to be is perishable, either simply ceasing
to be, or perishable in whatever category is being used
with regard to it, that is, with regard to place or quantity
or quality. Therefore, nothing which taken simply is imperishable is potential taken simply; though there is nothing
to prevent it from being potential in respect of quality or
place, and so forth. Accordingly, whatever is eternal is
actual. Nor is anything potentially which is necessarily, and
necessary beings[1a] are primary; for, without them, nothing
would be at all.

Moreover, if there is movement which is eternal, it cannot 20
be potentially. And if there is anything movable eternally,
it is not moving potentially; although it may move from
place to place, and there is nothing to prevent its being
material or potential with reference to the direction of the
movement. Hence, the sun and the stars and the other
heavenly bodies are in ceaseless operation, and there is no
ground for fearing, as do the naturalists, that they may at
some time cease to move. They do not become weary: their
movement is not subject to a power which may lead to
opposites, whereas perishable bodies may or may not move
and therefore become exhausted; their exhaustion is due[83]
to the fact that their being is material and potential. But
there are changing bodies which imitate the eternal, such
as earth and fire. For these are also ever active, since they
have their motion both of themselves and within themselves. 30
But the other powers, according to our previous distinctions,
all admit opposites; for whatever can move something else
one way can also move it contrariwise, at least, if it is
rational. And if it is a nonrational power, it is still subject
to opposite motions, depending on whether it is present
or absent.

Accordingly, if there are any natures or beings like those "ideas"[89] for which some argue, there must be something much more knowing than knowledge[179] itself and some- 1051a thing more moving than movement itself; for it is science and movement, rather, that are actual, and the ideas are corresponding powers. It is evident, then, that actuality is prior to potentiality and to every principle of change.

9

That the actuality of good is better and more valuable than the power for good is clear from the following con- siderations. Anything that is said to be a power has a potentiality for either of two contraries[50]: the same thing that is said to be potentially healthy is also at the same time potentially ill; for the same power pertains to health and illness, to rest and motion, to building and tearing down, to 10 being built and falling down. The potentiality of contraries, then, belongs to its possessor at the same time; but the contraries themselves cannot. It is likewise impossible for contrary actions to belong to an agent at the same time, such as health and illness. Consequently, the good must be the one or the other. But potentiality is both alike or neither; hence, actuality is better. Also, in the case of evils the end or action must be worse than the power; for the potential is both contraries alike. Accordingly, it is clear that evil is not something apart from[74] things[188c]; for evil is naturally posterior to power. In whatever is primordially and in 20 anything eternal there is, accordingly, no evil or defect[128] or corruption; for corruption is an evil.

It is also in action that geometrical proofs are discovered; for men discover them by drawing dividing lines in the given figures. If these lines had been there, the proofs would have been evident; but, as it is, they are in the figures potentially. Why is the sum of the angles of a triangle two right angles? Because the angles grouped about any one point of the triangle are equal to two right angles. If, then, the line parallel to the side had already been drawn in with the given triangle, the reason would have been clear to anyone immediately on seeing the construction. Why is an angle inscribed in a semicircle always a right angle? Given the three equal lines, two of which form the base and one the radius from the inscribed angle to the center, the reason is clear to anyone seeing the construction and having knowledge of triangles. Consequently, it is evident that one discovers what is potential by performing an operation. The 30 reason[83] is that knowing[169c] is an act. Hence a power is deduced from an operation, and therefore it is by making constructions that men come to know the possibilities; for in the order of genesis a particular demonstration is posterior to the figure on which it is based.

10

Now "being"[1] and "nonbeing"[1b] are used: first, according to the types[91a] of categories[25]; secondly, according to power[11] or actuality[9] of their contraries[50]; and commonly[55b], according to the true[7] or the 1051b false[8]. This use depends on things[188c] being combined[21b] or dissociated[75]; so that he who thinks that what is dissociated is dissociated, and what is combined is combined, holds the truth, whereas he whose thought is contrary to the state of affairs is in error. When, therefore, is there or is there not what is called truth or falsity?

We must inquire into what we mean by this. For it is not because we truly hold you to be white that you are white; but it is because you are white that we who assert this hold the truth. If, therefore, some things are always combined and cannot be dissociated, whereas others are always dissociated and cannot be combined[64g] and it is 10 possible for still other things to be either combined or dissociated, then to "be" is to be combined or to be united, whereas not to "be" is to be separated or to be more than one. Concerning contingencies[12b], then, the same opinion[175] or the same statement[90] comes to be false and true; for it can at one time be true and at another time false. But concerning matters that cannot be otherwise than they are, the same opinions cannot be at one time true and at another time false, but are always true or always false.

However, as to incomposites, what is it to be or not to be; and what is truth or falsity? For a being of this sort is not composite[64g], so as to "be" when it is combined or not to 20 "be" if it is dissociated, such as wood being white or the diagonal of the square being incommensurable with the side; nor will truth or falsity apply to them in the same way as it did to the previous cases considered. Indeed, as truth is not the same in these cases, so being is not the same. Here there is truth or falsity in the sense that what we "get"[137d] we also affirm or deny (for to affirm[47] is not the same as to speak[46]); and failure to "get" a thing is [not error, but] ignorance[190]. For it is not possible to be in error concerning what a thing is, except incidentally. Likewise, concerning incomposite beings it is not possible to be in error. They are all actual, not potential, since otherwise they could come to be or be destroyed; but as it is, being[1] itself is neither 30 generated nor destroyed, since it would then have had to be generated out of something. Therefore, concerning actual being it is not possible to be in error, but only to know[169a] or fail to know it. But concerning such being we can ask what it is; that is, whether it is of a certain sort or not.

As to "being" in the sense of the true and "not being" in the sense of the false, there are two cases: in one case there is truth if the combination [of subject and attribute] exists, and falsity if there is a dissociation; in the other case, however, [the noncomposites], whatever is, is as it is, or it is 1052a not at all. Here truth is the knowledge of these beings; and there is no error, but ignorance instead—but an ignorance not like blindness, which would imply a total lack of the power of thought.

As to changeless beings[109e], it is evident that there can be no error with regard to time, if we take them to be unchanging. For example, if we suppose that the triangle does not change, we shall not suppose that its angles at

one time equal two right angles, and at another time not;
for it would then change. But we may suppose something
of one class, and not of another; for example, we may suppose
that no even number is prime or suppose that some are and
that some are not. But we may not make even this sort of
supposition concerning something that is numerically
single; for we cannot, in this case, make a supposition con- 10
cerning a class as distinguished from others, but the truth
or falsity will always be whichever it is.

X. BOOK IOTA

I

WE HAVE SAID before,* in our explanations of the various meanings of terms[6a], that "unity" means several things. But apart from the accidental[3] ways, the primary[17a] and essential[2] ways of being "one" may be grouped under four heads. There is (1) being continuous[136a]: continuity may
20 be unconditional, or natural, instead of being united by contact or attachment; such continuity is primarily and more especially unity when the being's movement is quite indivisible and simple. (2) Things are especially units when they are concrete wholes[21] and have their own shape or form; most especially when this unity is natural, not by force, such as objects glued or nailed or bound together, that is, when it has in itself the ground[83] of its continuity. An object is of this sort when its movement is single and indivisible in place and time; so that it is evident that if an object has its own natural source of the primary kind of motion (locomotion), and if its motion is of the most unified kind (circular), then that object is in the primary sense a "unit" quantity.

Some things are units in one of these ways, being either continuous or concrete wholes; others are united by their
30 definition. Such a unity exists among the things comprehended by a single thought[169c], that is, an indivisible thought; it may be indivisible either in kind or in number. (3) Numerically any individual[40] is indivisible; (4) in kind[20], things are indivisible when they are unified in

* v.6.

intelligibility or in knowledge. Hence things are "one" in the primary sense when their unity is the reason[83] for the unity of some primary being[26].

These are the four ways of being "one": being naturally continuous, being a concrete whole, being numerically one, and being generically[43] one. All these are unities, either because their movement is indivisible or because their 1052b conception or definition is indivisible.

However, it must be thoroughly understood that the question "What sorts[28] of things are said to be one?" is not to be taken as having the same meaning as the question "What is it[87] to be[88a] one?" or "What is the definition[90] of unity?" On the one hand a thing may be said to be a unity in any of these ways; so that whatever is in one of these ways is "one." On the other hand, "to be one" may mean merely to be one of these things, or it may mean something even closer to the meaning of the word than the things are to which the word is applied. So, also, "element" or "explanatory factor" mean both the things[188c] thereby designated[72e] and also the definitions[72b] of the terms. For fire is, in a sense, an element (as is, perhaps, also the in- 10 definite[130] or anything else thus taken by itself[2]), but there is a sense in which it is not; since to be fire and to be an element are not the same, though as a particular[4] being[188c] or nature[101] fire is an element, the name "element" means that it has the attribute of being that of which something is composed or primarily constituted. So, also, "explanatory factor" and "one" and any such term has a connotation.

In this sense "to be one" means "to be indivisible"[75a], that is, to be essentially[1] a "this"[4a], to be discrete[73b] in place or form or thought[170], or, also, "to be a whole and indivisible." But it is especially "to be a first measure within any kind"[19], and chiefly a measure of quantity[27]; for it is from quantity that "unity" has been extended to the other categories. For a measure is that by which quantity 20 becomes known[181a]; and quantity as quantity becomes

known either by a unit or by a number, and any number comes from "one." Consequently, all quantity as quantity becomes known by unity, and that by which quantities primarily become known is unity itself; hence, unity is the beginning of number as number. Hence, it is also among the other kinds of being that "measure" means that by which each first becomes known, and the measure of each is a unit: in length, in breadth, in depth, in weight, in speed. Now, "weight" and "speed" apply equally[92] to contraries, since each of these terms has a double meaning: "weight" applies both to anything that tends downward at all and to what has an excessive downward tendency, and "speed,"
30 both to any motion and to what has excessive motion; for even what is slow has a certain speed, as even what is light has a certain weight. In all these matters the measure, or beginning, is something one and indivisible; for even in measuring lines by feet we treat a one-foot line as indivisible[41]. Thus, we always seek as a measure something one and indivisible, something simple either in quality or in quantity. An exact measure is one from which nothing can be subtracted and to which nothing can be added. Hence,
1053a number is the most exact measure; for we assume that a numerical unit is in every respect indivisible. Therefore, in other cases this sort of measure is imitated. For, in the case of a furlong or a talent or anything relatively large, an addition or subtraction might more readily escape our notice than in the case of some relatively small measure. Consequently, it is the first thing from which no appreciable quantity can be taken away that all men take for a measure, whether of liquids or solids or of weight or of size; and they think they know[182] a quantity when they know it by means of this measure. They also measure motion by the simplest and fastest motion, since it takes the least time.
10 Hence, in astronomy this sort of unit is a starting-point and measure, for astronomers assume celestial motion to be of uniform and greatest velocity and estimate other motions by it; in music, it is the half tone, because that is the smallest

interval; in speech, the letter. It is in this way that all such things are unified, not by having "one" in common, but in the way which has been explained. However, the measure is not always numerically one, but is sometimes more than one: there are two half-tone intervals, measured, not by ear, but by ratio. And the vocal sounds by which we measure are more than one, and the diagonal of the square and its side are measured by two quantities; and so with all spatial magnitudes.

Therefore, all things are measured by unity; for we get to know the elements of which any primary being consists by division either in quantity or in kind. And the unit is 20 indivisible, because the first of each kind is indivisible. But it is not in the same way that every unit is indivisible, such as a foot and a unity: the latter is absolutely indivisible; but the former is used, as already said, as an apparently indivisible thing, for any continuous magnitude may be divisible.

Then, too, a measure is always homogeneous with what is measured, for the measure of magnitudes is a magnitude; in particular, length is measured by a length, breadth by a breadth, articulate sounds by an articulate sound, weight by a weight, units by a unit. For we must take it in this way and not say that numbers are measured by a number, as we would have to if we were to use a similar form of words, for the cases are not analogous; measuring numbers by a number is like measuring units by units, not by a single unit, for 30 numbers are pluralities of units.

Similarly, we say that science and sense measure things, because by them we get to know things; whereas they really do not measure, but are measured. We feel as though someone were taking our measure, and we get to know our size because the measuring tape is repeatedly applied to us. But Protagoras says, "man is the measure of all things," as if he had meant to say "the man of science" or "the man of sense"; for 1053b such men are measures because they possess science, or sense, which we know to be measures of whatever is submitted[85] to them. Therefore, this saying, though it seems to say something, really says nothing.

It is evident, then, that unity, according to the strictest definition of the term, is a measure, especially of quantity, and then also of quality. Some things are united by being indivisible in quantity, and others, in quality. Thus, unity is indivisible, either absolutely or in so far as it is a unit.

2

Concerning the very being[26] of unity and its nature, 10 we must examine which of two ways properly describes its being. This is precisely the question which in our list of problems * we raised when we asked what unity is and how we must take it: whether unity itself is in some sense a primary being, as the Pythagoreans of old and more recently Plato say; or whether rather some natural being is referred to as the principle of unity, such as the natural philosophers speak of, one of whom finds unity in friendship; another, in air; and still another, in the indefinite.

Now, if primary being cannot be generic[43], as we said in our accounts of being and primary being,† and if being itself cannot be primary in the sense of being one and apart from the many (since it is something they have in common), 20 but only a predicate, it clearly follows that unity cannot be a primary being; for being and unity are of all categories the most generally predicated. Consequently, genera are not natures or primary beings separable from other things; hence, unity cannot be a genus, for the same reasons for which being and primary being cannot be genera.

This must be true of unity in all its meanings. Now, there are as many ways of being one as there are of being; so that since in qualitative being unity is something definite[4] and has a definite nature, likewise in quantitative being it is clear that we must investigate in general what this definite kind of unity is, just as we investigate what being is. For it is not an adequate explanation to say that the nature of

* iii.4.1001a4–b25. † vii.13.

unity is to be one or simply to be. For in colors unity is a color, for example, white, if the colors seem to come from white and black and if black is the privation of white, as 30 darkness is of light. Hence, if all things were colors they would all be a number. But a number of what? Clearly, of colors. And the unit of colors would be a definite color, white. Similarly, if things were tunes, they would be a number, but a number of half tones; their primary being would not be a number, and their unity would be something whose primary being is not unity, but a half tone. Similarly, 1054a if things were articulate sounds, they would be a number of letters, and their unity would have been a vowel. And if things were rectilinear figures, they would be a number of figures, and their unity would be the triangle. And the same account applies to other kinds[19] of being. Consequently, although there are numbers and unity in attributes, qualities, quantities, and movements, yet their unity is not to be[26] unity, but to be a number of things definitely united, their unity being a united something[4]; and the same must be true also of primary beings, for this truth applies to all forms of being alike.

It is evident, then, that in each genus unity is a definite 10 nature and that the nature of its unity is in no case mere unity; but, as the unity which is sought among colors is a color, so unity itself in primary being is one primary being. It clearly follows that "one" means the same as does being, for it has meanings corresponding to the categories and is not to be found within any one category—not in primary being[87], or in quality—but related to them, just as being is; and "one man" is not predicated as something in addition to "a man," just as being is nothing beyond a being or a quality or a quantity. So "to be[88a] one" is to be something definite.

3

The one and the many are opposed in several ways, one 20 of which is the opposition between the one as the indivisible[75a] and the many as the divisible; anything that is divided or divisible is called a plurality, whereas the indivisible or undivided is called a unity. Of the four kinds of opposition, this one is opposition by privation[106]; such terms are contraries, not contradictories and not correlatives. The meaning of unity becomes clear when contrasted with what is divisible, for plurality or the divisible is more perceptible than the indivisible, so that the definition of plurality is prior in sense experience to that of the indivisible.

In addition, as we have recorded in our distinction of the 30 contraries,* unity is associated with sameness, likeness, and equality, and plurality with otherness, unlikeness, and inequality. Let us consider sameness[15]: to be "the same" may mean to be the same numerically, but it may also mean to have a single definition as well as the same number; for example, you are one with yourself in both form and matter. Or things are the same if the definition[90] of their primary 1054b being[26] is identical: equal straight lines are the same, and so are equal and equal-angled quadrilaterals, though there are many of them; here it is their equality in which they are one and the same.

Things are "alike"[57] when, though they are not absolutely the same and though they are different individuals, they, nevertheless, have the same form[20]: the larger square is like the smaller, and unequal straight lines are alike; they are alike, but not absolutely the same. Then, too, things of the same form, which are subject to quantitative variations, are "alike" when their quantities are the same. Or even when they are quantitatively different they may be 10 alike if they share a common form, for example, whiteness. And we also call objects "alike" if they have more attributes[35a] in common than not, whether these attributes be prominent or not: tin is like silver in color, and gold is like fire in so far as it is yellow and red.

Similarly, there are several meanings of "other"[16] and

* iv.2.1004a2.

"unlike." In one sense the other is opposed to the same; so that anything is either the same as or other than everything else. In another sense one thing is other than another unless their matter, as well as their definition, is identical; thus, you are other than your neighbor. A third use of "other" is found in mathematics. In the case of "being one"[24] or "being"[1], all things are said to be other than or the same as other things. For "other" is not the contradictory of "same"; which is why nonexistent things are not said to be 20 "other" than existent things[1a], though they may be said to be "not the same." Thus, "other" applies to all beings; for what is and is one is naturally one or not one with everything else. These are the distinctions between "other" and "same."

But difference[76a] is distinct[16b] from otherness[16a]. For a thing and its "other" need not be other in a definite respect, since everything that has definite[4] being is either other or the same; but what is different, is different from something definite in a definite respect, so that something must be identified by which they differ. And this identity is a genus or a species; for everything that differs, differs in genus or in species. Things differ in genus if they do not have their matter in common and are not generated out of each other; that is, if they belong to different categories. When they have the same genus, they differ in species, and 30 their common genus identifies them as being essentially[26] alike, with specific differences.

Things "contrary"[50] are "different"; for contrariety is one kind of difference. That we are right in this supposition may be proved inductively[113e]; for in cases of contraries there are specific differences, not mere otherness; some are generically other, and others are in the same category and therefore in the same genus or generically the same. But 1055a we have distinguished elsewhere † what things are generically the same or other.

† v.9.

4

Since things which differ[76] may be more or less different, there is a greatest difference; this I call [strict] contrariety[50b]. We can show inductively that contrariety is the greatest difference. For when things differ from one another generically, they have no way of access to one another, but are isolated and incomparable[58a]; whereas, when things differ specifically, the extremes[18a] meet, and generation takes place. Hence the distance between extremes is a 10 maximum, and this constitutes the relation of contrariety.

Now, in any genus the greatest is the most complete[14]. For that is greatest which cannot be exceeded, and that is complete beyond which nothing can be had; so, like all other things, difference, too, comes to a complete end or fulfillment. But there is nothing beyond the end[100]; for an end is always an extreme, including all within it. Hence, there is nothing beyond the end; one cannot add to perfection[14]. From these considerations, then, it is clear that contrariety is perfect difference. Since contraries are in several ways, the ways in which they are complete will be correlative to their ways of being[23].

All this being so, it is evident that one thing can have 20 only one direct contrary; for nothing can be more extreme than the extreme, nor can one distance have more than two extremities. This is equally clear taken generally: a difference separates two things; therefore contrariety, being complete difference, is a relation between two things.

There are other definitions of true contraries. We have shown that complete difference is the greatest possible, since beyond such difference and between things generically different no difference is definite and there is no difference between anything and things of another genus; hence, a complete difference between different things in the same genus is the greatest possible. We have shown also that such complete difference is contrariety; for a complete difference is one which separates the species of the same genus. Similarly, things that are extremely different, but have the

same material, are contraries; for contraries have the same 30
matter. So things that are extremely different in the same
power are contraries; for a single science covers a single
genus and therefore deals with the complete differences in
that genus.

Now the basic form[17a] of contrariety[50b] is that
between a positive state[33a] and its privation[106]; that is,
its complete privation (for privation has several senses).
Other contraries are derived from this type: some, because
they possess it; others, because they produce or can produce
it; and still others, because they are acquisitions or losses of
this or of other contraries. So, opposition may take the form
of contradiction or of privation or of contrariety or of
relation. The first of these is contradiction[49], and contra- 1055b
diction admits of no intermediate[138a], whereas contraries
do; it is clear that contradictories and contraries are not the
same. But privation is a contradiction; for a thing suffers
privation either generally[44] or in a determinate[72d] way,
either when it is generally incapable of possession or when it
fails to have what it naturally has (here we are using "privation" in more than one way, according to the distinctions
we have made elsewhere *). Thus, privation is a contradiction or a determinate[72e] incapacity[11d] received[65h]
by some subject[12]. Though contradiction has no intermediate, privation sometimes does: for everything is equal or
not equal, but not everything is equal or unequal, or if it 10
is, it is only within the realm of what is receptive[12] of
equality. If, therefore, it is from contraries that things are
generated in material, and if their becoming proceeds either
from the form and the possession of the form or from the
privation of the form and the shape, it is clear that every
contrariety must be a privation. But perhaps not every
privation is a contrariety, for the reason that what has
suffered privation may have suffered it in more than one
way; and only the extremes from which changes proceed
are direct contraries.

* v.22.

This is evident also by way of induction. For of every pair of contraries, one is a privation. But not all cases are alike; for inequality is the privation of equality, and unlikeness, of 20 likeness, but vice is the privation of virtue. So cases differ in the way which has been described. Sometimes we mean that a thing has suffered privation completely; at other times we mean that it has suffered privation at some time or in some respect, for example, at some age or in some dominant aspect, or throughout. Hence, there is sometimes an intermediate, and there is a man who is neither good nor bad; at other times there is no intermediate, for a number must be either odd or even. And sometimes a determinate[72] thing is the subject[85], sometimes not. However, it is evident that one of the two contraries always denotes a privation; and it suffices if this is true of the first or generic contraries, for example, the one and the many, since the others may be reduced[113a] to these.

5

30 If for each thing there is one direct contrary, one might raise the question how the one can be opposed to many and how the equal can be the opposite of both the greater and the less. For it is always in an antithesis[64b] that we ask "whether," for example, whether something is white or black, or whether it is white or not white; but we do not ask whether it is a man or white, except when we proceed on the assumption of an alternative and ask, for example, whether it is Cleon or Socrates that has come; but this is not a necessary antithesis between members of the same kind, though it is an extension of an antithesis. For it is only opposites that cannot belong[82f] to the same thing at the same time, and we employ this principle of opposition 1056a here in asking *which* of the two has come; for if both might have come, the question would be absurd. But even if they might, the question involves the antithesis between the one and the many, that is, whether it is both or one of them that has come.

Similarly, if the question "whether" is always concerned with opposites, and if it is asked whether something is greater or less or equal, where is the antithesis between the equal and the other two? Equal is not the contrary either of only one or of both; for why would it be contrary to the greater rather than to the less? It is to the unequal that the equal is contrary; hence, if contrary to the greater and the less, it would have more than one contrary. But if the unequal means the same as both the greater and the less, the equal would be opposed to both; thus, the difficulty would 10 favor those who assert that the unequal is a dyad, and it would follow that one affair is contrary to two, which is impossible. Thus, equal appears to be intermediate between greater and less, but contrariety appears not to be intermediate, nor can it, by definition, be so: for it would not be a complete contrary if it were intermediate between two terms; it is rather an extreme which implies an intermediate between it and its opposite. In that case it must be an opposite either as a negation[48] or as a privation[106]. It certainly cannot be the negation or privation of one of the two; for why would it be of the greater rather than of the less? Hence, it must be the privative negation of both. Hence, the "whether" here refers to both, not to one of the two, that is, whether greater or equal and whether equal or less; there are always the three alternatives. But the privation is not a 20 necessary one; for not everything which is not greater or less is equal, but only those things that are naturally equal or greater or less. The equal, therefore, is what is neither greater nor less, but what may naturally be either; and it is opposed to both as a privative negation and is therefore also intermediate between them.

So, also, what is neither good nor bad is opposed to both, but it has no name; for these terms have many meanings, and their subjects[12] have no unity. There is a unity in what is neither white nor black, though even this has no single name. However, the colors to which this privative negation applies are limited[72]; for they must be gray or

30 yellow or some other color. Consequently, those objectors are wrong who regard all expressions of this sort as contraries, so that what is neither a shoe nor a hand would be intermediate between a shoe and a hand, precisely as what is neither good nor bad is intermediate between good and bad—as if there must be an intermediate in all cases. But this does not necessarily follow. For what is neither good nor bad is a negation of[48a] both opposites at once, and they have an intermediate because they have a natural distance between them; but the other expression mentions two things un-
1056b related in this sense, since the two things both denied are of different kinds[19], so that there is no common subject[85].

6

One might raise similar questions about the one and the many. For if the many are opposed absolutely[105] to the one, a number of impossibilities follow. The one would then be little or few; for the many are also opposed to the few. And two would be many, since the double is multiple, and double is derived from two. And the one will be few; for relative to what would the two be many, except relative to the one, which would then also be few? For there is
10 nothing fewer. Again, as are the long and the short in length, so are the much and the little in plurality; and what is much is also many, and the many are much. The little is, accordingly, in a sense, a plurality, except where an easily bounded continuum makes a difference. Consequently, the one is in a sense a plurality if it is few; and this it must be, if two are many. But perhaps the many are in a sense also said to be much, but with a difference; for example, water is much, but not many.

However, "many" sometimes applies to what is divisible: in one way, if there is a plurality which has an excess either absolutely or relatively, and so "few" is said if there is a plurality which has a deficiency; in another way, as number, and it is in this way alone that the many are opposed to the
20 one. For it is in this way that we say "one or many"; just

as if one were to say "one and ones," or "white object and white objects," or were to compare objects which have been measured with the measure and the measurable. It is in this way that multiples must be interpreted. For each number is said to be many because it consists of ones and because each number is measurable by one; and it is many as opposed to the one, not to the few. It is in this way, then, that even the two is many; but it is that, not as a plurality which has an excess (either relatively or absolutely), but as the first plurality. But two is absolutely few; for it is the first plurality which has a deficiency. Hence, Anaxagoras was not right in dismissing these problems with the remark "All things were together, boundless both in plurality and in smallness"; instead of "and in smallness" he should 30 have said "and in fewness," for they could not have been boundless in fewness. And it is not because of the one, as some say, that there are few, but because of the two.

The one is, therefore, opposed to the many in number as measure to the measurable; and these are opposed as are those relatives[29] which are not of themselves[2] relatives. We have elsewhere * distinguished the two meanings of relatives: on the one hand, as contraries; on the other hand, as knowledge[179] to what is known. And that is relative to which something else is said to be relative.   1057a

However, there is nothing to prevent the one from being fewer than something, for example, than two; for, if it is fewer, it is not therefore also few. But plurality is, as it were, a kind[19] including number; for plurality is number measurable by one. And one and number are in a way opposed, not as contrary, but as some relatives have been said to be opposed; for they are opposed inasmuch as one is measure and the other measurable. Hence, not everything that is one is a number; that is, if it is indivisible.

On the other hand, although knowledge is similarly said to be relative to the knowable, these relatives are not related in a similar way. For knowledge might, indeed, be thought

* v.15.1021a26–30.

to be a measure; and the knowable, the measured. But it
10 happens that all knowledge is knowable; but not everything
knowable is knowledge, because knowledge is in a way[55c]
measured by the knowable.

Also, plurality is not contrary to the few, the many being
contrary to the few as excessive plurality to exceeded plurality; nor is plurality contrary to the one in every way. But
these are contrary in one way, as has been said, because the
former is divisible and the latter is indivisible; and in another
way they are relative, as knowledge is to the knowable, if
plurality is a number and the one is a measure.

7

Since there may be something intermediate between
contraries, and in some cases there is, the intermediates
must be composed of the contraries. For all intermedi-
20 ates[138a] are in the same genus as are the contraries between
which they are intermediate. For we call those things intermediate into which what changes[115] must change first:
if one were to pass from the highest string of a harp to the
lowest by the smallest intervals, one would first come to
the middle notes; and if in colors one were to go from white
to black, one would come to crimson and gray before coming
to black; and similarly in other cases. But there is no changing from one genus to another, except incidentally[3]; for
example, from color to figure. Accordingly, intermediates
must be in the same genus both with one another and with
the things between which they are intermediate.
30 All intermediates are between opposites; for such change
can take place only between opposites. Hence, it is impossible
for intermediates to be between nonopposite things; since
there would then be change which would not be from one
opposite to another. However, of opposites contradictories
cannot have intermediates, for that is what contradiction is:
an antithesis, one or the other part of which is present to
anything whatever; that is, an antithesis which has no
intermediate. Of the rest of the opposites, some are relative,

others privative, and still others contraries. Of relatives, those which are not contrary have no intermediate, for the reason that they are not in the same genus. For what would be intermediate between knowledge and the knowable? 1057b Between great and small, however, there is an intermediate.

If, therefore, intermediates are in the same genus, as has been shown, and are intermediate between contraries, then they must be composed of these contraries. For either there will be a kind including the contraries, or there will be none. If there is a kind such that it is prior to the contraries, then the differentiae which mark the species of a genus as contraries would be prior contraries; for species are composed of the genus and the differentiae. For example, if white and black are contraries, and the one is a differentiating color and the other a confusing color, then these differentiae, "differentiating" and "confusing," are prior, so that these 10 are contraries prior to each other. Yet the kinds which differ in a contrary way are, nevertheless, more especially contraries, and the others, which are intermediate, will be composed of their genus and their differentiae: all colors which are intermediate between white and black must be said to be composed of their genus (color) and of certain differentiae. But these differentiae will not be the primary contraries; otherwise, every color would be either white or black. These differentiae are, accordingly, different from the primary contraries; and they will, accordingly, be intermediate between the primary contraries. And the primary differentiae are "differentiating" and "confusing."

Consequently, it is with reference to those contraries which are not in the same genus that we must first ask of 20 what their intermediates are composed. For those which are in the same genus cannot have their genus among the constituents of which they are composed, or else they must themselves be incomposite. Contraries, then, are not composed of one another, and they are consequently first principles[82]; but either all intermediates are incomposite, or none of them are. Now, when something is generated out of the contraries there can be a change to it sooner than to the contraries themselves; for this product will have less of one quality than does the one contrary, and more than does the other. This differentia will accordingly also be an intermediate between contraries. All the other intermediates will accordingly also be composite[64g]; for whatever has more of a given quality than *A* has and less than *B* has is in a way compounded of *A* and *B*. And since there are no other things homogeneous with the intermediates and prior 30 to the contraries, all the intermediates must be compounded out of the contraries. Consequently, both the contraries and their intermediates will also be compounded out of the primary contraries to which they are all subordinate. It is clear, then, that intermediates are all in the same genus, that they are intermediate between contraries, and that they are all composed of the contraries.

8

To be of a different[16] species[20] implies difference within something, and this something must belong to both; for example, animals of different species are both animals. Things which vary in species must, accordingly, be in the same genus[19]. For I call a genus whatever unites things into being one and the same, though it has differentiae that 1058a are not accidental[3], whether it unites them as matter or in another way. For not only must the common trait belong to both, for example, that both are animals; but this animality itself must also be different for each, for example, that of a horse and that of a man. Therefore, what they have in common is differentiated into species, one animal as such[2] being one sort[5], and the other another sort—one a horse, and the other a man. This difference, accordingly, must be an otherness intrinsic in the genus, that is, a difference which marks the genus itself with variety.

This difference is, therefore, a contrariety as we can show 10 by induction. For all things are divided by opposites, and

it has been shown * that contraries, though they are completely different, are in the same genus. But every difference
as to species is a distinction within something, so that this
something is the same for both and is their genus. Hence,
all contraries differ as to species, not as to genus, and are
of the same category. They are in the highest degree different; their difference is complete, since they cannot occur
at the same time with one another. To be different in species
is, accordingly, a contrariety.

In short, things are different in species when they are in
the same genus, and are not further divisible[41], and are
contraries. On the other hand, things are the same as to
species when they are indivisible, but are not contraries.
For in the process of dividing[75], contrarieties arise even
in the intermediate stages before we come to the indivisibles. 20
Consequently, it is evident, with reference to what is called
a genus, that none of its species is the same as it is or differs
from it as one species to another. And this is correct, as is
evident if we put it negatively. The genus is the matter of
that of which it is said to be the genus—not in the sense in
which the children of Heracles belong in the same generation,
but as one in nature. What has been said is evident also with
reference to things not in the same genus, whose species will
differ as to genus, since things in the same genus will not
be of their species. To be different in species, things must
be contraries; and this is true only of things that are in the
same genus.

9

One might raise the question why woman does not differ
from man in species, when female and male are contrary 30
and their difference is a contrariety; and why a female and
a male animal do not belong to different species, since this
difference is a property[2] of animals, not an accident, such
as white and black. This question is almost the same as the

* x.4.

question why one contrariety divides[34] things into species, and another does not; for example, footed and winged but not white and black. Is it not because the former pair are modifications[35a] peculiar[55] to the genus, and the latter are less so? We should recall the distinction between a 1058b thing's definition[90] and its matter[84]. Contrarieties which are in the definition mark a difference as to species; but those which are in the individualized[65h] matter do not. Hence white or black does not divide men into species; white men are not a different species from black men, even if each class were denoted by a single word. For in this case men are being taken as matter, and the matter does not make the difference; since color does not make different kinds of men. The flesh and the bones of which this and that man consist are different, to be sure, and any concrete individual[21a] is, indeed, distinct, but not therefore of another species, because there is no contrariety in the definition; and whatever can 10 be defined without contrariety is ultimately[18a] indivisible[41]. But "Callias" implies definition together with matter and so does "the white man"; because it is Callias who is white, whereas "man" is white only incidentally[3]. Similarly, a ring of bronze and one of wood do not differ as to species; but between a triangle of bronze and a ring of wood there is a contrariety in the definition, not merely in matter.

But may not a difference in species be due to some kind of material difference? May there not be cases when difference in matter causes difference in species? In the case of "this horse" and "that man," though each is a union of definition and material, may not their being of different species be due to the material factor? But even in this case, is their contrariety not due to a difference in definition? For though a white man and a black horse are contraries, they are 20 so, not on account of color, but of species; since they would be of different species even if they had the same color. Similarly, male and female, though peculiar to animals, do not make an essential[26] difference, but only a difference of matter or body. Hence, the same seed may produce either male or female, depending on circumstances.

We have now shown what it means to be of different species and why some things differ in this way, others not.

10

Some contraries differ in form[20]; the perishable and the imperishable are contraries (since privation[106] is a specific[72e] incapacity[11d]), and hence the perishable and the imperishable necessarily differ in genus. We are here speaking of the names generally[43], and hence it might be held unnecessary for imperishable things to differ from 30 perishable things in form, just as this is not necessary for white and black things. For something general may be both at the same time, as "man" may be white and black; and an individual[40] may be both, though not at the same time; the same man may be now white and now black. Here white is contrary to black; and these are among the contraries that belong to certain things accidentally[3]. But there are contraries which are not accidental; among them, the perishable and the imperishable. For nothing is perishable 1059a accidentally. It is possible for the accidental not to belong to its possessor, whereas perishableness is one of the traits which necessarily belong to those things to which they belong; or else one and the same thing would be both perishable and imperishable, for then perishableness might not belong to it. Perishableness must, accordingly, be the primary being of anything perishable or must belong to it as inherent in its primary being. And the same account may be given of imperishableness; for both are traits which belong to their possessors by way of necessity. There is an antithesis, accordingly, in the traits by which and in primary accord with which one thing is perishable and another is imperishable; so that these are necessarily different in genus. 10

It is evident, therefore, that there cannot be forms of the

sort in which some believe; for then one man would be perishable and another imperishable. For such forms are said to be the same in form as an individual[4], not merely the same in name. But things which differ in genus are farther apart than things which differ in form.

XI. BOOK KAPPA

I

THAT wisdom[180] is a science[179] dealing with first principles[82] is clear from our introductory discussions,* in which we stated the difficulties[200a] raised by the statements of others concerning first principles; but still the 20 question remains † whether wisdom is to be taken as one science or more than one. If one, then the same science always deals with contraries[50], though first principles are not contraries. If not one, how can such[28] sciences be distinguished[64]? Take the principles of demonstration[63a]: does one theory[187] cover them all? If there is one such science, why *this* one rather than another? If more than one, how can such sciences be distinguished?

And does wisdom deal with all primary beings[26], or not? If not with all, it is hard to state with what sorts; but if in a single theory it embraces all, it is not clear how the same science can be a science of so many subject matters. Does it include accidents[3a] as well as primary beings? 30 Certainly, if there is a demonstrative theory of accidents, there is none of primary beings. But, if the two sciences are different, what is each, and which is wisdom? For, as a demonstrative science, the theory of accidents is wisdom; but as primary[17a] science, the theory of primary beings is wisdom.

The science we are seeking must not be supposed to cover all four of the basic factors of explanation[83] which we distinguished in the *Physics*.‡ For it does not deal with

* i.3–10.　　† iii.2, 3.　　‡ *Physics* ii.3.

the wherefor[96] or the good, which is relevant[82f] to the arts[188a] or to primary beings in movement; an end[100] is a first mover. But of the immovable there is no first mover.

This raises the general[44] difficulty, whether the science 1059b we are now seeking deals with sensible[165c] primary beings, or only with others. If with others, it would deal either with "ideas"[20] or with mathematical entities. It is by this time clear that there are no "ideas." But even if one were to posit them as being, there is still the difficulty why mathematical entities do not have the same kind of being[33] that other things have of which there are "ideas." I mean that men place mathematical entities between "ideas" and sensible things as a third kind of entity distinct from both "ideas" and from familiar objects. But there is no "third man" besides "man" and the individual[40] man, any more then there is a "third horse." Accordingly, if mathematics 10 has no "third" subject matter, what is it that concerns[197] the mathematician? Surely not familiar objects; for they are not the kind of thing which the mathematical sciences investigate. Similarly, the science we are now seeking does not deal with mathematical entities, for they have no independent[73] being. But neither does it deal with sensible primary beings; for they are perishable. In general, one might ask what sort of science should raise questions about the matter[84] of mathematical entities. Not natural[101a] science, because the whole enterprise of natural scientists concerns things which have within themselves their source of motion and rest; nor the analysis of demonstration and science, for it is just this question of how demonstration and 20 science are related that is its peculiar concern. It remains, therefore, that the philosophy we have set before ourselves must examine this last-named question.

One might also ask whether the science we are seeking is to be supposed to deal with those principles which by some are called elements[103]; for all men suppose these to be the inner principles[82h] in compounds[64g].

On the other hand, one might hold that the science we

are seeking is to treat rather of general[43] considerations; for every definition[90] and every science involve generalization beyond the lowest orders[18a], and hence might be supposed to treat of the primary kinds[19] of being. And these happen to be "being"[1] and "unity"[24]: it is these especially that may be supposed to contain all things[1a] and to be most like principles, for they are first by nature; 30 if they should perish, everything else would be destroyed with them, since everything is and is united. However, if being and unity are interpreted as genera, all the different species of being necessarily exhibit them, but no differentia[76a] belongs[93] to the whole of its genus; hence, it would seem that being and unity should not be interpreted as genera or principles. On the other hand, if we regard as a principle whatever is most simple, and if the least general beings are simpler than their genera, since they are undivided and genera are divided[75] into many and differing species, the species, rather than their genera, might seem to be principles. Inasmuch as species, however, are destroyed with their genera, the genera would seem to be like their principles; for whatever can involve the destruction of something else in its own destruction, is a principle. These 1060a and similar questions suggest the difficulties which confront us.

2

Must * we believe in being which is other than individual being[40], or does the science we are seeking deal only with individuals? They are infinite in number. Apart from individuals, there are genera and species; but the science we are now seeking deals with neither of these, for we have just stated † why this is impossible. Indeed, it is in general difficult to say whether or not one must suppose primary being to be separate from sensible primary beings, that is, those with which we are familiar. Should we suppose these beings to be what is[1a] and wisdom to be about them? We 10 seem to be investigating some other primary being, and this

* iii.4–6.   † xi.1.1059b24–38.

is the issue before us; I mean, to see if there is something that is itself[2] separate and does not belong to anything sensible.

Now, if there is some other primary being apart from sensible primary beings, from what sort of sensible things must such being be supposed to be separate? Why should one believe it to be apart from men or horses or other animals and not also apart from inanimate objects in general? Nevertheless, it would seem quite unreasonable to set up[149c] eternal primary beings equal in number to those which are sensible and perishable.

On the other hand, if the principle we are now seeking is 20 not separate from bodies, is it likely to be anything besides matter? But matter is not actual[9], but is potential[11]. A form[20], or shape[91], seems to be a more genuine[55b] principle; but it is perishable, so that, if it is a principle, there is no eternal primary being at all that is separate and self-existent[2]. However, this is absurd: for nearly all the investigations carried on by those most cultivated seem to be based on the belief in such a principle and primary being; for how would there be order[207a] unless there were something eternal, separate, and abiding? But if there is a primary being and principle of such a nature as we are now investigating, and this is one and the same for everything, whether eternal or perishable, there is the difficulty why on the basis 30 of the same principle some things are eternal, and others not; for by any single principle this would be absurd. But if there is one principle for the perishable and another for the eternal, we shall be in a similar difficulty; for if an eternal principle can, nevertheless, be the principle of the perishable, why, if the principle is eternal, are not the things it governs also eternal? But if perishables are governed by a principle which is itself perishable, something else must be its principle, and another, of that, and so there will be an infinite regress. If we take those principles which are held to be most evidently immovable, being and unity, then, in 1060b the first place, if either of these does not apply to a concrete "this-something"[4b] and to a primary being, in what way is it separate or self-existent? But inasmuch as it is an eternal and primary principle, our theory demands that it be of this sort. And if either of them does apply to a concrete "this-something" and a primary being, then all things[1a] are primary beings; for being[1] is predicated of all things, and unity of many. But it is false that all things are primary beings.

Besides, how can they be right who say that the first principle is unity and that this is a primary being and who generate number as the first product out of unity and matter and assert that number is primary being? How are two and each of the rest of the numbers that are composed of units 10 to be conceived[169a] as one? On this, they have nothing to say; nor is it easy to say anything. And if someone were to take as principles lines or their derivatives, primary surfaces, they are certainly not separate primary beings, but segments and divisions of surfaces and of bodies, respectively, as points are of lines, and they are, again, limits of the same entities; all of these belong inherently to other things, and none of them is separate. Or how conceive[65i] of the primary being of unity or of a point? For every primary being has a genesis, but a point has none, being a division.

There is also the difficulty that all scientific knowledge is 20 of what is general[43] and qualitative[5], whereas a primary being is not general, but is rather a separate this-something; so that if there is a knowledge of principles, how can these principles be primary beings? So the question is: Is there any being besides the concrete[21a], or not? I mean, besides matter and what accrues to it. If not, then all things that are in matter are perishable. If there is something else, it would be form or shape. Now, it is difficult to determine when forms are separate and when not; for it is clear that the form is sometimes not separable, as in the case of a house.

Finally, are principles the same in kind or in number? If in number, then all things will be the same.   30

3

Since * the philosopher's science is about being[1] as being[1], that is, about being in general[43], not some part of it, and since "being" has more than one meaning, it follows either that the term is used equivocally and without any common reference, in which case there is no single science of being (since there is no single kind of being uniting its varieties), or that "being" refers to something its meanings have in common, in which case all come under one science. Now "being," as we have analyzed it, is used like "medical" and "healthy"; for though each has several
1061a meanings, each has some common reference, as everything medical to medical science, and everything healthy to health, and so forth, in each case to a single object. For a discourse and a knife may both be "medical," the former being derived from medical science, and the latter being useful to it. Similarly, one thing may be called "healthy" because it is a sign of health, and another, because it is a means to it, and so forth. Everything that is[1], similarly, refers in one way or another to being, because it is an attribute or a state or a disposition or a movement, and so forth,
10 of being as being.

Moreover, as everything that is may eventually be referred[113a] to one and common being, so each of the contraries[50b] may be referred to the first differences and contraries of being, be these basic contrasts in being such as plurality and unity, or similarity and dissimilarity, or others; these matters we have considered[187] elsewhere. And it makes no difference whether what is[1] be referred to being or to unity. For even if they are not the same, but different, they are certainly convertible: what is one must also be; and what is must also be one. Since it is always one and the same science that considers contraries and in
20 each pair of contraries one is a privation (though in cases such as "just and unjust," where there is an intermedi-

* iv.1, 2.

ate[138] being[4], the privation may not always be evident), a definition[90] of a being must always indicate[64] the privation, not necessarily of the whole[21], but at least of a[100a] species[20]. Thus, if the just man is defined as "disposed to be obedient to the laws," the unjust man will not have the whole definition denied of him in every way, but may in some respect be deficient in obedience to laws; and the privation will belong to him in this respect. It is the same in other cases.

Mathematics, too, [shows how a science is one]; for it is always abstractions[118c] that the mathematician studies. The mathematician, in his thinking, eliminates all aspects of sense perception, such as weight and lightness, hardness 30 and its contrary, and also heat and cold and the other sensible contraries, and leaves only the quantitative and continuous, sometimes in one dimension, sometimes in two, sometimes in three, and the attributes of these entities as quantitative and continuous, and does not study them in any other respect; he investigates sometimes relative positions and their implications[82f], sometimes commensurabilities and incommensurabilities, and sometimes ratios. 1061b Nevertheless, we believe that one and the same science, geometry, covers all these matters. So it is, also, with regard to being. No science except philosophy studies the attributes[3a] of being as being and the contraries in being as being. For natural science studies things, not in so far as they are beings, but rather in so far as they are in movement. Dialectic and sophistic deal with attributes of being, but not with attributes as being or with being itself as being. Hence, it remains that the philosopher must study 10 these things as being. Hence, since all beings, though in different ways, have a single and common reference[39a] and all contraries may be referred[113a] to the first contraries and differences of being, and since all these matters can come under one science, the difficulty stated at the beginning † seems to have been solved; I mean how there

† xi.1.1059a20–23.

can be a single science of things which are many and different in kind[19].

4

Since * the mathematician in his own way uses the common principles of being, first philosophy must examine the principles of mathematics. For it is common to all
20 quantitative being that taking equals from equals leaves equal remainders; but mathematics begins its study by concentrating on some aspect of its proper subject matter[84], such as lines, angles, numbers, or some other quantity, and examines, not how they are, but what properties they have as continuous quantities in one or two or three dimensions. Now, philosophy investigates these things, not in part, in so far as each of them has certain attributes, but asks how such beings exhibit the properties of anything as a being.

Natural science proceeds much as mathematics does: for it, too, studies the attributes and principles of beings,
30 in so far as they are moved, and not in so far as they are. But the first science, we have said, deals with these subject matters[85] in so far as they represent being, and not in any other respect. Hence, both natural and mathematical science must be regarded as only parts of wisdom.

5

There ** is in things[1a] one principle[82] concerning which it is impossible to be mistaken—a principle, I mean, whose truth it is necessary always to. recognize; namely, the principle that the same thing cannot at one and the same
1062a time be and not be or have any other similar opposites[13]. Of such a principle there can be no demonstration in the strict[105] sense; though there may be relative to an individual[4a]. For it is not possible to draw this truth itself as a conclusion[62] from a more certain principle, as would be required in a strict demonstration. But if anyone undertakes to prove to another who asserts opposites why he is mistaken,

* iv.3, 4.   ** *Ibid.*

he must take something which will be identical with this
principle (that the same thing cannot at one and the same
time be and not be), but which will not seem to be identical
with this principle; for thus only may the demonstration be
made to one who declares it possible for opposite statements 10
to be true of the same thing.

Those, therefore, who are to communicate[92] with one
another by way of argument[90] must have some common
understanding; for if this does not happen, how will it be
possible for them to communicate with one another by way
of argument? Every word must therefore be intelligible[181d]
and indicate[59] something definite, not many things, but
only one; and if it has more than one signification[38], it
must be made plain in which of these the word is being used.
He, therefore, who says that "this is and is not" denies
what he affirms, with the consequence that he declares the
word to signify what it does not signify; but this is impossible. Consequently, if "this[4a] is"[23] signifies something, it is impossible to assert truly its contradictory.

Accordingly, if a word signifies something, and this is 20
truly asserted, this [connection] must be necessary; but
what necessarily is cannot ever not be; and so opposite
statements concerning the same thing cannot be true
together. Thus, if an affirmation is no truer than the corresponding denial, he who says "man" speaks no more truly
than he who says "not man." Hence, it would seem that he
who asserts that man is not a horse would not speak less
truly than he who asserts that man is not a man; consequently, he who asserts that this same man is a horse will
also speak truly, since opposite statements were supposedly
equally true. It follows, therefore, that the same individual
is a man and a horse, or some other animal. 30

Although there is, then, in the strict sense, no demonstration of this principle, there is demonstration, nevertheless, against one who believes such suppositions. Perhaps
if Heraclitus had been questioned in this way, he might
have been compelled to agree that opposite statements

concerning the same thing can never be true together; but, as it is, because he failed to understand what his assertion implied, he adopted this opinion. In general, however, if what was said by him is true, not even this itself would be 1062b true; I mean that the same thing may at one and the same time both be and not be. For, just as when the statements are separated the affirmation is no truer then the denial, in the same way, also, since the conjoined or complex statement is like a single affirmation, the whole taken as an affirmation will not be truer than its denial. Again, if it is impossible to affirm anything truly, then this will also itself be false; namely, to declare no true affirmation to belong to anything. But, if there is any true affirmation, it would 10 appear to refute what is said by those who in raising such objections, would altogether annihilate conversation.

6

The * saying of Protagoras is like the views described; for he said that man is the measure of all things[163], whereby he meant no more than that there really is what seems to any man to be. But if this is the case it follows that the same thing both is and is not, or is bad and good, and so with what is said in all other opposite statements; because what appears to each man is the measure, and things often appear to be beautiful to some and the contrary to others.

20 This difficulty may be resolved, however, if we examine the source[82] of this opinion[174]. For it seems to have arisen in some cases out of the doctrine of the writers on nature, and in other cases out of the circumstance that not all men recognize[181a] the same features in the same objects, but that something appears pleasant to some and the contrary to others. For that nothing arises from non-being[1b], but that everything arises from being[1], is virtually the universal opinion of those who deal with nature. But white cannot arise from what is already com-

* iv.5–8.

pletely[14] white and in no sense nonwhite; hence, becoming white would be whiteness arising from nonwhiteness. And so whiteness would come from nonbeing, according to them, unless nonwhiteness and whiteness were[82f] the same. But 30 it is not hard to solve this difficulty, for it has been stated in the *Physics* † how birth comes from nonbeing and how from being.

But it is foolish to occupy oneself equally with all the doctrines and fancies of those who dispute with one another; for it is clear that some of them must be in error. And this is evident from the facts of sense; for the same thing never appears sweet to some and the contrary to others unless in 1063a some the organ by means of which the flavors mentioned are sensed and discriminated has been corrupted and injured. This being so, some must be taken as the measure; the others must not. And so I say the same about good and bad, beautiful and ugly, and other qualities of the sort. For to maintain the view in question is no different from insisting that what appears to those who push a finger under their eye and make one object appear to be two must therefore be two, because it appears to be two, and yet it is also one, because the same object appears to be one to those who 10 do not so manipulate their eye.

In general, it is absurd to present the fact that familiar objects appear to change and never to remain in the same state as a criterion[164] of truth. For in the pursuit of truth one must start from whatever is always in the same state and does not undergo change. Such beings are the celestial bodies; for they do not appear to be now of one sort and then of another, but are always the same and share in no change.

Besides, if there is movement, there is also something that is moved, and everything is moved out of something and into something; and what is moved must accordingly be in that out of which it is moved and then not be in it, but move into the other and come to be in it, and contra- 20 dictories cannot, as these men say, be true together. And

† *Physics* i.7–9; *On Generation and Corruption* i.3.317b14–319b5.

supposing familiar objects are quantitatively in continuous flux and motion, even though this is not true, why could they not endure qualitatively? For contradictory predications about the same thing appear to have arisen largely from taking quantities of bodies as not enduring; because the same thing is taken both to be and not to be four cubits long. But essential being[26] is qualitative, and such being is determinate[72] by nature; whereas quantitative being is indeterminate[72c]. Why is it that when the physician prescribes some particular food men take it? And why is this bread rather than not bread? If it is either, it would make no difference whether men ate or not. But, as it is, men take the food prescribed, assuming that they know the truth about it, and they eat what they believe to be bread. Yet they should not if there were no definite constant nature in perceived objects, but all natures were always moved and in flux.

And if we always change[120] and never remain the same, what wonder is it if to us, as to the sick, things never appear the same? For, because the sick are not in the same condition as when they are in good health, things do not appear alike to them in sense perception; yet the perceived objects need not for this reason share in this change[115], though they produce different, not the same, sensations[165b] in the sick. So, also, in other cases in which change occurs. However, if we do not change, but remain the same, there will be something that abides.

As for those, then, who derive the difficulties mentioned from reasoning[90], the solution is not easy, unless there is something they are willing to posit and for which they no longer demand a reason[90]; it is thus that all reasoning and all demonstration come to be, since those who posit nothing destroy conversation and all reasoning. Consequently, there is no reasoning with such men; whereas, for those who are troubled by the difficulties handed down, it is easy to meet and resolve the considerations that produce their difficulties. This is clear from what has been said.

It is evident from these considerations, therefore, that contradictory statements cannot be true about the same thing at one time; neither can contrary statements, because every contrariety implies[39a] a privation. This is clear to those who reduce the definition of contraries to their principles. Similarly, no intermediate[138] between the contraries can then be predicated of one and the same thing. 20 For, if a given thing[85] is white, and we say that it is neither white nor black, we shall speak falsely, since it would follow that it is and is not white; for the second of the complex terms [not black] is true of it, but this [not white] is the contradictory of white.

Accordingly, it cannot be correct to agree either with Heraclitus or with Anaxagoras. If it were, it would follow that contraries may be predicated of the same thing; for, when Anaxagoras declares a part of everything to be in everything, he declares nothing to be sweet rather than bitter, and so with any other contraries, since everything belongs inherently to everything—not potentially only, but actually and separately. So, too, neither can all statements 30 be false, nor can all be true, because of many other difficulties that might be brought forward on this basis, and because if all were false it would not be true for anyone to assert even this, and if all were true, it would not be false to say that all are false.

7

Any * science investigates whatever principles[82] and explanations[83] pertain to its particular subject matter; for example, medicine, gymnastics, and the other sciences, 1064a whether applied[189] or mathematical. For each, having marked off some kind of being, deals with it as something factual[82f] and as being[1], but not with its being as such; hence there is a special science that does this and is thereby distinguished from the other sciences. Each of the sciences referred to determines what the particular kind of being
* vi.1.

is[87] which it is investigating, and then makes inferences as best it can concerning the other properties of its kind. Some state[65] what their subject matter is in terms of sense perception, and others in terms of assumptions[64h]; clearly, such procedures[113e] can yield no systematic knowledge[63a] of primary being[26] or of what being is[87].

10 Now, since there is a science of nature, it is clear that it must be different from both practical science and applied science [or art]. For as to applied science, the changes which it studies originate in some artist or maker[34], not in what is made. This maker may be an art[171] or some other power[11]. Similarly, as to practical science, the changes come, not from the deeds done, but from their doers[188a]. But natural science deals with the things which have the source of their changes within themselves. It is clear from these considerations, therefore, that natural science is necessarily neither practical nor applied, but theoretical; for it must come under some one of these three kinds. Now,

20 since each of the sciences must know[182] how to know[179] what[87] it knows and use this knowledge as a principle, we must not overlook how the natural scientist must know[72] and how he explains[90] the primary being of the nature which he investigates; whether it exists as "snub" does or as "concave." That is, whether like "snub" it must be defined with reference to some matter, or whether like concave, without reference to a matter: for, since to be "snub" means to be a kind of a nose, its definition must refer to "nose"; thus, to be "snub" means to be a concave nose. So, too, the definition of "flesh" or "eye" or any other organ cannot be given without referring to an organism.

Now, since there is a science of being as being and separate, we must inquire whether this science is a natural science or

30 different. Natural science deals with things that have their source of motion within them; and mathematical science, though it is theoretical, deals with immovable and inseparable entities. Concerning separate and immovable being, accordingly, there is a science different from both natural

and mathematical, provided there is[82f] such separable and immovable being[26]; and this we shall endeavor to show.† And if there is any such nature in beings[1a], we would here, if anywhere, find the divine[208], which is the first[17a] and most lordly[55b] principle[82]. It is clear, 1064b therefore, that there are three kinds of theoretical sciences: natural, mathematical, and divine[211]. The theoretical kind of science is best, and of these the best is the last mentioned, for it deals with the most honored[159a] things[1a], and each science is called better or worse according to its subject matter[179b].

One might also raise the question whether the science of being as being should be regarded as a general[43] science or not. For each of the mathematical sciences deals with a determinate class of beings; whereas general mathematics is common to them all. If, then, natural beings[26] are first things[1b], the natural sciences will also be first; but, if 10 there is a different nature and a separate and immovable being, the science of it must also be different from natural science and prior to it, and being prior, it must be general as well.

8

Since * "being"[1], when unspecified, may mean several ways of being, among which is what is called "accidental"[3] being, we must first inquire into what "is" in this way. It is clear that none of the traditional sciences concerns itself with the accidental; for architecture does not inquire into what will happen to those who are to use the house, that is, whether they will live sadly in it or not. Nor does weaving 20 or cobbling or cooking inquire into the like; but each of these sciences inquires only into what is peculiar[42] to it[2], that is, its proper end. Suppose a musician became a grammarian; being still a musician, and having become a grammarian, he will be both at the same time, though previously he was not both. Here is a case of something

† xii.6, 7.　　* vi.2–4.

becoming what it was not; therefore, some say, he must have become both a musician and grammarian at the same time. Such accidents none of the recognized sciences investigates, but sophistic exploits them; so that Plato did not express it badly when he said † that the sophist spends his time on
30 nonbeing.

However, that a science of the accidental[3a] is not even possible[12b] will be evident to those who try to see exactly what the accidental is. We say that everything is (1) always and of necessity (not the necessity of compulsion, but that of demonstrations), or (2) usually[125], or (3) neither usually nor always and of necessity, but by chance[126a]; for example, it may be cold in the dog-days, but this does not
1065a occur always and of necessity or even usually, though it may sometimes happen[3b]. The accidental, therefore, is what occurs, but not always and of necessity or usually. This states what the accidental is and makes clear why there is no science of anything of the sort; for every science is of what is always or usually, and this excludes the accidental.

It is clear also that of being[1] as accident[3] there are no grounds[83] or principles[82] as there are in the case of essential[2] being[1]; otherwise everything would be of necessity. For if A is when B is, and B is when C is, and C is
10 not by chance or necessity, then also A and B, which are explained by C, will be of necessity, and so on to the last item that needs explanation[83b] and was supposedly accidental. Hence, everything would be of necessity, and all chance would be altogether eliminated from the realm of events, together with all possibilities[12b] that a given event may or may not occur. Even if the supposed[64h] explanatory factor[83] were not a being[1], but another event[116], the same consequences would follow, and all events would occur of necessity. For suppose tomorrow's eclipse will follow if A occurs, and A will follow if B occurs, and B will follow if C occurs; if we allow only the finite[131a] time between now and tomorrow, we must in this way

† Plato *Sophist* 254A.

eventually arrive at what is now occurring[82f]. Hence, since this is a fact, everything after this will come about of neces- 20 sity; so that all events would occur of necessity.

When "being" means "being truly," rather than accidentally, it refers to relations established mentally[170], and such being is a kind of mental happening[35a]; hence, a science of principles, which is concerned with external and independent beings, can afford to ignore such "true being." As for accidental being, which, as explained, is not necessary, but indeterminate[72c], the circumstances which would explain it are chaotic and indefinite[130].

Things ‡ happen to some purpose or end[96], either by nature[101] or by design[170]. They happen by chance[126] when they come about by accident[3]. Thus, just as anything may be[1] either essentially[2] or accidentally[3], so explanatory events or factors[83] may also be of either kind. 30 An accidental or chance factor may intervene in events otherwise directed to an end in accordance with some plan[178]. Hence chance and thought[170] affect the same things; for planning takes thought. But the explanatory factors in events that occur by chance are indeterminate; and therefore chance is obscure to human calculation[176] and is an accidental factor—but this is, in the strict sense, an explanation of nothing. Moreover, it is good or bad luck when the result is good or evil; and prosperity or mis- 1065b fortune, when the results are on a grand scale.

Moreover, since nothing accidental is prior[17] to the essential, neither are accidental factors prior. Accordingly, if chance or spontaneity[127] is a fundamental factor of the universe[143a], mind[169] and nature[101] are factors prior to it.

9

Being,* whether primary or quantitative, and so forth, may be only actual[9], or [only] potential[11], or both actual and potential. There is no movement apart from things[188c];

‡ *Physics* ii.5, 6.   * *Physics* iii.1–3.

for when they change, they always change according to some category[25] of being[1]; and there is nothing which, because it is common to all, falls into no one category. But 10 the categories apply[82f] to anything in one of two ways: by form or by privation. This is true of any specific primary being[4a], and also of any quality (white or black), any quantity (complete or incomplete), any spatial change (up or down, light or heavy). Consequently, there are as many kinds[20] of movement[109] and change[115] as there are of being[1]. Since any kind[19] of being may also be either potential or completely realized[10], I call the kind of being which is functionally[9] potential "being in movement."

The truth of this can be shown as follows. When building materials are actually functioning as building materials there is something being built; and this is the process of building. Similarly, learning, healing, walking, leaping, 20 aging, ripening are movements whenever something is being completed or fulfilled, neither earlier nor later. The fulfilling, therefore, of the potential, is movement when there is actually something being realized, not as itself, but as movable. By "as," I mean this: bronze is potentially a statue; nevertheless, the complete being[10] of bronze as bronze is not exhausted in its being changed[109]. For to be[88a] bronze and to be a certain potentiality are not the same; since if they were strictly the same in definition the complete being of bronze would be a movement. But they are not the same. This is clear in the case of contraries; for to be capable of being healthy and to be capable of being diseased are not the same (if they were, being healthy and 30 being diseased would be the same). But it is the same subject[85] that may be either healthy or diseased, such as blood or some other bodily fluid. Since, therefore, to be bronze and to be a potentiality are not the same, as color and the visible are not the same, the complete realization of the potential as potential is movement. Clearly, this is movement; and it takes place whenever complete realization 1066a does, and not earlier or later. For any power may sometimes function and sometimes not, for example, building materials and building; their functioning as building materials is the process of building. For their functional or actual being[9] is either this process, or it is the house. But when the house is built, it is no longer buildable; hence, the buildable exists in building. Its actuality[9], accordingly, must be the process of building; and the process of building is a movement. And the same account applies to other movements.

The truth of this argument is clear also from what others say about movement and from the fact that it is not easy to define it in any other way. For one cannot include it in any other kind[19] of being. And this is clear from what those 10 say who call it "otherness" or "inequality" or "nonbeing." None of these, however, is necessarily moved; and things do not change toward these or from these more readily than from their opposites. The reason movement is referred to such kinds of beings it that it is held to be something indefinite; and the principles governing the privative type of contraries are indefinite, since no privation is a "this" or a "such" or fits into any of the other categories. And another reason why movement is held to be indefinite is that it cannot be classified as either a potentiality or an actuality of things[1a]; for movement does not apply necessarily to, let us say, a quantity, either in its potential or in its actual 20 state. Movement is supposed to be a sort of imperfect actuality, for the reason that the potentiality, whose actuality it is, is incomplete. And therefore it is hard to grasp what movement is; for it must be classified either under "privation" or under "power" or under "pure actuality," and none of these appears to be possible. Consequently, what has been said remains plausible: movement is the kind of actuality which has been described, which is hard to discern, but which is capable of being.

It is clear also that movement is in the movable; for its movement is its being perfected[10] by some agent[109c], and the functioning of an agent is identical with the actualization

of the potential. For movement must be the complete
realization of both; since a thing is movable because it can
30 function in this way, and a thing is an agent for the same
reason. An agent acts upon something movable so that the
operation of both is one, just as the intervals from one to
two and from two to one are the same, and the steep ascent
and descent are one, although their being is not identical.
Similarly, with the mover and the moved.

10

The infinite * is (1) what by its very nature[101c] cannot
be spanned, as a voice is naturally invisible, or (2) what
may be endlessly spanned, or (3) what can scarcely be
spanned, or (4) what can naturally be spanned, but is not
1066b actually spanned or has no limit. There is, besides, an infinity
by addition, and one by subtraction, or both.

Now, the infinite cannot be something that is separate and
independent. For if infinity[130] is neither a magnitude nor a
plurality, but is itself a primary being, not an accident of it,
then it will be indivisible[75a]; since the divisible is either a
magnitude or a plurality. But, if indivisible, it is not infinite;
except as the voice is invisible. But it is not usually so
regarded, nor are we analyzing it in this sense; we regard it
as incapable of being traversed. And how can the infinite
be by itself[2], unless number and magnitude, of which
infinity is an attribute[35a], are also by themselves? And if
the infinite is an accident[3], it cannot as infinite be an
10 element[103] of things[1a], any more than the invisible is an
element in conversation because voices are invisible. And it
is clear that the infinite is not an actuality, for then any
given part of it would be infinite; since "to be[88a] infinite"
and "infinite" would be the same if the infinite were itself a
primary being and not attributed to a primary subject[85].
Consequently, it is either indivisible or, if it has parts, it is
divisible into infinites. But the same thing cannot be many
infinites; for as a part of air is air, so a part of the infinite

* *Physics* iii.4, 5, 7.

would be infinite, if the infinite were a primary being or a principle. Accordingly, the infinite must be without parts and indivisible. But an infinite in its completeness cannot be indivisible; for it must be quantitative. Accordingly, subjects must be accidentally infinite. But, if so, then, as has been said, infinity cannot be itself a principle, though it may be 20 accidentally related to a principle such as the air or even numbers.

We seem to be inquiring into something general. That the infinite is not among sensible things is clear from the following considerations. If the definition of a body is "what is bounded by planes," there cannot be an infinite body, whether perceptible or intelligible[169b]; nor a separate and infinite number, since the number of what has number is numerable. What has been said may also be clarified concretely by the following considerations. The infinite can be neither composite nor simple. It cannot be a composite body, since the elements are quantitatively limited. For contrary elements must balance each other, hence neither can be infinite; since if one of the two contrary forces should 30 fall short of the other in power, the finite would be destroyed by the infinite. And it is impossible that each should be infinite: for a body is what has extension in every direction, and the infinite is boundlessly extended; so that, if the infinite is a body, it will be infinite in every direction. Nor can an infinite body be one and simple or, as some say, something apart from the elements out of which bodies are supposed to be generated, such as fire or some other such element, for there is no such body apart from the elements; everything can be resolved into that of which it consists, except in the case of the simple bodies, which certainly have 1067a no external elements. Aside from the question how any body can be infinite, the All, even if it is finite, cannot be or become any one of them, as Heraclitus maintains that all things sometimes become fire. The same argument applies here as to the One which the natural philosophers present as independent of the elements. For everything changes from one contrary to another; for example, from hot to cold.

Then, too, a sensible body, such as the earth, is somewhere; its whole and its parts have their same and proper places. Consequently, if the infinite body is homogeneous[57a], it must be immovable or else constantly moving. But this is impossible; for why would it rather rest than move, or go down than up, or move anywhere? For example, if there were a clod in it, where would this move or rest? For the proper place of this homogeneous body is infinite. Will a clod in it then occupy the whole place? And how? What, then, is its rest or movement? Will it rest everywhere? Then it will not move. Or will it move everywhere? Then it cannot stop. On the other hand, if the All has unlike parts, their proper places will also be unlike; first, the body of the All is not one except by contact, and, secondly, the parts will be either finite or infinite in kind. They cannot be finite, for then some will be infinite in quantity, such as fire or water, and others not, if the All is infinite; but such an infinite element would destroy those contrary to it. But if the parts are infinite and simple, their proper places are also infinite, and the elements will be infinite in number; and, if this is impossible, and the places are finite, the All must also be finite.

In general, there cannot be an infinite body and also a proper place for bodies if every sensible body has either weight or lightness. For it must move either toward the center or upward, and either the whole or a half of the infinite cannot do either; for how will you divide it? Or how will part of the infinite be down, and part up, or part extreme, and part central? Again, every sensible body is in a place, and the kinds of place are six; but these cannot be in an infinite body. In general, if there cannot be an infinite place, neither can there be an infinite body; for what is in a place is somewhere, and this means either up or down or one of the others, and each of these is a limit.

The infinite is not the same in the sense of being a single nature, in extension, in change, or in time. But what follows[18] in any of these three ways is called infinite with regard to the antecedents[17]: in change, it is the size of the distance covered by the motion or alteration or growth; and in time, it is the quantity of the change.

11

Changes * are of three types: (1) accidental[3] change[115], 1067b as when a musician turns from his music to take a walk; (2) internal[105] change due to a change in a part[22], which changes the whole, as when the whole body is restored by the healing of an eye; (3) essential[2] change, as when a being is moved which is essentially movable. There are the same kinds of agents or movers: accidental, partial, and essential. Any movement involves an immediate agent, a thing moved, a time of change, a starting-point, and a culmination. The forms, the modes, and the places into which things are carried by their movements are themselves 10 unmoved: knowledge and heat do not move; the movements which end in them are [knowing and] heating.

Nonaccidental changes are not to be found inherently in all things, but take place between contraries or their intermediates and between contradictories. We may convince ourselves of this by induction. Changes take place (1) between substantives[85], (2) between nonsubstantives, (3) from a nonsubstantive to a substantive, and (4) from a substantive to a nonsubstantive. By a "substantive" I mean what is referred to in a positive assertion. Since change from one nonsubstantive to another nonsubstantive is really 20 not a change, involving neither contraries nor contradictories and hence no opposition[64b], this leaves three types of change. A change from a nonsubstantive into a substantive (its positive contradictory) is generation. Such change, when absolute[105], is the generation of a whole new subject or substantive; when partial, it is a partial[4] generation. Change from a substantive to a nonsubstantive is destruction, an absolute change being absolute destruction and a partial change being partial destruction.

* *Physics* v.1.

243

Though "nonbeing"[1b] has several senses, there is no way in which a nonbeing can be in process[109a], whether it be the nonbeing involved in [false] predication[64g] or disjunction[75], or whether it be the nonbeing of potentiality[11], which is opposed to complete[105] being[1]. To be sure, nonwhite and nongood can undergo movement accidentally, in so far as a "nonwhite" may be a moving man; but in so far as it is not a positive substantive, or "this"[4a], it cannot
30 be moved. Hence, nonbeing cannot be moved; and, if this be so, generation cannot be movement, since it is from nonbeing that generation starts. For, even admitting that such generation is accidental, it remains true that any absolute generation must begin[82f] in nonbeing. Similarly, nonbeing cannot come to rest. These consequences are troublesome; and so is the fact that everything that is moved is in a place, but "nonbeing" is not in a place, for then it would be somewhere. Hence, destruction is also not movement; for the contrary of a movement is another movement or rest, and
1068a of destruction the contrary is generation.

We must conclude, therefore, that since processes are changes and changes are of the three types mentioned, those changes which are generations and destructions are not processes. A process moves from one thing to its contradictory; hence, only the change from one substantive to another is a process. And these substantives are either contraries or their intermediates, for even privation is to be put down as a contrary; and privations can be expressed[59] positively, such as "naked," "bald," "black."

12

If * the categories are divided into primary being, quality, place, activity or passivity, relation, quantity, there must
10 be three kinds of change[109]: in quality, in quantity, in place. There is no change with regard to primary being, because primary being has no contrary; nor is there change in relation, since it is possible that if one correlative
* *Physics* v.2, 3.

changes[115] what was true of the other is no longer true, although this other does not itself change, so that in such cases the change[109] is accidental. Nor is there change from agent to patient, or from mover to moved; because there is no movement of movement or generation of generation or, in general, change of change.

Now there could be movement of movement in two ways: first, as change of subject matter[85], in the sense in which, for example, a man is a changed being when he changes from fair to dark; similarly, a change might be said to become hot or cold or to change its place or to increase. But this is impossible; for a change is not literally[4] a subject. 20 Or, secondly, some other subject might change from a change into some other state of being[20]; for example, a man changes from becoming ill to recovering health. But this, too, is impossible, except accidentally. For every movement is change from something to something else; and so are generation and destruction, except that these are changes into opposites of one sort, whereas movements are changes into opposites of another sort. A thing that changes from health to illness would, then, change at the same time from this very change into another. Accordingly, it is clear that at the time it has become ill it will have changed to some other change (although it is, indeed, possible for it to remain at rest), and moreover to a change that is never fortuitous; and that further change will be from something to something else. Consequently, it would be the opposite change, that of 30 recovering health. But such change is accidental: there is a change from remembering to forgetting because that to which the process belongs undergoes change—at one time to knowledge, at another to ignorance.

Besides, if there is to be change of change and generation of generation, the process will go on to infinity. Thus, whatever a later stage is, the earlier must be also; that is, if generation itself was ever being generated, then what was 1068b becoming generation itself was also at one time being generated. Consequently, it was not yet the process of generation itself, but only the generation of some particular being[4], past or present. If this were true, there was a time when generation was being generated; consequently, it was not yet generated at that specific time when it was being generated. But since there is no first in the infinite the first will not be; consequently, there will not be a second either. Neither generation, then, nor movement would be possible, nor any change.

Whatever suffers a given change or state of rest also suffers the contrary change or state; so what is generated is destroyed. Consequently, what is being generated begins to perish when it has been in the process for some time; for it does not begin to perish either in the very first stage of being generated or later, since what is perishing must for a while
10 be. And there must remain some material constant underneath the generation and changes. What, then, can it be? What is it that is generated as movement or generation, as a body or a self is what undergoes alteration? And again, what is it into which they move? It must be the movement or generation of something[4a] from something to something. And how? For the movement of learning cannot be learning, and the movement of generation cannot be generation.

Since there is no movement, therefore, in primary being or relation or activity and passivity, it remains that movement is in quality and quantity and place; for each of these can have contrariety. By quality[28], I do not here mean what is in the primary being (for even the differentia is a quality), but a passive quality[35c] with regard to which something
20 is said to be acted upon[35] or to be incapable of being acted upon[35d].

The "immovable" is (1) what is wholly incapable of being moved, or (2) what is moved with difficulty after a long time or begins slowly, or (3) what can naturally be moved, but is not moved when and where and as it naturally would be. Only this last kind of immovable being I would call being at rest; for rest is contrary to movement, so that it must be a privation in what is capable of receiving[12] movement.

Things are "together in place" when they are in one primary place; and "apart," when they are in different places. Things "touch" when their extreme ends are together. That is "between" at which a thing undergoing change, if it undergoes continuous change according to its nature, arrives naturally before it arrives at the extreme into which it is changing. That is "contrary in place" which is most distant 30 in a straight line.

That is "in succession" which is after a beginning, as determined by position or form or in some other way, and has nothing of the same kind between it and what it succeeds; for example, lines if it is a line, units if it is a unit, or a house if it is a house. But there is nothing to prevent something of a different kind from being between. For what is in succession is in succession to something and comes after it; for one does not succeed two, nor does the first day of the 1069a month succeed the second.

That is "contiguous" which is in succession and touches. Also, since all change is between opposites, and these are either contraries or contradictories, and contradictories have no middle term, it is clear that what is "between" is between contraries. The "continuous" is something contiguous. I call things "continuous" when their limits touch and become one and the same and are contained in each other; so that it is clear that continuity belongs to things out of whose mutual contact a unity naturally arises.

It is clear also that of these concepts it is being "in succession" that comes first; for what is in succession does not necessarily touch, but what touches is in succession; and if 10 anything is continuous, it touches, but if it touches, it is not necessarily continuous. But there is no natural union[101f] in things in which there is no touching. Consequently, a point is not the same as a unit: for touching belongs to points, but not to units, which are only in succession; and there is something between points, but not necessarily between units.

XII. BOOK LAMBDA

I

THIS is the theory[187a] of primary being[26]; for what we are investigating are the principles[82] and explanatory factors[83] of primary beings. For though all [being] constitutes, in a sense, a totality[21], still there is a part which is 20 primary; and though all things are merely successive, primary being comes first even so, and afterward come quality and quantity. For these are not even beings in the strict sense, but are the qualities, movements, and so forth, of primary being. Even "not white" and "not straight" can be included here; at any rate, we say that even these "are," for example, "there is that which is not white." And none of the others is independent[73]. The ancients themselves bear witness to this in their practice; for they investigated the principles, elements, and explanatory factors of primary being. Some of our contemporaries, to be sure, prefer to regard universals[43] as primary beings, since genera are general; they seem to prefer such principles and primary beings because of the abstract[36] manner of their investigations. The earlier thinkers, however, believed in particular[40] primary beings, such as fire and earth, not in 30 what is common to both, that is, body.

Now, there are three kinds of primary being. One is sensible being. It includes, besides the eternal sensible bodies, the perishable bodies which all men acknowledge, such as plants and animals. But there is also eternal sensible being, whose elements we must grasp, whether they are one or many. And there is also immovable being. Certain men believe that this is capable of being independent; some divide it into two, whereas others identify "ideas"[20] and mathematical entities as being of one nature, and still others posit only the mathematical entities. The first two kinds of being belong to natural science (since they have 1069b movement), whereas the third belongs to another science, if there is no principle common to the third and the others.

2

Sensible primary being is changeable. Now, though change proceeds from opposites or from intermediates, it does not include all opposites, such as the opposition between white and voice (which is nonwhite); but from genuine contraries there must be something which changes into the contrary state; for the contraries themselves do not change. And since the contraries pass away into each other, there must be some third thing in addition to them which persists throughout the change; this thing is the material.

Changes are of four sorts: in a being itself[4], in quality, in quantity, and in place. A change involving the being of a 10 specific "this-something"[4a] is absolute generation or destruction; a change in quantity is increase and decrease; a change in quality is alteration; and a change in place is locomotion. These changes will all be from certain states into their contraries in some one of these several categories[40]. The material which changes must therefore be capable of receiving both states. Moreover, "being"[1] is either potential or actual; hence everything that changes. changes from what is potentially[11c] to what is actually[9b]; for example, from potentially white to actually white. Similarly also, in the case of increase and decrease.

Consequently, though things may come to be accidentally[3] out of nonbeing[1b], everything comes to be out of being[1]; that is, out of potential being, which is not actual. 20 And this is what was meant by the One of Anaxagoras (better than his "all things were together") and the "mixture" of Empedocles and of Anaximander and something like what Democritus says. For all things were together potentially, though they are not actually together. Hence, these men seem to have intended something like matter.

Though all things that change have matter, they have different matter. Things eternal and not generable, but subject to locomotion, have matter; though it is not the matter of generation and is only matter of locomotion.

One might also raise the question from what sort of "nonbeing" generation arises; for "nonbeing" has three meanings. Though generation arises from the nonbeing of potentiality, such nonbeing is, nevertheless, not potentially any thing whatsoever; for different things come from different things. Nor is it adequate to say that "all things were 30 together"; for things differ in their matter, and why on that view did an infinite number of things come to be, instead of but one? For "mind" is one; so that if matter also were one, whatever matter was potentially should have become actual.

The factors and principles of explanation thus appear to be three: two contraries, one being the definition or form, and the other being the privation, and the third, matter.

3

We note next that neither the material nor the form of a thing comes into being [when the thing comes into being]; and I mean this even of the matter and form closest[18a] to things. For everything that changes is something[4] that is 1070a changed by something into something. That by which it is changed is its first mover; what is changed is its material; and that into which it is changed is its form. Now there would be an infinite regress if when some brass becomes a sphere not only that brass sphere, but also brass and spheres then came into being; therefore this coming into being must stop somewhere.

We note next that all primary beings (both those generated naturally and otherwise) come into being out of something with the same name. Things come into being by

art or by nature, or else by fortune or by chance. When they
are generated by art, their source is in something else;
when by nature, their source is internal to them (thus,
it is man that generates man); and when they become by
fortune, they do so by privation of art; and when by chance,
by privation of a natural factor.

Primary beings are of three sorts: material, which only
seems to be something in particular[4b] (for when things are 10
merely contiguous and not in organic unity, they are materials or subject matters); secondly, there are natures or
particulars in which changes culminate when they reach
their positive state; and thirdly, there are individual beings[40], such as Socrates or Callias, which are composed of
these other two. In some cases the particular nature is not
something apart from the composite individual; for example, the particular form of a house is only in a given house,
unless one means the art of building a house. Nevertheless,
such forms of artefacts are neither generated nor destroyed
[with the objects in which they are embodied]: for a house
(apart from its material) either exists or does not exist;
whereas in quite a different way [that is, gradually, the
material becomes a house]; so also health or any other art
[though not itself generated or destroyed, is in individuals].
On the other hand, if there are beings whose natures or
forms are separable from individuals, they must be natural
beings. And so it was not badly that Plato said that there
are as many ideas[20] as there are natural beings, if, indeed,
there are ideas, and ideas only of such beings. Let us consider, for example, fire, flesh, and head. All these are materials 20
of beings; but a head, the last in order of these, is most
properly a material of a primary [natural being, namely, an
organism].

The factors[83] that produce change[109a] are things that
have come into being before; but the formal[90] factors in
explanation are simultaneous with their objects. For when
a man is healthy, there is also health at that time; and the
shape of a brass sphere is at the same time with a particular

brass sphere. But it is a question for special inquiry whether any shape endures after [the destruction of the individual whose shape it was]: for in some cases there is nothing to prevent this; for example, if the soul[154] is of this sort, it may not be the whole soul, but only reason[169], since such endurance seems impossible for the whole soul. It is evident, therefore, that for these reasons ideas need not have their own being. For man generates man; this particular man, that particular man. So it is also with the arts;

30 for it is the medical art [not the idea of health] that is the reason or form[90] of health.

4

In a sense, explanatory factors or principles differ in different cases; but in a sense, if one speaks on the whole and analogically, they are the same in all cases. For one may raise the question whether the principles and elements are different or the same for primary beings and for relations; and similarly in the case of each of the categories. But it would be absurd if they were the same in all cases, for then relations and primary being would have the same elements.

1070b What, then, could this common element be? Now, there is nothing outside the realm of primary being which could thus serve as an element for them all; but an element must be prior to the things of which it is an element. So, also, primary being is not an element of the relations; nor is any one of the relative categories an element of primary being. Anyway, how can all things have the same elements? For none of the elements can be the same as what is composed of elements; for example, *b* or *a* cannot be the same as *ba*. And therefore for intelligibles[169b], such as unity or being, there is no element; for these are found among the compounds as well. No universal element, accordingly, can be either a primary being or one of the relatives; but it must be the one or the other. Accordingly, there is no element

10 common to all things. Or, as we are accustomed to saying,

there are in one way such elements, but in another way, not: perhaps in all perceptible bodies there are the elements of form, the hot, and its privation, the cold, and there is material in them all, since it directly and of itself possesses potentially the forms of bodies; in any primary being there are these and the compounds derived from them as principles, and in any unity which arises out of the hot and the cold, such as flesh or bone, there are these elements, since the product must be different from the elements. These cases, then, all have the same elements and principles; though different kinds have also each its own elements. Hence, it is not in this way that all are said to have the same elements, but analogically; that is, one might say that there are three universal principles—form, privation, and matter. But each of these is different for each kind[19]: in the case 20 of color there would be form (white), privation (black), and material (surface); in the case of day and night, form would be light, privation would be darkness, and material would be air.

Then, since it is not only the inherent elements that are explanatory factors but in addition there is an external factor, the moving factor, it is clear that "principle" and "element" differ, though both are explanatory factors. Principles are divided into these two kinds [internal and external], and whatever produces movement or rest is a principle and a primary being. Analogically, therefore, there are always three elements and four explanatory factors or principles; but the elements are different in different cases, and the immediate source of motion is different in different cases. For example, the form, health, the privation, disease, the material, body, and the moving factor, medicine; or the shape of a house, its privation consisting of a certain amount of disorder, its material, bricks, and its moving factor, the art of building. Thus, principles can be classified. But since the moving factor is in the case of natural objects 30 a natural object (such as man, in the case of man), whereas in the products of intelligence[170] it is the form (or its contrary), there will be in one way three explanatory factors, and in another way, four. For the mover (medical art) is in a way also the form of health, and the building art is in a way the form of the house, and man generates man; again, there is, besides these, that which as first of all moves all things.

5

Now some things exist separately, others not; the former 1071a are primary beings[26]. Hence, what explains[83] these explains all things, since without primary beings there would be neither active[109] nor passive change[35a]. Perhaps all things may be explained in terms of their souls and their bodies, or of reason, desire, and body.

There is another way, analogically, in which all things have the same principles, namely, actuality[9] and capacity[11]; but not only are they themselves different, but they apply differently to different beings. For in some cases the same thing is at one time actual and at another time potential, such as wine or flesh or man. These two principles can also be related to the three explanatory factors distinguished above. For a form is actual if it can be separate, and so is anything composed of form and matter, and so, 10 also, is a privation, such as darkness or illness; but a material is potential, for it becomes either one of two contraries. But the actual and the potential differ in quite another way whenever either the material or the form is not the same, but different: what explains a man is (1) his elements (fire and earth), which are his material; (2) his peculiar form; also (3) something external to him, that is, his father; and (4) besides all these, the sun and its ecliptic, a factor which is not his material or form or privation or even of his species[57a], but which produces changes[109a] in him.

We should also observe that some explanations are stated[36a] in general terms[43], and others not. Thus, the

direct or proximate sources of a change are always a particular and actual "this"[4a] as well as something else that
is potential. There are, thus, no general explanatory factors; 20
for it is an individual[40] that is the direct source of another
individual. Though man generally is the source of men
generally, there is no general man, but only Peleus the
father of Achilles, and your father of you. So this *b* begins
this *ba*, although *b* in general is the beginning of any *ba*.

These observations[20] all concern primary beings. But the
explanatory factors and the elements of other kinds of being
are different, as has been said,* except analogically; for
example, those of things not in the same genus[19], such as
colors and sounds, or primary beings and quantities. And
even the explanatory factors of things in the same kind[20]
are different, not in kind, but because those of different
individuals are different: your matter and mover and form
differ from mine; but they are the same in so far as they have
a common[43] formula[90].

If we ask, therefore, what are the principles and the 30
elements of primary beings and of relations and qualities,
whether they are the same or different, it is clear that when
we distinguish their different meanings they are not the
same, but different in different cases. However, in the
following ways they are the same in all cases: they are the
same analogically in the sense that matter, form, privation,
and mover are common to all; also in the sense that the
same factors that explain primary beings may be regarded
as explaining all others, because without primary beings
there would be nothing; and finally, in the sense in which all
things are explained by that which is the first in perfect
actuality[10]. But from another point of view there are
always different first factors for different things: (1) each
thing has its own pair of contraries, which is neither generic
nor subject to diverse meanings; (2) each thing has its
own material.   1071b

* xii.4.1070b17.

We have now stated the nature and number of the principles of sensible things, and we have stated how they are the same and how different.

6

Since we have * distinguished three sorts of primary being[26], two natural and one changeless, we must show concerning this third sort that there necessarily is eternal changeless primary being. For primary beings are the first of all things[1a], and if all primary beings are perishable, everything is perishable.

However, it is impossible for the process of change[109] itself to have come into being or to cease to be; for it has always been. And so with time; for there could be no before or after, if time were not. Accordingly, change is as con-
10 tinuous as is time; for time is either the same as change or is in some way bound up[35a] with it. But there is no continuous change except locomotion, and no continuous locomotion except cyclical.

Now, if there is something merely capable of moving[109c] things or acting[189] upon them, but which does not actually do[9a] so, there still is no movement; for a capacity[11] does not imply its exercise. Hence, the need is not supplied if we posit[34] eternal primary beings such as the ideas[20], unless there is in them a principle[82] capable of effecting change[115]. And even then they are not adequate, nor is any other primary being such as the ideas; for if they are not exercising their power, there will still be no movement. And even though active, they are inadequate if their essential being[26] is potential, for then movement will not be eternal; since what is only potentially may as well fail to be.
20 There must, accordingly, be a principle such that its very nature[26] is to be in act[9].

And these primary beings must be without material. For they must be eternal, or else nothing is eternal. Accordingly, they must ever be actual.

* xii.1.1069a30.

However, there is a difficulty here; for it seems that everything that acts is capable of acting, but not everything capable of acting actually does so, so that capacity is prior. But if this is so, none of the things that are[1a] would need to be; for it would be possible for them to be capable of being without actually being.

And if it is as the theologians say, that everything was generated out of night, or as the writers on nature say, who declare that all things were mixed together, the same impossible consequence follows. For how will motion come about if there be no actual mover[83]? For building material will not move itself, but it needs the builder's art; nor does 30 menstrual blood generate life without semen, nor does the soil without seeds.

This is why some have posited an eternal action, for example, Leucippus and Plato;† for they declare that movement is eternal. But why[203a] and what this movement is they do not say, or how it is, or what explains[83] it. For movement certainly does not originate in chance[126a], but something must always be responsible[82f] for it; a movement is always being directed either naturally, or forcibly, or intelligently[169], or in some other way.

Then, too, what sort of movement is primary? For this makes an enormous difference. It is scarcely consistent for Plato,‡ at any rate, to say, as he sometimes does, that what 1072a moves itself is the source of all movement; for he agrees § that the soul is secondary[18] to the source of motion, since it originates with the heavens.

In short, to suppose potentiality prior to actuality, is in a way right, but in another way not right; and we have stated what these ways are. That actuality is prior, is maintained by Anaxagoras (for mind[169] is actual) and by Empedocles, with his love and strife, as well as by those who testify that movement is eternal, such as Leucippus. Accordingly there was not originally, for an unlimited time, chaos or night; but things have always been the same, either in successive

† Plato *Timaeus* 30A. ‡ Plato *Phaedrus* 245C; *Laws* 894E. § Plato *Timaeus* 34B

self-repeating periods or in some other way, since what they actually are is not evolved out of a prior potential state. If, 10 therefore, there is an eternal self-repeating sameness, something must remain always active in the same way. But if there is to be generation and destruction, there must be something which, though it is actual, acts in two different ways. This must, accordingly, be self-moving, on the one hand, but, on the other, it must move in accordance with something else, and therefore it is either in accord with another source of motion or with the first. But it must be in accord with the first; for otherwise this would in turn influence[83] both the second and the third. Better, therefore, the first; for this explains[83] the eternal sameness, whereas the second explains diversity. These are the facts of the movements. What need is there, then, to look for further principles?

7

Since this is a possible account, and if it were not so the 20 world would have proceeded out of night and "all things together" and nonbeing[1b], these questions may be taken as solved. It is clear, therefore, not in argument[90] only but also in fact[9c], that there is something which is always moved with unceasing and cyclical motion. Consequently, the first heaven[143a] must be eternal. There is therefore also something which moves it. And since a moved mover is intermediate[138], there is, therefore, also an unmoved mover, being eternal[135a], primary[26], and in act[9].

Now such a mover must impart movement as do the desirable[156] and intelligible[169b], which impel movement without themselves undergoing movement. But what is primary for desire and for intelligibility is the same; for what is desired[158] is what appears[173b] good[99], and the primary object of rational choice[177] is what is[1] good. Certainly, an end is desired because it seems good; it does not seem good because it is desired. So the starting-point 30 is the activity of knowing[169c]. Moreover, intelligence[169] is moved by the intelligible. Of the two series of opposites,* one series comprises the intrinsic[2] objects of thought; and first in this series comes primary being; and first among primary beings is what is simple and actual. (The simple is not the same as the one; for the one means a measure, and the simple means a thing as it is in itself.) The beautiful, too, and what is in itself desirable are in this same series; and the first is always the best or is analogous to it.   1072b

We can prove[75] how there may be a final good[96] even in the realm of the unchanged[109e]. The "wherefor" is both for something and of something; in the latter case it may be the good "of" something changeless, but it cannot be "for" something changeless; such a good "of" the change-less can move it as an object of love[159b] moves us, whereas other movers can move in so far as they undergo movement or are moved. Now, whatever is moved can be otherwise than as it is. Hence, if first locomotion is actual when it is in motion, it can be elsewhere than it is, even if it cannot be something else[26]. But, since there is something which moves without being moved, a being[1] purely actual[9b], this being can in no way be otherwise than as it is. For, though loco-motion is the primary kind of change, as circular motion is the primary kind of locomotion, it is induced by a first mover. The first mover, accordingly, is a necessary being[1]; 10 that is, it is well that it is necessary, and it is thus a first principle[82]. For necessity is attributed not only to what is necessary by compulsion because contrary to impulse but also to that without which there can be no good and to that which simply cannot be otherwise.

On such a principle, accordingly, the heavens and nature depend. It is a life [113i] such as ours is in its best moments. It is always at its best, though for us this is impossible. The first mover's action[9] is enjoyable[162], even as we, too, most enjoy being awake, conscious, and thinking, whence come the joys of hope and memory. Thus, knowing[169c], by its very nature[2], concerns what is inherently[2] best;

* i.5.986a22.

and knowing in the truest sense concerns what is best in
20 the truest sense. So intellect finds its fulfillment in being
aware[65d] of the intelligible; for it becomes itself intelligible by contact[137d] with the intelligible and in its exercise of knowledge, so that mind and the intelligible are the
same. For what is capable of receiving[12] intelligible or
essential being is mind. But mind is active in so far as it has
the intelligible as its possession. Hence, the possession of
knowledge rather than the capacity for knowledge is the
divine[208] aspect of mind, and it is the activity of intellectual vision that is most pleasant and best. If the divine,
then, is always in that good state in which we are at times,
this is wonderful[191]; and if it is in a still better state,
this is ground for still more wonder. Now, it is in this better
state that the divine has its being and its life. For the
activity[9] of mind[169] is also its life[152], and the divine
is that activity. The self-sufficient[2] activity of the divine
is life at its eternal best. We maintain, therefore, that the
divine is the eternal best living being, so that the divine
30 is life unending, continuous, and eternal.

Those, then, have a wrong opinion who suppose, as the
Pythagoreans and Speusippus do, that supreme beauty and
goodness are not in the beginning[82], because the beginnings
both of plants and animals are explanatory factors[83],
whereas beauty[99] and completeness[14] are in what
proceeds from those beginnings. For the seed comes from
other individuals which are prior and complete, and the
1073a first is not a seed, but a complete being; for example, we
must admit that a man is prior to his seed, not the man
generated from the seed, but he by whom[86] the seed
was generated.

It is evident, then, from what has been said, that there is a
primary being, eternal and unmovable and separate from
sensible things. It has also been shown that this primary
being cannot have magnitude, but is without parts and
indivisible. For the unmoved mover moves in unlimited
time, and nothing limited has unlimited power. Since every

magnitude is either unlimited or limited, the prime mover cannot have a limited magnitude for the reason given, and 10 he cannot have an unlimited magnitude, because there is no such thing as an unlimited magnitude. It has also been shown that the first mover cannot be moved[35d] and is unalterable; for all other movements are posterior to locomotion. It is clear, then, that these things are as they are.

8

We must not neglect the question whether we are to posit a unity or a plurality of such beings[26] and, if the latter, how many. We must say that the statements made by others about their number cannot even be clearly formulated. The theory[174] of ideas[89] includes no special inquiry into this problem: those who speak of ideas consider them to be numbers, and they speak of the numbers now as un- 20 limited[130], now as limited[72] by the number ten; but, as to[83] why there should be just so many numbers, nothing is said by way of proof[63a].

We, however, must discuss the question on the basis of the assumptions[85] and distinctions[72a] made. For the first principle or first being[1a] cannot be moved either in itself[2] or accidentally[3], but induces the first eternal and single movement. Now, since what is moved must be moved by something, the first mover must in itself be unmovable, and eternal movement must be induced by something eternal, and a unitary movement by something unitary, and since we observe, besides the world-movement as a whole which we say the first and unmoved being induces, other 30 eternal movements[121], those of the planets (the bodies moving in a circle being eternal and unresting, as we have shown in the physical treatises * concerned with these matters), each of these movements must also be induced by an unmovable and self-dependent[2] and eternal primary being. For the nature of the stellar bodies is eternal, being a primary being, and the mover is eternal and prior to the

* *Physics* viii.8, 9; *De caelo* i.2; ii.3-8.

moved, and what is prior to a primary being must be a primary being. It is evident, therefore, that there must be primary beings equal in number to such independent movements, eternal in nature, unmovable in themselves, and
1073b without magnitude, for the reason[83] previously stated.†

It is evident, then, that the movers are primary beings and that one of them is first and another is second according to the order[207a] of the stellar movements. But the inquiry into the number of these movements must depend upon that mathematical science which is most akin[55] to philosophy, upon astronomy; for this science examines[187a] the kind of primary being which is sensible, but eternal, whereas the others, such as arithmetic and geometry, do not deal with primary being. Hence, it must be evident even to those who have but a moderate grasp of the matter, that the move-
10 ments are more numerous than the bodies moved; for each of the bodies has more than one movement. But we can best give some notion of how many these movements happen to be if we now repeat what some of those mathematicians say who give us a definite number as a basis for our theory[170]; as for the rest, we must both investigate for ourselves and gather information from other investigators, and if there seems to be disparity between what those who concern[197] themselves with these matters believe and what we have said, we must treat both sides with due consideration[159c], but follow those who are more accurate.

Now, Eudoxus taught that the paths of the sun and of the moon each encompassed three spheres, the first of these being the sphere of the fixed stars, the second being along
20 the middle line of the zodiac, and the third being inclined across the breadth of the zodiac;‡ the path of the moon is

† xii.7.1073a5–11.

‡ The motion of the first sphere of each planet produces the daily rising and setting along with the stars. The second sphere for the sun is tilted to produce the yearly north and south swing along the center part of the zodiac. The second sphere for the moon, tilted like the sun, causes the similar monthly north and south swing of the moon. The third spheres provide for motion north and south of the center line of the zodiac (the zodiac is a belt 16° wide). There is really no need for the third sphere for the sun; but Eudoxus may have thought the sun would

inclined [to the center line of the zodiac] at a greater angle
than the path of the sun. And the path of the planets is in
each case within four spheres, the first and the second of
these also being the same as the first two just mentioned
(for the sphere of the fixed stars moves all the spheres, and
the sphere placed next inward from this and having its
path bisecting the zodiac is common to all),§ but the third
sphere of each planet having its poles in the circle bisecting
the zodiac, and the fourth sphere having its path inclined
to the equator of the third; the poles of the third sphere 30
being different for each of the other planets, but the poles
of Venus and Mercury being the same.

Callippus made the position of the spheres the same as did
Eudoxus and assigned the same number as did Eudoxus to
Jupiter and to Saturn; but he held that two more spheres are
to be added to the sun as well as to the moon, if one is to
account[46d] for the phenomena, and one more to each of the
other planets.

However, if all the spheres combined[64g] are to account
for the phenomena, there must be for each of the planets 1074a
other spheres, one less than those enumerated, moving
counter to these and bringing back to the same position the
outermost sphere of the star [or planet] located inwards
from the respective [or further] star [or planet]; for thus alone
can all the movements combine to produce the complex
movement of the planets.‖ Summing up, the spheres required by the movements of the planets themselves are: for
Saturn and Jupiter, eight; for the others, twenty-five; and
of these only those need to have countermoving spheres

---

have a slight motion north and south of this line, or he may have given the sun
three spheres because the moon has three.

§ It would seem that it is the axis of the second sphere of each planet that is common to all, since each planet has its own set of spheres; likewise, the axis of the
first sphere of each planet would seem to be common.

‖ The outer sphere of the planet appears to be regarded as disturbed by the spheres
of the planet next beyond. Aristotle's spheres moving in opposite directions may
have been used to transfer the motion of the fixed stars down along the line, or
they were to counteract disturbing forces among the spheres.

which are required by the movement of the innermost
planet, that is, the spheres moving counter to those of the
next two must be six, and the spheres moving counter to
10 those of the next four must be sixteen; so that the total
number of moving and countermoving spheres is fifty-five.¶
But if one does not add to the sun and to the moon the movements we have suggested, all the spheres will number only
forty-seven.

Let this be the number of the spheres. We may, then,
reasonably assume that there are as many unmoved beings
and principles as our theory of sensible objects suggests;
whether this conclusion be necessary we leave to those
better equipped to decide. But if there can be no locomotion
which is not related to some stellar movement and if there is a
finality[100] in every nature and every primary being which
20 undergoes no change but has itself achieved its best state,
there can be no other ultimate beings or processes in addition
to these; hence, we have determined the number of those
beings. For if there were others, they would induce movement in the sense of being the final state of locomotions.
But there cannot be other locomotions besides those mentioned; for this is a reasonable inference from the analysis
of bodies in motion. For if every mover exists naturally for
the sake of what it moves and every movement inheres in
what is moved, there can be no movement in and of itself or
of another movement, which is not ultimately in and of the
stars. For, if there is to be a movement of a movement, the
latter must in turn be of another; so that, since there cannot
30 be an infinite regress, the end of every movement must be
one of the divine bodies moving in the sky.

Now, it is evident that there is but one sky. For even if
there were many heavens, as there are many men, the
principle governing each would be uniform, though numerically many. But all things that are numerically many have a
material; for the definition of such beings, for example, of
man, is one and the same for all, whereas the material

¶ Mercury, the innermost planet, having no countermoving spheres.

Socrates is unique. But being's first essential character[88] contains no material, since it is complete actuality[10]. Accordingly, the unmoved first mover is one both in definition and in number; accordingly, what is first moved is always and continuously one, and there is, accordingly, but one sky.

However, our ancestors in the remotest ages have handed 1074b down to their posterity traditions in mythical form that these celestial bodies are gods and that the divine encompasses the whole of nature. And the other traditions have been added in mythical form for the persuasion of the multitude and for their legal and social uses; for they say that these gods are in the form of men or are like some of the other animals, and they give further details such as those mentioned. But if we take only the first essential point, separately from the rest, that the first primary beings are traditionally held to be gods, we may acknowledge that this has been divinely said and that, though arts and philoso- 10 phies may have been often explored and perfected, but lost, these myths and others have been preserved to the present day like ancient relics. It is only in this way that we can explain and accept the opinions of our ancestors and forerunners.

9

The inquiry into mind[169] is fraught with certain difficulties; for although the mind is held to be the most divine of anything within our ken[173b], the question of how it is so contains certain riddles. For if this mind knows nothing, what dignity does it have? It is like one asleep. And if it knows, but something else controls[55b] its thought, it would not be the best being, since its fundamental being[26] 20 would then not be the actual knowing, but a mere power; for it is because of its knowing that it is honored. But whether it is essentially a knower[169] or a knowing[169c], in either case what does it know? Either itself or something else. If something else, either always the same thing or different things. Does it make any difference, then, or not, whether it know the noble[99] or any chance thing? And are there not even some things which it would be absurd that it should know? Clearly, it knows what is most divine and most honorable; and it does not change, for any change would be for the worse and would imply some kind of process. First, therefore, if it is not an actual intelligence, but an ability to be intelligent, it would be reasonable to suppose that its continuous thinking would be laborious. Secondly, it 30 is clear that something else would be more honorable than the mind; namely, its object. For knowing and knowledge are found even among those who know the worst. If this is to be avoided (since there are things which it is better not to see than to see), the act of knowing would not itself be the best of things. Accordingly, a divine mind knows itself, since it is the supreme excellence; and its intelligence is the intelligence of intellect.

However, knowledge and perception and opinion and reason appear to be always of something else and only incidentally of themselves. And if knowing and being known are different, in which of these ways is knowledge a kind of well-being? Though knowing and being known are not the 1075a same thing, may there not be some cases in which a knowing[179] aims at itself[188c]? Even the productive sciences aim at knowing a thing's primary being[26] and essential character[88], aside from its material[84]; and the theoretical sciences aim at the explanation[90] or understanding[169c] of an object. Hence, wherever things are immaterial the mind and its object are not different, so that they are the same; and knowing is united with what is known.

But there remains the question whether what is known is composite; for then the thought might shift[115] from one part of the whole to another. Is not everything indivisible[75a] which is immaterial? Hence, even as the human mind, or rather that of composite beings, is at times aware of its supreme and enduring good, not the good of this

or that moment, but something quite different, so throughout
eternity is that mind which knows itself. 10

10

We must also inquire in which way the nature of the
whole enjoys its good or highest good: whether as something
separate and by itself, or as its own order, or in both ways,
as does an army. For an army's good lies both in its order
and in its commander, more especially the latter; for he is
not the result of the order, but it results from him. All things
are somehow ordered together, but not all in the same way:
fishes, birds, and plants are different orders. The world is
not such that a thing is unrelated to another, but it is always
a definite something[4]. For all things are ordered together
around a common center[24a], as in a household, where the
free men are the least free to do as they please, but all or 20
most of their activities are determined by the household;
whereas the slaves and the animals do only a little in view
of the common good, but for the most part act as separate
beings. This is the sort of principle that governs the nature
of anything. I mean that all things must at least be resolved
at last into their elements; and so there are other ways in
which all participate and contribute to a whole.

We must, however, not overlook the impossible or absurd
consequences of the different accounts given by others,
even the most refined accounts which pose the fewest
difficulties. For all these thinkers present all things as composed of contraries[50]. But neither "all things" nor "composed of contraries" is right. For these men fail to tell us
how all things which have contraries can be inherently 30
composed of contraries, since the contraries do not act
upon[35d] each other. With us, however, this difficulty has a
reasonable solution; for we say that there is a third something, the material, which they present as one of the two
contraries, as those do who present the unequal as the
opposite of the equal, or the one, of the many. But this

difficulty, too, we solve in the same way; for their common material is contrary to nothing. For them, all things, with the exception of the one, would partake of evil; for the bad itself is one of the two elements. The others * do not even present good and bad as principles[82]; whereas in all things it is especially the good that is a principle. The former say rightly that it is a principle; but how the good is a principle

1075b they do not say, whether as end or mover † or form.

Another absurd account is that of Empedocles; for he presents love as the good. But love is a principle both as mover, since it attracts[113h], and as material, since it is a part of the mixture. Now even if the same thing happens to be[88a] a principle both in the material sense and as a mover, at any rate the being of the two is not the same. In which of the two respects, then, is love a principle? And it is absurd also to suppose that strife should be imperishable; but for him the nature of evil is strife itself.

Anaxagoras presents the good as a principle in the sense of a mover; for mind moves things. But it moves them for the sake of something, which must therefore be something other than mind; unless it is conceived in our way, for we

10 would say that, for example, the medical art is in a way health. It is absurd, too, that he does not present a contrary to the good, that is, to mind. But all those who speak of contraries fail to make use of the contraries unless someone were to bring their statements together into an intelligible harmony. And no one says why some things are perishable and others imperishable, for they speak as if all things[1a] came from the same principles. Some say that things[1a] are derived from nonbeing[1b]; whereas others, in order to avoid the necessity of this, say that all things are one.

And no one explains why there should always be a coming into being and what kind of factor would account for a coming into being. And those who posit two principles must have another, a more controlling principle; and so must those who posit the ideas[20], because there is another

* xii.7.1072b31.   † Cf. 1075b8.

principle, more controlling, for why do things participate or come to participate in the ideas? And others need a 20 principle contrary to wisdom[180], that is, to the highest knowledge; whereas we do not, since for us nothing is contrary to what is primary. For all contraries involve[33] a material, and whatever is material is potentially; ignorance[190] may be a contrary and lead to contraries, but what is primary has no contrary.

And if there is to be nothing besides the sensible, there will be no principle or order or coming into being or celestial system; but every principle will be the principle of a principle, as in the accounts of the theologians and of all the writers on nature. But if there are to be ideas[20] or numbers, they explain[83] nothing; or if not nothing, at least not movement. And how can magnitude or a continuum consist of nonextended parts? For numbers will not, either as movers or as forms, produce a continuum. Nor can any 30 contrary as such serve as a productive or moving principle; for it would be possible for it not to be. In any case, its activity[34] would be posterior to its power. Accordingly, there could be nothing eternal. But there is; hence something in these theories must be rejected[118]. How this is to be done we have shown.‡

And no one has thrown light on what it is to which numbers, or soul and body, or, in general, form[20] and thing[188c] owe their unity. Nor is it possible to explain this unless one says as we do that this is due to the mover. And those who say that mathematical number is first and that hence there must always be one thing after another and different principles for each, present the being[26] of the 1076a universe[150] as a series of episodes, in which none, by being or not being, contributes anything to another. Thus, their first principles are many, but actually things[1a] do not wish to be misgoverned. "Multiple sovereignty is not good. Let there be one sovereign!"

‡ xii.6.1071b20.

XIII. BOOK MU

I

We have now stated what sensible primary being[26] is; having discussed its material[84] aspect in our treatise on natural sciences * and then † its actual being in operation[9]. Since we must still inquire into the problem whether or not there is besides sensible primary being immovable and eternal primary being and if there is, what it is, we must first make a critical study[187] of what is said on this subject by others; in order that if they make any statement that is wrong, we may not be entangled in the same mistakes, and if there is any opinion common to them and us, we may not on that account be especially dissatisfied with ourselves, for it is a satisfaction to state something better than others have done or at least no worse.

Two doctrines are held on these matters: some believe that it is mathematical entities, that is, numbers, lines, and so forth, that are the primary beings; some believe it is ideas[89]. Some regard ideas and mathematical numbers as two different kinds[19]; others regard both as having the same nature; and still others believe that the mathematical are the only primary beings. Therefore, we must inquire first into mathematical entities, not attributing[64f] any other nature to them and not asking whether or not they happen to be ideas, or whether or not they are primary beings and principles of things[1a], but only whether as mathematical entities they are or are not and, if they are, how they are. After this we must inquire, secondly and

* *Physics* i. † *Metaphysics* vii–ix.

separately, into ideas by themselves, taken generally[105] and in their usual meaning. But these issues have been much debated in the nonacademic discussions. We must here devote most of our attention to what concerns the present 30 inquiry: namely, whether primary beings and the principles of things are numbers and ideas; for this remains, after the critique of ideas, as a third inquiry.

If there are mathematical entities, they must either be in sensible objects, as some say, or be separate from sensible objects (and this also is said by some); but if they are not in either of these ways, they either are not at all, or are in still some other way. Hence, we shall be concerned less with whether they are than with how they are.

2

In our account of difficulties we pointed out that it is impossible for mathematical entities to reside in sensible things and that this doctrine is a fanciful one: first, because two solids cannot be in the same place; and secondly, be- 1076b cause the other powers and natures would by the same argument also reside in sensible things, and hence none of them would be separate. These arguments we have already presented.* But it is evident, besides, that in this case it would be impossible to divide[75] things. For a thing would have to be divided at a plane, and this at a line, and the line, in turn, at a point; but if the point cannot be divided neither can the line, nor the plane, nor the solid. What difference does it make, then, whether sensible things are themselves indivisible entities or are indivisible because 10 they have such beings resident in them? In either case the difficulty is the same: if the sensible things are divided, the mathematical objects, too, must be divided; otherwise the sensible things cannot be divided.

On the other hand, it is impossible for such natures to be in isolation[73]. For if besides sensible things there are other beings separate from them and prior to them, it follows

* iii.2.998a7–19.

from the same argument that in addition to the sensible surfaces there must be separate mathematical planes, points, and lines. Then, if these must be, there must also be, separate from the planes and the lines and the points of the mathematical solid, another set prior to both. For simples are prior to compounds; and if there are bodies prior to sensible 20 bodies, and beyond the reach of sense, then by the same argument there must also be planes prior to those of the mathematical compound, existing separately from it[2]. Hence, these planes and lines must also be separate from the sensible solids, whose planes and lines belong with the mathematical solids; for this third set has priority to the mathematical solids. These planes will in turn have separate lines, and, by the same argument, there must be points prior to these lines; and, prior to these points in the prior lines there will have to be other points, though there need not be any others prior to them.

Now, this heaping up of beings becomes absurd: we need 30 one set of solids apart from the sensible; three sets of planes apart from the sensible—those apart from the sensible, those in the mathematical solids, and those apart from those in the mathematical solids; four sets of lines; and five sets of points. Which of these are the objects of mathematical sciences? Surely not the planes and lines and points in the mathematical solid, for science always seeks the ultimates. The same analysis applies to numbers: for apart from each set of points there will be other units[24c], as there will also be other units apart from each set of sensible beings, and then, also, of the intelligible; so that the kinds of mathematical entities will be unlimited.

1077a Does this help us solve the questions propounded in our list of difficulties? † For the objects with which astronomy deals will be separate from the sensible bodies, and the same holds for the objects of geometry; but how is it possible for the heavenly sphere and its parts, or for anything else that has movement, to be in this way? And so with the

† iii.2.997b12–34.

objects of optics and of harmonics; for there will be both voice and sight apart from those which are sensible and particular[40]. Hence, it follows that the other sciences, too, and their objects will be more and more remote from the concrete; for why should one set of them be separate and not another? Then too, since the senses are involved, there must also be corresponding sets of animals.

There are some mathematical theorems which are general[43] and extend beyond these primary beings. Here, 10 then, there will be another intermediate[138a] primary being which is separate both from the ideas[89] and the intermediates and which is neither number, point, spatial magnitude, nor time. But, if this is impossible, it is evidently impossible also for the other changeless beings which we have discussed to be separate from sensible things.

In general[44], consequences follow which are contrary to truth and to the usual views, if one supposes that mathematical entities are thus separate natures. Were they in this way, they would have to be prior to sensible magnitudes, but they must in truth be posterior; for though an incomplete spatial magnitude is prior in the order of genesis, it is posterior in complete being[26]. Thus, the inanimate is posterior as a complete being to the animate. 20

And how and when is it that mathematical magnitudes have unity? Our bodies have unity in terms of a self[154] or some aspect of the soul or something else equivalent; otherwise, they would be multiplex and disintegrate. But what reason[83] can be given for the stability and unity of the entities in question, which are divisible and quantitative?

These questions are further clarified by noting the ways in which these entities are generated. For the first dimension generated is length, the next is breadth, and the last is depth, with which the process is completed. If, then, the last in the order of genesis is first in complete being[26], the actual body will be prior to the plane and the line and will in this way also be a more complete[14] whole[21], because it is that which becomes animate; but how could a line or a

30 plane be animate? The supposition would be unimaginable. A body is a primary being, for it has a certain completeness; but how could lines be primary beings? Neither as a form or a shape (a sort of soul) nor as matter (body); for there is nothing tangible that can be put together out of lines, or planes, or points. But if these were complete material beings, they ought to be able to generate bodies.

1077b   Let the mathematical, then, be prior in concept[90]. But not everything logically prior is also prior in being[26]. For priority in being belongs to whatever when separated from others surpasses them in independent being; whereas things are logically prior when their definitions are needed to construct the definitions of others; and these two priorities are[82f] not coextensive. So attributes[35a] (such as mobile or white), which are not independent of primary beings, may be logically prior, as "white" may be logically prior to "a white man," but they are not prior in being, since they cannot be in isolation, but are always an aspect of the concrete[21a]; and by the concrete I mean, for example, a white man. Hence, it is evident that the abstract[118c] 10 "white" is not a prior being and that what is added to it, "a white man," is not posterior.

3

We have said enough to show that mathematical entities are not more primary beings than bodies; that they are only logically prior, not prior in being, to sensible things; and that they cannot be somewhere in isolation. But since they cannot be resident in sensible things, they must either not be at all, or they must be in some special way, which does not imply being independently[105]; for "to be" has many meanings. Now, just as general[43] statements in mathematics do not refer to anything that is apart from magnitudes and numbers, but to something that is *with* the magnitudes 20 and numbers (to something *about* them, though not essentially *in* them as magnitudes or numbers), so statements and demonstrations may clearly *be about* sensible magnitudes;

they are not *in* them as sensibles, though *in* them as qualitatively definite beings[5]. For just as there are many statements about things taken only as in motion, abstracted from what each thing is and apart from its accidents, and as this does not imply that there must be something mobile separate from sensible things or any definite mobile nature resident in them, so statements and sciences are applicable to mobile things, not as mobile but only as bodies, or planes, or lines, or as divided, or as undivided things having position, or 30 only as undivided.

Consequently, since it is strictly true not only that there are separable entities but also that there are nonseparables (for example, that there are movements), so it is also strictly true that there are mathematical entities and that they are such as mathematicians say they are. And just as it is also strictly true that other sciences are *about* so-and-so, such as health, so geometry, too, is *about* something. Such a subject matter cannot be merely accidental: the science of health is not *about* white things, even though healthy things may be white; and the science of man is not about health, though 1078a men may be healthy. So geometry, though its subject matters happen to be sensible, does not deal with them as sensible beings, and the mathematical sciences are therefore not sciences of sensible things; but neither are they therefore sciences of things that are separate from sensible things. So there are many traits that things have because they are what they are: a living being has the peculiar attributes of being female or male, yet there is no female or male being separate from living beings; thus, there are peculiar attributes that things have when taken only as lengths or as planes.

To the extent that a science deals with what is logically prior or simpler, to that extent it has greater accuracy, that 10 is, simplicity. Hence, it has greater accuracy if it abstracts from spatial magnitude than if it occupies itself with it; and it has the greatest accuracy if it abstracts from motion. But if it occupies itself with motion, it is most accurate if it occupies itself with a primary motion, for this is the simplest; and the simplest primary motion is uniform motion.

The same account may be given of harmonics and optics; for neither studies its respective subject matter as being sight or sound, but as lines and numbers, which are attributes proper to sights and sounds. And mechanics proceeds in the same way. Hence, if one takes attributes in abstraction from others and confines one's inquiry to what concerns them in such abstraction, one will not for this reason be in error any more than if one draws a line on the ground to 20 represent a foot of length, though it is not precisely of this length, for the error is not relevant to the premises.

A theory, therefore, makes progress best when, like arithmetic and geometry, it takes in abstraction what does not exist separately. A man as a man is one and undivided; so the arithmetician postulates an undivided unity and then inquires into whatever attributes belong to a man as an undivided being. So the geometer studies him, not as man or as undivided, but as a volume. For it is clear that the attributes of a man when he is not undivided, can still be his even when undivided. Hence, geometers speak correctly: 30 they talk about beings[1a], and these beings really are; for being is twofold, completely actual[10] and material.

Moreover, those who assert that the mathematical sciences have nothing to say about the beautiful[99] or the good[98] are mistaken. (The good and the beautiful are not the same, since the good is always practical, whereas the beautiful may be motionless.) For these sciences have much to say and to prove about them; merely because they do not expressly mention them, and only exhibit their workings[9c] and connections[90], it does not follow that they have nothing to say about them. The chief forms[20] of the 1078b beautiful are order, symmetry, and definiteness, which the mathematical sciences especially investigate. And since order and definiteness serve to explain[83] many facts, it is clear that these sciences inevitably deal with the beautiful as an essential factor in their explanations. But we shall

speak more informatively[181d] about these matters elsewhere.

4

We have discussed mathematical entities sufficiently,
having stated that they are[1a], how they are, how they are
prior, and how not prior. We come now to the discussion of
ideas[89]. First we must inquire into the doctrine[175] of
ideas itself, not connecting it in any way with the nature of
numbers, but considering it in the sense in which it was
taken in the beginning by those who first expounded the
being of ideas. The doctrine of ideas[20] appealed to those
who maintained it because they were convinced of the truth
of the Heraclitean teachings that all sensible things[165c]
are always in flux; so that, if there is to be knowledge[179]
and intelligence[172] about anything, there must be other
and permanent natures remaining over and above the
sensible, since there is no knowledge of anything in flux.

It was Socrates, however, who first seriously investigated[197] how the moral virtues with which he was concerned might be given general[43] definition[72]. Of the
writers on nature, Democritus, in his groping, got as far as to
define the hot and the cold; meanwhile the Pythagoreans
had dealt with such problems as What is[87] opportunity?
What is justice? What is marriage? And the definition[90]
of these ideas they connected with numbers. But Socrates is
rightly said to have examined the question What is[87]? For
he tried to think syllogistically, and the principle on which
syllogisms are based is the attempt to state what is. In his
day dialectic was as yet not sufficiently developed to enable
men, even apart from the question What is? to analyze contraries[50] and to include the knowledge of contraries in a
single science. But there are two contributions which one
justly credits to Socrates: inductive arguments and general
definitions, both of which are scientific principles.

Socrates, however, did not regard general terms or
definitions as having independence[73]; it was other

philosophers who separated them from things and gave them the name "ideas"[89]. And they concluded by practically the same reasoning that there is an idea for each general term; as if they thought it was easier to count many than few.* For their ideas are precisely equal in number to, 1079a or not fewer than, the objects which they are supposed to explain by referring each object to its idea. For corresponding to each thing there is something which has the same name and is independent of it, whether it be a primary being or a composite being, and whether sensible or eternal.

As for the various ways in which we prove the existence of ideas, none is clear: from some the conclusion does not necessarily follow; from others it would follow that there are ideas even of matters of which we believe there are none. For according to the arguments from the sciences there would be ideas of all matters of which there are sciences; according to the unity-out-of-multiplicity argument there 10 would be ideas even of negations; and according to the argument that we can think of something that has perished there would be ideas of things that have perished, since we have images of such things. Of the more accurate arguments, some imply ideas of correlatives, of which we admit that there are no separate classes; others assert a "third man" [between the perceptible and the ideal].

In general, the arguments for the ideas destroy the very principles on which those who believe in the ideas rely much more than they rely even on ideas. For it would follow that number would be prior to duality, that being relative would be prior to being independent, and all the other contradictories with their own principles on which those have stumbled who have followed the doctrine of the ideas.

On the assumption according to which we prove the being 20 of ideas there would be ideas not only of primary beings but also of many other things (for not only primary beings, but other things, too, are intelligible, and sciences deal not only

* The text of xiii.4.1078b34–1079b3 is identical with that of i.9.990b2–991a8.

with primary being but also with others); and a thousand other such difficulties arise. But by logical necessity as well as by doctrinal tradition, if there is participation in the ideas, then there can be ideas only of primary beings; for participation is not incidental, but is in an idea in so far as the idea is not an attribute ascribed to a subject. I mean, for example, that if something participates in the idea of "double," it also incidentally participates in the idea of the "eternal"; for "double" happens to be eternal.   30

Hence, there are ideas only of primary being; but the same terms designate primary being both temporal and eternal—or else what would it mean to declare that a thing's unity is apart from the multiplicity which it unifies? And if the ideas and the things participating in them have the same idea, it will be something they have in common; for why should "duality" be identical with the perishable twos or with those dualities which, though eternal, are many and not be identical with "duality itself" and with a particular two? But if they do not have the same idea in com- 1079b mon, then they have only the same name, and it would be analogous to calling both Callias and a wooden figure a "man" without observing any interrelation.

We must also ask whether it is not altogether futile to suppose[64] that there are still other ways in which common definitions correspond to ideas[20]: let us suppose, for example, that "the circle itself" includes not only "plane figure" and the other parts of the definition of a circle but also some being of which "circle itself" is the idea. Where can this being be added[64f] in the definition: to "center," to "plane," or to all parts together? Since everything contained in any essential being[26] has its idea[89] (as "animal" and "biped" must each have its idea in the essential idea of "man"), there is not only a "plane-itself" related to a "circle-itself" but there must also be an "idea[15a] of being[23] an idea"[4], which would serve[82h] as a sort of 10 genus for all ideas[20].

5

Then,* above all, one might raise the question what on earth the ideas contribute to the sensibles, either to the eternal or to those that come to be and cease to be. For the ideas do not explain any movement or change in perceptible objects. And as for imperceptibles, the ideas do not in any way help toward their knowledge (for they do not constitute the definition of their being, else they would have been in them), or toward their being, if they do not belong inherently to the things which participate in them—although if they did inhere in them, they might even be thought to be explanatory factors, like the white with which a white object
20 is painted. But this argument, which first Anaxagoras and later Eudoxus and some others used, is quite easily upset; for it is easy to being many impossibilities to bear upon a doctrine of this sort.

In addition, other things do not come "from" the ideas in any of the usual senses of "from." But to say that the ideas are patterns and that other things participate in them is to use empty words and poetical metaphors. For how does one go about "looking up" to the ideas? For anything may be and come to be like something else without being copied from it, so that, whether Socrates exists or not, a man like Socrates might come to be; and clearly this might
30 be so even if Socrates were eternal. Also, there will be more than one pattern of the same thing, therefore more than one idea: of man, for example, animal and biped and at the same time also man-himself. Again, the ideas will be patterns not only of perceptible objects but also of the ideas themselves: a genus would include its species, so that the same thing would be both pattern and copy.

Again, it would seem impossible for primary being and that whose primary being it is, to be dissociated. How could
1080a the ideas, if they are the primary being of concrete things, be in isolation? In the *Phaedo* † this doctrine is stated by

* The text of xiii.5.1079b12–1080a8 is identical with that of i.9.991a8–b9.
† Plato *Phaedo* 100D.

saying that the ideas are explanations for being and becoming. But though the ideas are, the things that participate in them do not come to be unless there is something to set things going; and many other things come to be, such as a house and a ring, of which we deny that there are ideas. Clearly, therefore, even the other things may be and come to be because of the same factors which govern the being and becoming of the things just mentioned; not because of the ideas[20].

Thus, it is possible to criticize the doctrine of ideas[89] and, by even more abstract arguments, to collect many 10 other objections like those considered.

6

Having now criticized the doctrine of ideas, we might well examine the consequences which follow for the theory of numbers[141] from the doctrine that numbers are themselves primary beings and that they explain[83] all things[1a].

Now, if a number is itself a nature, not a number of something, but just number, as some declare, then a necessary consequence is that each number must include what is before and what is after, for each number is different in kind[20]. Now, either this trait belongs to all integers[24c] directly, so that all the integers are essentially inadditive[58a], or else all the integers are inherently in series, so 20 that the integers are all additive[58], as is said to be the case with mathematical number, since no integer in mathematical number is wholly separate from another. Or else some integers are additive and others are not, for example, those in a dyad add together, those in a triad add together, and so forth; but the integers in two-itself cannot be added to those in the three-itself, and likewise in the case of the other successive numbers. Thus, mathematical numbers are 30 counted as follows: after one, two (which consists of another one besides the former one), then three (which consists of another one besides these two), and so forth, whereas numbers-themselves are counted thus: after one, a distinct[16] two, which does not include the first one, a three, which does not include the two, and so forth. Possibly some numbers fit the series first described, others the series which the mathematicians describe, and still others the kind of series we have just described.

It is further necessary that these numbers either be
1080b separate from objects[188c] or that they be not separate, being in sensible things[165c]; not in the way in which we first supposed,* but so that sensible things consist of numbers as their inherent constitutents[82h]. Only some of the numbers, not others, or all of them may be such constituents.

These, then, are necessarily the only ways in which it is possible for numbers to be. Now, almost every one of those who say that the one is the principle[82] or the primary being[26] or the element[103] of all things and that number is formed from the one plus something else has described number in one of these ways, except for the view that all
10 the units are unlike. And the reason is clear; for there can be no other way.

Some, then, say that there are both kinds of numbers: the kind which includes a before and after are ideas[89]; the mathematical kind is different from[74] ideas and from sensible things; and both are separate from sensible things. Others say that mathematical number only is the first among things[1a] and separate from sensible things. And the Pythagoreans limit number to one kind, the mathematical; they do not take it to be separate, but say that sensible beings are composed of it. For they build up[149c] the whole universe[143a] out of numbers, but not out of numbers consisting of abstract units, for they take[65i] units as
20 having spatial magnitude. How the first one was constituted as having spatial magnitude they seem unable to explain. There is another philosopher who believes in the being of only the first kind of number, the general forms[20]; whereas others believe that mathematical number is the same as form.

* xiii.2.1076a38–b11.

It is similar, also, with lines, planes, and solids. For some believe that the mathematical ones are different[16] from those which come after the ideas[89]; whereas, of those who speak differently, some speak of the mathematical in a mathematical way, that is, they do not regard ideas as numbers or believe that ideas exist; others speak of the mathematical, but not in a mathematical way, since they say that neither is every spatial magnitude divisible into magnitudes nor do any two random units make two. But 30 all who believe that unity is an element and principle of all beings posit numbers as being composed of abstract units, with the exception of the Pythagoreans, who posit numbers as having spatial magnitude, as has been said before.

It is evident from this account in how many ways number may be described. All these ways have been mentioned, and all are impossible; some more so than others.

7

First, then, we must inquire if integers[24c] are additive[58] or not; and if not, in which of the two ways that we have 1081a distinguished. For it may be that no unit is additional to any other; or it may be that those grouped in a dyad-itself are unlike those grouped in a triad-itself and that therefore in this way those grouped in any archetypal[17a] number are unlike those in any other. Now, if all integers are additive and undifferentiated[76b], number and only number is mathematical, and the ideas[89] cannot be numbers. For what sort of number would man-himself or animal-itself or any other general form[20] be? There is only one idea[89] in each case, one man-himself, one animal-itself, and so 10 forth; whereas similar and undifferentiated numbers are infinitely many, so that no "three" is, let us say, "man-himself" any more than is any other "three." And if ideas are not numbers, they cannot be at all. For from what principles would the ideas be derived? Number is derived from the one and the indefinite[72c] dyad, and principles and elements are said to be principles and elements of number; whereas ideas cannot be ranked either as prior or as posterior to numbers.

On the other hand, if integers or units are discrete[58a] in the sense that any one is unlike any other, numbers of this sort cannot be mathematical numbers. For mathematical 20 number consists of undifferentiated units, and mathematical proofs are in harmony with this trait. Nor can the sort of nonmathematical number described be classed among general forms[20]. For two does not proceed directly from "the one" and "the indefinite dyad," and then from other successive numbers, as when we count "two, three, four"; since the units in the archetypal two are generated at the same time, whether, as the first proponent of the view said, out of unequals (that is, generated when these have been equalized), or in some other way. If one unit, therefore, is to be prior to the other, it must be prior also to the two composed of these; for, when there is a prior and a posterior, the combination will be prior to the one and posterior to the other.

And since "one-itself" is first, and then there is a par- 30 ticular[4] one which is first among the others and is next after the one-itself, and again a third which is next after the second and is next after the successor of the first "one," therefore the units must be prior to the numbers in which they are intertwined: there will be a third unit in "two" before there is "three", and a fourth and a fifth in "three" before the numbers four and five are. Hence, none of these men have said that the units are unlike in this way; but it is reasonable on their principles that they should be so even 1081b in this way, although it is in fact[7a] impossible. For it is reasonable both that the units should be prior and posterior if there is a first unit or first one, and also that the twos should be if there is a first two; for it is reasonable and necessary that after the first there should be a second, and if a second, then a third, and so in succession. And it is impossible to say both that a unit is first and another is

second after "one" and at the same time that a two is first
after it. But they admit a first unit, or one, but not also a
second and a third, and a first two, but not also a second
and a third.   10

Also, it is evident that it is impossible, if all the units are
unlike, that there be a two-itself and a three-itself, and so
with the other numbers. For whether the units are undifferentiated or different each from each, number must be
counted by addition: two, by addition of another one to
one; three, by addition of another one to the two; and four,
similarly. This being so, there can be no genesis of numbers
in the way in which they generate them out of the two and
the one: for the two becomes part of the three; the three, of
the four; and the same happens in the case of the succeeding 20
numbers. But according to them the four came from the
first two and the indefinite two, so that there are two twos
besides the two-itself; if not, the two-itself will be a part of
four, and one other two will be added. And, similarly, two
will consist of the one-itself and another one; but if this is
so, the other element cannot be an indefinite two, since it
generates one unit, not a definite two.

And how can there be, besides the three-itself and the
two-itself, other threes and twos? How can they consist of
prior and posterior units? All these are fictitious; and there 30
cannot be a first two and then a three-itself. Yet there would
have to be if the one and the indefinite two are the elements.
But, if these consequences are impossible, it is impossible
for those to be the principles.

If the units, then, are differentiated each from each, these
and other consequences of the sort follow of necessity. But
if the units grouped in different numbers are differentiated,
but those grouped in the same number are alone undifferentiated from one another, the perplexities which follow
are, even so, no less formidable.

In the ten-itself, for example, there are ten units, and the 1082a
ten is composed of them as it is of two fives. But, since the
ten-itself is not any chance number and is not composed of

any chance fives any more than of any chance units, the units in this ten must differ. For, if they do not differ, neither will the fives differ of which the ten consists; but since these differ, the units also will differ. But if they differ, will there be no other fives in the ten than just these two, or will there be others? If there are not, this is absurd; and if there are, what sort of ten will consist of them? For there is no other ten in the ten than itself. It follows necessarily that the four must not consist of any chance twos; for the indefinite two, as they declare, received the definite two and thus made two twos, since it was of the sort to double what it received.

And how is it possible for the two to be a nature apart from its two units, or the three apart from its three units? Either by participation, as "white man" differs from "white" and "man" because it participates in them, or when one is a differentia of the other, as "man" is different from "animal" and "two-footed."

Some things are one by contact, others by intermixture, and others by position, but none of them can belong to the units of which the two or the three consists; but as two men are not a unit[24] apart from both, so it must be with the integers[24c]. And it will make no difference that they are indivisible; for points too are indivisible, and yet a pair of them is nothing apart from the two.

We must not overlook another consequence, that there must be prior and posterior twos; and the same with the other numbers. For though the twos in the four be simultaneous, they are still prior to those in the eight, and as the two generated them, so they generated the fours in the eight-itself. Hence, if the first two is an idea[89], these twos will also be ideas of some sort. And the same account applies also to the units; for the units in the first two generated the four in the four, so that all the units come to be ideas, and an idea will be composed of ideas. This would imply that things, too, like their ideas, will be composite; for example, one might declare animals to be composed of animals, if there are ideas of them.

In general[44], to present the units as somehow different[76] from one another is absurd and fictitious (and by "fictitious" I mean forced with reference to an assumption[64h]), for neither in quantity nor in quality do we see unit differing from unit; but numbers must be equal or unequal—every number, but especially that which consists of abstract units. Hence, if a number is neither greater nor less than another, it is equal to it; but things equal and altogether undifferentiated we take to be the same, as far as number is concerned. If not, then not even the twos in the ten-itself will be undifferentiated, though they are equal; for what reason[83] can be given for believing that they are undifferentiated?

If any unit and another unit are two, a unit from the two-itself and a unit from the three-itself will form a two; this will consist of differentiated units, and will it be prior or posterior to the three? It would seem rather to be necessarily prior; for one of the units is simultaneous with the three, and the other is simultaneous with the two. And we ourselves take one and one to be two, in general, whether the things are equal or not, such as good and evil, or man and horse; but those who speak in the way under consideration say that not even two units are two.

And it would be strange if the number of the three-itself were not greater than that of the two; and, if it is greater, then it is clear that there is in it a number equal to the two, so that this is undifferentiated from the two-itself. But this cannot be so if there is a first and a second sort of number.

Nor will the ideas be numbers. For, as we said above, they are right who require[46c] units to be differentiated if there are to be ideas[89], since an idea[20] is unique. But if the units are undifferentiated, the twos and the threes also will be undifferentiated. And this is why they must also say that in counting "one, two" we do not add to a given number: numbers can then not be generated out of the indefinite dyad, nor can a number then be an idea[89], since one idea will then inhere in another, and all the general forms[20] will then be parts of one general form. Therefore they make a right assumption, but otherwise they are wrong; for they undermine[118] much mathematics if they doubt even whether when we count "one, two, three" we are counting by addition, not by separate parts. For we do both; and therefore it is ridiculous to raise so great a difficulty[76a] in the very being[26] of number.

8

1083a It is well to determine, first of all, in what numbers differ and in what, if in anything, units differ. Now units would have to differ[76] either in quantity or in quality, and neither of these appears to be possible. Of course, numbers as numbers differ in quantity. And, if the units also differed in quantity, then number would differ from number even when equal in number of units. Are the first units greater or smaller, and do the later increase or diminish? All these suppositions are irrational.

Neither can the units differ in quality. For no attribute can belong to them; even to number, quality is said to belong posterior to quantity. Quality would not come to the units either from the one or from the dyad; for the former is not qualitied, and the latter is essentially quantitative, since its nature is the plurality principle itself, in terms of which plural things[1a] are intelligible[83].

Accordingly, if the facts are quite different, this ought to be stated at the very outset[82], and it ought especially to be determined why it is necessary for difference to belong to a unit; but, if this is not necessary, what difference do they mean? It is evident, then, if the ideas are numbers, that the units cannot all be alike and that they cannot be unlike one another in either of the two ways before distinguished.*

There are others, too, who are confused on the theory of numbers. These are the men who do not think that there are ideas, either as ideas simply or as identical with certain numbers; but who think that there are mathematical

* xiii.6.1080a18–20, 23–35.

entities, that numbers are the first of all things[1a], and that the beginning of numbers is the one-itself. For it is absurd that there should be a one which is first among ones, as these men say, and not a two which is first among twos, or a three which is first among threes; for the same reasoning applies to all.

If we have told the truth concerning numbers and can maintain that there is only mathematical number, then its principle is not "the one." For this sort of "one" must differ from other units; and, if this is so, then there would also be 30 "the two" first among twos, and so forth. But if "the one" is the principle or source of all number, then the truth would be as Plato described it, and there would be a first two and three, and the numbers would not be like one another. But on such suppositions many impossible consequences follow, as has been said.† But either this [Platonic] or the other assumption must be true; otherwise number cannot be separate.   1083b

It is evident also, from these considerations, that the third system [that of Xenocrates] is the worst; namely, that numbers as general forms[20] and mathematical numbers are the same.‡ For two mistakes must then meet in one doctrine: mathematical number cannot be thus general, hence it becomes necessary to make additional peculiar assumptions[64h]; and it also becomes necessary to maintain all the consequences which follow for those who interpret numbers as general forms.

On the other hand, the Pythagorean approach contains fewer perplexities than do those previously mentioned, yet contains other perplexities peculiar to itself. For to present number as not separate removes many impossible conse- 10 quences; but it is, on the other hand, impossible for bodies to be composed of numbers that are mathematical numbers. For it is not true to speak of indivisible[41] spatial magnitudes; however much there may be magnitudes of this sort, integers at any rate do not have magnitude, and how can

† xiii.7.1080b37–8.1083a17.   ‡ xiii.6.1080b22.

magnitude be composed of indivisibles[75a]? But mathematical number certainly consists of integers. Hence, when the Pythagoreans interpret things[1a] as numbers, or at any rate apply their maxims to bodies, they talk as if bodies
20 consisted of those numbers. If number, to be independent[2], must be in one of these ways,§ and it cannot be in any of these ways, it is evident that there is no such nature of number as those conceive who think that number is separate being.

We must now ask whether each unit comes from the great and the small equalized, or one from the small and another from the great? If the latter, then nothing consists of all the elements, and the units are undifferentiated; for the great belongs inherently to one, and the small, being by nature contrary to the great, belongs inherently to the other. And what are the units in the three-itself? One of them is an odd unit. Probably it is to avoid this difficulty that they interpret the one-itself as a mean[138] between even and the other odd
30 numbers.

But if each of the two units consists of both the great and the small equalized, how can the dyad, which is a single nature, consist of the great and small? Or in what will it differ from unity? Besides, unity is prior to the dyad; for when it is destroyed, the dyad is destroyed. It must, then, be the idea[89] of an idea, since it is prior to an idea, and it must have come into being before it. But from what? Certainly not from the indefinite dyad; for it generates the double.

Number must be either infinite or finite; for since these
1084a men think of number as separate, it is impossible to avoid one of these alternatives. Now it is clear that number cannot be infinite, since infinite number is neither odd nor even, but the generation of numbers is always the generation of an odd or of an even number: adding one to an even number, we get an odd number; and we get even numbers either by doubling any two after one or by doubling any odd number.

§ xiii.6.1080a15–b36.

And if every idea is an idea of something, and the numbers are ideas, then infinite number will also be an idea of something, sensible or otherwise. Yet this is not possible either on their thesis or in reason[90], and hence they interpret ideas as they do.   10

On the other hand, if number is finite, how far does it extend? For this limit must be stated and also explained[203]. But if number extends only as far as ten, as some say, then in the first place it will be disastrous for "ideas"[20]: thus, if three is man-himself, what number under ten will be horse-itself? The numbers for the things-themselves can go only as far as ten. Therefore one of the numbers among these up to ten, which are primary[26], must correspond to each primary idea[89]. But there will not be enough, since even the forms[20] of animal outnumber ten. At the same time, it is clear that, if "the three" is thus "man-himself," the other "threes" are so also, since those in the same number are similar, so that there will be an infinite number of men: if 20 each of the threes is an idea[89], it is man-himself; if not, they will at any rate be men. And if the smaller number is part of the greater, where the units in the same number are alike, then, if the four-itself is an idea of something, for example, of horse or white, man will be part of horse, if man is two. Also, it is absurd that there should be an idea of ten, but not of eleven and not of the succeeding numbers. Again, there are supposed to be or become things of which there are no general forms[20]. Why, then, are there no general forms of them? Certainly the general froms do not answer[83] this question. Again, it is absurd if number up to ten is more of a[4] being[1] and a general form than is the ten-itself; yet 30 there is no genesis of the former as one thing, but there is of the latter. But they imagine number up to ten as a complete series. At any rate, they generate the derivatives, such as void, proportion, odd, and others of the sort, within the series of ten; for they attribute some things, such as movement, rest, good, bad, to the originating principles, and the others to the numbers. That is why they say that the odd is based on unity; for if the odd were based on the triad, how could the five be odd? Again, spatial magnitudes and all 1084b entities of this sort are confined within a definite number: the first dimension, the indivisible line, then the second dimension, and so forth; and these entities together would also extend only up to ten.‖

Besides, if number is separate, one might ask whether it is the one or the three or the two that is separate. Now, inasmuch as number is composite, the one is prior; but, inasmuch as generals[43] and general forms[20] are prior, a number is prior. For each of the units is a material part of a number, and a number is their general form. So the right angle is also in a way prior to the acute angle, because it is determinate and because of its definition; but the acute angle is prior in another way, because it is a part and the right angle is divided into acute angles. As matter, then, the acute angle 10 and the element and the unit are prior; but, with regard to the general form and to the essential being[26] expressed in the definition[90], the right angle and the whole composed of matter and form are prior, since the compound is nearer to the form and to what is expressed in the definition, although it is posterior in genesis.

How, then, is unity a principle? Because it is not divisible they say. But both what is general and what is partial or an element are indivisible. But they are principles in different ways: one of them, in definition; the other, in time. In which of these ways, then, is unity a principle? As has been said, the right angle is held to be prior to the acute angle, and the acute angle to the right angle, and each is one. And so they present the one as the beginning in both ways. But this is impossible; for what is general is one as form or essential 20 being[26], whereas an element is one as a part or as matter. For each of the two units of a dyad is, in truth, one only potentially, at least if the number is a unity and not like a heap, that is, if different numbers consist of different units,

‖ xiv.3.1090b21–24.

as they say; but each of the two units is not in complete realization[10].

And the reason[83] for the mistake which followed for them is that they conducted their pursuit from the standpoint both of mathematics and of definitions of general terms. From the former standpoint, therefore, they regarded unity as the starting *point*, as if it had spatial location. These men, then, just as some others have done, put things[1a] together[64g] out of the smallest parts. In consequence, the unit becomes the matter of numbers and at the same time one is prior to two; on the other hand, it is posterior, inasmuch as the two is a whole, a unity, and a form. But because 30 they were also seeking what is general, they spoke of the one which is predicated of a number as also a logical part of the number. But it is impossible for these traits to belong to the same thing at the same time.

And if it is only the one-itself that is nonspatial (since it differs from the other ones in nothing except in being a beginning), and if the two is divisible, whereas the unit is not, then the unit must be more like the one-itself than is the two. But, if the unit is more like the one-itself, the one-itself must be more like the unit than like the two; so that each of the units in the two must be prior to the two. But this they deny; at any rate, they generate the dyad first. Again, if the two-itself is a unity, and the three-itself is also, both 1085a form a two. From what, then, is this two derived?

9

One might also ask: Since numbers are discrete and in succession, do successive units, for example, those in the two and those in the three, between which there is nothing, succeed the one-itself or not? And in case some succeed it, which comes first, the two or one of its units?

Similar perplexities follow concerning the kinds[19] of things to which numbers apply[18]: line, plane, and solid. For some regard them as derived from the kinds[20] of

10 things great and small: lines, from the long and the short; planes, from the broad and the narrow; volumes, from the deep and the shallow.* These are species of great and small. Moreover, different thinkers explain[64] in different ways how such things come from a principle analogous to unity. Here, too, the impossibilities, the fictions, and the contradictions of all that is reasonable are evidently countless. For geometrical entities are severed from one another, unless their principles go together in such a way that broad-and-narrow is also long-and-short; but if this is so, the plane will be a line, and the solid, a plane. And then how can angles and

20 figures and the like be defined[46d]? Then, too, the same consequence follows as in the case of numbers; for long-and-short, and so forth, are attributes of magnitude, but magnitude does not consist of them, any more than the line consists of straight-and-curved or solids consist of smooth-and-rough.

Common to all these views, also, is the difficulty which occurs with respect to the species of a genus whenever one[64] generalizes[43], whether it be animal-itself or something other than animal-itself that is in an animal. For this will occasion no difficulty if what is general is not separate; but, if "the one" is a separate being from numbers, as those who say these things maintain, it is not easy to solve the difficulty—if one may say of the impossible that it is not easy.

30 Thus, is the conception[169a] of the-one-that-is-in-two or in number in general the conception of a thing-itself or of something else?

Some generate spatial magnitudes from this kind of material; and others generate them from the point (and the point seems to be, not the one, but something like the one) and from a matter which, though like plurality, is not plurality. Nonetheless, the same difficulties follow concerning these principles. For if their matter be one, then a line, a plane, and a solid must be the same; since from one and the same thing can come only things that are the same. But if

1085b the matters are more than one, and there is one for the line

* i.9.992a10-19.

and another for the plane and still another for the solid, the same consequences will follow even so; for these matters either are consecutive or not, so that the plane will either not contain a line or will be a line.

They also fail to explain how number can consist of the one and plurality; but however they express themselves, the same perplexities follow as for those who derive number from the one and the indefinite dyad. For the one account generates number from plurality in general, not from a particular plurality; whereas the other generates it from a particular plurality, but from the first, since two is said to be the first 10 plurality. Consequently, there is no difference worth mentioning, and the same difficulties follow: intermixture or position or blending or generation, and so forth.

Especially, if each unit is one, one might persist in asking from what it comes; for each is, indeed, not the one-itself. It must, therefore, come from the one-itself and plurality or a part of plurality. To declare the unit to be a plurality is impossible, since it is indivisible; and to derive it from a part of plurality is fraught with many other perplexities. For each of the parts must be indivisible, or it will be a plurality, and the unit will be divisible; and the elements will not be the one and plurality, since each unit does not come from 20 plurality and the one. Besides, such an explanation merely constructs another number; for the plurality of indivisibles is a number. So we must investigate whether the number proposed by this theory is infinite or finite.† For, as it seems, there is a finite plurality from which and from which unity came the finite number of units; and there is another plurality that is plurality-itself, infinite plurality. What sort of plurality, then, is this element that together with unity produces numbers?

Similarly, one might also investigate concerning the point, that is, the element out of which they make the spatial magnitudes; for this is, indeed, not the one and only point. From what, therefore, do the other points, at any rate, 30

† xiii.8.1083b37.

come? Surely not from "extension" or from point-itself. There can be no indivisible parts of extension, like the indivisible parts of the plurality from which the units are said to be derived; for although number consists of indivisibles, spatial magnitudes do not.

All these and similar considerations make it clear, therefore, that it is impossible for number and spatial magnitudes to be separately. Again, the disharmonies between the 1086a various ways of dealing with numbers are an indication that it is the false conception of the facts[188c] themselves which brings confusion into these views. For those who regard the mathematical entities as being independent of sensible things, seeing the perplexity and the artificiality surrounding the general forms, abandoned the belief in archetypal[20a] number and then regarded all number as mathematical. But those who wanted to think that general forms are at the same time numbers, and who did not see how on these principles mathematical number could be apart from the archetypal, regarded archetypal and mathematical number as logically[90] identical, since mathematical 10 number had in fact[9c] been annihiliated; for they state assumptions[64h] which are peculiar to themselves and are not mathematical. Accordingly, he who first believed that there are general forms, that these general forms are numbers, and that there are mathematical entities separated the two, and reasonably so. Consequently, it follows that all are to some extent right, but not entirely[44] right. And they themselves confirm this in that they do not give identical, but conflicting, accounts. The reason is that their assumptions and principles are false. And it is hard to give a good account when one has made a poor beginning; according to Epicharmus, "As soon as it is said, it is seen to be wrong."

However, as to numbers, the difficulties and the distinctions we have formulated are sufficient; for whereas he 20 who is already convinced might be more convinced by further arguments, he who is not yet convinced would not come any nearer to being convinced. But as to the first

principles[82], the grounds[83], and elements[103], what
those say who deal with sensible primary being has been in
part set forth in the writings on nature ‡ and in part does
not belong to the present exploration[198]; but what those
say who assert that there are other primary beings besides
the sensible must occupy our reflection[187] next after what
we have been saying. Since some say that ideas[89] and
numbers are of this sort and that their elements are elements and principles of [sensible] things[1a], we must inquire
into what they say about this and how they say it.

Those, then, who posit numbers only, and these mathematical, must be considered later;§ but those who believe in 30
ideas[89], their way of speaking, and the difficulty confront-
ing them must be examined now. They regard ideas as
primary beings that are general[43] and at the same time
separate and particular[40]. That this is not possible, has
been proved before.‖ However, the reason why those who
describe the ideas as general combined[137c] all these beings
into one type is that they did not regard their primary beings
as identical with sensible ones. They regarded the particulars in the realm of sense as in flux and none of them as
persisting; but what is general, as being independent[74] 1086b
of them and as being something different[16]. Socrates urged
this view, as we have said before,¶ in his definitions, though
he did not separate the general from the particular; and he
was right in not separating them. This is clear from the
results[9c]: for without the general it is not possible to get
knowledge[179]; but separating it is the reason for the
consequent perplexities concerning ideas. His followers,
however, thinking it necessary to believe in the separation,
if there are to be any primary beings besides those sensible
and in flux, believed in these general beings, since they knew 10
no others; so that it follows that generals and particulars
have almost the same natures. This, then, is in itself one
perplexity among those to which we have referred.

‡ *Physics* i.4–6; *De caelo* iii.3, 4; *On Generation and Corruption* i.1.

§ xiv.2.1090a7–15, 3.1090a20–b20.   ‖ iii.6.1003a7–17.   ¶ xiii.4.1078b17–30.

10

Let us now state the source of a certain difficulty both for those who do and for those who do not believe in ideas[89], though we have stated it before, at the beginning, among the problems.* If we do not believe[64] in primary beings[26] as separate and as being in the way in which particular beings are, we undermine[118] primary being in the way in which we wish to speak of it; and if we believe in primary beings as
20 separate, how can we conceive the being of their elements and principles?

If these beings are particular[40], not general[43], there must be as many things[1a] as there are elements, and the elements will not be knowable[179b]. For let the syllables in speech be its primary being, and their elements be elements of primary beings, then there would have to be but one *"ba"* and only one of each of the syllables; since they are not general or the same in form, but each is numerically single and a "this-something"[4b], and each has no common name. And so they believe that what anything is itself is in each case a unity. But if this is so for syllables, it is so also for the parts of which they consist; and there will accordingly not be more *a*'s than one or more than one of any of the other elements—by the same argument by which there
30 cannot be more than one identical syllable. But if this is so, there are only elements and no other beings[1a] besides them. And these elements will not even be knowable; for they are not general, whereas knowledge is of generals. And this is clear from demonstrations and definitions: for no syllogism, for example, that the sum of the angles of this triangle is two right angles, is generated unless the sum of the angles of every triangle is two right angles; nor, for example, that this man is an animal unless every man is an animal.

On the other hand, if the principles are general, then either
1087a the primary beings composed of them are also general, or what is not primary being will be prior to primary being.

* iii.4.999b24–1000a4, 6.1003a5–17.

For what is general is not primary being, whereas an element or principle is general; and an element or principle is prior to the things of which it is an element or principle.

All these consequences follow reasonably, indeed, when they regard ideas as composed of elements and at the same time insist that there are also independently[74] of the primary beings of the same form ideas as single separate entities[4]. But if, for example, in the case of the elements of speech, there is nothing to prevent the *a*'s and *b*'s from being many and nothing to prevent there being, besides the many, no *a*-itself or *b*-itself, there may be, so far as this is concerned, an infinite number of syllables that are similar. 10

Now the statement that knowledge is general, so that the principles of things[1a] must also be general, not separate primary beings, of all the arguments we have stated contains the greatest difficulty; but the statement is, nevertheless, in a way true, though it is in another way not true. For "knowledge," like "knowing," means two ways of being: one, potentially[11]; the other, actually[9]. The power, or material, being general and indefinite, is a principle of the general and the indefinite; but the actual is definite[72] and is a principle of the definite—being a "this-something"[4b], it is of something definite[4b]. However, sight can see general color incidentally[3], because "this"[4a] color which it sees 20 is a color; and so "this" *a* which concerns[187] the grammarian is "an" *a*. For if the principles must be general, then whatever is derived from them must also be general; as in demonstrations. And if this is so, it will not be possible for anything to be separate or primary being. But it is clear that knowledge is in one way general and in another way not.

XIV. BOOK NU

I

So much, then, for this [unchanging] primary being.

30 Now all agree in regarding first principles as contraries, whether in natural things, or in the case of unchanging[109e] primary beings. If nothing can be prior to these first principles of all things, then such a principle cannot itself be a separate[16] thing[4]: if one were to say that "white" is a principle, not something white, but merely "white," and that this white, nevertheless, is in[39a] a subject matter[85], in something which is white, then the subject matter must be prior to the "white." So anything that is generated from its contrary belongs to some subject matter, and hence necessarily implies, especially in the case of contraries, some 1087b subject matter[82f]. All contraries, accordingly, are contraries of some subject matter, and none of them is itself a separate[73] thing. Now, it is both obvious[173b] and demonstrable[90] that nothing is contrary to a primary being. Therefore, none of the contraries, but something else, must be the chief principle of all things.

Moreover, these men present matter as one of the contraries. And some regard the unequal, which they interpret as the nature of plurality, as the matter of unity and of equality; others regard plurality as the matter of unity. According to the former, numbers are generated out of the dyad of the unequal or of the great and the small; according to the latter, out of plurality; according to both, by the agency of the primary being of unity. For even those who 10 say that inequality and unity are the elements and that the

300

unequal dyad is composed of the great and the small describe the unequal or the great and the small as if they were one and fail to make the distinction between being one in concept[90] and being numerically one, which latter does not apply to them.

They do not even give a good account of the principles, which they call "elements": for some name the great and the small together with unity, these three, as the elements of numbers, the first two being their matter, and the unity being their form; others begin with the many and the few, because they think the great and the small are more naturally the elements of magnitude; still others begin with elements even more general, namely, excess and deficiency. None of these variations makes a difference worth mentioning from most points of view, but logically they raise difficulties, 20 which these men avoid because their own proofs are of the logical kind. There is, however, one exceptional, real issue between those who begin with excess and deficiency and those who begin with the great and the small: on the more general basis of excess and deficiency number is a more primary derivative than duality is; for number is the more general. But, as it is, these men admit one part of the argument without the other.

Others regard separateness[16] and otherness[16b] as the opposites of unity; whereas still others regard plurality as the opposite of unity. But if things[1a] are composed of contraries, as they want them to be, and there is nothing contrary to unity, unless it be plurality, and inequality is contrary to equality, separate to same, and other to this, 30 then those who hold unity as the opposite of plurality maintain the best opinion, although even theirs is not adequate; for unity might still be few, which is also opposed to many or plurality.

What is clear in all this is that "one" indicates a measure. And it always applies to some subject matter or other: in the scale it is a half-tone; in spatial magnitude, a finger or a foot or something of the sort; in rhythms, a beat or a syllable;

and similarly, in heaviness, a definite weight. And so in all
1088a cases: in qualities, some quality; in quantities, some quantity. And the measure is indivisible: the former, in kind[20];
and the latter, to the sense[165a]; so that unity is not in
itself the primary being of anything. And this is reasonable;
for "one" indicates a measure of some plurality, and number,
a measured plurality or a plurality of measures. Therefore,
it is reasonable that the "one" is not a "number"; for a
measure is among things measured. Hence, both the measure
and the one belong among principles. But the measure must
always have an identity with what it measures: in the case
of horses, the measure is a horse; in the case of men, a man.
10 In the case of a man, a horse, and a god, the measure is,
perhaps, a living being; and their number will be a number of
living beings. In the cases of man, white, and walking, there
can be no adding them together, because each belongs to
the same individual, numerically one, although they may
from a number of kinds or aspects of a thing.

Those who regard inequality as a unity, and the dyad as an
indefinite compound of great and small, say something very
remote from what is probable or possible. For these are not
subjects of measurement, but are rather modifications or
accidents of numbers or magnitudes: many and few modify
number, and great and small are accidents of magnitude; so
20 also, even and odd, smooth and rough, straight and curved.

And besides this mistake, the great and the small, and so
forth, must be relative to something; but the relative belongs
least of all to the category of a nature or primary being, and
comes after quality and quantity; thus, the relative is a
modification of quantity, as has been said, not its matter,
whether we take matter as something distinct or matter as of
relation in general or of its parts and kinds. For nothing is
great or small, many or few, or, in general, relative to something else, which can be so without being something distinct.
An indication that the relative is least of all a primary[26]
30 and distinct being[4c] is the fact that only what is relative
has no generation or destruction or movement of its own:

quantities can increase and diminish; qualities can change; there is locomotion from place to place; and there can be a total generation or destruction of a primary being. But not with regard to relation; for without undergoing change a thing may become now greater and now less or equal, that is, when its correlative[16] has undergone change in quantity. The matter, too, of anything (for example, of primary 1088b being) must be potentially that being; but the relative is neither potentially nor actually primary being. It is absurd, then, or rather impossible, to regard what is not primary being as an element of and prior to primary being; for it is in all categories posterior to primary being. Another argument against its being an element is that an element would not also be an attribute[25a] of the same thing of which it is an element; whereas "many" and "few" are each and both attributes of number, and "long" and "short" are attributes of lines, and "broad" and "narrow," of planes.

Finally, how can a number consist of "few" and "many"? There would then have to be a certain number which could always be called "few," and another would be absolutely "many." But if two is "many," one is "few"; and if there were no greater number than ten, it would be "many," and 10 the same would be true of ten thousand. Thus, either "many" or "few" may be attributed to any number; but if both were elements of number, any number ought to be both or neither.

2

In general[105], the question arises whether it is possible for eternal things to be composed of elements. If so, they would have matter; because everything composed of elements is put together. Since a thing, whether it is eternal or not, necessarily comes to be out of that of which it is composed, and since everything becomes what it is from what it was potentially (for it could not have become from something impossible, nor could it be composed of that), and since it is possible for the potential to become actual or not, then number or anything else having matter, however eternal it 20 may be, would possibly not be. For it might cease to be, whether it is a day old or has continued for many years. And if this is so, then even what has lasted for an infinite time might perish. Therefore, such things cannot be eternal, since nothing is eternal which may possibly not be, as we had occasion to conclude in other discussions.* And since what we are now saying is true universally, that no primary being is eternal unless it is actual, and since the elements are the matter of primary beings, then no eternal primary being can be composed of elements which constitute[82h] it. There are those who, being understandably dissatisfied with the assumption that "inequality" can serve with "unity" as an 30 element, because this assumption has impossible consequences, assume[34] that there is with "unity" an "indefinite dyad." But they have removed only those perplexities which follow necessarily from the assumption that the unequal or the relative can be an element; whereas the perplexities which follow even without this assumption still trouble these men, whether it be archetypal or mathematical number that they assume to be composed of such elements.

1089a There are many reasons why they are led astray into such explanations; in particular, because their problem has been formulated in an obsolete way. For it seemed to these men that all things[1a] would be one, mere being-itself, unless they directly attacked and refuted the saying of Parmenides: "For never will this be proved that things that are not, are." And so it seemed to them necessary to prove that there is nonbeing[1b]; for if there are many things, they can be only because they are composed of being[1] and of something else. But, we ask, in the first place without assuming the being of nonbeing, what kind of unity do things constitute? For "being" has several meanings and may indicate primary being, quality, quantity, or one of the other categories. Is 10 it primary beings or their attributes that are one? And so with the other categories and all of them together. When the

* ix.8.1050b7–19; *De caelo* i.12.

"this"[4a], the "such"[5], the "so much"[6d], and all the other categories designate something that is one, are they therefore all unified? It is absurd, or rather impossible, that the emergence of some single nature could explain how a thing is not only "this," but also "such," "so much," "somewhere," and so forth.

Secondly, of what sort of nonbeing and being are things composed? For since "being" has several meanings, so has "nonbeing": not being a man means not being a certain "this"; not being straight means not being a certain "such"; not being three cubits long means not being a certain "so much." Of what sort of being and nonbeing, then, are the many things composed? It is true that Plato † meant by the kind of nonbeing which, together with their being, con- 20 stitutes things, "the false" and the nature of falsity. This is why he said that we must assume[64h] something false, just as geometers assume a line not a foot long to be a foot long. But this cannot be so. For it is not true either that geometers thus posit something false (since the proposed assumption[62a] is not a part of the reasoning), or that nonbeing, in the sense of the false, is that out of which things come to be and into which they pass away. But since a thing can nonbe in as many ways as there are categories, and since "nonbeing" may mean either the "false" or the "potential," it is the latter meaning that is relevant to generation: man comes from what is not man, but is potentially man; white, from what is not white, but is po- 30 tentially white; and this is true whether a single being is generated or many.

Now it is evident that the kind of being which concerns us in the question how "being" is "many" is primary being. For it is numbers, lines, and bodies that are generated. Now, it is absurd to investigate only how "being" is many in the primary kind of being[87], not how qualities or quantities are many. For the indefinite dyad, or great and small, certainly does not explain how there are two whites or many colors or

† Plato *Sophist* 237A, 240.

1089b flavors or shapes; for then these, too, would be numbers and units. But had men gone on to these categories, they would have been able also to explain primary beings; for the reason is the same or analogous. This aberration is also the reason that in seeking the opposite of being and the one, from which, together with being and the one, all things are to be derived, they supposed it to be the relative or unequal, which is neither contrary nor contradictory to being and the one and which, like the "what"[4] and quality, is a nature in things. These men should have investigated how the relative is many, not one. But, instead, they investigate only how there

10 are many units besides the first "one," not also how there are many "unequals" besides "the unequal." Yet they use relatives and speak of great and small, many and few, as the sources from which numbers are derived; of long and short, from which the line is derived; broad and narrow, from which the plane is derived; deep and shallow, from which volumes are derived; and so they speak of still more kinds of relatives. What is the reason, then, why these are many?

Here it is necessary, we maintain, to consider[64h] the potential being of each. He whose views we are criticizing also maintained that any "this" or primary being has potential being which is not in itself being; but he identified it with the relative—just as if he had said things are potentially "qualitative." Such being is neither potential unity and potential being nor the negation of unity and being, but

20 is one among the many ways of being. What he should rather have done, as has been said,‡ if he were investigating how beings are many, was, instead of taking beings in the same category and asking how primary beings are many, how qualities are many, and so forth, to investigate how beings in general are many; that is, some are primary beings, some are attributes, some are relations, and so forth. In the dependent categories there is a special problem of explaining how beings are many; for qualities and quantities are many because they are not separate from the things to which they belong and

‡ xiv.2.1089a35.

which become many or are many. Though there ought to be some matter for each category, it cannot be separate from primary beings. But in the case of "thises" it is possible to explain how a "this" is many things, unless something particular is regarded as being both a "this-something" and 30 a nature of a certain sort. However, the difficulty arising about primary beings is rather how there are actually many primary beings, not only one.

Then, too, if a "this" and a quantity are not the same, their theory does not explain how and why these beings are many, but only how quantities are many. For all "number" indicates a quantity; and so does a unit, unless it indicates a measure or the indivisible in quantity. If, then, quantity and "what is"[87] are different, they fail to explain whence or how the "what is" is many; and if anyone says that they are 1090a the same, he must assert many inconsistencies.

As regards "numbers," we may well ponder how one is to justify the conviction that there are such things. To one who believes[64] in ideas[89] numbers provide an explanation, since each number is an idea, and an idea is somehow or other (let us admit[85] for the sake of the argument) an explanation for the being of other things. But why should one who does not think so, seeing the perplexities involved in the doctrine of ideas, and who does not have this reason for believing[34] in numbers and regards[34] number as merely mathematical, why should he try to convince us that there are "numbers," 10 and of what use is it to believe this? For in believing in numbers, he neither holds them responsible[83a] for anything, since he describes them as being themselves a nature, nor does he enable us to see how they could be responsible for anything; for all the theorems of arithmeticians will be found applicable to sensible beings, as has already been said.§

3

Those, then, who believe[64] that there are ideas and that they are numbers at least try, by their method of abstract-

§ xiii.3.

ing[64a] terms from their instances and by their assumption[65] that each is something unified, to explain how and why there are numbers. But since their reasons are neither 20 necessary nor possible, it is at least not for these reasons that we must believe in numbers.

Now the Pythagoreans, seeing that many attributes of numbers belong also to sensible bodies, believed[34] that things[1a] are themselves numbers, not separate numbers, but composed of numbers as their elements. Why? Because the attributes[35a] of number belong inherently to musical scales, to the heavens, and to many other things.

On the other hand, those who say that only mathematical numbers are cannot, on their assumptions[64h], say anything of that sort; for they are caught by the old saying that there can be no science of sensible things. We, however, believe there can be, as we have said before.* And it is clear that mathematical entities are not separate; for had they been 30 separate, their attributes could not belong inherently to bodies.

The Pythagoreans, then, are not open to attack on this score; but in believing natural bodies to be composed of numbers, things light and heavy to be composed of things not having heaviness and lightness, they seem to be speaking about other heavens and bodies, not about those perceived.

However, those who believe that number is separate assume that number must be, in order to be separate, because the axioms of mathematics would not apply to sensible things, though mathematical theorems are true and content 1090b the mind[154]; and it is the same with the spatial magnitudes of mathematics. It is clear, then, that the opposite[50] account † must say the opposite of this; and also that those who think in this way must solve the difficulty just suggested, why it is that if numbers in no way belong inherently to sensible things their attributes, nevertheless, belong inherently to sensible things.

There are also some who think that because a point is the

* xiii.3.   † xiv.3.1090a20–25.

limit and extreme of a line, and a line, of a plane, and a plane, of a solid, there must be natures of this sort. We must therefore examine whether this view is not uncommonly weak. For extremes are not primary beings, but limits, since there is a limit even of walking and of movement in general. Any limit would, then, be a "this-something" and a primary being. But that is absurd. If they were primary beings, they would belong to the familiar sense objects; for the argument applied to them. Why, then, must they be separate? 10

And if we were to be stubborn, we might persist in investigating number of every sort and mathematical entities, to show that they contribute[58b] nothing to one another, that the earlier do not explain the later: for even if there were no number, there would still be spatial magnitudes to be explained by those who believe that only mathematical numbers are; and even if there were no spatial magnitudes, there would still be conscious life[154] and sensible bodies. For nature's show is not episodic, like a poor tragedy. 20

However, this objection does not apply to those who believe in ideas: they believe that spatial magnitudes are derived from matter and number; lines, from the two; planes, probably from the three; solids, from the four.‡ Or they derive them from other numbers; for this makes no difference. But will these magnitudes be ideas? Or what is the mode of their being? And what do they contribute to things?[1a] They contribute nothing, any more than do the mathematical entities. Not even theorems belong to them exclusively, unless there is to be a new mathematics to accommodate these strange doctrines. Of course, it is not hard for those who accept arbitrary assumptions to string out a long tale. But they are mistaken if they intend to combine mathematical thinking with their ideas. 30

Nor were those who first assumed two kinds of numbers, the general forms[20] and the mathematical, more successful in explaining how mathematical number is and of what it is

‡ xiii.8.1084b2.

composed. For they place it between the archetypal and the sensible. Now, if it is composed of the great and the small, it will be the same as the number of the ideas. And he maintains that spatial magnitudes are composed of some other "small and great." § But to introduce these other elements makes elements rather many. And, if unity is the principle of each of the two sorts of number, unity will be something common to them. So we have still to find out how the one is these many things. And number cannot at the same time, according to him, he generated except from one and an indefinite dyad.

All this is irrational and conflicts both with itself and with what is reasonable, and there appears to be in it Simonides' "long tale"; for a long tale, like those of slaves, is born when men have nothing sound to say. And the elements themselves, the great and the small, appear to cry out against the maltreatment to which they are subjected; for they cannot generate any number except that derived from the one by doubling.

It is absurd, also, to ascribe generation to what is eternal, or rather, it is impossible. There need be no doubt, then, whatever the Pythagoreans do or do not say, that they clearly ascribe generation to it when they say that in the construction of the one, whether out of plane or surface or seed or things difficult to express, the nearest part of the unlimited at once began to be constrained and limited by the limit. But since they are cosmologists and want to speak naturalistically, it is fair enough to test what they say about nature, but to exempt them from the present exploration, since we are seeking principles in the realm of the unchanging, and it is therefore numbers of this sort whose genesis concerns us.

4

These men deny generation of odd number, as though it were clear that there is generation of the even; and some

§ xiv.3.1090b21, 22.

construct the even initially from unequals and then, when these have been equalized, from the great and the small. The inequality must, then, belong to them before they have been equalized. But if they had always been equalized, they would not have been unequal before; for there is nothing before that which is always. Hence, it is evident that they do not introduce[34] the generation of numbers for the sake of theoretical[187] interests.

There is also the difficulty, which it is a reproach to treat 30 lightly, how the elements and the first principles are related to the good and the beautiful. The difficulty is whether any of the elements is the sort of thing that we mean by the good itself and the best, or whether, on the contrary, these beings are later in origin than the elements.

Now, the theologians seem to agree with some men of the present day,* who give a negative answer and declare that it is, on the contrary, only after the nature of things[1a] has moved forward that the good and the beautiful appear in it. And this they do because they shrink from the genuine perplexity which follows for those who say, as some do, that the one is a first principle. But that perplexity is not due to 1091b the portrayal of the good as belonging to the first principle, but to the portrayal of the one as a principle, and as a principle in the sense of an element, and of number as derived from the one.

The old poets speak similarly, inasmuch as they say that it is, not those who are first in time, such as night and heaven or chaos or ocean, but Zeus who reigns and rules. However, these poets happen to say things of this sort only because they describe the rulers of the things that are changing[115]. However, those whose accounts are mixed and who do not express everything in mythical form, such as Pherecydes and some others, suppose that the best was the first gener- 10 ating agent; and so do the magi and also some of the later sages, for example, both Empedocles and Anaxagoras, the former regarding love as an element, and the latter,

* xii.7.1072b31.

mind[169] as a principle. But some of those who maintain
that there are unchanging primary beings maintain that the
one-itself is the good-itself, although they believe that its
fundamental being is primarily its unity.

The difficulty, then, is this: Which of the two accounts
ought to be given? It would be a wonder if what is first and
eternal and most self-sufficient possessed these very traits in
some other way than as good. It cannot be indestructible
or self-sufficient for any other reason than because it is
good. Consequently, it is probably true to declare the first
20 principle to be good.

However, it is impossible that unity should be this principle or, if not that, an element, and an element of numbers;
for then considerable perplexity arises. To avoid the latter,
some have surrendered that position, agreeing that the one
is a principle and an element, but of mathematical number
only. For otherwise any unit would become something good,
and there would be goods in superabundance. And if the
general forms[20] are numbers, all the general forms would be
good. Now, let a man posit ideas[89] of anything he pleases.
If these ideas are of goods only, they will not be primary
beings; and if they are ideas of primary beings as well, then
30 all animals, plants, and things participating in the ideas will
be good. Added to these absurdities is also the implication
that the contrary element is the bad-itself, whether it is
plurality or the unequal or the great and the small. And that
is why one of these men avoided relating[137b] good to
unity, because it would be necessary, since generation is
from contraries, to regard the bad as the nature of plurality.
And there are others who say that inequality is the nature of
the bad. It follows, therefore, that all things[1a] partake of
the bad except one, unity itself; that numbers partake more
1092a fully of the bad than do spatial magnitudes; that the bad
serves as the space for the good; and that the bad partakes
in and desires what destroys it, since one contrary is destructive of another. And if, as we said,† matter is what is poten-

† xiv.1.1088b1.

tially anything, for example, the matter of fire in operation is what is potentially fire, then the bad will be precisely what is potentially good.

All these consequences follow from the tendency these men have to interpret[34] every principle as an element; or because they interpret contraries as principles; or because they interpret unity as a principle; or because they interpret numbers as the first primary beings, as separate, and as general forms.

5

Now, since it is equally impossible to exclude the good from first principles and to include[64] it among them in the manner of these men, it is clear that there is something wrong in the way principles[82] and the most primary[17a] be-ings[26] have been conceived[46d]. No one has the right grasp[65i] on them who co-ordinates the universal[21] principles with those of animals and plants, on the ground that the more complete[14] always evolves from the in-definite[72c] and incomplete; the philosopher * who declares such a doctrine about things primordial[17a] is forced to conclude that unity itself is not even something that is[4c]. On the contrary, even among plants and animals organisms are generated by others which are complete; for it is man that generates man, and it is not the seed that comes first.

It is also absurd to regard place as coexistent with mathe-matical volumes: for place is relative to individual things[40], and hence they are separate in place; whereas mathematical entities are nowhere. And it is absurd to say that they must be somewhere if one cannot say where.

Moreover, those who say that things[1a] come from their elements and that this is true first of all about numbers should have distinguished the various ways in which one thing may come from another, and then they could have said in which way number comes from its first principles.

Is it by mixture? But some things cannot be mixed; and

* xii.7.1072b31.

when they are, they produce something different. Thus, the one would not be a separate or distinct nature, as these men want it to be.

Or is it by juxtaposition[64g], like a syllable? But this implies position, and then it would be possible to have an idea[169a] of unity, and another of plurality, which are independent[73a] of each other. Number would then be a unit plus a plurality, or unity and inequality.

30   Besides, some things are generated in such a way that their elements inhere in the product, but of others this is not true. In which of these ways is number derived? It is only things that are generated that can come from things that inhere in them. Does number come thus, as from seed? But nothing can be detached from unity, which is indivisible.

Or does number come as one contrary[50] replaces its other? But such a change implies a basic material which persists in the change.† Now, since some regard[64] unity as
1092b contrary to plurality, and others regard unity as contrary to inequality (one being equal), number is apparently being treated as coming from contraries. There must, accordingly, be something else which persists and from which, in addition to the contrary, the compound is or has come to be. And why is it that whereas other things perish which come from or have contraries, even when they exhaust tne entire contrariety, number does not? They say nothing about this. But whether a contrary be inherent in the compound or not, it is destructive of the compound; for example, [according to Empedocles] strife destroys the primordial mixture; though really it ought not do so, since it is not to the mixture that strife is contrary.

Thus, there is no clarification[72e] of the way in which numbers are responsible[83a] for primary being or for any
10 being. Is it as limits[72b] (as points are limits of spatial magnitude)? It was in this sense that Eurytus determined the number of anything; for he computed the number of a man or that of a horse or of any living being by outlining

† xii.2.1069b3-9; *Physics* i.7.

its shape with pebbles, as one would number the sides of a triangle or of a square.

Or are men and other things harmonies, being composed of ratios[90] of numbers? In that case, how could their attributes also be numbers, such as white, sweet, hot? Clearly, it is not the numbers, then, that are the essential being[26] of or responsible[83a] for the form[91]; for the ratio is the essential being, whereas the number is the matter. The essential being, for example, of flesh or bone, is number only in this way: three parts of fire and two of earth. And a number, whatever number it is, is always a number of some- 20 thing, for example, of parts of fire or earth or of units; but the essential being is the relative amounts[6d] in the mixture, and this is no longer a number, but a ratio of mixture of numbers, whether these are corporeal or of any other sort.

Number, then, whether number in general or the number consisting of abstract units, is not responsible for things, whether as agent[34] or as matter[84], as ratio[90] or as form[20]—nor, indeed, as their wherefor[96].

6

One might also raise the question why it should be good to have things compounded in such a way that a number, either one that is readily calculable or a complicated one, will express its structure. Honey-water is no more salutary when it is mixed in the proportion of three times three; in fact, it would be more beneficial if it were well diluted in no particular ratio than it is when well proportioned, but too 30 strong. Besides, the ratios of mixtures are not simple numbers, but additions of different numbers: three parts of *A* to two parts of *B*; not three times two. For in any multiplication there is a single factor; thus, the product of one, two, and three must be divisible by one, and the product of four, five, and six, by four; and so forth. The number of fire, then, cannot be the product of two, five, three, and six, if the number of water is two times three; [for then water would be 1093a a factor in fire].

And if all things must share[92] in "number," it must follow that many diverse things must be the same and that the same number must belong to two different things. Is number then, fundamental[83] in things, and is it because of its number that a thing[188c] is; or is this hidden in obscurity? For example, the revolutions of the sun have a certain number, as do also those of the moon and even the life and prime of each animal. What is there, then, to prevent some of these numbers from being squares and others cubes, some equal and others double? For there is nothing to prevent this; but they must circle around within these forms, if all things supposedly share in number. And it was supposed possible for diverse things[76] to fall under the same number. Hence, if the same number belonged[3b] to certain things, these would be the same, since they would have had the same form[20] of number; for example, sun and moon would be the same.

But how do numbers explain[83] things? To be sure, there are seven vowels, seven harmonic chords, seven stars in the Pleiades, every seven years certain animals shed their teeth (though others do not), and seven were the heroes against Thebes. Is it, then, because the number happens[101c] to be the sort[5] it is that the heroes were therefore seven or the stars of the Pleiades are seven? Or may not the heroes have been seven because there were seven gates or for some other reason; and are not the stars of the Pleiades seven because we count them thus, as we count twelve in the Greater Bear, whereas others count more in both?

It is even said that Xi, Psi, and Zeta are chords and that they are three because there are three chords. But these men ignore altogether that there might be a thousand letters of this sort; for *Gr* might be combined in one symbol. But if each of the three double consonants is equal to two single consonants, and no other is so, and if the reason is that there are three places in each of which one letter is pronounced directly before *s*, then it is for this reason that there are only three double consonants; but not because there are three chords, for there are more than three chords, but there cannot be more than three double consonants. These men, therefore, are like the old Homeric scholars who see small resemblances, but fail to see significant ones.

Some also say that there are many cases of this sort: that the middle strings are represented by nine and eight; that the epic verse has seventeen syllables, the same as the 30 number assigned to the two strings; and that the scansion is nine syllables in the right and eight in the left half of the 1093b line. Also, that the distance in the letters from Alpha to Omega is equal to that from the lowest note of the flute to the highest and that the number of this note is equal to the whole choir of heaven. But it must be noted that no one could have difficulty in stating coincidences of this sort and even in discovering them in the realm of the eternal, since they can be traced even in the realm of the perishing.

However, the natures extolled in numbers, along with those contrary to them and together with mathematical features in general, as some describe them and think that they explain nature, seem, when we investigate them in this way, to disappear; for none of them is a "factor"[83] in 10 any of the ways we have distinguished * with reference to the "beginnings"[82]. But this much these men do, indeed, make evident, that goodness[98a] prevails[82f], that the odd, the straight, the equal, and the powers of certain numbers belong in the column of the beautiful; for the seasons and a number of a certain sort go together, and all the correspondences they collect on the basis of mathematical considerations have this validity[11]. This is why they are like coincidences[122]: they are accidents[3a]; but the correspondences are all appropriate to one another and are one by analogy. For there is in each category of being that which is analogous: as the straight is in length, so is the level in surface, perhaps the odd in number, and the white in color. 20

However, it is not by the ideal[20] numbers that musical facts and the like are explained; for equal numbers in music

* v.1, 2.

differ from one another in form[20], since even their units do. Consequently, it is not for these reasons, at least, that we posit ideas[20].

These, then, are the consequences which follow; and even more might be brought together. But the many troubles which these men have with the generation of numbers, and their inability to bring them together in any coherent way, seem to indicate that mathematical entities are not separate from sensible things, as some would have them be, and that they are not the first principles.

ANALYTICAL INDEX OF
TECHNICAL TERMS

I. BEING

1. ὄν, *ens*, *existens*, being: defined, v.7; vi.2.1026a32–b2; ix.10.
1051a34–b2; Democritus, i.4.985b4–10; iv.5.1009a29; unity, i.5.
986b, 6.987b23, 7.988b2; iii.1.996a4–9, 3.998b10–999a23, 4.
999b26, 1001a4–b25; iv.2; v.10.1018a35; vii.4.1030a1–13, 6.
1031b1–1032a11, vii.16; viii.6; x.1, 2, 3.1054b19; xi.1.1059b24–
34, 2.1060a36–b6; xii.4.1070b7; xiv.2; Parmenides, 1.5.986b27–
987a2; good, i.7.988b10, 12; xii.7.1072a28, 9.1075a9; Pythagoreans, i.8.990a4; becoming, ii.2.994a28; iii.4.1000b16; iv.5.
1010a20, 8.1012b28; ix.10.1051b28–30; xi.6.1062b24–33, 8.
1064b23–26, 1065a14; xii.2.1069b19; first, ii.2.994b7; being-
itself, iii.4.1001a4–b25; ix.10.1051b29, 35; nonbeing, iii.4.
1001a32, 6.1003a4; iv.2.1003b10, 1004b28, 4.1007b27, 28, 1008a,
5.1009a32, 34, 1010a4, 7.1011b25–29, 1012a7; vii.4.1030a25,
26; x.3.1054b21; xi.6.1062b24–33, 11.1067b27; xii.10.1076a2;
xiii.5.1079b29; xiv.2.1089a; bodily, iii.4.1001b7–25; mathematics, iii.5; xiii.6.1080a18; as being, iv.1, 2; vi.1, 4.1028a1–6;
xi.3, 7; axioms, iv.3, 7; priority, v.11.1018b37; categories of
(*see also* 4–6, 25–35), v.28; vi.2.1026a35–b1; vii.1, 3.1029a21;
ix.1.1045b27–33; xi.9.1065b8, 14; xiv.2.1089a14, 6.1093b19;
accidental (*see also* 2, 3), vi.2.1027a11, 4.1027b17; xi.8; as true
(*see also* 7, 8), vi.4; ix.10; xi.8; knowledge, subject, vii.4.1029b10,
6.1031b1–28, 13.1038b5; primary being, vii.16; x.2.1053b18;
xi.2.1060b1–6; potential, actual (*see also* 9–11), ix.1.1045b32,
4.1047b8, 8.1049b20; xi.9.1065b6, 22; xii.2.1069b15; xiii.3.
1078a30, 31; definite, x.3.1054b25, xiii.8.1084a30; xiv.1.1087a35,
1088a28; necessary, xi.5.1062a21, 8.1065a5; xii.7.1072b10;
infinite, xi.10.1066b2; essential attributes of (*see* 12–24)

traits, iii.1.995b26, 4.1007a8–b18; iv.5.1010b21; vii.5.1030b21; x.1.1052b13; xi.4.1061b26; xiii.3.1078a5, 25; rest, iv.5.1010a35; factors, v.2.1013b4, 36; being, etc., v.6, 7, 9, 12, 15, 30; vi.2, 3; vii.6.1031b25; xi.8.1065a1; impossible, ix.4.1047b11; x.5.1056a11, 6.1056b5; change, etc., xi.9.1065b20, 34, 10.1066b21, 12.1068a31; xii.10.1075b4; perplexities, xiii.9; xiv.1.1087b19, 2.1088b32, 4.1091a37, b22; number, xiii.7.1081b20; xiv.6.1093a11

4. τί, *quid, aliquid*, something, what: contrasts, i.5.986b1, 4; being, unity, i.6.987b23, 8.989a28, b12, 9.992a8, b11; iii.1.996a7, 4.1001a5–b25; iv.2.1003b27, 4.1006a19, 21, b17, 5.1010a18–20; vii.1.1028a30; viii.6.1045b1; x.2.1054a7, 18, 25; xi.3.1061a22; xii.2.1069b9, 3.1069b36, 8.1084a30; xiv.1.1085a35, 2.1089b8; independent, i.9.991a1; xi.10.1066b2; particular, i.9.990b5; iii.3.999a6; v.14.1020b15, 19, 18.1022a29, 32; vi.1.1026a23–32; vii.7.1032a14, 18, 13.1038b33; x.1.1052b12, 10.1059a13; xii.3. 1070a29; xiii.7.1081a30; xiv.2.1089b30; material, form, i.9. 991b14; iii.4.999a33; vii.4.1030a2; ix.7.1049a35; beginning, principle, ii.2.994a1; xiv.1.1087a33; definite, iv.4.1008a34, 7.1012a14, 8.1012b29; xii.10.1075a18; respect, v.9.1018a12; unit, v.13.1020a8; and appearance, v.29.1024b24; category, predicate, vi.2.1026a36; vii.3.1029a20, 24; ix.1.1045b33; whole, vii.17.1041b16; actuality, ix.6.1048a27, 8.1050a1; other, x.8. 1057b35; "idea," plurality, xiii.4.1079b10, 9.1085b9, 10.1087a6

4a. τόδε, τοδί, *hoc*, this: particular, i.1.981a8, 8.990a22; vii.7. 1032a14, 15.1039b25; x.9.1058b12; xi.5.1062a3; sensible, i.9. 990b1, 8; iii.2.997b35; xiii.2.1077a8, 4.1079a4, 10.1087a20, 21; xiv.3.1090b12; in change, etc., ii.2.994a3, 22; vii.8.1033b3, 4; viii.3.1043b17; xi.11.1067b30; xii.2.1069b11, 5.1071a19; syllable, iii.6.1002b19; vii.17.1041b26; being, iv.4.1006a30; v.6.1017a12, 13; vii.1.1028a15, 4.1030a15, 5.1030b18, 11.1036b24, 13.1038b24, 26; viii.6.1045a2; xi.9.1065b10, 1066a16; fact, event, v.2. 1013b12, 30.1025a23; vi.3.1027a33; number, v.15.1020b35; xiv.6.1093a3; beginning, vi.2.1027a15; condition, matter, form, vii.7.1032b7, 19, 20, 8.1033b5–29, 1034a6, 10.1035b29, 1036a2, 11.1036b23, 17.1041a26, b2, 6, 7; viii.1.1042a29, 4.1044b19; x.1.1052b13, 16; potential, ix.4.1047b5, 6.1049a19, 24; xiv.2. 1089b17; moment, xii.9.1075a9; category, xiv.2.1089a11, 14, 17, b32

4b. τόδε τι, *hoc, hoc aliquid*, this-something: primary being,

9.1065b17, 11.1067b33; being, i.8.989b7; iv.4.1007b26; v.7; vi.2.1026a35, vi.4; ix.10; xi.8.1065a21–26; philosophy, discourse, iv.2.1004b17, 3.1005a30, iv.4, 7; xi.5.1062a36, b1; appearance, iv.5, 6; and false, iv.4, 5, 7, 8; v.12, 29; vi.4; ix.10; xi.5, 6; mathematical, xiii.2.1077a15, 18, 3.1077b31, 33, 35, 8.1083b14, 9.1086a2, 10.1087a14; xiv.3.1090a36; eternal primary being, xiv.2.1088b24, 4.1091b20

7a. ἀλήθεια, *veritas*, truth: philosophy, i.3.983a3, 984b10, 7. 988a20; ii.1; iv.3.1005b3, 5.1009b37; xiii.4.1078b13; difficulty, iii.3.998a21; knowledge, opinion, iv.4.1008b29, 31; change, xi.6.1063a12; fact, xiii.7.1081b1, 8.1084b21

7b. ἀληθεύειν, *verum dicere, verificare*, iv.4.1008a27–b12, 5. 1010a8–9, 6.1011b16, iv.7; ix.10; xi.5, 6, 12.1068a12

7c. ἀληθινός, *verus*, genuine, xiv.4.1091a37

8. ψεῦδος, *falsum*, falsehood, the false: defined, v.29; and truth (*see* 7); not being (*see* 1b); impossible, ix.4.1047b12–14; primary being, xi.2.1060b6; abstraction, number, xiii.3.1078a17–21, 9.1086a16

8a. ψεύδεσθαι, *mentiri*, be mistaken, tell lies, i.2.983a3; iv.3. 1005b12, 31, 4.1008a27–b12, iv.7; v.29.1024b34; ix.3.1047a13, ix.10; xi.5, 6.1063b21, 34; xiii.3.1078a34

9. ἐνέργεια, *actus*, activity, operation, actuality, act: defined, ix.6; principles, iii.1.996a11; prior, good, v.14.1020b20; ix.8, 9; xiv.4.1092a4; movement, v.15.1021a14–25, 20.1022b4, 21. 1022b18; ix.1.1046a1–4, 2.1047a17–b5, 6.1048b8, 18–35; xi.9; constituents, v.26.1023b34; being, material, form, primary being, viii.1.1042a28, viii.2, 3, 6; ix.6.1048b9, 10.1051a35; xi.2.1060a21; xiii.1.1076a10; xiv.1.1088b2, 2.1088b26, 1089b31; incomposites, ix.10.1051b28, 31; contraries, infinite, xi.6. 1063b29, 10.1066b11; change, xii.2, 5; eternal prime mover, xii.6, 7; knowledge, xiii.10.1087a15–25

9a. ἐνεργεῖν, *agere, operari, actuari*, act, operate, exercise, become actual, v.2, 14, 15; ix.3.1046b29, 30, 1047a8, 5.1047b34, 8. 1049b13, 1050a18, b22, 29; xi.9.1065b23, 1066a1; xii.6, 7. 1072b22; xiv.2.1088b19

9b. ὂν ἐνεργείᾳ, *ens actu*, actual being, ix.8.1049b23, 25; xi.9. 1065b6; xii.2.1069b16, 20, 7.1072b8

9c. ἔργον, *opus, operatio*, activity, action, practice, working, i.3.984a12, 8.990a1, 11; ii.1.993b21; iii.2.996b7; iv.2.1003b3; v.2.1013b3, 4.1015a9; vii.4.1029b5, 1030b2, 11.1037a15; xii.1.

1069a25; and definition, vii.10.1035b17, 11.1036b31; xiii.9. 1086b5; being, ix.1.1045b34; end, ix.8.1050a21–34; fact, xii.7. 1072a22; xiii.9.1086a9; good, beautiful, xiii.3.1078a35

9d. ἐργαζόμενον, *opus*, go about doing, i.9.991a23; xiii.5.1079b27

9e. πρὸ ἔργου, προύργου, *prae opere*, profitable, important, i.3.983b4; iii.1.995a28; iv.2.1003b26; vii.4.1029b3, 6.1031a16, 12.1037b10

9f. πάρεργον, *accessorium*, incidental, xii.9.1074b36; περίεργον, *superfluum*, futile, vii.11.1036b23, 12.1038a21, 32

10. ἐντελέχεια, *endelechia, actus, perfectio*, actuality, fulfillment: and indefinite, infinite, iv.4.1007b28; xi.10.1066b18; and contraries, iv.5.1009a36; being, becoming, movement, primary being, v.4.1015a19, 7.1017a1–9; vii.13.1038b6, 1039a3–17, 16. 1040b12; viii.3.1044a9; ix.1.1045b35, 2.1047a30, b2, 7.1049a5, 8.1050a23; xi.9.1065b14–35, 1066a27, 29; xiii.3.1078a30; priority, v.11.1019a7–14; vii.9.1034b17; known state, vii.10.1036a7; first, xii.5.1071a36, 8.1074a36; not units in dyad, xiii.8.1084b22

11. δύναμις, *potestas, potentia*, power, potency, potentiality: defined, v.12; experience, i.1.981a1; principles, iii.1.996a11, 6.1002b32–1003a5; philosophy, iv.2.1004b24; contraries, iv.5. 1009a34; x.4.1055a31; xi.6.1063b29, 10.1066b30; factors, v.2. 1014a21, 24, 4.1014b28, 1015a18; being, material, form, v.7. 1017a1–9, 10.1018a30, 26.1023b34; vi.2.1026b1; vii.9.1034a34; viii.1.1042a28, 2.1042b10, 1043a15, 5.1044b29–1045a6, 6. 1045a23–b23; ix.1.1045b32–35, ix.7, 10.1051a35; xi.2.1060a21, 11.1067b27; priority, v.11.1018b21–26, 1019a7–14, 19.1022b2; vii.9.1034b19; xii.10.1075b32; and art, vi.1.1025b22, 2.1027a5–8; vii.7.1032a28, b21, 8.1033b8; xi.7.1064a13; primary being, vii.3. 1029a13, 13.1039a3–7, 16.1040b6, 12, 14; xiv.1.1088b1, 2; movement, ix.1–5 (cf.1.1045b35–1046b4), 6.1048a25–30, b8; v.15.1021a14–30; xi.9; and act, ix.6.1048a30–b17, ix.8, 9, 10.1051b28; application, validity, x.1.1052b7; xiv.6.1093b16; change, xii.2, 4, 5; xiv.2.1089a28–30; and eternal prime mover, xii.6.1071b13, 24, 1072a3, 9, 7.1073a8, 9.1074b20, 28; sense, knowledge, xiii.2.1076b2, 10.1087a15–25; unit, xiii.8.1048b21; numbers, xiv.6.1093b14

11a. δύνασθαι, *posse, valere*, can, be able: to explain, etc., i.1.981b, 2.982a10, 7.988b18, 9.990b3; ii.1.993a31, b6, 3.993a9; iv.6. 1011a7, 7.1012a19; xiii.4.1078b35; to be independent, iii.3. 999a18; v.6.1016b2; vii.10.1035b23; to act, move, v.2.1014a8,

INDEX OF TECHNICAL TERMS

7.1017a4, 6, 14.1020b21; vii.9.1034a15, 20, b5, 11.1036b31; ix.3.1046b30, 31, 1047a17, 5.1048a, 8.1049b14, 1050b32, ix.9; xi.9.1065b29, 1066a10, 30, 12.1068b23; and power, v.12.1019a25, 30, 32, b14, 15.1021a17; ix.1.1046a5; to speak falsely, v.29. 1025a7; to produce, become, vii.7.1032b9; xii.2.1069b14, 5. 1071a11; xiii.2.1077a35, 36; xiv.3.1091a10, 6.1093a26, b27; eternal prime mover, xii.6.1071b15, 23, 26; dialectic, xiii.4. 1078b25

11b. δυνατόν, *possibile*, possible, potential, capable: defined, v.12; genesis, i.8.990a10; iii.4.999b6; not infinite regress, ii.2. 994a3; "intermediates," iii.2.997b30; and actual, iii.6.1003a2, 4; xiv.2.1088b19; being, not being, v.7.1017b8, 10.1018a26; vii.7.1032a21; x.2.1053b17; movement, power, vi.1.1025b27; ix.1.1046a20, 2.1046b23, 3.1046b35, 1047a20–26, ix.4–6, 8, 9.1051a6; xi.9.1065b33, 1066a19, 21, 12.1068a23; not separate, vii.1.1028a24; x.2.1053b19; xiii.2.1076b12, 1077a4, 13, 3. 1077b14, 28, 8.1083b16; xiv.1.1088a16, b14, 2.1090a19; opposites, x.5.1056a13; xi.5.1062a34, 6.1063b31; perfected, xii.8. 1074b11

11c. ὂν δυνάμει, *ens in potentia*, potential being, iv.4.1007b28; vii.16.1040b12; viii.6.1045a30; ix.7.1049a6, 8.1049b24, 9. 1051a29; xi.9.1065b6, 22; xii.2.1069b15, 19, 6.1071b19; xiv.2. 1088b

11d. ἀδυναμία, *impotentia*, incapacity: defined, v.12; and power, ix.1.1046a29–31; privation, x.1055b8, 10.1058b27

11e. ἀδυνατεῖν, *non posse*, be unable, vii.11.1036b7, 12.1038a13

11f. ἀδύνατον, *impossibile*, impossible, what cannot be done: defined, v.12; forms, "ideas," i.6.987b6, 8.989b13, 9.991a18, b1–3, 992a1, 10, b19; iii.2.997b20, 22, 998a9, 19, 4.1001b2, 6.1002b32; xiii.5.1079b22, 36, 8.1084b19; infinite regress, ii.2. 994b4, 6; iv.4.1007b1; movement, becoming, iii.1.995a32, 4. 999b8, 11, 15, 6.1003b5; vii.7.1032b30, 9.1034a14, 16, b6; vii.3.1044a13; xi.11.1067b30, 12.1068a20, b21; xii.5.1071b6, 8.1074a24; contradictories, iii.2.996b30; iv.3.1005b, 4.1006a, 1007b18, 6.1011b16, 20–22, 7.1012a11, 8.1012a30, b1, 2, 9, 28; xi.5.1062a18, 19; demonstration of everything, iii.2.997a7; iv.4.1006a8, 6.1011a15; predication, iii.3.998b24, 4.999a31; iv.4.1007a14; v.29.1024b18; vii.15.1040a26; xi.2.1060a6; principles, iii.4.1000b27, 31, 6.1002b32; xiv.1.1087a32; and necessary, iv.4.1006b32, 5.1015a22, b9; v.5.1015b9; vi.2.1027a16;

327

18. ὕστερον, *posterius*, later, posterior, after, derivative: philosophers, i.3.984a13, 8.989b20, 9.991a17; iii.5.1002a11; xiii.5. 1079b21; xiv.4.1091b11; elements, i.8.988b34, 989a15–18; proposition, truth, ii.1.993b27, 994b19; difficulties, i.10.993a27; iii.1. 995a28; as attribute, iii.1.995b22; iv.2.1005a16; in series, iii.3. 999a6–14; ix.7.1049a21; being, unity, iii.5.1002a31; v.6.1016b35; vii.3.1029a31; factors, v.2.1013b32; part, whole, vii.10, 12. 1038a34; potential, actual, ix.8.1050a5, 9.1051a18, 32; movement, xi.9.1065b22, 35, 10.1067a34, 12.1068a35, b35; xii.6. 1071b8, 7.1073a12, 10.1075b32; soul, xii.3.1070a24, 6.1072a2; mathematical, xiii.2.1077a17–20, 6.1080b12, 7.1081, 1082a27, b14, 8.1083a7, 1084b, 9.1085a7; xiv.3.1090b16; categories, xiii.8.1083a10; xiv.1.1088a24, b4

18a. ἔσχατος, *ultimus*, last, ultimate, extreme: conclusion, end, ii.2.994a11–18, b11; v.10, 16, 26; vii.7.1032b9; ix.8.1050a24; x.4.1055a14; genus, species, iii.3.998b14–999a23, 4.999a31; v.24; xi.1.1059b26, 35; limit, iii.4.999b7, 1000b2; v.11, 17; vii.7.1032b28; xiv.3.1090b5, 9; belief, iv.3.1005b33; elements, v.3; subject, v.6, 8; vii.3.1029a24; ix.7.1049a34; matter, form, vii.10.1035b30; viii.6.1045b18; xii.3.1069b36; contrariety, x.4. 1055a, 9.1058b10; xi.12.1068b29; infinite, xi.10.1067a28

19. γένος, *genus*, (inclusive) kind, genus, class: defined, v.28; of explanatory factors, i.3.983b5; v.2; beings, i.8.989b26; iii.2. 997a21, 3.998a32, b4, 10; iv.2.1003b18–22, 1004a5, 3.1005a21–26, 34, b9; vi.1.1025b8, 12, 16, 19, 1026a21, 24, 4.1028a1; vii. 8.1034a1; xi.3.1060b34, 7.1064a2, 6, b8, 9.1065b15, 1066a10; xiv.1.1088a13, 2.1089b28; "ideas," mathematical entities, i.9. 990b17, 991b28, 992a10–24, b12–18; x.6.1057a3; xiii.1.1076a19, 2.1076b39, 4.1079a13, b11, 9.1085a7; xiv.5.1092b33; species, i.9.991a31; iii.3.998b4–14; iv.2.1003b21, 22; v.6, 10, 24, 25, 28; vii.4.1030a12, 14.1039a26, b11, 15.1040a20; viii.1.1042a14; x.3.1054b30, 7.1057b7, x.8; xi.1.1059b34–39, 2.1060a5; xiii.5. 1079b34, 35, 9.1085a24; primary beings, iii.1.995b16, 2.997a1, b15; iv.2.1005a17; v.6.1015b33; vii.3.1028b35; viii.1.1042a14, 15, 22; xii.1.1069a27; principles, beginnings, elements, iii.1. 995b27–31, 3.998a20–999b23; iv.2.1005a2; v.3, 11; xii.4.1070b20, 5.1071a25; subjects, iii.2.997a6, 9, 29; iv.2.1004b22; and definition, iii.3.998b4–14; vii.7.1033a4, vii.12; science, iv.2.1003b35; xi.7.1064a19, b2, 4; and predication, iv.2.1004a13; v.6, 15, 16, 22; unity, being, v.6; viii.6.1045b6; x.1.1052b18, 2.1053b20–24,

1054a5, 10, 3.1054b27–1055a2; xi.1.1059b24–34; and difference, v.9; viii.2.1042b32; x.4, 5.1056b1; xi.1.1059b33, 3.1061b17; opposites, v.10; x.5.1055b36, x.7; xi.12.1068b33; xii.5.1071a36; power, ix.8.1049b9; perishable, x.10.1058b28, 1059a10; of questions, xi.1.1059b20

19a. συγγενής, ὁμογενής, *cognatus*, alike, innate, homogeneous, iii.1.995b12; ix.5.1047b31; x.1.1053a24, 7.1057b29; xi.10. 1067a12; xiii.1.1076a18

20. εἶδος, *species*, (included) kind, species, idea, form, general form: art, knowledge, i.1.981a10; v.23; iv.5.1010a25; vii.7.1032b, vii.8, 9.1034a24; of being, i.3.983b19; iv.2.1003b34, 1005a17; xi.9.1065b14; "doctrine" of "ideas," i.6, 7.988b1–6, i.9; iii.1. 995b17, 2.997b1–14, 3.999a24–b24; xii.1.1069a35; xiii.4, 5; and indefinite, i.8.989b13, 18; iv.6.1011b12; factors, ii.2.994a2, b27; iii.2.996b8, 997a3; v.2; viii.4.1044a36, b12; xii.10.1075b27; principles, iii.1.996a1, 4.999b25–1000a4; xi.2.1060a22, 12. 1068b31; xii.8.1074a32, 10.1075b1, 19; and "intermediates," iii.2.997b, 998a; xi.1; and genera (*see* 19); indivisible, iii.3.999a3, 4; primary being, iii.6.1002b; v.4, 18, 24; vii.2.1028b20, 3. 1029a6, 29, 6.1031b14, 15, 7.1033a3, vii.8–11, 14.1039a26, 27, b18, 16.1040b27–34, 17.1041b8; viii.1; xi.1; xii.5.1071a24; xiii.2.1077a32, 10.1087a6; elements, v.3; xiii.10.1086b25; unity, v.6, 9; x.1, 3; xii.10.1075b35; separate, v.8.1017b26; xi.2. 1060b26–28; and other, v.9; x.8, 9; parts, etc., v.16, 17, 19; xi.10.1067a18, 29; and becoming, change, movement, v.18; viii.5.1044b22, 33; x.4.1055b11–13; xi.11.1067b9, 12.1068a22; xii.2.1069b34, xii.3–5, 6.1071b14–17; and matter, v.28; vii.11; ix.7.1049a35, 8.1050a15, 16; xii.3; and numbers, vii.2.1028b24–27; xii.10.1075b27, 30; xiii.6.1080a18, 22, 7.1081a9, 21, 1082b26, 32, 8.1083b3, 7, 1084a, 9.1085a9, 12, 1086a1–18; xiv.3.1090b33, 4.1091b26, 27, 1092a8, 5.1092b25, 6.1093a12, b21–24; nature, vii.7.1032a24; power, act, ix.1.1046a9, 8.1049b18, 29, 1050a4–6, b2; difference, x.4.1055a8, 26; perishable, x.10.1058b31, 1059a10–14; and privation, xi.3.1061a24; xii.4; beauty, xiii.3.1078a36; relatives, xiv.1.1088a26, 2.1089b14

20a. εἰδητικός, archetypal, xiii.9.1086a5, 8; xiv.2.1088b34, 3. 1090b35

21. ὅλον, *totum*, whole: defined, v.26; nature, i.3.984a31, 9.992b8; iv.3.1005a32, 5.1010a28; xii.8.1074a3, 10.1075a11; truth, ii.1. 993b6; and parts, iv.2.1005a17; v.2, 11, 20, 23–27; viii.4.1044b19,

6.1045a8–12; ix.6.1048a33; xi.10.1067a8; xii.1.1069a19, 20,
9.1075a6; xiii.8.1084b2–13; unity, v.6, 8; x.1; and concepts,
vii.10; statement, xi.3.1061a23, 25, 5.1062b6; good, xii.9.
1075a9, 10.1075a25; xiv.5.1092a12; mathematics, xiii.2.1077a28,
1080b18, 8.1084b30
21a. σύνολον, *synolon, totum*, composite: material, form, iii.1.
995b35, 3.999a32, b16, 24; vii.3.1029a5, 9.1035a6, 21, vii.10,
11; x.9.1058b8; xi.2.1060b24; xiii.2.1077b8; true, false, vi.4.
1027b19
21b. συγκεῖσθαι, *componi*, be composed, combined, put together,
iii.3.998a24, 29, b2, 5.1002b2; iv.2.1004b30; v.3, 6, 25, 29;
vi.4.1027b21; vii.14.1039b6; ix.10; x.3.1054b5, 7.1057b; xii.4.
1070b6; xiii.2.1076b18, 7.1081b29, 1082a, 8.1083b12, 15, 9.
1085b34; xiv.2.1088b15
22. μερισμός, *partitio*, relation, vi.4.1027b20, 22; μέρος, *pars*,
μόριον, *pars, particula*, part, aspect, κατὰ μέρος, *particulariter*,
about some part: defined, v.25; elements, i.4.985a28; iii.3.
998b2; iv.5.1009a29; v.3.1014a30, 31; vii.2; xii.10.1075b6;
xiii.8.1084b20; astronomical, i.5.986a5, 8.990a1, 23; iv.5.1010a30;
viii.1.1042a11; xiii.2.1077a3; particular, i.8.989b12; v.14.
1020b16, 19; truth, ii.1.993b6; in series, ii.2.994a18; philosophy,
iv.1, 2.1004a3, 8, 17, 3.1005a29; xi.3.1060b32, 4.1061b22, 25,
33; of a pair, antithesis, iv.8.1012b11, 13; v.6.1015b25, 27;
ix.6.1048b5; x.7.1057a25; of definition, v.2.1013a29; vii.15.
1040a18; viii.1.1042a18–21; xiii.4.1079b5; and whole (*see* 21);
of living being, v.4, 6, 8, 18; vii.2, 16.1040b5–16; viii.1.1042a9,
10; xi.7.1064a27; xiii.2.1077a22; and complete, v.6, 16, 19, 27;
process, vii.7.1032b21–32, 9.1034a9–30; xi.11.1067b4, 7; and
concepts, vii.10, 11; infinite, xi.10.1066b12, 16; xii.7.1073a6;
number, form, xiii.7.1081b18, 23, 32, 8.1084a, b, 9.1085b12–22,
32, 33; xiv.1.1088a26
22a. ὁμοιομερής, *similium partium*, composed of similar parts,
i.3.984a14, 7.988a28, 9.992a7
23. εἶναι, *esse, existere, subsistere* (the property of existing as
"substance"), be, exist: defined, v.7; viii.2; "ideas," mathematics, i.9; iii.2.998a16, 6.1002b30; xii.3.1070a28; xiii.1, 3.
1077b13, 4.1079b10, 5.1079b16, 1080a2–8, 8.1083a14; and
truth, ii.1.993b31; iv.5.1010a17; xi.6; becoming, ii.2.994a27,
b1; iii.2.996a25, 3.999b3–16, 4.1001a17, 6.1003a4, 5; iv.5.
1010a19, 27; v.4, 5; vii.17.1041a32; viii.5; ix.4; xi.6; xii.2.

II. CATEGORIES

25a. κατηγορεῖν, *praedicare*, predicate: number, i.5.987a18, 9.992b3; and material, iii.1.995b35, 3.999a33; vii.3.1029a21, 22; viii.2.1043a6; ix.7.1049a35; species, genus, iii.3.998b14–999a23; being, unity, iii.4.1001a29; v.7, 10; vii.1.1028a13, 33, 4.1030a20; x.2.1053b19, 21, 1054a16; xi.2.1060b5; xiii.8.1084b31; common, iii.6.1003a10, 16; xii.4.1070b1; axiom, iv.4.1007b18; xi.6.1063a25, b20, 26; general, v.26; vii.13.1039a1, 15.1040a22–26; xiii.9. 1065b8; not element, xiv.1.1088b4–13

26. οὐσία, *substantia*, (*indivisum in se et divisum ab aliis*), primary being: defined, v.8; vii.3.1028b33–36; viii.1; ix.1.1045b27–32; xii.3.1070a9–13; being, i.5.986b8, 6.987b22, 25, 7.988b13, 8.989b7; iii.1.996a7; v.9.1018a14, 27.1024a20; vii.10.1035b13; ix.7.1049a36, 8.1049b11, 1050a4–1051a3; xi.7.1064a35, b10, 11; xii.7.1072b7, 10.1075b38, 1076a1; xiii.2.1077a19, b1–11, 6. 1080a16; and matter, sensible, body, i.3.983b10, 4.985b10, 9.992b1–7; iii.4.999b14; v.24.1023b2; vii.2, 3; viii.1, 4; ix.6. 1048b9, 7.1049a27; xiii.1, 2.1077a35, 3.1077b12, 6.1080b18, 9.1086a23; xiv.1.1088b2; and mathematics, i.5.987a18, 19, 9.992a8, 10, b1–7; iii.1.996a12–15, 2.997a25–998a19, 4.1001b3, iii.5; vii.2; viii.3.1043b32–1044a14; xii.1.1069a35, 36; xiii.1–3, 6, 7.1082b37, 8.1084a16, b10, 9.1086a25; xiv.3.1090b9, 11, 4.1092a8, 5.1092a11, b9; change, becoming, i.8.989b3, 23, 9. 992a26; iii.5.1002a28–b11; iv.5.1009a37, 1010a27; vi.1.1025b20, 27, 1026a28, 29; vii.7–9; viii.4; xi.12; xii.3–5; xiii.2.1077a27; "ideas," i.9; iii.2.997b1–12, 4.999b20–23, 6.1002b; vii.2, 8; ix.8.1050b35; xii.1.1069a35, 6.1071b14, 16; xiii.1, 4, 5, 9, 10; xiv.4.1091b29; elements, i.9.992b22; xii.1.1069a29; xiii.10; principles, explanation, iii.6.1003a5–17; v.1.1013a21; xii.1. 1069a18, xii.5; xiii.10; xiv.1; difficulties, iii; xi.2; and science, philosophy, iii.2; iv.2, 3; vi.1.1025b14; xi.1.1059a26–b1, 7. 1064a9, 22; xii.1, 9.1075a2; xiii.10; order, iii.3.998b12; unity, being, iii.3.998b21, 4.1001a4–b25; v.6, 9; vii.2, 16; x.1.1052a33, 1053a19, x.2, 3.1054b1, 4; xiii.6.1080b6; xiv.1.1087b9, 1088a4, xiv.2, 4.1091b13–15; "this," iii.6.1003a9; vii.1.1028a15; soul, vii.2, 11.1037a5–10; viii.3.1043a29–b3; essential being, character, concept, definition, nature, i.3.983a27, 7.988a35, 10. 993a18; iv.6.1011b19; v.4, 27, 30; vii.4, 8.1033b17; x.2.1053b9, 3.1054b31, 9.1058b22; xi.6.1063a27; xii.6.1071b18, 20, 7.1072b22; xiii.4.1079b8, 5.1079b17, 8.1084b10, 19; xiv.5.1092b17, 18, 20; "what is," i.5.987a23, 8.988b28; v.17; vii.4.1030a19; formal

being, i.3, 4, 8; iii.5; iv.2; v.6; vii.1, 3–6, 13; viii.6; ix.7; xi.3; xii.5; xiii.2; xiv.2; 5; of numbers, magnitude, i.5.985b29, 32, 8.990a19, 27; iv.2.1004b11; v.15.1021a9; xi.3.1061a34, 10. 1066b8; xiii.8.1083a10, 9.1085a21; xiv.1.1088a17, 24, 3.1090a21, 23, 30, b4; and change, movement, iv.5.1010b20, 21; v.12, 14; xi.11.1067b9; xii.2.1069b12, 6.1071b10

35b. πάθημα, *passio*, behavior, process, i.2.982b16, 4.985b12

35c. τὸ παθητικόν, *passivum*, suffer, passive, patient, v.10.1018a33, 15.1020b30, 1021a14–25; ix.1.1046a13, 5.1048a6, 13, 15; xi.12. 1068b19

35d. ἀπαθής, *impassibilis*, without attributes, impassive, ἀπάθεια, *impassibilitas*, insusceptibility, i.9.991b26; v.12.1019a27, 31; ix.1.1046a13; xi.12.1068b20; xii.10.1075a30; first mover, xii.7. 1073a11, 8.1074a19

36. λέγειν, *dicere*, say, i.4.985a17; *et passim;* what terms "mean" and what things are "said" to be, v.1–30; explanatory factor, i.3.983a26; being, iv.2.1003a33, b5, 5.1009a32; unity, iv.2. 1004a22–25, 1005a5; λογικός, *logicus*, dialectical, abstract, logical, iv.3.1005b22; xiii.5.1080a10; xiv.1.1087b20, 21; λογικῶς, *logice*, from the standpoint of discourse, vii.4.1029b13, 1030a25, 17.1041a28; xiii.1.1069a28

36a. εἰπεῖν, *dicere*, aio, say, i.8.989b7; *et passim;* ὡς εἰπεῖν, *ut dicam*, so to speak, i.1.980a25; iii.3.998b32; iv.5.1010a30; vi.2. 1026b9, 16; vii.1.1028b7, 17.1041a28; xiii.4.1079a1, 9.1085b19; ὡς ἔπος εἰπεῖν, *ut est verisimile dicere*, so to speak, iv.5.1009b16; vii.14.1039b7

36b. εἴρειν, *dicere*, say, i.1.981a25; *et passim;* ἀπείρειν, surrender a position, xiv.4.1091b23; συνείρειν, *colligere*, make hang together, i.5.986a7; ii.3.993a10; xiv.3.1090b30, 6.1093b27

36c. διαρθροῦν, *articulare, dearticulare, corrigere*, articulate, make explicit, συνδιαρθροῦν, *articulare*, coherently articulate, i.5. 986b6, 8.989a32, b5; iii.6.1002b27; vii.17.1041b2

37. καλεῖν, *vocare*, προσαγορεύειν, *appellare*, call, i.5.985b23, 6.987b8, 8.989b29, 990a5, 992a21; ii.1.993b19; iii.2.996b9, 5.1002a14; iv.3.1005a20, 4.1006b20; v.3.1014a9, b3; vii.7. 1032b10, 15, 8.1033b5; x.8.1057b38, 1058a21; xi.1.1059b23, 12.1068b23; xiii.4.1079b2; xiv.1.1087b13

37a. ὀνομάζειν, *nominare, denominare*, expressly mention, xiii.3. 1078a35; ῥῆμα, *verbum*, word, vii.16.1040b34; ὄνομα, *nomen*, name, word, term, i.6.987b7–14; iii.4.1000a13; iv.4.1006a30;

340

(species): and mathematics, i.9.992a22; x.1.1052b33; vii.13.
1039a10; xiii.8.1083b13, 1084b1; definition, ii.2.994b21; v.10.
1018b6; classification, iii.1.995b29, 3.998b14–999a23; xi.1.
1059b36; form, vii.8.1034a8; contrariety, x.8.1058a17–21, 9.
1058b10

42. ἴδιον, *proprium*, peculiar, special, i.3.984b1, 5.987a15, 6.
987a31, b27, 8.989a22, 990a18; iv.4.1006b5, 1008a27; viii.4.
1044b3; xi.4.1061b18; xii.5.1071a14, 8.1073a18; xiii.8.1083b5,
9, 9.1086a10; xiv.3.1090b29, 5.1092a19; science, iii.2.996b34,
997a2; xi.8.1064b22; attributes, iv.2.1004b11, 15, 16; xiii.3.
1077a7; and sense perception, iv.5.1010b3, 16; primary being,
vii.9.1034b16, 13.1038b10, 23

42a. ἰδίᾳ, *singulariter*, special, especially, iv.3.1005a23; viii.1.
1042a7, 11; xiii.1.1076a15

43. καθόλου, *universale*, *universaliter*, whole, general term, generally: art, science, philosophy, i.1, 2, 6.987b3; iv.1, 3.1005a35;
vi.1.1026a23–32; ix.9.1051a27; xi.1.1059b24–27, 2.1060b20, 7.
1064b6–14; principles, iii.1.996a10, 2.997a12, 3.998b17, 999a20,
22, 4.1001a1, 6.1003a5–17; being, unity, iii.4.1001a20–22, 28;
iv.1, 2.1004b9; v.6.1060b32; x.1.1052a36, 2.1053b20; and accidents, iv.4.1007a34; v.6, 9; element, v.3; and particular (*see*
40); primary being, vii.3.1028b34, vii.13, 16.1041a4; viii.1;
x.2.1053b16; xi.2.1060b21; xii.1.1069a26–28; xiii.4.1078b30;
xiv.2.1088b26; nature, definition, vii.7.1032a22, 11.1036a28,
1037a22; xiii.4.1078b19, 29; perishable, x.10.1058b29; infinite,
xi.10.1066b22; change, explanation, xii.4, 5.1071a17; "ideas,"
mathematics, xiii.2.1077a9, 3.1077b17, 4.1078b33, 8.1084b,
9.1085a25, b8, 1086a21–b13; xiv.1.1087b17, 24

44. ὅλως, *totaliter*, *omnino*, in general, (not) at all, i.1, 2, 8, 9;
ii.2; iii.2, 5, 6; iv.4, 5; v.2–4, 6–11, 14–16, 22, 26, 27; vi.1; vii.4,
8, 10, 11, 13, 14; viii.2, 5, 6; ix.1, 3, 8, 10; x.2, 4; xi.1, 2, 5, 6, 10,
12; xii.5, 7, 10; xiii.2–4, 7–9; xiv.1, 3, 5, 6

45. τύπῳ, *typo*, briefly, vii.3.1029a7

46. φάναι, *dicere*, *repraesentare*, *aio*, speak, φάσις, *dictio*, *reprae-
sentatio*, statement, i.3.983b11; iii.1.995b9, 2.996b29; iv.6.
1011b14, 7.1011b24, 1012a14, 8.1012b9, 11; ix.10.1051b24, 25;
xi.5.1062a23, 24; *et passim*

46a. φάσκειν, *dicere*, pronounce, assert, i.3, 7.988b12, 8.989a30,
9.992a33; iii.4.1001b19; iv.5.1010a35, 6.1011a29, 8.1012a31;
et passim

46b. ἀποφαίνεσθαι, *asserere, pronunciare, enuntiare,* express oneself, proclaim, i.3.984a3, 5.986a30, b2, 11; iv.5.1009b21, 36, 1010a28; viii.1.1042b7

46c. ἀξιοῦν, *dignari, dignificare, significare,* regard as worthy, welcome, insist, demand, require, i.3.984a3, 5.986b29, 8.989a5; ii.3.995a1, 8; iv.4.1006a, b15, 5.1009a36, 6.1011a; v.29.1024b32; x.1.1053a29; xi.6.1063a7; xiii.7.1082b25, 10.1087a6

46d. διδόναι, *dare,* grant, ἀποδιδόναι, *reddere, assignare,* give, credit, speak about, explain, attribute, warrant, define, conceive, i.8.990a12, 9.990b11, 12; iv.2.1004a29, 4.1006a24; viii.6. 1045a22; x.1.1052b9; xi.1.1059a27, 7.1064a28; xiii.8.1084a35; xiv.1.1087b13, 4.1091b2, 5.1092a11; *et passim*

47. καταφάναι, *affirmare,* affirm, κατάφασις, *affirmatio,* affirmation: and deny, iii.1.995b10, 2.996b29; iv.4.1007b18–1008b2, 6.1011b20, iv.7, 8.1012b9, 11; v.7.1017a31–35; vi.4.1027b21; xi.5.1046b2–9; and "speak," ix.10.1051b24; and substantive, privation, xi.11.1067b18, 1068a6

48. ἀποφάναι, *negare,* deny, ἀπόφασις, *negatio,* negation: and "ideas," i.9.990b13; xiii.4.1079a10; and affirm (*see* 47); and primary being, iv.2.1003b10; vii.3.1029a25; of being, iv.2.1004a, 4.1007a9; xiv.2.1089b19; nothing its own negative, iv.4.1007b31; and privation, iv.6.1011b19; v.22.1022b32; ix.2.1046b13; x.5. 1056a15–30; genus, x.8.1058a23; statements, xii.8.1073a16

48a. συναπόφασις, *connegatio,* negation of both, x.5.1056a35, b2

49. ἀντίφασις, *contradictio,* contradictories, opposition: opinions, iv.3.1005b29; axiom, iv.4.1007b, 1008a25, 6.1011b16, iv.7, 8.1012b2, 10; xi.5.1062a19, 6.1063a21, 24, b24; and sense perception, iv.5.1009a24; opposition, v.10.1018a20; x.3.1054a25, 4.1055a38–b11, 7.1057a34; relation, vi.4.1027b20, 22; eventuation, ix.8.1050b; not same, other, x.3.1054b20; and change, xi.11, 12.1069a3; one, xiv.2.1089b7

49a. ἀντιλέγειν, *contradicere,* contradict, v.29.1024b34

49b. ἀντειπεῖν, *contradicere,* contradict, iii.2.996b11

50. ἐναντίον, *contrarium,* contrary, opposite: defined, v.10; beginning, end, i.2.983a12, 17; v.1.1013a1; elements, i.3.984b8; xi.10.1066b29, 1067a20; good, bad, i.4.984b32; v.14.1020b22; xiv.4.1091b31, 1092a3; and principles, explanation, i.4.985a31, 5.986b3; iii.2.996a20; iv.2.1004b27–1005a13; v.5.1015a32; x.7. 1057b23; xi.1.1059a23; xii.5.1071a37, 10.1075a28–38; xiv.1, 2.1089b6; facts, theories, i.6.988a1, 8.989a15–18; v.12.1019b23–

INDEX OF TECHNICAL TERMS

33; vii.14.1039b4; ix.10.1051b4; xiii.2.1077a14, 9.1085a15, 1086a15; states, i.8.989a29; vi.3.1027b10; and philosophy, science, iii.1.995b27, 2.996a20; iv.2.1004a1, 2, 27, b3; ix.1. 1046a4–24; xi.1.1059a22, 3.1061a10–28; xiii.4.1078b26; axiom, iv.3.1005b26–32, 5.1009a10, 6.1011a, b15–22, 7.1012a9, 8.1012b; xi.5.1061b35, 6.1063b; sense perception, iv.5.1009a22–25; xi.6. 1062b19, 1063a1; power, iv.5.1009a35; ix.1.1046a30, 5.1048a9, 22, 9.1051a4–21, 10.1051b1, 11; xi.9.1065b28; difference, opposition, v.9.1018a14; x.3.1054b32, x.4, 6.1056b36, x.7, 9.1058a30; xi.11.1068a7, 12.1068b30; change, v.5.1015a32, 9.1018a17; viii.5. 1044b25, 29; xi.10.1067a7, xi.11, 12; xii.2, 4.1070b32; xiv.4. 1091b34; form, species, vii.7.1032b2, 12.1037b20; x.8.1058a10, 14; common to, x.1.1052b27; one, many, x.2.1054a, 5.1055b30, 6.1057a5, 12–17; xi.3.1061b13; perishable, x.10; number, xiii. 8.1083b27; xiv.3.1090b2, 5.1092a33–b8, 6.1093b8

50a. ἐναντιότης, contrarietas, contrast, contrariety, i.5.986a32; iii.1.995b22; iv.2.1004a20, 21; x.3.1054b32, 4.1055a17, 22, b1, 8.1058a11, 9.1058b1; xi.6.1063b17

50b. ἐναντίωσις, contrarietas, contrariety, v.10.1018b3; x.4. 1055a5, b14, 18, 5.1055a12, x.8, 9; xi.3.1061a12, 32, b5, 13, 6.1063b28, 12.1068b18; xii.2.1069b6, 13, 33; xiv.2.1090a2

50c. ἐναντιοῦσθαι, opponere, oppose, i.9.990b22; xiii.4.1079a18

51. ἀμφισβητεῖν, διαμφισβητεῖν, dubitare, debate, quarrel, contend, oppose, i.9.993a4; iii.1.995b3; iii.2.996b27, 3.998b17; iv.4.1006a13, 5.1010a17, b20; xi.6.1062b34; xiii.1.1076a36

52. ὁμολογεῖν, confiteri, agree, admit, confirm, ὁμολογουμένως, confessae ratione, consistently, i.3.984a33, 4.985a23, 5.986a4, 8.989a3, 4, 990a3, 9.991b27; iii.4.1000a25, b18, 2.1004b30, 4.1007a12, 1008a29; vii.3.1029a33; viii.1, 2.1042b9; xi.5.1062a33, 8.1064b27; xiii.9.1086a11; xiv.4.1091a34, b23

53. ἀπολογία, responsio, defense, iii.4.1001b15

54. ἀναλογία, analogia, proportio, analogy, proportion, v.6, 9; viii.2.1043a5; ix.6.1048a36, b7; xii.4.1071a26, 33, 7.1072b1; xiii.8.1084a33; xiv.6.1093b19, 20

55. οἰκεῖον, proprium, familiar, proper, intimately related, i.5. 986b18, 8.989b22, 9.993a10; iii.3.998b25; iv.2.1004b22; v.2, 16, 29; vii.12.1038a24; viii.4.1044a18; x.9.1058a37, b22; xi.4. 1061b22, 7.1064b6, 8.1064b23; xii.8.1073a4; xiii.3.1078a16; xiv.1.1087b17, 6.1093b17

55a. ἀλλότριον, strange: object of perception, iv.5.1010b15

55b. κύριος, *principalis*, controlling, authoritative, lordly, κυρίως, *proprie*, chiefly: sense, thought, i.1.981b10; iii.2.997a12; iv.2. 1003b16, 5.1010b13, 15; xii.9.1074b19; meanings, v.4, 5, 12, 14; vi.4.1027b31; ix.1.1045b36, 8.1050b6, 10.1051b1; x.1.1052b19, 1053a5; part, aspect, v.9, 27; vii.10.1035b25; x.4.1055b22; desire, ix.5.1048a10, 12; principle, xi.2.1060a22, 7.1064b1; xii.10.1075b18, 19; xiv.1.1087b4

55c. τρόπον τινά, *quodammodo*, *aliquo modo*, in a way: factors, i.4.985a7, 7.988b7, 19, 10.993a14; xii.4.1070b32; xiii.3.1078b5; being, iv.2.1003b14; 5.1009a31; v.6, 11; vi.2.1026b14; vii.3. 1029a2; form, vii.7.1032b3, 11, 8.1034a21, 13.1039a21; ix.2. 1046b13; change, vii.11.1037a14; ix.6.1048a29; measured, x.6. 1057a11; mathematical entities, xiii.3.1077b16

56. ἁρμονία, *harmonia*, harmony, musical scale, i.5.986a; v.27. 1024a21; xiv.1.1087b35, 6.1093a14

56a. ἁρμόττειν, *congruere*, be suited to, be in harmony with, i.8.990a7; iv.5.1010a6; v.16.1022a2; xiii.7.1081a20

56b. ἐφαρμόττειν, *adaptare*, exhibit harmony, correspond, i.5. 986a6; xiii.4.1079b4

56c. συναρμόττειν, *congruere*, be connected with, i.5.986b13

57. ὅμοιος, *similis*, like, similar, alike, congenial: defined, v.9; x.3; knowledge, opinion, i.1.981a2; iii.4.1000b6; iv.4.1008b35, 5. 1009a7, b11, 1010b12, 15, 6.1011a30; xi.6.1062b33; xii.10. 1075b16; beings, unity, numbers, i.5.985b27, 6.987b17, 9. 991a24; v.15; ix.9.1051a14; x.1.1053a21, 28, 29, 2.1053b24, 26; xi.3.1061a13; xiii.7.1081a10, 10.1087a10; xiv.6.1093a27; speech, iii.3.995a2; attributes, iii.1.995b21; iv.2.1003b36, 4.1008b17, 5.1009a26, 28; xi.5.1062a28; analogies, iv.6.1011a6; v.15. 1021a33; vii.10.1035b9, 11.1036a35, b10, 28, 13.1039a12; viii. 3.1043b8; ix.1.1046a7; generate, v.12; vii.8.1033b34

57a. ὁμοειδής, *ejusdem speciei*, *conformis*, alike, i.9.991b23–992a2; iii.6.1002b16; v.2, 3, 28; vii.7.1032a24; xii.5.1071a17

57b. ὁμοιοτρόπως, *simili modo*, similarly, analogously, iv.2.1004b4; *et passim*

57c. ἀφομοιοῦν, *assimilare*, model, outline, i.5.985b33; xiv.5. 1092b13

57d. παραπλήσιος, *similis*, like, i.6.987b23, 8.989b20; iii.2.997b9, 5.1002b5; v.3, 6; xi.6.1062b12; xii.8.1074b7; xiii.4.1078b34

57e. εἰκών, *imago*, copy, i.9.991b1; xiii.5.1079b35; εἰκότως, *merito*, properly, naturally, iv.3.1005a32; vii.11.1036a26; viii.3.1044a7

57f. ἀνόμοιος, *dissimilis*, unlike, dissimilar, iii.1.995b21; iv.2. 1004a18; v.27; x.4.1055b19; xi.3.1061a14, 10.1067a15

57g. ἄνισος, *inaequalis*, unequal, iii.4.1001b23; iv.2.1004a18; x.4.1055b19, x.5; xi.9.1066a11; xii.10.1075a33; xiii.7.1081a25, 1082b6, 17; xiv.1, 2, 4.1091a23–29, b32, 35, 5.1092a29, b1

58. συμβλητός, like: units, xiii.6–8

58a. ἀσυμβλητός, *incomparabilis*, unlike, incomparable, x.4. 1055a7; xiii.6–8

58b. συμβάλλειν, *conferre*, contribute, i.9.991a9; iii.1.993b14; xii.10.1076a2; xiii.5.1079b13; xiv.3.1090b15, 25, 27

58c. ἐπιβάλλειν, *immittere*, contribute, ii.1.993b2

58d. ἀποβάλλειν, *abjicere, expellere*, lose, avoid, i.3.983b15; iv.5.1010a18; v.5, 10; ix.3.1047a1

59. δηλοῦν, *ostendere, demonstrare*, discern, illuminate, illustrate, reveal, clarify, express, i.1.980a27, 10.993a24; ii.1.993b6, 3. 995a4; iii.1.995a31, 4.1000b17; iv.2.1003b24, 27, 31; v.6, 14, 19, 25; vi.1.1025b16, 4.1028a2; vii.5.1030b16, 7.1032b5, 9. 1034b8; viii.3.1043b16; ix.1.1046a3, 2.1046b8, 14; x.3.1054a26, 8.1058a23; xi.2.1060b4, 5.1062a14, 11.1067b18, 1068a6; xii.7. 1072b2; xiii.2.1077a24, 9.1086b5

59a. δῆλον, *manifestum, apertum, palam*, clear, i.1–3, 7–9; ii.2, 3; iii.1, 2, 4, 5; iv.1–7; vi.1–3; vii.1, 3, 5, 6, 8–17; viii.1–4; ix.2–4, 6, 8, 9; x.2–4, 7, 8; xi.1, 2, 6–10, 12; xii.4, 5, 7, 9; xiii.2–5, 7, 8, 10; xiv.3–5

59b. ἄδηλον, *non manifestum*, not clear, obscure, iv.5.1009b10, 12; vi.1.1026a9, 20; vii.3.1029a10, 7.1033a14, 11.1036b8, 15. 1040a2; viii.4.1044b13, 16; ix.8.1050a20; xi.1.1059b28, 8. 1065a33; xiv.6.1093a4

59c. σαφῶς, *manifeste, plane*, clearly, διασαφεῖν, *explanare*, make a clear statement, i.4.985a13, 5.986b5, 22, 30, 7.988a35, 8.989b19, 10.993a23; vii.10.1035b4; xii.8.1073a17

59d. φανερόν, *manifestum, palam*, evident, i.2, 3, 5, 9; ii.1; iii.3, 4; iv.2, 4–6, 8; v.2, 6, 9, 17, 20; vi.1–4; vii.1–4, 6, 8, 11–14, 16, 17; viii.2, 3, 6; ix.1–4, 8–10; x.1, 2, 4, 8, 10; xi.5–8; xii.3, 7, 8; xiii.2, 3, 6–10; xiv.1, 3, 4, 6

60. ἔνδοξον, *probabile*, probable: dialectic, iii.1.995b24

60a. ὀρθός, *rectus*, right, i.7.988b16, 8.989a15, 26, b19; ii.1.993b19; iv.5.1009a31, 6.1011a6; v.5; vii.4.1030a34, vii.10, 12.1038a30, 13.1039a9, 16.1040b28, 29; viii.3.1043b7, 4.1044b4; ix.7.1049a36;

x.5.1056a30, 6.1056b28; xii.7.1072b34, 10.1075a29, 38; xiii.3.
1078a29, 7.1082b24, 33, b4; xiv.5.1092a10, 11

60b. δίκαιος, *justus*, just, i.2.982b28, 5.981b29, 8.990a24; ii.1.
993b12; iii.2.996b12; iv.5.1010a31; v.22; xi.3.1061a22, 24;
xiii.4.1078b23, 28; xiv.3.1091a19

60c. εὔλογος, *rationabilis*, reasonable, i.6.988a2, 8.989a26, 9.
991b26; iii.2.996b33,˙997a18, b19, 998a11, 4.999b13, 1000a23,
b31; vi.2.1026b13; xi.2.1060a18; xii.8.1074a24, 9.1074b28,
10.1075a31; xiii.2.1077a22, 4.1078b23, 6.1080b10, 7.1081a37,
b4, 9.1085a15, 1086a12, 10.1087a4; xiv.1.1088a6, 2.1088b30,
3.1091a7, 4.1091b20; ἄλογον, *extra rationem*, unreasonable,
irrational, iii.4.999b23, 5.1002a29; xiii.8.1083a8; xiv.3.1091a6

60d. ἄξιον, *dignum*, fitting, ἀξίως, *digne*, completely, i.2.982b31;
ii.1.993a31; iii.4.1000a19, 5.1002a14; iv.5.1010a25, b4

60e. ἱκανός, *sufficiens*, sufficient, adequate, i.3.983a34, 984b9,
4.985a23, 5.986b9, 9.990a33; iii.2.998a10; iv.3.1005a25; vi.4.
1027b18; vii.3.1029a9, 8.1034a4; x.2.1053b28; xii.2.1069b29,
6.1071b16; xiii.3.1077b14, 9.1086a18; xiv.1.1087b31

61. ἄτοπον, *absurdum*, *inconveniens*, absurd, strange, i.8.989a33,
9.991b24; ii.3.995a13; iii.2.997b5, 998a17, 4.999b21; iv.4.
1007b30; vii.5.1030b34, 6.1031b28, 13.1038b24, 14.1039b6, 17,
15.1040a32; ix.3.1046b33; xi.2.1060a24, 31, 6.1063b11; xii.3.
1070a35, 9.1074b25, 10.1075a26, b1, 6, 10; xiii.2.1076b28,
7.1082a9, b8, 8.1083a24, 1084a25, 29; xiv.1.1088b2, 2.1089a12,
34, 3.1090a11, 1091a12, 4.1091b31, 5.1092a17

61a. γελοῖον, *ridiculosum*, *derisio*, ridiculous, absurd, iv.4.1006a13;
x.5.1056a1; xiii.7.1082b37

61b. εὐηθής, *stultus*, simple-minded, v.29; xi.6.1062b34

62. συλλογισμός, *syllogismus*, syllogism, conclusion, reasoning,
i.9.990b10; iv.3.1005a7, 7.1012a20; v.3, 5, 18; vii.9.1034a30–32;
viii.1.1042a3; xi.5.1062a4; xiii.4.1078b24, 1079a6, 10.1086b34;
xiv.2.1089a25

62a. πρότασις, *propositio*, assumption, premise, proposition,
iii.2.996b31; iv.3.1005b28; xiii.3.1078a20; xiv.2.1089a25

63. δεικνύναι, *demonstrare*, *monstrare*, show, ἐπιδεικνύναι, *ostendere*,
exhibit, i.5.986a4, 8.990a13, 9.990b9, 992b10; iii.1.995b8, 2.
996a29, b28, 997a10, 30; iv.4.1006a9, 1007b17, 5.1010a34,
8.1012b27; vii.15.1039b26; viii.3.1043b16; ix.8.1050a18; x.4.
1055a26, 7.1057b2, 8.1058a11; xi.7.1064a6, 36; xii.7.1073a5,

INDEX OF TECHNICAL TERMS

8.1073a32; xiii.3.1078a34, 36, b1, 4.1079a5, 7.1081a20; xiv. 2.1089a5

63a. ἀπόδειξις, *demonstratio*, proof, demonstration, i.8.990a24, 9.992b31; iii.2.996a30, b19, 26–997a15, 15–25, 25–34, 3.998a25– 27, 4.1000a20; iv.3.1005a26, b32, 4.1006a, 6.1011a10, 13; v.1, 3, 5; vi.1.1025b13, 14; vii.15; xi.1.1059a24, 31, 32, b19, xi.5, 7.1064a9; xii.8.1073a22; xiii.3.1077b21, 10.1086b34, 1087a23; xiv.1.1087b21

64. θέσις, *positio*, position, i.4.985b13–20; viii.2.1042b14, 19; xi.6.1063b32, 12.1068b31; xiii.3.1077b30, 7.1082a21, 8.1084a9, 9.1085b12; xiv.5.1092a27; τιθέναι, *ponere*, posit, believe, assume, take, rank, i.3–5, 7–9; iii.2–4, 6; iv.3, 4; v.6, 18, 19, 26, 27; vii.4, 6, 7; viii.3; ix.4; x.1, 9; xi.1–9; xii.1, 8; xiii.2–4, 6, 8–10; xiv.2–5

64a. ἐκτιθέναι, suppose, ἔκθεσις, *expositio*, setting out terms apart, explication, abstracting: method, i.9.992b10; vii.6. 1031b21; xiv.3.1090a17; "this," iii.6.1003a10; "ideas," xiii.9. 1086b10

64b. ἀντιτιθέναι, oppose, ἀντίθεσις, *oppositio*, opposition, antithesis: one, many, x.3.1054a23, x.5; xiv.1.1087b26, 31; contraries, contradictories, x.7.1057a35, 10.1059a10 (perishable, imperishable); xi.11.1067b21

64c. διάθεσις, *dispositio*, condition, disposition, iii.5.1001b30; v.12, 19, 20 (defined); xi.3.1061a9

64d. ἐπιτιθέναι, *imponere*, bring to conclusion, viii.1.1042a4

64e. μετάθεσις, *transpositio*, transposition, v.26.1024a4

64f. πρόσθεσις, *additio*, *appositio*, *adjectio*, addition, i.2.982a27, 3.984a9, 5.986b16, 987a15; ii.2.994b30; iii.4.1001b7–25; iv.2. 1003b31, 4.1007a9, 13; vii.4.1030a33, 5.1030b15, 16, 1031a2, 16.1040b33; x.1.1052b36, 1053a4; xi.10.1066b1; xii.8.1073b36, 1074a12; xiii.1.1076a23, 2.1077b9, 10, 7.1081b12–17; xiv.6. 1092b31; in definition, vii.4.1029b30, 15.1040a30; viii.1.1043a17, 3.1044a2, 4.1044b14; xiii.4.1079b6, 7

64g. συντιθέναι, *componere*, compound, put together, associate, σύνθεσις, *compositio*, synthesis, union, juxtaposition, i.9.993a9; iii.5.1002a1; iv.7.1012a4; vi.4.1027b19; ix.3.1047a31, ix.10; x.7.1057b20–29; xi.1.1059b24, 10.1066b26–34; xii.4.1070b8, 8. 1073b38, 9.1075a5, 8; xiii.2.1076b19, 8.1084b28; matter, form, primary being, v.2, 4, 24; vii.13.1039a17, 15.1040a18, 17. 1041b11; viii.2.1042b16, 1043a13, 18, 3.1043a30, b29, 6.1045b7–

16; xii.3.1070a14; xiv.2.1088b16; state of affairs, v.29; ix.10. 1051b10; and categories, vii.4.1029b23

64h. ὑπόθεσις, *suppositio, conditio,* postulate, assumption, premise, i.5.986b14, 7.988a25, 8.990a14; iv.2.1005a13, b14, 17; v.1. 1013a16, 2.1013b20; vi.1.1025b11; xi.4.1047b10; x.1.1053a11, 3.1054b33, 5.1055b35; xi.7.1064a8, 8.1064b15; xiii.7.1082b3, 32, 8.1083b6, 9.1086a11, 15; xiv.2.1086a22, 24, b6, 16, 1090a27, 3.1090b30

65. λαμβάνειν, *accipere, sumere,* take, employ, acquire, learn, believe, grasp, achieve, accept, i.2–5, 8, 9; ii.3; iii.3, 4, 6; iv.1, 2, 6; v.10, 16, 17, 29; vi.1; vii.9; viii.2; ix.3, 8; x.1, 2, 4; xi.7, 9, 10; xii.1, 8; xiii.7, 19; xiv.2, 3; axiom, iv.4.1006a3, 6.1011a14, 8.1012b7; xi.5.1062a6, 35

65a. ἀπολαμβάνειν; *assumere,* collect, v.5.1015a25; concentrate, xi.4.1061b21

65b. ἐπαναλαμβάνειν, *repetere,* take up again, vii.10.1035b4

65c. καταλαμβάνειν, *tradere,* hand down, xii.8.1074b2

65d. μετάληψις, *transumptio,* being aware, xii.7.1072b20

65e. παραλαμβάνειν, *accipere,* get, acquire, i.3.983b1, 5.986a28, 987a3, 8.989b31; ii.1.993b18

65f. περιλαμβάνειν, *comprehendere,* contain, i.8.990a4

65g. προλαμβάνειν, *praeaccipere,* precede, ix.8.1050b5; προσλαμβάνειν, add, xiii.7.1082b28–37

65h. συλλαμβάνειν, *concipere, coaccipere, colligere,* take together, relate, i.9.992a2; iii.3.998b28; vi.1.1025b32; vii.10.1035a25–b3, 11.1036a27, b5, 12.1037b31, 15.1039b21; x.4.1055b8, 9.1058b2

65i. ὑπολαμβάνειν (*see also* 174), *suscipere, putare,* take, think, grasp, believe, interpret, understand: sense, knowledge, i.1, 2, 6.987b1, 5; iv.5.1009b12, 27, 1010a26, b10; xi.1.1059a21; principles, i.5.986a27; iii.3.998a22, 999a16, 20; v.1.1013a6; xiv.5.1092a11; being, primary being, iv.2.1003b25, 3.1005b, 4.1006a, 1008b, 5.1009a; vii.16.1040b10; ix.10.1052a5; xi.1. 1059b28, 2.1060a8; xii.7.1072b31; *et passim*

66. ἀποδέχεσθαι, *recipere,* accept, endorse, i.6.987b4; ii.3.995a6, 13; iv.3.1005b3; viii.1.1043a22

67. ἀξίωμα, *dignitas,* axiom, iii.2.997a, 4.1001b7; iv.3; xiii.2. 1077a31; xiv.3.1090a36

68. βέβαιος, *firmus,* basic, certain: iv.3.1005b, 4.1006a4, 1008a16, 17, 1009a2, 6.1011b13

69. σχεδόν, *fere,* precisely, hardly, nearly, practically, i.2.982a23,

1076a11, xiii.2; against nature, v.5.1015b15; vii.8.1033b33; viii.5.1044b34; xii.7.1072b12; primary being, viii.3.1043b11; ix.8.1050a25, 9.1051a18; xi.2, 7.1064a4, 9.1065b7, 10.1066b35, 36, 1067a6; *et passim*

75. διαιρεῖν, *dividere, distinguere*, divide, distinguish, analyze, dissociate: in mathematics, ii.2.994b23; iii.5.1002a19; v.13; ix.9.1051a22, 23; x.1.1053a24; xi.2.1060b14, 19; xiii.2.1077a23, 3.1077b20, 29, 8.1084b, 9.1085b19; parts, elements, iii.1.995b28, 5.1002b1–4, 10; v.3, 25, 26; vii.16.1040b13, 17.1041b31; xiii.2. 1076b4–11; species, iii.3.999a4; x.8.1058a19; xi.1.1059b37; truth, falsity, iv.4.1008a19, 21, 27; vi.4.1027b19, 21, 30; ix.10; xi.5.1062b3; definition, v.6.1016a35; vii.10, 12; viii.3.1043b35; x.1.1052a16, 4.1055b6, 6.1056b34; being, v.6, 11; x.1.1053a19, 3.1054a20–29, 6.1056b16; xi.9.1065b14; xii.1.1069a34; categories, v.28; xi.12.1068a8; matter, form, vii.8.1033b12; ix.6. 1048a27; infinite, ix.6.1048b16; xi.10; contraries, opposites, x.3.1054a30, 8.1058a10; xi.11.1067b26; principles, xii.4.1070b24, 30, 5.1071a32, 6.1072b2

75a. ἀδιαίρετον, *indivisibile*, indivisible, indistinguishable, iii.3. 999a2, 4.1001b7–25, 5.1002b4; v.3, 6; and unity, v.6; vii.17. 1041a18; viii.3.1043b35; x.1, 3.1054a20–29, 6.1057a7, 15; xiii.7.1082a24, 8.1084b14; xiv.1.1088a2; and infinite, xi.10.1066b; first mover, xii.7.1073a7, 9.1075a7; and mathematics, xiii.3. 1077b30, 1078a23–28, 7.1082a5, 8.1083b15, 9.1085b; xiv.2. 1089b5, 5.1092a33

76. διαφέρειν, *differre, distinguere*, differ, be superior, be inferior: knowledge, i.1.981a13, b16; iv.2.1004b24, 4.1006a16; xii.9. 1074b24; elements, i.4.985b10–20, 8.988b34; v.3.1014a34; "ideas," numbers, i.6.987b16, 9.991b26; iii.6.1002b15; xiii.6–8; xiv.6.1093a10, b22; man, iv.4.1008b11; v.2; one, many, opposites, v.4, 10; x.4, 6.1056b12, 16, 7.1057b11; material, vi.1. 1025b32; ix.7.1049a27; xii.2.1069b30; genus, species, vii.12. 1037b21; x.3.1054b26–30, x.4, 8.1058a25, 27, 9.1058a29, b14, 25; xi.1.1059b37; actual, potential, xii.5.1071a12, 6.1071b17; οὐθὲν διαφέρει, *nihil refert*, makes no difference, i.9; ii.2; iii.4, 6; iv.2, 4; v.2, 7; vii.4, 6, 10–13; viii.3; xi.3, 6; xiii.2, 7, 9; xiv.1, 3

76a. διαφορά, διάφορον, *differentia*, difference, differentia: defined, v.9.1018a12–15; x.3; sense, knowledge, i.1.980a27, 981b26; Democritus, i.4.985b10–20; viii.2.1042b11–15; number, i.9.

III. PRINCIPLES OF EXPLANATION

84a. ἐν ὕλης εἴδει, of a material kind, i.3.983b7, 984a17, 4.985a32, 5.986b6, 987a7

85. ὑποκείμενον, *subjectum, suppositum,* subject, subject matter, thing spoken of, persistent being: defined, vii.3.1028b36, 37; knowledge, i.2.982a23, b4; iii.2.997a6, 20; x.1.1053b3; material factor, i.3.983a30, 5.988a12, 9.991b18; v.2.1013b21, 18.1022a19; viii.2.1042b9, 11, 1043a25; ix.7.1049a27–36; change, i.3.984a22, 29, 4.985b10, 8.990a9; viii.1.1042a32–b8; xi.11, 12; xiv.1. 1087a29–b3; predication, i.9.990b31, 992b1–7; iii.1.996a2, 5. 1001b31; iv.4.1007a35; v.8, 28; vii.4.1029b24; xi.6.1063b21, 10.1066b14; xiii.4.1079a28; being, iii.1.996a8, 4.1001a8; v.11. 1019a5; vii.1.1028a26, 11.1037b4; xi.4.1061b31, 9.1065b30; privation, iv.2.1004a15; vii.7.1033a9; viii.1.1042b3; x.4.1055b25; perception, iv.5.1010b34; unity, v.6.1016a17–24; vii.12.1037b16; x.2.1053b13, 5.1056b2; xiv.1.1087b34, 1088a18; genus, v.6, 28; primary being, vii.3, 6.1031b16–18, 8.1033a28, 31, 13.1038b; viii.1, 4.1044b9; ix.7.1049a27–36; xii.3.1070a11; xiv.2.1089b26; assumption, xii.8.1073a23; xiv.2.1090a7

86. ἐξ οὗ, *(principium) ex quo,* wherefrom: defined, v.24; element, i.3.983b8, 8.988b35, 9.992b18–24, 993a3; ii.2.994a3; iii.4. 1000a29, 1001a16, 5.1001b33; v.3.1014a26, 28, 10.1018a24, 25; viii.3.1043b30; xi.10.1066b37; "ideas," numbers, i.9.991a19, b20, 29, 992a10–24; basis of demonstration, iii.2.997a23; v.5. 1015b9; primary, iv.2.1003b16; material, v.2.1013a24, b21; vii.7.1032a17, 1033a5–23, 11.1037a29; nature, v.4; vii.7.1032a17; seed, xii.7.1073a3; *et passim*

87. τί ἐστιν, *quod quid est* (principle of cognition), *essentia, quidditas* (form of the whole), *(causa formalis),* (the question of) what is: in early philosophies, i.5.987a20, 6.988a10, 8. 988b29, 9.991a22; xiii.5.1079b26; being, primary being, ii.1. 993b29; iii.2.997a31, 5.1001b28; iv.2.1003b34, 1004b7; vi.1. 1025b7–18, 1026a32, 4.1027b32; vii.3.1029a8, 7.1032b19, 20, 9.1034a32, 17.1041b8; viii.2.1042b11, 1043a26; x.2.1054a15; xi.7; xiii.1.1076a8, 12; contrary, iv.2.1004b3; definition, v.13, 18, 28; vi.1.1025b31, 1026a4; vii.7.1033a2, 16.1041a3; viii.1. 1043a15, 22, 3.1043b23–28; ix.6.1048a26, b35; xiii.4.1078b21–27; accidental, vi.2.1027a27; xi.8.1064b31, 1065a3; incomposites, vi.4.1027b28; ix.10.1051b26, 32; unity, viii.6.1045a14;

INDEX OF TECHNICAL TERMS

x.1.1052b3, 2.1053b10, 9.1058b24; abstracted from, xiii.3. 1077b23

88. τὸ τί ἦν εἶναι, *quod quid erat esse*, what it meant to be something: essential character, i.3.983a27, 7.988a34, b4, 10.993a18; ii.2.994a11, b17; iv.4.1007a21; v.18.1022a25–27; xii.8.1074a35, 9.1075a2; and explanation, v.2.1013a27, b22; vii.17.1041a28; viii.4.1044a36; definition, v.6, 8, 17, 29; vi.1.1025b28; vii.4; viii.1.1042a17, 3.1044a1; primary being, vii.3.1028b34, vii.4–6, 7.1032b1, 14, 8.1033b7, 9.1035b14, 10.1035b32, 11.1037a1, 21–b7, 13.1038b1–6, 14, 17; viii.1.1042a13, 17, 3.1043b1–4, 6.1045a33–b23; matter, form, viii.6.1045a33

88a. εἶναι with the dative, *huic esse*, (*quod quid erat esse illius rei*): e.g., τὸ ἀνθρώπῳ εἶναι, *homini esse*, to be a man, τὸ ψυχῇ εἶναι, *animae esse*, being a soul, i.1.981a20; iv.4; vii.5.1030b21, vii.6; viii.3.1043b2–4; to be X, etc., i.5.987a26, 9.990b34; ii.2.994b27; v.6.1016b18, 15.1021b9, 11; vii.4, 6, 10.1036a1–25, 15.1039b25, 16.1041b6, 19, 17.1041a19; ix.3.1046b35; x.1.1052b, 2.1054a18, 4.1055a18, 8.1058a17; xi.9.1065b25–33, 10.1066b12; xii.10. 1075a5; xiii.4.1079a30

89. ἰδέα, *idea*, "idea": explanations, i.6.987b8, 7.988b1–6, i.9; xiii.4; duplicates, i.9.990b1–8; xiii.4.1078b34–1079a4; arguments (restricted, inconclusive), i.990b8–991a8, a8–b9; xiii.4.1079a4–b3, b12–1080a6; numbers, i.9.991b9–992a24; vii.11.1036b14; xii. 8.1073a17–22; xiii.1, 4.1078b22, 6.1080b, 7.1081a, 1082, 8. 1083a, 1084a, 9.1086a27; xiv.2.1090a2–15, xiv.3, 4.1091b27–30; principles, i.9.992a24–993a10; being, primary being, vii.3. 1029a5, 6.1031a28–b28, 14.1039a25, b12, 15.1040a22–27; viii. 1.1042a15, 22; ix.8.1050b34–1051a3; xii.3.1070a28; xiii.1, 2. 1077a11, xiii.3, 9.1086a21–10.1087a25; not definable, vii.15. 1040a8, 9, b3. *See also* 20

89a. παράδειγμα, *exemplum*, pattern, example, i.9.991a13–31; ii.3.995a7; v.2.1013a27; vii.8.1034a2; xiii.5.1079b23–35

90. λόγος, *ratio, sermo, oratio, mentio*, reason, i.1; xii.3 (art, science); ii.3 (exposition); iii.2 (wisdom); iv.5 (change); iv.6; xi.6 (not for everything); v.2 (form); vii.3 (priority), 17 (identity); ix.2 (power), 5, 8 (actual); xiii.8 (numbers); account, i.1 (knowledge), 5 (principles, explanations); iii.2 (good, bad), 5 (mathematics); iv.4 (being); v.29 (false), 30 (accidents); vi.1 (what is); vii.9 (production); x.2 (primary being), 10 (perishable); xi.9 (movement); xiii.2, 7; xiv.3 (numbers, science);

358

definition, i.3; v.8 (essential character); ii.2 (meaning); iii.2; v.2; xii.2 (form); iv.2, 4; v.6, 9; xi.9 (unity, being); v.3 (not of highest genera), 10 (differ), 11; xiii.2 (priority); v.13 (line), 18 (man), 25, 28 (parts of); vi.1, 4, 5, 7, 10, 15; viii.2–4, 6; xi.7, 10; xiii.8 (primary being); x.1, 3 (unity), 9 (otherness); xi.1; xiii.8 (general); xi.3 (privation), 6 (contraries); xii.8 (mover); xiii.2, 4 ("ideas"); view, theory, doctrine, teaching, i.3, 8 (mind); iv.4, 5 (axiom); ix.3 (power); xiii.2, 4; xiv.3 (mathematical); relations, i.5; discourse, dialectic, discussion, i.5; v.6 (unity); i.6; xiii.1 ("ideas"); i.8 (nature); iv.4 (axiom); vii.1; viii.1, 3; ix.8 (primary being); xi.3 (medical); xiv.2 (eternal); argument, i.8; iv.7 (mixture); i.9; iii.2; ix.8; xiii.4, 5 ("ideas"); i.9; iii.3, 4; iv.4 (principles); iii.4; iv.7 (being); iv.4–8; xi.5 (axiom); iv.5 (change); v.29 (Hippias); vi.2 (Sophists); vii.6, 17; viii.1, 3 (primary being); ix.8 (actuality); xi.10 (unity); xii.7 (first mover); xiii.2, 4, 10; xiv.1, 3 (mathematical entities); ratio, i.9; iii.5; x.1; xi.3; xiv.5, 6; articulated structure, i.10; difficulties, iii.1.996a17; explanation, iii.2, 5; iv.2; vi.1; viii.6; ix.2; xi.7; xii.9; xiv.2; order, rule, iii.3; v.11; analysis, iii.4; meaning, iv.4; ix.1; reasoning, vi.3; ix.8; xiii.4, 8; xiv.1; question, vi.4.1027b24; statement, saying, vii.4; ix.2, 10; xiii.3; xiv.2; term, vii.4, 5; pattern, vii.7; formula, viii.1; ix.1; xii.5; concept, logical, formal, vii.10–15; ix.1, 8; xii.3; xiii.2, 3, 9; connection, xiii.3.1078a35; long tale, xiv.3.1091a8

91. μορφή, *forma* (principle of "subsistence"), (*formae separatae et formae substantiales*), shape: or form, iii.4; v.4, 8, 24, 26; vii.3, 8; viii.1–3, 5, 6; x.1, 4; xi.2; xii.3; xiii.2; xiv.1, 5; and privation, xi.9.1065b10; of myth, xii.8.1074b2

91a. σχῆμα, *figura*, shape, figure, pattern, diagram: rhythm, i.4.985b13–20; viii.2.1042b14; species, genus, iii.3.999a9–12; v.6.1016a31; body, iii.5.1002a21; appearance, iv.2.1004b28; categories, v.6, 7; vi.2.1026a36; ix.10.1051a35; x.3.1054b29; mathematical, v.14, 28; vi.2.1026b11, 8.1033b14; viii.6.1045a35; x.2.1054a3; xiii.4.1079b5, 9.1085a19; xiv.2.1089a1, 5.1092b12; form, "idea," vii.3.1029a4, 7.1033a3

92. κοινωνεῖν, *communicare, participare*, agree, communicate, κοινωνία, *communitas*, interrelation, κοινός, *communis*, common: sense, definition, i.1.981b14, 2.982a12, 6.987b6; iii.6. 1003a9; v.1.1013a17, 3.1014b14; xiii.4.1079b4; "ideas," i.9. 991a2–8; xiii.4.1079a33–b3; elements, i.9.992a2–10; iii.3.998a25;

97. χάριν, *causa*, in behalf of, for the sake of, i.5.986a13, 9.992a33;
ii.1.993b12; iii.4.1000a16; iv.5.1009a21, 6.1011b2; vii.11.1037a13;
ix.8.1050a9; xii.8.1074a26, 29; xiii.1.1076a28

98. ἀγαθόν, *bonum*, good, excellent: science, i.2.982b6, 10, 983a11,
18; xiii.3.1078a31–b6; explanatory factor, i.3.983a32, 7.988b9,
15; ii.2.994b13; iii.2.996a20–b26; v.1.1013a22, v.2; xi.1.1059a36;
xiv.4, 5.1092a9;` and bad, i.4, 5.986a26, 33; iii.2.996b1; iv.4.
1008b17, 27, 7.1011b32, 33; v.5, 14, 16, 22; vi.4.1027b26, 27;
vii.1.1028a15, 28; ix.9; x.4; xi.6.1062b16, 1063a5, 8.1065a35;
xii.10; xiii.7.1082b18, 8.1084a35; xiv.4.1092a1–5; and mixture,
iv.7.1012a27, 28; general, supreme, v.18; vii.4.1029b6, 7, 6.
1031a31–b7; xii.9.1075a9, xii.10

98a. εὖ, (*quod*) *bene*, good, well, i.3.984b8–22, 6.988a14; v.12, 16;
ix.2.1046b24–28; xii.7.1072b12, 24, 9.1074b37, 1075a8, 10.
1075a14; xiv.4.1091b2, 19, 5.1092b26, 6.1093b12

99. καλός, *bonus*, *nobilis*, beauty, i.4; v.1.1013a23; xi.6.1062b18,
1063a6; xii.7.1072a28–34, 9.1074b24; xiii.3.1078a31–b6; xiv.4,
6.1093b13

99a. καλῶς, *bene*, beauty, well: explanation, i.3.984b8–22; said,
i.4, 5, 8; iii.1, 6; vii.2, 11, 12; x.3; xi.9; xii.6; xiii.1, 6, 8, 9;
xiv.1; turn out, v.12, 14; ix.1; beautiful, vii.6.1031b12; define,
vii.10.1035b17; first mover, xii.7.1072b11

100. τέλος, *finis*, end: explanatory factor, i.3.983a32; iii.2.996a20–
b26; v.2; viii.4.1044b1; xi.1.1059a38; of science, inquiry, ii.1.
993b21; iii.1.995a1; viii.1.1042a4; xi.8.1064b23; of process,
ii.2.994b5, 9–16; iii.4.999b10; v.4, 16, 17, 24; ix.6.1048b18–23,
8.1050a; xii.8.1074a20, 23, 30; xiii.2.1077a26; evils, ix.9.1051a16;
difference, x.4.1055a10–16; good, xii.10.1075b1; ἀποτελεῖν,
facere, acquire, perform, i.1.981a1; vii.11.1036b31; ἀποτελευτᾶν,
proficere, reach, i.2.983a18; διατελεῖν, *perseverare*, continue,
iv.5.1010a29; xi.6.1063b7; ἐπιτελεῖν, *perficere*, mature, do, ii.2.
994a26; v.12.1019a23; ἀτελής, ἀτελεύτητος, *imperfectus*, incomplete, endless, ix.6.1048b29; xi.9.1065b12, 1066a21, 10.
1066a37; xiii.2.1077a19; xiv.5.1092a13

100a. τελευταῖος, *ultimus*, *finalis*, final, remote, least, last, i.3.
983b9; ii.2.994a15; iii.1.995b30; iv.5.1010a12; v.6.1016a20, 30,
1017a5, 10.1018b5; vii.7.1032b17, 12.1038a19, 26, 29; xi.3.
1061a24, 8.1065a10; xiii.2.1077a25

IV. NATURE AND CHANGE

ix.7; xii.1, 5; xiv.5; water, i.3, 7, 8; ii.2, v.3, 5, 6, 24, 26, 27; viii.5; x.6; xi.10; xiv.6; air, i.3, 7, 8; ii.2; iii.4; v.6; x.2; xi.10; fire, i.3–5, 7, 8; ii.1; iii.4; iv.2; v.27; vii.1, 9; xi.10; xii.1, 3, 5; xiv.4, 5; four, i.3–5, 7–10; iii.1, 3–5; v.2, 4, 8; vii.2; viii.1; ix.7, 8; hot, cold, moist, dry, i.3, 5, 8; ii.1; iii.5; iv.2; v.14, 26; vii.7, 9; ix.1–3; xi.3, 10; xii.4; xiii.4; full, empty, i.4.985b4–20; of numbers, magnitudes, i.5.986a, b7, 8.989b29–990a32; xiii.7. 1081a15, b25, 32, 8.1083b26, 1084b9, 9.1085b, 1086a28; xiv.1, 3, 4, 5.1092a21; of "ideas," i.6.987b18–20; of bodies, i.8.988b25; not of all things, i.9.992b18–24; kinds or constituents, iii.1. 995b28, 3.998a20–b14; xi.1.1059b21–24; letter, iii.4; v.2, 24; vii.10, 12, 17; viii.3; x.1, 2; xiii.10; knowledge, iii.4.1000a5; vi.1.1025b5; being, unity, iii.4.1001a5–b25; iv.1; xiii.6.1080b7, 32; potentiality, iii.6.1002b32–1003a5; primary being, vii.2, 16, 17; viii.1, 3, 4; xii.1, 4; xiii.9, 10; xiv.1, 2; infinite, xi.10; explanation, xii.5.1071a13, 25, 30; and the eternal, xiv.2

104. συστοιχία, *coelementatio*, columns, i.5.986a23; iv.2.1004b27; x.3.1055a1, 8.1058a13; xi.9.1066a15; xii.7.1072a31, 35; xiv.6. 1093b12

105. ἁπλοῦς, *simplex*, (*absolutus*, vs. *relativus, relatio*); ἁπλῶς, *simpliciter*, (*absolute*, vs. *in ordine ad aliquid, secundum quid, ex conditione*), simply, absolutely, in itself, without qualification, explicitly, strictly: origination, destruction, i.3.983b14; viii.1.1042b7; xi.11; xii.2.1069b10; xiv.1.1088a33; factors, i.7. 988b15, 9.989b17; v.2.1014a19; vi.1.1025b7; xi.8.1065a34; bodies (*see also* 102), i.8.988b30; v.8.1017b10; xi.10.1067a1; definition, i.5.987a21; v.5, 11, 15; vii.4.1030a17–b13, 5.1031a13; "ideas," mathematical entities, i.9.991b29; xiii.1.1076a27, 3. 1077b31–34, 1078a10–13, 8.1083a22; statement, demonstration, iv.2.1004a12, 4.1007a9; v.5, 9, 29; vi.2.1027a5; vii.4.1030a16, 7.1033a21, 10.1036a16, 23; xi.5; xii.7.1072b13; decision, iv.4. 1008b26; contraries, opposition, iv.6.1011b22; v.10; x.6.1065b4; being, vi.1.1025b9, 2.1026a33; vii.1.1028a31, 11.1037a9, 17. 1041b1, 9; viii.1.1042a31, 6.1045b23; xi.8.1064b15, 11.1067b27, 29; xii.1.1069a22; xiii.3.1077b16; terms, vi.6.1027b27; vii.5. 1030b15; general, vii.10.1035b1, 12.1038a5; xi.1.1059b35, 36; xii.5.1071a24; xiv.2.1088b14; movement, ix.6.1048a29; potential, actual, ix.6–8; xi.9; continuity, measure, same, x.1.1052a19, 35, 1053a8, b8, 3.1054b, 6.1056b; xi.9.1065b26; infinite, xi.10;

998a29, b2, 5.1002a1; v.8; vii.9.1034a33; xiii.2.1077a35; primary being, vii.17.1041b30; viii.3.1043b22; xiii.6.1080b18; one, xiii.6.1080b21

112. ἀποβαίνειν, *contingere*, result, i.1.981a2, 2.982a16; xi.8.1065b1

112a. βαδίζειν, *ire, vadere*, walk, ii.2.994a8; iii.1.995a36; vii.1. 1028a20, 24; ix.3.1047a23, 6.1048a35, 7.1049a33; xiv.3.1090b10; infinite regress, iii.4.1000b28; v.20.1022b9; vi.3.1027b12, 8. 1033b4; vii.17.1041b22; process, vii.12.1038a16; ix.8.1050a7

113. ἄγειν, *adducere, deducere*, treat, arrive, v.23.1023a9; vii.7. 1032b9; xiv.5.1092b12

113a. ἀνάγειν, *reducere*, lead back, reduce, resolve, refer, i.3. 983a28, 9.992a10; ii.2.994b17; iii.4.1001a13; iv.2.1004b27–1005a1, 3.1005b32; vi.3.1027b14; vii.11.1036b12, 22, 16.1040b20 (to better known); viii.3.1044a13; ix.9.1050a30; x.4.1055b29 (contraries); xi.3.1061a2, 10–17, b14; xiii.7.1082b37

113b. ἀπάγειν, *abducere*, lead away, vii.11.1036b26

113c. εἰσάγειν, *introducere*, introduce, i.4.985a3, 30, 6.987b31

113d. ἐπάγειν, *inducere*, drive, cite, i.8.989a33; ii.3.995a8

113e. ἐπαγωγή, *inductio*, induction, i.9.992b33; v.29.1025a10; vi. 1.1025b15; ix.6.1048a36; x.3.1054b33, 4.1055a6, b17, 8.1059a9; xi.7.1064a9, 11.1067b14; xiii.4.1078b28

113f. προάγειν, *producere*, advance, i.5.985b24

113g. προσάγειν, *adducere*, add, xii.8.1074b4

113h. συνάγειν, *conducere, colligere*, bring together, unify, relate, attract, collect, i.4.984b30, 5.986a6, b5, 9.991a18; iii.4.1000b11; viii.1.1042a3; xi.6.1063b32; xii.10.1075b3; xiii.5.1079b22, 1080a10; xiv.6.1093b15, 25

113i. διαγωγή, *introductio, eruditio, deductio*, enjoyment, i.1. 981b18, 2.982b23; xii.7.1072b14

114. ἔρχεσθαι, *venire*, come, attain to, be extended, iv.7.1012a17; vii.12.1038a16, 15.1040a4; ix.3.1047a30, 8.1050a15; x.1.1052b19, 8.1058a21; xii.10.1075a24

114a. ἀπέρχεσθαι, *abire, abscedere*, pass out, vii.10.1036a6; xiv.5.1092a33

114b. διέρχεσθαι, *supervenire, pertransire*, go over, distinguish, enumerate, i.7.988b21, 9.992b19; iii.2.998a10; iv.2.1004a28, 4.1007a15; vii.4.1029b1; ix.6.1048a30; xi.10.1066a35; xiii.7. 1081a1; xiv.5.1092a22

114c. ἐπέρχεσθαι, *advenire, pertransire, tractare, aggredi*, go over, survey, consider, propound, i.5.986a13, 7.988a18; iii.1.995a24;

vii.13.1038b8; viii.1.1042a25; x.2.1053b10; xiii.2.1077a1; xiv. 2.1089b2

114d. ἐπανέρχεσθαι, *redire, resumere*, return, i.10.993a26; vii.13. 1038b1; viii.5.1045a4

114e. προέρχεσθαι, *procedere*, proceed, move, i.9.990b6; iii.1. 995a33; xiii.4.1079a2; xiv.4.1091a35

114f. συνέρχεσθαι, *convenire*, come together, iii.4.1000b2

114g. προϊέναι, *procedere*, progress, i.2.982b14, 3.984a18

114h. ἰέναι, *ire, procedere, progredi*, proceed: e.g., infinite regress, ii.2.994a3, 8, b4

115. μεταβολή, *mutatio, permutatio, transmutatio*, change: and persistence, i.3.983b10; iv.5.1010a37, 8.1012b22–31; viii.1. 1042a32–b8; explanatory factor, i.3.984a16–b8, 7.988b6, 8.990a10, 9.991a26; ii.2.994a24; iii.2.996b23, 4.1000b12–17; iv.5.1009b17, 18; v.1, 2, 4; vii.7.1033a21; "ideas," i.6.987b7, 9.991a11; xii. 6.1071b16; xiii.5.1079b15; truth, iv.5.1010a8, 9, 15; categories, being, iv.5.1010a23, b22, 24, 8.1012b29; v.14, 24; xi.9.1065b7, 14, xi.12; contraries, iv.7.1011b32–35, 1012a8; x.4.1055b16, x.7; xi.10.1067a6, 12.1068b27–1069a5; xii.2; power, v.12; ix.1. 1046a9–15, 2.1046b4, 7.1049a11, 17, 8.1049b6, 1050b28, 1051a3; material, viii.5; movement, xi.9.1066a12, xi.11, 12; xii.7.1072b9; definite, xii.3.1069b36; divine, xii.9.1074b26, 27, 1075a6; xiv.4.1091b7; μεταβλητικός, *permutans, permutativus*, of change, ix.8.1049b6, 1051a3

116. γίγνεσθαι, *fieri, evenire*, arise, be generated, come to be: and explanation, i.3, 4, 7–9; ii.2.994a19–b9; iii.2–4; iv.5.1010a20; v.1, 2, 18, 24; vii.17.1041a25; viii.4; ix.8; x.4.1055b12, 7.1057b24; xi.2.1060a35, 5.1062a12; numbers, "ideas," i.5.985b28, 8.990a20, 9.991a10, 25, b3–9; iii.4.99b, 1001b, 5.1002a28–b11; xiii.2. 1077a25, 29, 4.1079a7, 5.1079b, 7.1081, 1082a35, 8.1083a12, b35, 1084b28; xiv.2, 3.1091a4, 8, 4.1091b25, 5.1092a25; knowledge, syllogism, i.6.987b5, 9.990b10; iv.6.1011b5, 6, 7.1012a22–24; vii.4.1029b4; xi.1.1059b27, 6.1063b10; xii.7.1072b21; xiii. 4.1079a6, 10.1086b24; elements, i.8.989a; iii.4.999b23; xi.10. 1067a2–6; unity, i.9.992b9–11; iv.4.1007b10, 25; vi.4.1027b25; vii.12.1037b17, 16.1040b9, 11; xi.12.1069a6, 8; xii.4.1070b15, 16; and being (*see* 23); contraries, iv.5.1009a25; x.2.1053b30, 8.1058a16, 20, 9.1058b24; xi.3.1061a11, 16; xii.5.1071a11; xiv.1. 1087a36; and nonbeing, iv.5.1009a25, 32; xi.11.1067b31–34; xii.2.1069b26–32; xiv.2.1089a26; power, v.12; ix.3.1047a, 7.

1048a, 8.1049b35; xiv.2.1088b17–19, 1089a31; accidental, v.27, 30; vi.2, 3; vii.6.1031a24–28; xi.8; primary being, vii.3.1029a10, vii.7–9, 13.1039a10, 15.1040a34; viii.1.1042b7; and passing away, ii.2.994a31; iii.5.1002a28–b11; vi.3; vii.15.1039b20–31, 17.1041a31, 32; viii.3.1043b14–23; ix.10.1051b28–30; xii.6. 1071b7; xiv.2.1089a26; change, xi.6.1063a20, b6, 7.1064a25, 12.1068b8; xii.3; man, xii.7.1073a3; *et passim*

116a. γένεσις, *generatio*, becoming, generation, production, origination: individual, i.1.981a17; viii.6.1045a31; philosophy, i.2. 982b17, i.8; end of, i.3.983a32; v.4.1015a11; ix.8.1050a9; elements, i.3.984a20, i.8; nature, growth, i.3.984a32; v.4.1014b16, 1015a16, 27.1024a27, 28.1024a, b7; mathematics, i.8.990a10; iii.5.1002a28–b11; xiii.7–9; xiv.3–6; being, nonbeing, ii.2.994a27, b1; iii.4.999b6, 9; x.3.1054b29; xii.2.1069b27; destruction, ii.2.994b6, 7; iii.5.1002a29; iv.2.1003b29, 5.1010a29, 30, 7. 1012a7; v.10.1018a22, 11.1019a11–14; vi.2.1026b23, 15.1039b20–31; viii.1.1042a29–b8, 3.1044a11, 12, viii.5; xi.11, 12; xii.2. 1069b10, 11, 3.1070a15, 6.1072a11; xiv.1.1088a29–33; movement, iii.2.996b22; primary being, iv.5.1009a38; vii.7–9, 13. 1038b28; xi.2.1060b18; xiii.2.1077a; contraries, iv.7.1012a1; x.4.1055a8, 11; xiv.4.1091b34; accident, vi.3.1027b13; power, ix.3.1047a14, 7.1049a12, 8.1050a3, 4, 9.1051a32; xiv.2.1089a29; always, xii.10.1075b

116b. ἐγγίνεσθαι, *fieri, esse in*, occur in, ix.2.1046b16, 7.1047a31; x.3.1054b8

116c. ἐπιγίγνεσθαι, *supervenire*, come, be found, i.6.987a29; vii.11.1036a31, b6

116d. γεννᾶν, *generare*, generate: things, i.3.984b9, 5.986b15, 17, 8.989b34; iii.5.1000a28; iv.5.1010a21; iv.5.1010a21; xii.6.1071b27; xiv.4.1091b10; mathematical, i.6; xi.2; xiii.7–9; xiv.1, 3; ungenerated, iii.4.999b7; primary being, iv.2.1003b8; vii.8; xiv. 2.1089a33; men, v.12, 28; vii.7, 9; xiii.3, 4; xiv.5; concepts, vii.15.1039b27; viii.3.1043b17; bodies, xi.10.1066b35; and matter, xii.2.1069b25, 26

117. φθείρειν, *corrumpere*, destroy, corrupt, φθείρεσθαι, perish, cease to be, be corrupted: return to elements, parts, i.3.983b9; iii.4.1000b26; vii.10.1035a18–34; and "ideas," mathematical entities, i.9; iii.2, 5; xiii.4, 5; xiv.5, 6; becoming (*see* 116); being, ii.2.994b6–9; iv.5.1010a20; v.2.1014a24; xi.1.1059b30; xii.1. 1069a31; perishable, imperishable, iii.1, 2, 4; v.16; vii.16;

allatio, adduce (explanations), iii.4.1000a14; μεταφέρειν, *transferre*, transfer: metaphor, i.9.991a22; v.3, 4, 12, 13, 16, 26; xiii.5.1079b26

122. πίπτειν, *cadere*, fall, be related to, iv.2.1005a2; v.2.1013b17; xi.2.1060a18, 7.1064a19; xii.5.1070b7; xiii.8.1084a5; xiv.6. 1093a10

122a. ἐμπίπτειν, *cadere*, fall, i.5.986a15; iv.4.1008b17; xiii.8. 1084a5; συμπίπτειν, *accidere*, vi.2.1026b13; σύμπτωμα, coincidence, xiv.6.1093b17

123. ἀνάγκη, *necessitas*, necessity: explanation, principles, i.4, 5, 8–10; iii.3; reasoning, science, i.9; iii.1, 2; ix.2; xi.7; xiii.4, 10; perishable, imperishable, ii.2; vi.1; vii.15; x.10; unity, being, iii.4; iv.5; v.4; vii.6, 7, 17; x.2–4, 6; xi.1, 5; change, iii.4; iv.8; viii.1, 4; xi.11, 12; xii.3; in speech, iv.4, 6, 7; v.10, 17; vii.4, 5, 10, 15; and impossible, iv.4; v.5; ix.4; primary being, iv.4; vii.1, 3, 9, 14; viii.3; ix.8; xii.1, 2, 4, 6, 8, 10; truth, falsity, iv.5, 8; v.12; xi.6; priority, iv.5; v.11; vii.7; compulsion, v.5; and accidental, v.30; vi.2, 3; xi.8; power, act, ix.2, 5, 8, 9; xi.9; xiv.2; antithesis, x.5, 7, 8; xiv.1; infinite, xi.10; "ideas," mathematical entities, iii.6; x.4; xiii.1–4, 6–10; xiv.1–6

123a. ἀναγκαῖον, *necessarium*, necessary: defined, v.5; conditions, i.1, 2; knowledge, philosophy, i.2; iv.4; xi.7; elements, i.4; xiv.2; logic, formal, i.9, 10; iii.2; iv.3–5, 7, 8; vi.1; vii.15, 16; viii.1; xi.5; xiii.4; "ideas," numbers, etc., i.9; iii.4, 6; vii.6; xiii.2, 7–10; xiv.2; principles, explanation, ii.1, 2; iii.4; iv.1; difficulty, iii.1, 2, 4, 6; change, iii.4; xi.6; being, unity, iii.4; iv.5; x.2; possible, accidental, iii.6; v.12; xi.8; perishable, imperishable, x.10; categories, xii.4; first mover, xii.7, 8; good, xiv.4

123b. ἀναγκάζειν, *cogere*, force, i.3.984b10, 5.986b31; v.5.1015a31; xi.5.1062a33; xii.10.1075b16

123c. συναναγκάζειν, *cogere*, coactively force, i.3.984a19

124. δεῖν, *oportere*, *egere*, should, must, i.2.982a18, b9, 983a11, 17, 9.992b32; ii.3.995a12; iii.1.995a25, 33, 36, 2.997b18, 3.998a21, b15, 999a16, 17, 6.1002b12; iv.2.1003b18, 3.1005b4, 4.1006a7, 8, 10, 1008b23; vi.1.1025b28, 1026a4; vii.9.1034b2, 11.1037a11, 12.1037b27, 15.1040a5, 17.1041b2; viii.3.1043a29, 4.1044a15; ix.6.1048a36; xi.6.1063a13; *et passim*

125. ἐπὶ τὸ πολύ, *secundum magis*, for the most part, v.30.1025a15, 20; vi.1.1025b28, 2.1026b24–1027a27; xi.8

125a. ἐπὶ πλέον, *in plus*, (have application) beyond, ix.10.1046a1
126. τύχη, *fortuna*, luck, chance, i.1.981a5, 3.984b14; vii.7.1032a29;
ix.7.1049a4; xi.8.1065a26–b4; xii.3.1070a4–9
126a. τυγχάνειν, *contingere*, *sortiri*, *adipisci*, happen, achieve, get
at, ἐπιτυγχάνειν, *proficere*, succeed: experience, i.1.981a14;
truth, i.2.981a22, 5.987a12; ii.1.993a31; iii.3.998a20; vii.6.
1032a10; xii.9.1074b24; random, accidental, i.5.986a33, 8.989b2;
v.11, 27, 30; vi.2.1027a17, 3.1027b13; vii.8.1033a28; xi.8.
1064b36, 1065a9, 12; xii.10.1075a20, 22; beings, iii.2.997a1;
xiii.1.1076a24; change, xi.12.1068a29; xii.2.1069b28, 6.1071b34,
8.1073b11, 8.1074a20; number, xiii.7.1082a2–5, 12, 37
126b. δυστυχής, *infortunatus*, unfortunate, i.2.983a1; xi.8.1065b1
126c. ἀποτυγχάνειν, *fallere*, miss, ii.1.993b1
127. αὐτόματον, *automaton*, *casus*, automatism, i.2.983a14, 3.
984b14; vii.7.1032a13, 29, b23, 9.1034a10, b4; xi.8.1065b3;
xii.3.1070a4–9
128. ἁμαρτάνειν, *delinquere*, go wrong, fail, διαμαρτάνειν, *peccare*,
miss the mark, ἁμαρτία, ἁμάρτημα, *peccatum*, defect, mistake,
i.1.981a23, 8.988b24; ii.1.993b5; iv.2.1004b8; vii.15.1040a29;
ix.9.1051a20; xiii.8.1083b4, 24; xiv.1.1088a21, 3.1090b32
129. κωλύειν, *prohibere*, iv.4.1009a4; v.5, 23; ix.5.1048a16–21,
ix.7; nothing to prevent, iv.4.1007a10, 8.1012a32; vi.2.1026b8
(accidents); vii.6.1031b31 (being immediately), 11.1036a35,
15.1040a14; ix.4.1047b8, 17, 8.1050b17, 22 (possible); xi.12.
1068b34; xii.3.1070a25 (endure); xiii.10.1087a7; xiv.6.1093a6, 8
130. ἄπειρον, *infinitum*, infinite, innumerable, unlimited: defined,
xi.10; early views, i.3, 5–8; x.6.1059b29, 32; infinite regress,
ii.2; iii.4.999b10, 1000b28; iv.4.1006a9, 1007b1, 9, 5.1010a22,
7.1012a12, 8.1012b22; v.20; vii.5.1030b35, 6.1032a3, 8.1033b4,
17.1041b22; xi.2.1060a36, 12.1068a33; xii.3.1070a2, 8.1074a29;
principles, statements, iii.3.998b32, 6.1002b21; iv.4.1006b6,
8.1012b20; individuals, beings, iii.4.999a27; iv.6.1011b12; vii.
1.1028b6, 14.1039b; xi.2.1060a4; xiii.10.1087a10; and limit,
iv.2.1004b33; xiv.3.1091a17; accidents, iv.4.1007a14; vi.2.
1026b7; xi.8.1065a26; division, viii.3.1043b35; potentially,
ix.6.1048b9–17; element, x.1.1052b10; x.2.1053b16; and change,
xi.12.1068b4; xii.2.1069b30, 6.1071b7; first mover, xii.7.1073a7–
11; mathematics, xii.8.1073a20; xiii.2.1076a39, 7.1081a11, 8.
1083b36–1084a10, 9.1085b23–27
131. πέρας, *terminus*, *finitum*, limit, i.5.986a23, 8.990a8, 9.992a23;

10.1067a25, 28, 12.1069a4; xii.7.1072a24, xii.8; xiii.4.1079b7, 8.1083b30; xiv.6.1093a29

138a. μεταξύ, *medius, intermedius,* between, intermediate: mathematical entities, i.6.987b16, 29, 9.991b27–31, 992b16; iii.1. 995b17, 2.997a34–998a19, 6.1002b; xi.1; xiii.2.1077a11, 9. 1085a4; xiv.3.1090b35; process, ii.2.994a20, b4; v.7; vii.7. 1032b18; kinds, iii.3.998b28; x.8.1058a20; excluded middle, iv.7.1011b; x.4.1055b, 5.1056a12–24, x.7; means, v.2; state, v.22; and change, xi.11, 12.1068b27–35; xii.2.1069b4

139. μειγνύναι, *permiscere,* mix, μῖγμα, *mixtum, mixtura,* mixture, i.8.989a30–b21, 990a24, 9.991a15; iv.5.1009a27, 7.1012a27, 28; v.4; vii.14.1039b6; viii.2.1042b29, 1043a1, 11, 13, viii.3; xii.2.1069b22, 10.1075b6; xiii.5.1079b19, 7.1082a21, 9.1085b11; xiv.4.1091b8, 5.1092a24, 25, b7, 21, 22, 6.1092b27, 31

140. μαθηματική, *mathematica, doctrinalis,* mathematical (science): in Egypt, i.1.981b23; Pythagoreans, i.5.985b, 8.989b32, 990a15; entities, i.6.985b15, 9.992b16; iii.1.995b17, 6.1002b; xi.1; xiii.8, 9; xiv.2–4; philosophy, i.9.992a32; iv.1.1003a25, 2. 1004a6–9; xi.3.1061a28–b3, 4.1061b17–27; xi.7; xii.8.1073b4, 11; being, primary being, i.9.992b1–7; iii.2.997a29, b2; v.14; vii.2.1028b20, 11.1036b32–1037a5; viii.1.1042a12, 22; x.3. 1054b18; xii.1.1069a35, 36, 10.1075b38; xiii.1–3, 4.1078b7, xiii.6, 7; explanation, ii.3.995a6, 15; iii.2.996a29–b1; vi.1. 1025b5; axioms, iv.3.1005a20; theoretical, vi.1.1026a; xi.7; and sensibles, vii.10.1036a4, 12; xiv.5.1092a18, 19, 6.1093b27

141. ἀριθμητική, *arithmetica,* arithmetic, ἀριθμός, *numerus,* number: and geometry, i.2.982a28, 9.992a10–24, b12–16; iii.1.996a13; iv.3.1005a31; xii.8.1073b7; xiii.3, 9; explanations, i.5, 6.987b12, 24, 8.990a18–32, 9.991b9–12; xii.10.1075b29, 38; xiii.6; xiv.1–3, 5, 6; and unity, i.5.986a19–21; iii.4.1001a24–27, b5–27; v.6, 9; viii.6.1045a8; x.1, 2, 3.1054a32, 33, x.6; xii.10.1075b34; xiii.7, 8, 9.1085a28; xiv.1, 2, 4, 5; independent, i.6.987b27–34; iii.3. 998a8, 4.1001a25; xiii.2.1076b36–39, 1077a12; xiii.6–9; xiv.4. 1092a8; and "ideas," i.9.990b1–8, 991b9–992a24, b16; vii.2. 1028b24–27, 11.1036b7–1037a5; xii.8.1073a17–22, 10.1075b27; xiii.4.1078b11, 22, xiii.3, 4.1092a8; count, ii.2.994b25; v.6, 12, 13; xiii.4.1078b34, 36, 6.1080a30, 7.1081b14, 1082b28–37; xiv. 6.1093a19; of principles, iii.1.996a1, 4.999b24–1000a4, 6.1002b; xi.2.1060b29; and primary being, iii.5; iv.2.1004b6, 10; v.8; vii.2.1028b23, 11.1037a12, 13.1039a11–14, 14.1039a28; viii.3.

INDEX OF TECHNICAL TERMS

1043b32–1044a14; x.2; xi.2.1060b6–12; xiii.6, 7.1082b37; xiv.2, 4.1092a8; odd, even, iv.7.1012a10; vii.5.1031a3, 6; quality, relatives, totality, v.14, 15, 26, 27; and infinite, xi.10.1066b8, 24–26

141a. δύο, *duo*, two, i.2.983a5, 3.984b, 4.985b21, 5.986a31, b33, 987a, 6.988a9; vii.4.1000a4; v.2; δυάς, *dualitas*, two, duality, dyad, i.6, 9; iii.3.999a8; vii.11.1036b12–20; x.5.1056a10, x.6; xiii.4, 6–9; xiv.1–3; διχῶς, *dupliciter*, in two ways (meanings), ii.2; iv.5; v.4, 8, 24, 26; vii.4, 13; viii.4; x.1, 6; xi.9; συνδυάζειν, *copulare*, couple, vii.5.1031a6; join, viii.2.1043a4; διπλάσιος, *duplus*, double, διπλασιάζειν, double, i.5.987a22–27, 9.990b32–34; v.29.1025a1; vii.13.1039a6; x.6.1055b6–8; xiii.4.1079a28–30, 8.1084a6; xiv.3.1091a12, 6.1093a22

142. γεωμετρία, *geometria*, geometry: and arithmetic (*see* 141); diagonal of the square, i.2; iv.8; v.7, 12, 29; ix.4, 10; x.1; and demonstration, iii.2.996b34, 997a25–34; xiv.2.1089a21–25; geometrical entities, iii.2.997b, 998a; vi.1.1026a26; xiii.2.1077a3; Zeno, iii.4.1001b7–25; and primary being, iii.5; iv.2.1004b6, 1005a11; xi.2.1060b12–19; power, v.12; ix.1.1046a8; and accidents, vi.2.1026b10–12; one, xi.3.1061b3

142a. μέγεθος, *magnitudo*, magnitude: material, sensible, i.8. 988b23, 990a12, 26; iii.2.997b32–35; xii.10.1075b29; xiii.2, 3.1077b21; xiv.3.1090b1, 1091a1; truth, ii.1.993b3; and being, unity, iii.4.1001b7–25; v.6, 13, 16, 17, 21; vii.2.1028b23, 13. 1039a10; x.1.1052a28, 1053a7, 18, 25; xiii.2.1077a21, xiii.3; xiv.1.1087b35, 4.1092a1, 5.1092b10; infinite, xi.10; and movement, xii.7.1073a5–11, 8.1073a38; and numbers, xiii.6.1080b, 8.1083b13–17, 1084b37, 9.1085a21, 22; xiv.1.1087b17, 3.1090b

143. ἀστρολογία, *astrologia*, astronomy, i.2.982b, 983a, 8.989b33; iii.2.997b16–20, 35, 998a5; vi.1.1026a26; x.1.1053a10; xii.8. 1073b5, xiii.2.1077a1–6

143a. οὐρανός, *caelum*, sky, heaven, cosmos, i.5.986a, b24, 8. 989b34, 990a; iii.2.997b, 998a; iv.5.1010a28; v.23; vii.2.1028b12, 27; viii.1.1042a10; ix.8.1050b23; x.1.1053a11; xi.8.1065b3; xii.6.1072a2, 7.1072a23, b14, 8.1074a31–38, 10.1075b26; xiii. 2.1077a3; xiv.3.1090a25, 34, 6.1093b4

144. ἁρμονική, *harmonica*, music, (mathematical) harmony, i.5. 985b31; iii.2.997b20–26; xiii.2.1077a5, 3.1078a14; xiv.6.1093b22

145. μηχανῇ, *artificialiter*, mechanically, i.4.985a18; xiii.3.1078a16

146. μετρεῖν, *commetiri*, measure, μέτρον, *metrum*, measure,

ἀσυμμετρία, *incommensuratio*, incommensurability, i.2.983a12–20, 5.987a10; v.6, 13, 15; vii.10.1034b33; xi.3.1061a6; xiv.5. 1092b34; symmetry, beauty, xiii.3.1078b1; diagonal of square (*see* 142); one (*see* 24); man (*see* 151)

147. τὸ μέγα καὶ τὸ μικρόν, *magnum et parvum*, great-and-small, i.6, 7, 9; iii.3.998b10; v.3, 13; x.5, 7.1057b1; xiii.8.1083b23–26; xiv.1–4; μᾶλλον, *magis*, more, rather, higher, i.9.992b2; ii.2. 994b18; iii.3.998b17, 999a1, 4, 5.1002a26; iv.4.1008b32; vii.2. 1028b19, 3.1029a6, 11.1037a17, 16.1040b21; viii.1.1042a14; x.3.1054b8, 7.1057b23–29; xi.2.1060a15, 10.1067a10; xii.1. 1069a27, 10.1075a14; xiii.2.1077a7, 8.1084a30; *et passim*; μάλιστα, *maxime*, most, especially, ii.1.993b24; iii.2.996b3, 3.998b14, 5.1001b32, 1002a26; vii.1.1028a36, b6, 5.1031a13, 13.1039a20; x.2.1053b21, 8.1058a15; xii.7.1072b19; *et passim*

148. ὑπεροχή, *excedentia, excessus, superabundantia*, excess, too much, ὑπερέχον, *continens, superparticulare*, ὑπερεχόμενον, *contentum, subparticulare*, i.9.992b6; iv.2.1004b12; v.11, 15; viii.2.1042b25, 35; x.1.1052b29, 30, 6.1056a13, b17, 26, 1057a14; xiii.8.1084a17; xiv.1

148a. ἔλλειψις, *defectio, defectus*, deficiency, too little, i.9.992b7; iv.2.1004b12; viii.2.1042b25, 35; x.6.1056b19, 27

149. κόσμος, *mundus*, order, cosmos, celestial bodies, i.3.984b16, 8.990a22; xi.6.1063a15

149a. διακόσμησις, *ornatum*, arrangement, i.5.986a6

149b. κοσμοποιία, *mundi generatio*, create the world, i.4.985a19; xiv.3.1091a18

149c. κατασκευάζειν, *facere, constituere*, establish, give an account of, set up, i.1.981b21, 4.984b25, 9.991b28; vii.8.1034a3; xi.2. 1060a18; xiii.6.1080b18, 8.1083b22; xiv.4.1091a25

150. πᾶν, *omne*, every, everything: knowledge, i.2, 9.992b29; iv.2.1004a34, b20, 3.1005b6; unity, being, i.3–5, 8, 9; iii.4; iv.14; vii.4, 8, 11, 17; xi.1, 2, 10; xii.2, 10; xiv.2; genesis, i.4. 984b26, 5.986b17; iii.4.1000a28; numbers, i.5.985b; vii.11.1036b; xiv.6; "ideas," i.6.987b19; iii.4.999b18; in process, i.8.988b27; iii.4.1000b19; iv.5.1010a36, 8.1012b22–31; mixed, i.8; iv.5; x.6; xi.6; xii.2, 6, 7; factors, iii.2.996b5; primary beings, iii.2. 997a16; principles, iii.3, 4.1001a1; xi.2.1060a8; xii.4, 5, 10. 1075b14; perceived, iii.4.999b2; iv.5.1010a30; and contraries, iv.2.1005a3; xii.10.1075a28–38; accidental, iv.4; true, false, iv.7–9; xi.6.1063b30–35; necessary, xi.10; xii.1, 8, 10; the

"All," xi.10; xii.1, 8, 10; *et passim*; πάντῃ, *omnino*, in every respect, πάντως, *omnino*, *quocunque modo*, *qualitercumque*, in every way, iii.4.1001b11; v.1016b25, 27; vii.10.1035b24, 11. 1036b30; ix.5.1048a18; x.1.1053a1, 23, 4.1055b22, 6.1057a14; xi.3.1061a25, 10.1066b32, 33; etc.

V. HUMAN NATURE AND SOUL

151. ἄνθρωπος, *homo*, man: and wisdom, i.1; "third," i.9.990b17, 991a28, b9–21; vii.13.1039a2; xi.1.1059b8; xiii.4.1079a13; animal, iv.4; v.2, 14, 18, 27–29; vi.2.1026b37; vii.5, 12, 13.1038b18, vii.14, 17.1041a21; viii.3.1043b10, 6.1045a14–20; xiii.4.1079b9, 5.1079b32, 7.1082a19; and opinion, iv.6.1011b; nature, v.4; viii.6; unity, v.6.1016b5; primary being, vii.1, 10, 11, 14; viii.3; actual, potential, ix.8; "measure," x.1.1053a36; xi.6

151a. ἀνθρώπινος, *humanus*, human, suited to man, i.2.982b28, 5.986a31; xii.9.1075a7

151b. ἀνθρωποειδής, *humanae speciei*, *conformis hominibus*, like men, iii.2.997b10; xii.8.1074b5

152. ζωή, *vita*, living, ix.8.1050b1; ζῆν, *vivere*, live, i.1.980b26; v.5, 26; vi.3.1027b9; ix.6.1088b25–27; ζῷον, *animal*, living being, animal: nature, intelligence, iv.5.1009b7; v.1, 4, 6; vi.1.1026a2; x.8.1058a2–8; man (*see* 151); primary being, v.8; vii.2, 4.1031a4, vii.10, 16.1040b14; viii.1.1042a10; xi.2.1060a16; xii.1.1069a32; xiii.2.1077a8; production, vii.9.1034b18; xii.7.1072b33; and death, viii.5; divine, xii.7.1072b26–30

153. βίος, *vita*, life, iv.2.1004b24; xiv.6.1093a6

154. ἄψυχος, *inanimatus*, inanimate, i.1.981b1–6; v.12; ix.2. 1046a36, 3.1047a4; xi.2.1060a16; xiii.2.1077a20; ἔμψυχος, *animatus*, animate, iv.5.1010b31; v.14; vii.11.1036b32, 16.1040b10; ix.5.1048a4; xiii.2.1077a20; ψυχή, *anima*, soul, i.5.985b30; v.18; vi.1.1026a5; vii.10, 11, 16.1040b11; viii.3.1043a29–b3, 6.1045b9– 16; ix.2, 7.1049a30, 8.1050b1; xi.12; 1068b12; xii.6.1072a2, 10.1075b35; xiii.2.1077a21, 22, 34; xiv.3.1090b18; mind, ii.1. 993b10; vii.15.1040a4; xii.3.1070a26; xiv.3.1090a37; and primary being, v.8; vii.2.1028b23; xii.5.1071a3; and art, vii.7. 1032b1, 5, 23

155. ὁρμή, *impetus*, impulse, v.5, 23; xii.7.1072b12

156. ὀρέγεσθαι, *appetere*, *desiderare*, have an impulse, ὄρεξις,

appetitus, desire, i.1.980a21; ix.5.1048a10–15; xii.5.1071a3, 7.1072a26–29; xiv.4.1092a2

157. ἔθος, *consuetudo*, habit, practice, i.1.981b5; ii.3; ix.5.1047b32, 34

157a. εἰωθός, *consuetum*, usual, familiar, i.9.991a20; ii.3.995a1; iv.3.1005b28; vii.8.1033b27, 11.1036b25; viii.6.1045a21; xiii.2. 1077a15, 5.1079b24.

158. ἐπιθυμεῖν, *cupere*, desire, ἐπιθυμητόν, *concupiscibile*, desirable, ἐπιθυμία, *desiderium*, desire, i.4.984b24; ix.3.1047a34, 5.1048a21; xii.7.1072a27

159. ἀγαπᾶν, *diligere*, prize, ἀγάπησις, *dilectio*, delight, i.1.980a22, 23; xiii.1.1076a15

159a. ἐπιτιμᾶν, *increpare*, censure, object, reproach, iv.5.1010a13, 26; x.5.1056a31; xiv.4.1091a30; τίμιος, *honorabilis, nobilis*, i.1.981a31, 2.983a2–11, 3.983b32, 33; vi.1.1026a21; ix.8.1051a4; xi.7.1064b4; xii.9.1074b21, 26, 30, 10.1075b20

159b. ἔρως, *amor*, love, i.4.984b23–31, 7.988a34; ἐρώμενον, *amatum*, object of love, xii.7.1072b3

159c. φιλία, *amicitia*, love, friendship, νεῖκος, *lis, odium*, strife, i.4, 7; iii.1, 4; iv.2; x.2; xii.6, 10; xiv.4, 5; treat with consideration, xii.8.1073b16

160. διώκειν, *persequi*, pursue, i.2.982b21; iv.5.1009b38

161. φεύγειν, *effugere*, διαφεύγειν, *diffugere*, escape, elude, baffle, disappear, i.2.982b20; iii.5.1001b28, 1002a27; vii.3.1029a11; ix.4.1047b5; xii.9.1074b32; xiv.3.1090b21, 4.1091b23, 33, 6. 1093b10

162. ἡδονή, *voluptas, delectatio*, pleasure, i.1.981b21; xiii.7.1072b16

163. χρεία, *utilitas*, utility, i.1; χρῆσις, *usus*, action, ix.8.1050a24, 20; xii.8.1074b5; χρῆμα, *res*, thing; possession, iv.4.1007b26; viii.1.1043a17; x.6.1056b29; xi.6.1062b13; χρήσιμος, *utilis*, useful, xi.3.1061a5; xiv.2.1090a11; χρῆσθαι, *uti*, use, make use of, treat, i.4.985a17–23, 33, 5.987a12, 6.988a9, 8.989a30 (explanations); iii.2.997a4, 10, 3.998b10; x.5.1055b38 (principles); iv.3.1005a23–27, 4.1006a2; xi.4.1061b18 (axioms); v.7, 9, 11; vii.8.1033b28, 10.1035b7; ix.1.1045b36; x.1.1052b33; xi.7.1064a20, b20, 8.1064b34; xii.10.1075b12; xiv.2.1089b11, 5.1092b1

164. κρίνειν, *judicare*, judge, determine, advocate, estimate, i.4.984b32, 8.989a7, 990a24; iii.1.995b3; iv.5.1009b2, 6.1011a5; x.1.1053a12; xi.6.1063a13

INDEX OF TECHNICAL TERMS

166. βλέπειν, *videre*, see, i.5.986b28; ἀποβλέπειν, *respicere*, gaze, look up, i.5.986b24, 9.991a23; xiii.5.1079b; ἐπιβλέπειν, *inspicere*, observe, i.9.991a8; xiii.4.1079b27; ὁρᾶν, *videre*, see, i.8. 989a23; iii.5.1002a16; vii.11.1036b1, 16.1041a1; ix.6, 8; xii.5. 1071a17, 8.1073a28, 9.1074b32, 33; xiii.7.1082b5, 9.1086a3, 6, 10.1087a19; xiv.2.1090a8, 3.1090a19, b8, 6.1093a28, b5; παρορᾶν, *praetermittere*, overlook, fail to see, iii.1.995a27; xiv.6.1093a28; συνορᾶν, *conspicere*, comprehend, ix.6.1048a37; ἰδεῖν, *videre*, examine, see, viii.1.1042a20; ix.3.1046b33, 9. 1051a26, 28; xi.2.1060a12, 8.1064b31, 9.1066a26; xiv.2.1089b3; ἀκούειν, *audire*, attend to studies, iv.3.1005b5; ἀκρόασις, *auditio*, instruction, ii.3.994b32

167. μνήμη, *memoria*, memory, i.1.980; iv.5.1009b26; xii.7.1072b18

168. ἐμπειρία, *experientia*, *experimentum*, experience, ἀπειρία, *inexperientia*, inexperience, i.1; infinity, i.7.988a28

VI. MIND

169. νοῦς, *intellectus*, mind: explanation, i.3.984b15, 4.985a18–21, 5.985b30, 7.988a34, b8, 8.989b15, 9.992a30; ii.2.994b14–16; vi.1.1025b22; vii.9.1034a24; xi.8.1065b4; xii.5.1071a3, 6.1072a5, 10.1075b8–13; xiv.4.1091b12; blind, ii.1.993b11; sound, iv.5. 1009b5; actual, xii.2.1069b31, 3.1070a26, 6.1072a5; and movement, xii.6.1072a5, 7.1072a30, b18–30, xii.9

169a. νοεῖν, *intelligere*, think, know, understand, i.9.990b14; xiii.4.1079a10 ("ideas"); ii.2.994b23, 24, 26; iv.4.1006b10, 1008a23 (not indefinite); v.6; vi.4.1027b23; vii.7.1032b8 (and production), 12.1038a33; ix.6.1048b23, 24, 34, 10.1051b32–1052a4 (actuality); x.1.1052b2; xi.2.1060b11; xii.7.1072b18–30, xii.9; xiii.9.1085a30, 31; xiv.5.1092a28

169b. νοητός, *intellectualis*, *intelligibilis*, intelligible, conceived, i.8.990a30; iii.4.999b2; iv.7.1012a2; xii.4.1070b7, 7.1072a26, 30, b18–30, xii.9; and perceptible (*see* 165c)

169c. νόησις, *intelligentia*, thought, conception, denotation, knowing, i.9.991b27; v.6; vii.7.1032b15–17, 10.1036a6; ix.9.1051a30; x.1.1052a30, b1; xii.7.1072a30, b17, 18

169d. νόημα, *intelligentia*, intelligible, i.9.990b25; xiii.4.1079a21

169e. ἐννόημα, *conceptio*, item of information, i.1.981a6

170. διάνοια, *mens*, *intellectus*, *meditatio*, intellect, intention, meaning, judgment, thinking, thought, i.3.984a5, 4.985a4,

INDEX OF TECHNICAL TERMS

2.1026b4; xi.7; and opinion, vii.15.1039b31–34; power, act, ix.2.1046b2–24, 8.1049b33–1050a2, 20; measure, x.1.1053a31–b3, 6.1057a7–12, 16; and opposition, x.4.1055a32, 6.1056b36; xiii.4.1078b27; and the accidental, xi.8; xiii.3.1077b34; and movement, xi.11.1067a11, 12.1068a33; principles, xiii.4.1078b29; and the sensible, xiv.3.1090a27

179a. ἐπίστασθαι, *scire, studere,* know, i.2; ii.2.994a28–30, b20; iii.2.996b15, 4.999b26; iv.3.1005b5, 4.1008b27, 30; v.7; vii.6. 1031b20, 21; viii.6.1045b11; ix.6.1048a34; x.1.1053b1; xiii.10. 1087a15

179b. ἐπιστητόν, *scibile,* intelligible, known, i.2; iii.2.996b13, 6.1003a14; v.15; vii.4.1030a33, 34; x.6.1057a7–12, 16, 7.1057b1; xi.7.1064b6; xiii.10.1086b22, 32

180. σοφία, *sapientia,* wisdom, i.1, 2, 9.992a24; iii.1.995b12, 2.996b2–26, 4.1000a18; iv.2.1004b19, 3.1005b1; xi.1.1059a18–34, 2.1060a10, 4.1061b33; xii.10.1075b20

180a. σοφός, *sapiens,* wise, sage, i.1, 2, 5.987a3; iii.5.1002a11; xiv.4.1091b11

181. γνῶσις, *cognitio, notitia,* knowledge, i.1.981a16, b11; iii.4. 1000b6 (like by like); v.11, 17; vii.1.1028a33; ix.6.1048b15, 8.1049b17

181a. γινώσκειν, *cognoscere,* know, understand, recognize, i.2. 982a11, 9.992b28, 31; ii.2.994b22, 29, 3.995a5; iii.1.995b1, 2.997a2, 4, 4.1006a7; iv.5.1010a25; v.1.1013a19; ix.9.1051a32; x.1.1052b20–27; xi.6.1062b23

181b. γνῶναι, *nosse,* know, understand, recognize, i.2.982a10, 9.993a8; iii.4.1001a5; v.1, 6; vi.1.1026a11; vii.1.1028a37, b2, 6.1031b7, 4.1029b10, 11, 10.1036a9, 15.1040a11; x.1.1052a32

181c. γνωρίζειν, *cognoscere,* know, take cognizance of, recognize, i.1.980a26, 981a22, 30, b6, 2.982a24, b3, 5, 3.983a26, 9.992b25, 30, 993a2; ii.2.994b30; iii.2.996a21, b16, 997a1, 4, 28, 3.998b3, 5, 4.999a29, 1000b4; iv.2.1004a20, 23, b7, 3.1005a28, b8, 14, 16; v.6.1016b19; vii.10.1036a6, 8, 11.1037a16, 15.1040a25; viii.4. 1044b5; x.1.1053a19, 32, 34

181d. γνώριμος, *notus,* familiar, i.9.992b33, 993a7; ii.3.995a3; iii.4.1000a14, 1001a13; iv.3.1005b13, 4.1007a17; vii.1.1029a1–12, 16.1040b20; x.2.1053b14; xi.5.1062a14; xiii.3.1078b5

181e. γνωριστικός, *sciens,* philosophy, iv.2.1004b26

182. εἰδέναι, *scire, noscere,* know, i.1, 2, 3.983a25, 4.985a16, 9.

992b27, 32; ii.2.994b21, 29; iii.2.996b19, 20; v.29; vii.1.1028a36, b1, 12.1038a11; ix.9.1051a28; x.1.1053a7; xi.7.1064a20

183. πειθώ, *persuasio*, persuasion, iv.5.1009a17; xii.8.1074b4; πίστις, *fides*, conviction, πιστεύειν, *credere*, rely on, believe, i.3.983b6; iii.2.997b18; iv.5.1010a34, 6.1011a3, 10, 14; xi.3. 1061a26; xii.8.1073b16; xiii.4.1078b13, 9.1086a20; xiv.2.1090a3, 10

184. μανθάνειν, *discere, addiscere*, learn, μαθητικός, *disciplinabilis*, teachable, i.1.980, 2.983a19, 9.992b24–993a10; ii.2. 994a28–30; v.1.1013a1–4; vi.2.1027a22; vii.4.1029b4; ix.3. 1046b37, 5.1047b33, 6.1048b18–35, 8.1049b31–1050a2; xi.12. 1068b15

184a. παιδεύειν, *erudire*, train, ii.3.995a12

185. διδάσκειν, *docere*, teach, δίδαξις, *doctrina*, instruction, διδασκαλικός, *doctrinalis*, educative, i.1.981b, 2.982a; vi.2. 1027a22; vii.17.1041b10; viii.3.1043b26; ix.8.1050a17–22

186. ἐπαΐειν, *obviare, audire*, understand, i.1.981a24; iii.2.996b34; iv.2.1004b10

187. θεωρεῖν, *speculari, considerare*, see, understand, examine, inquire into, reflect: eliminate amazement, i.2.983a14; explanatory factors, i.3.983a34, 4.985b3; ii.3.995a20; iii.1.995b5, 2.996a19, b25; forms, mathematical entities, i.5.985b27; iii. 2.998a10, 4.999a25, 1001b14; vi.1.1062a10; xi.3.1061a30, 35; xiii.3.1078a15, 21, 24, 5.1080a11, 6.1080a13, 9.1086a31; xiv.4. 1091a28; elements, i.5.986b10; truth, ii.1.993a30, b23; vi.4. 1027b28; difficulties, iii.1.995a34, b25, 4.1001a4; attributes, accidents, iii.2.997a20, 22, 24, 32; vi.2.1926b11; xi.4.1061b29; being, primary being, iv.1–3; vi.1.1026a31; vii.1.1028b7, 3. 1029a26, 4.1029b2; xi.3.1061b6, 4.1061b27; xiii.1.1076a13, 9.1086a26; soul, vi.1.1026a5; general, vii.13.1038b34; xiii.10. 1087a20; potentially, actually, ix.6.1048a34, 8.1050a12–14, 36; demonstration, xi.1.1059a24; contrariety, principles, opinion, definition, xi.3.1061a15, 19, 4.1061b19, 6.1062b20, 7.1064a26

187a. θεωρία, *theoria, theorica, contemplatio, speculatio*, theory: about beings, primary beings, i.8.989b25; iii.1.995b19, 2.997a26; vii.11.1037a16; xi.3.1061b7; xii.1.1069a18, 8.1073b6; axioms, iv.3.1005a29; accidental, vi.2.1026b4; in knower, ix.8.1050a36; about abstractions, xi.3.1061a29, 4.1061b22; the best, xii.7. 1072b24

187b. θεωρητικός, *speculativus, speculatrix, theoricus*, theoretical, i.1.982a1, 2.982a29, b9; ii.1.993b20; iv.2.1005a16, 3.1005a35; vi.1, 2.1026b5; ix.8.1050a12–14; xi.3.1061b11, xi.7; xii.9.1075a2

187c. σχολάζειν, *vacare*, have leisure, i.1.981b23, 24; ἐλεύθερος, *liber*, free, i.2.982b26, 27; ii.3.995a12; μελετᾶν, *meditare*, be trained, ix.8.1050a13

188. πρακτικός, *activus, practicus*, practical, i.1.981b5; ii.1.993b21; vi.1, 2.1026b5; xi.7

188a. πράττειν, *agere, operari*, do, act, i.1.980a24, 25, 981a13; ii.2.994b14, 15; v.23; vi.1.1025b24; xi.1.1059a36, 7.1064a14, 15

188b. πρᾶξις, *actus*, action, activity, i.1.981a17, 7.988b6; iii.2. 996a26, 27, b22; iv.6.1011a11; v.17, 20; vii.4.1029b6; ix.6. 1048b18–23; xiii.3.1078a32

188c. πρᾶγμα, *res*, thing, concrete thing, state of affairs: memory of, i.1.980b29; and explanation, principles, i.3.984a18, b15; iii.1.996a10, 2.996b4, 3.998b18, 4.1000b1; iv.3.1005b10; v.1; movement, production, i.4.984b30; v.1; vii.9.1034a13; xi.9. 1065b7; definition, concepts, i.5.987a23; iii.2.996b16; v.6; vii.5.1030b31, 10.1034b20–24, 11.1036a31, 1037a19, 20, 12. 1038a20; x.1.1052a18, b12; xi.7.1064a24; numbers, "ideas," formal being, i.6.987b28, 9.991b2, 10.993a18; v.18; xii.10. 1075b35; xiii.5.1080a1, 6.1080b1; xiv.5.1092b25, 6.1093a4; discourse, knowledge, iv.4.1006b, 5.1009a26; v.17; ix.1.1046b8; x.1.1053a31; xii.9.1075a1, 3; true, false, v.29; vi.4.1027b26, 31; ix.10.1051b2, 5; xiii.9.1086a1; primary being, vii.16.1040b19, 17.1041b29; art, actuality, ix.3.1047a2, 6.1048a31, 9.1051a18; traits, xiii.3.1078a5

189. ποιητής, *poeta*, poet, i.2.982b32, 3.983b32, 9.991a22; ii.3. 995a8; v.23; xiii.5.1079b26; xiv.4.1091b4; ποίημα, ποίησις, *factio*, doing, making, ποιητικός, *factivus, activus, effectivus*, productive, poetic, active, applied: art, science, i.1.982a1, 2. 982b11; vi.1, 2.1026b5, 1027a6; xi.3.1061a6, xi.7; xii.9.1075a1; and primary being, iv.2.1003b8; vii.3.1029a13; contraries, v.10; xii.10.1075b31; agent, v.15; ix.5.1048a6, 8; making, vii.7.1032a25–b21; power, ix.2.1046b3; xii.6.1071b12

190. ἀγνοεῖν, *ignorare*, be ignorant of, ignore, εὐτέλεια, *parvitas*, limitation, ἀπαιδευσία, *ignorantia, apaedeusia*, lack of training, i.1.981a22, 2.982b, 3.984a4; iii.1.995a30, 36; iv.2.1005b3, 4. 1006a6, 5.1009a19, 31, 1010b13; vii.15.1039b33, 1040a7; viii.3. 1043a29, b24; ix.10.1051b25, 1052a2; xii.10.1075b23

191. θαυμάζειν, *mirari, admirari*, wonder, find strange, i.1.981b14,

i.2, 9.993a1; iv.5.1010b4; xi.6.1063a36; xii.7.1072b25, 26; xiii.7.1082b21, xiv.4.1091b16

192. μῦθος, *fabula*, myth, μυθώδης, *fabularius*, mythical, μυθικῶς, *fabulose*, in mythical form, i.2.982b19; ii.3.995b4; iii.4.1000a18; xii.8.1074b1, 4; xiv.4.1091b9

193. φιλοσοφεῖν, *philosophari*, philosophize, φιλοσοφία, *philosophia*, philosophy, φιλόσοφος, *philosophus*, philosopher: first philosophers, 1.2, 3, 6, 10; truth, i.3.983b2; ii.1.993b20; iv.5. 1001b37; mathematics, i.9.992a23; xii.8.1073b4; being, axioms, iv.2, 3; xi.1.1059b21; first philosophy, vi.1.1026a18–32; vii.11. 1037a15; xi.4; arts, xii.8.1074b11

194. ζητεῖν, *quaerere, inquirere*, seek, search, investigate, ζήτησις, *quaestio, inquisitio*, search, investigation, ἐπιζητεῖν, *quaerere, investigare*, seek to discover: wisdom, science, i.2; ii.3; iii.1, 2; vi.1; xi.1; principles, i.3–10; iv.1; vi.1; vii.16, 17; viii.1, 2, 4, 6; xi.7; xii.5, 6; xiii.4; xiv.3; general truths, i.6; iv.3, 4; xiii.4, 8; elements, i.9; iv.1; primary being, iii.1; vii.1, 3, 9, 11; viii.3; xii.12; xiv.2; unity, being, iii.4; ix.10; x.2; xi.8; number, magnitude, "ideas," iii.4, 6; vii.8; xiii.9; xiv.2, 3; demonstration, contraries, iv.4, 6; x.5, 7; power, ix.3, 6; measure, x.1; accidents, xi.8; infinite, xi.10; movement, xii.8

195. σκέπτεσθαι, ἐπισκέπτεσθαι, *perscrutari, considerare*, inquire, σκέψις, ἐπίσκεψις, *perscrutatio, inquisitio*, inquiry: philosophy, i.2; xi.7.1064a29; beings, i.3.983b2, 8.989b27; iv.2.1004b2, 16; vi.4.1027b29, 1028a3; xi.8.1064b16; explanations, i.5.986b13, 18, 8.989b29; vi.3.1027b16; xi.1.1059b21; dialectic, i.6.987b32; iii.1.995b24; nature, i.9.992b9; ii.3.995a17; primary beings, iii.1.995b18; vii.2.1028b15, 31, 3.1029a33, 4.1029b25, 6.1031a16, 17, 7.1032a32, 9.1034b34, 11.1037a12, 13.1038b1; viii.1.1042a23; xii.8.1073a18; xiii.1; axioms, iv.3, 4.1008a31; definitions, vii. 11.1037a20; true, false, ix.10.1051b6; "ideas," mathematical entities, xii.3.1070a25, 10.1075a11; xiii.4.1078b10, 7.1080b37, 9.1086a28, 30; xiv.2.1090a2, 3.1091a22

195a. σκοπεῖν, *intendere, perscrutari*, examine, ἐπισκοπεῖν, *intendere, investigare, perscrutari*, examine, look upon, σκοπός, *quaestio*, search: goal of search, i.2.983a22; generation, i.8. 988a30; science, ii.1.993b22; iv.1.1003a23, 3.1005a29, 33; xi.1.1059b18, 8.1064b19, 22; xiii.3.1078a18, 4.1078b26, 1079a6; myth, iii.4.1000a19; being, primary being, iv.2.1004b9, 5.1010a2; vii.3.1029a19, 4.1030a27; xi.4.1061b26; definition, vii.12.

1037b28; mathematics, xi.3.1061a36; xiii.6.1080b2; xiv.6. 1093b10; movement, xii.8.1073b5; elements, xiv.2.1088b14

196. πειρᾶν, *tentare*, try, iii.1.995b23; iv.2.1004b25; vii.4.1029b11, 11.1037a14, 15.1040b3; xi.7.1064a6, 36, 8.1064b31; xiii.8. 1084a31; xiv.3.1090a18

197. πραγματεύεσθαι, *tractare, versari*, pursue, πραγματεία, *negotium*, enterprise, system, i.5.986a8, 987a21, 6.987a29, b2, 8.989b33, 9.992b1; iii.1.995b32, 2.997b21; vi.1.1025b9, 17; xi.1.1059b10, 18, 7.1064a3, 8.1064b18, 28; xii.8.1073b15; xiii.4. 1078b18; xiv.2.1088b25

198. μέθοδος, *methodus*, exploration, i.2.983a23, 3.983b4, 984a28; xiii.1.1076a9, 9.1086a24; xiv.3.1091a20

199. μαρτυρεῖν, *testari*, attest, i.2.982b22, 7.988b17; ii.3.995a8; xii.1.1069a25, 6.1072a5; xiv.1.1087b3

200. ἀπορία, ἀπόρημα, διαπόρημα, *dubitatio, defectus*, difficulty: statement of, iii.1.995a30; philosophy, explanation, i.7.988b21, 10.993a27; iii.1.995b4–6, 2.996a18–b26; philosophy, demonstration, iii.1.995b6–10, 2.996b26–997a15; iv.6.1011a6, 7, b2; philosophy, primary being, iii.1.995b10–13, 2.997a15–25; kinds of primary being, iii.1.995b13–18, 2.997a34–998a19; xi.1. 1059a39, b3, 2.1060a7; xiii.2.1076b1, 1077a1; primary being, essential attributes, iii.1.995b18–27, 2.997a25–34; iv.2.1003b22–1005a18; principles as genera or constituents, i.9.993a4; iii. 1.995b27–29, 3.998a20–b14; principles as genera or species, iii.1.995b27–31, 3.998b14–999a23; independent non-material being, iii.1.995b31–36, 4.999a24–b24; number and kinds of principles, iii.1.996a1, 2, 4.999b24–1000a4; perishable and imperishable, iii.1.996a2–4, 4.1000a5–1001a3; xi.2.1060a29; being, unity, iii.1.996a4–9, 4.1001a4–b25; x.2.1053b10; principles whole or individual, iii.1.996a9, 10; principles potential or actual, iii.1.996a10–12; numbers, geometrical entities, iii.1.996a12–15, 5.1001b26–1002b11; definition, vii.5.1030b14, 28, 11.1036b21, 12.1037b9, 11; viii.3.1043b24, viii.6; general, vii.13.1039a14; xi.3.1060b20; xiii.10.1078a13; potentiality, viii.5.1044b29, 34; xii.6.1071b22; unity of individual, viii.6; contraries, x.5.1056a10, 9.1058a34; xii.10.1075a27; wisdom, xi.1.1060a1, 3.1061b15; appearance, xi.6.1062b20; becoming, xi.6.1062b31, 1063b7–15; mind, xii.9.1074b15, 1075a5; "ideas," mathematical entities, xiii.7.1082b34, 9.1085a27, b11, 1086a32, 10.1086b14; xiv.2. 1089b31, 3.1090b3; good, xiv.4.1091a29, 31, b15

1028a3; vii.3.1029a31, 10.1034b34; ix.1.1046a7; xii.8.1074a17; xiv.3.1091a20

205. λανθάνειν, *oblivisci, latere,* escape notice, fail to notice, overlook, neglect, i.9.993a1; ii.2.994b12; vi.1.1025b29; vii.5.1031a7, 15.1040a28, 17.1041a33; viii.3.1043a29, 4.1044a15; x.1.1053a3; xi.7.1064a21; xii.8.1073a15, 10.1075a27; xiii.7.1082a26

206. εὑρίσκειν, *invenire, reperire,* discover, find, i.1.981b13–25, 3.983b5, 4.984b5, 9.992b19; iii.1.995b1, 2.996b21; v.30; ix.9. 1051a21–33; xii.8.1074b10; xiv.6.1093b6

206a. λύσις, *solutio,* solution, ἀναλύειν, *resolvere,* analyze, solve, διαλύειν, *dissolvere,* analyze, solve, resolve, disintegrate: difficulties, iii.1.995a29; vii.6.1032a6–10; viii.6.1045a22; xi.3. 1061b15, 6.1062b20, 31, 1063b8, 13; xii.7.1072a20, 10.1075a31, 33; xiii.2.1077a1, 9.1085a29; xiv.3.1090b3; logical, iv.3.1005b4, 7.1012a18; xi.5.1062b9; xiv.2.1089a3; whole, v.11; other in genus, v.28; separate, vii.17.1041b14; xiii.9.1085a16; materials, principles, elements, viii.4.1044a22, 24; xi.6.1063b18, 10. 1066b37; bodies, xiii.2.1077a23

207. μετατάττειν, *transponere,* change the order, vii.12.1038a30; προστάττειν, *jubere,* prescribe, xi.6.1063a28, 32; συντάττειν, *coordinare,* order together, xii.10.1075a16, 19; τάττειν, ἐπιτάττειν, *ordinare,* rule, order, i.2.982a18, 5.986b7; vi.2. 1026b15; xi.8.1065a26; xii.8.1073b, 1074a, 10.1075a21; xiii.7. 1081a16, 8.1083a10; xiv.5.1092b10

207a. ἀταξία, *inordinatio,* disorder, xii.4.1070b28; τάξις, *ordo,* order, i.3.984b17, 4.984b33, 985a1, b; v.11, 19; vii.12.1038a33; viii.2.1042b15; xi.2.1060a26; xii.8.1073b2, 34, 10.1075a11–25, b25; xiii.3.1078b1, 3

VII. THE DIVINE

208. θεῖον, *divinum,* divine, i.2.982b28–983a11; vi.1.1026a16–23; xi.7.1064a37; xii.7.1072b23, 9.1074b16, 26; xii.8.1074a30, b3, 9

209. θεός, *Deus,* God, θεοί, gods, i.2.982b28–983a11, 3.983b31, 4.984b27, 5.986b24; iii.2.997b10, 4.1000a9–14, 24–b6; iv.4. 1008a24; v.26.1023b32; vii.1.1028a18; xii.7.1072b24–30, 8. 1074b2, 9; xiv.1.1088a10

210. θεολογεῖν, *theologizare,* theologize, i.3.983b29; iii.4.1000a9; vi.1.1026a19; xii.6.1071b27, 10.1075b26; xiv.4.1091a34

211. θεολογική, *theologica,* theological, xi.7.1064b3

INDEX OF NAMES